Maimonides' Political Thought

SUNY Series in Jewish Philosophy
Kenneth Seeskin, Editor

MAIMONIDES' POLITICAL THOUGHT

Studies in Ethics, Law, and the Human Ideal

Howard Kreisel

STATE UNIVERSITY
OF NEW YORK PRESS

And he planted a tamarisk in Beer-Sheva,
and there he called out in the Name of God,
Lord of the World.

GENESIS 22:33

For Shoshanah

Published by
State University of New York Press, Albany

Printed in the United States of America

For information, address the State University of New York Press,
State University Plaza, Albany, NY 12246

Marketing by Fran Keneston • Production by Bernadine Dawes

Library of Congress Cataloging-in-Publication Data

Kreisel, Howard T. (Howard Theodore)
Maimonides' political thought : studies in ethics, law, and the human ideal / Howard Kreisel.
p. cm. — (SUNY series in Jewish philosophy)
Includes bibliographical references and index.
ISBN 0-7914-4189-X (alk. paper). — ISBN 0-7914-4190-3 (pbk. : alk. paper)
1. Maimonides, Moses, 1135–1204. 2. Political science--Philosophy. 3. Philosophy, Jewish. 4. Philosophy, Medieval. 5. Intellect—Religious aspects—Judaism. 6. Common good. 7. Perfection—Religious aspects—Judaism. 8. Ethics, Jewish. 9. God (Judaism) I. Title. II. Series.
B759.M34K74 1999
320'.092—dc21 99-13651
CIP

1 2 3 4 5 6 7 8 9 10

CONTENTS

ACKNOWLEDGMENTS

Several years ago I observed that much of my research on Maimonides gravitated toward the same basic area—political-ethical thought. I hoped one day to gather these studies together in a single volume. Last year I began working on this project. Rather than simply collecting the articles and introducing a few cosmetic changes, I decided to reedit all of them. This resulted in extensive revisions in the studies that comprise the chapters of this volume. I eliminated much of the duplicate material, added a great deal of new material, and also reworked many points in my analysis. Two of the studies originally appeared in Hebrew and I translated them into English. I also wrote an introductory essay for the purpose of this volume. The excellent suggestions of the anonymous readers of the manuscript led to further revisions, as well as to the attempt to tie together the chapters more tightly. This brought more of a unity to the work.

It has been my fortune to have studied at Brandeis University under some of the leading Maimonidean scholars of our generation, the late Prof. Alexander Altmann, the late Prof. Marvin Fox, and Prof. Alfred Ivry. I owe each of them a debt of gratitude. For the past fifteen years I have had the privilege to belong to the faculty of the Program of Jewish Thought at Ben-Gurion University of the Negev. I would like to take this opportunity to thank in particular two of my distinguished colleagues, Prof. Daniel Lasker and Prof. Gerald Blidstein. Over the years they have contributed much to my understanding of Maimonides, as well as many other areas of Jewish thought. I would like also to thank Prof. Kenneth Seeskin who encouraged me to send this manuscript to SUNY Press, and to Mr. James Peltz, Ms. Bernadine Dawes, and the rest of the editorial staff of SUNY Press for their assistance and patience. Our sages remind us that if there is no flour there is no Torah. I am indebted to the Harry Walsh Q.C. Career Development Chair for its financial support over the years.

Earlier versions of my studies appeared in the following publications, and I would like to thank the publishers for granting me permission to reprint them.

Chapter 2 appeared as "The Practical Intellect in the Philosophy of Maimonides," *Hebrew Union College Annual* 59 (1988): 189–215. [Reprinted with the permission of Hebrew Union College.]

Chapter 3 appeared as "The Problem of 'Good' in the Philosophy of Maimonides" (in Hebrew), *Iyyun* 38 (1989): 183–208. [Reprinted with the permission of the S. H. Bergman Center for Philosophical Studies, Hebrew University.]

Chapter 4 appeared as "*Imitatio Dei* in Maimonides' *Guide of the Perplexed*," *AJS Review* 19 (1994): 169–211. [Reprinted with the permission of the Association for Jewish Studies.]

Chapter 5 appeared as "Individual Perfection vs. Communal Welfare and the Problem of Contradictions in Maimonides' Approach to Ethics," *Proceedings of the American Academy for Jewish Research* 58 (1992): 107–141. [Reprinted with the permission of the American Academy for Jewish Research.]

Chapter 6 appeared as "Intellectual Perfection and the Role of the Law in the Philosophy of Maimonides," in *From Ancient Israel to Modern Judaism: Intellect in Quest of Understanding*, ed. Jacob Neusner, Ernest S. Frerichs, Nahum Sarna (Atlanta: Scholars Press, 1989), 3:25–46. [Reprinted with the permission of Brown Judaic Studies.]

Chapter 7 appeared as "Love and Fear of God in Maimonides' Thought" (in Hebrew), *Daat* 37 (1996): 127–51. [Reprinted with the permission of Bar-Ilan University Press.]

My thanks also to University of Chicago Press for allowing me to cite *Moses Maimonides, The Guide of the Perplexed*, trans. Shlomo Pines (Chicago: University of Chicago Press, 1963).

ONE

MAIMONIDES' POLITICAL THOUGHT
Introductory Essay

I

When one thinks of Jewish philosophers, Maimonides' name immediately comes to mind. Maimonides, however, would demur from being described as such. "Philosopher" for him designated a disciple of the Aristotelian tradition who investigated the world with the impartial tools of reason. The apprehension of reality is the goal, the *telos,* of the philosophic pursuit. Aristotle, *the* philosopher, laid the foundations and built most of the structure for understanding the world as it truly is. Maimonides was deeply impressed by this picture, and makes no effort to hide the fact. Nevertheless, he does not define himself as belonging to the philosophic camp. He sees himself as belonging to a particular religious tradition, and as being bound by that tradition. When Maimonides speaks in terms of "we," he is addressing his coreligionists. The philosophers are invariably referred to as "they." The theoretical issue that concerned Maimonides more than any other was the relation between the teachings of the Jewish tradition and the picture of the world painted by the philosophers—the relation between "our" view and "theirs."

Many scholars, I among them, have interpreted Maimonides' relation to the medieval Islamic Aristotelian philosophers as that of a fellow traveler. They shared the same essential view of God, the world, and the human being's place in the world. This interpretation is opposed to the one that views Maimonides as building a conceptual scheme occupying the "middle ground" between the radical naturalism of the Aristotelian philosophers and the view of a personal, miracle-working deity who holds central stage in traditional conceptions.[1] Yet even if one concludes that for Maimonides, "our" view—that is, the Jewish view of the world when properly understood—and "their" view are essentially the same, a crucial distinction between the views remains. The philosophic worldview entails no commitment to Judaism. It is this commitment, more than any other factor, that defines Maimonides' identity.

The commitment to philosophy and the commitment to Judaism, or to any religious tradition, are not necessarily mutually exclusive. The Islamic Aristotelians who so impressed Maimonides—Alfarabi in particular—continued to see themselves as loyal to their religious tradition. If Maimonides saw the philosophic and Jewish worldviews as being essentially the same, he must have viewed the commitments to philosophy and Judaism as coexisting in complete harmony, if not coinciding. Moreover, it is not unreasonable to maintain that when Judaism and philosophy teach opposing beliefs, the one considered more reliable by an individual may be treated as a sign of where the individual's loyalties lie. By being more prone to reinterpret Judaism in order to conform to philosophic views than to reject philosophic views in order to uphold traditional Jewish ones, Maimonides shows where his preferences lie. Yet it is not this type of loyalty to which I am referring. Commitment defines a person's concerns and activities. Maimonides' primary commitment was not to a further exploration of the frontiers of knowledge illuminated by Aristotle. He did not take upon himself the task to expand the borders of philosophy. Maimonides' principal effort was directed to the understanding and strengthening of Judaism.

This point is crucial for any proper evaluation of Maimonides' thought. Leaving aside his medical treatises,[2] almost all of Maimonides' literary corpus is Jewish in nature. Most of it deals with Jewish law. While still a young man, Maimonides completed a commentary on the *Mishnah*, the second-century compilation of the Jewish Oral Law. The *Book of the Commandments* followed, in which Maimonides enumerated and summarized the 613 commandments derived from the Torah. This work paved the way for Maimonides' greatest one—the groundbreaking *Mishneh Torah*. The *Mishneh Torah* was the first complete, systematic code of Jewish law.[3] Numerous legal responsa and epistles to Jewish individuals and communities were penned by Maimonides throughout his lifetime.

Maimonides' most famous "philosophic" work, *The Guide of the Perplexed*, should also be defined as a Jewish treatise.[4] The impartial investigation of the issues of philosophy was not Maimonides' concern in this work. The *Guide* was not designed to serve as an alternative to the treatises of the philosophers, in the way that the *Mishneh Torah* was designed to serve as an alternative to previous texts of Jewish law.[5] The *Guide* was addressed to those Jews who, like Maimonides, were committed to Judaism while at the same time engaged in philosophic studies. The perplexity experienced by them, and which Maimonides attempts to resolve, involves those issues on which philosophy and Judaism are in evident conflict.[6] Maimonides enters into formal philosophic discussions to the extent that he feels it important to define or defend the "Jewish" view, whether it be on such issues as God's incorporeality, creation, or the problem of evil and individual providence.

The relation between Maimonides the student of philosophy and Maimonides the great Jewish legal authority has posed a particularly vexing problem to those who have studied him. In the eyes of staunch Jewish traditionalists, Aristotelian philosophy is synonymous with heresy. How could a person so totally at home in the world of rabbinics engage in the study of such thought, let alone *openly* embrace it on several religiously sensitive issues? Many Jewish rationalists, on the other hand, viewed Jewish legal studies at best as secondary to the philosophic pursuit, upon which depends one's true felicity. As we shall see, Maimonides, too, subscribes to this view of where true felicity lies. Why then would he devote most of his literary efforts to the former area, painstakingly studying and codifying even those laws that had no practical relevance in his own day? Why would he pay so little attention to the latter area, at least as far as his literary activity is concerned? What is the "key" that allows us to understand this exceptional personality, so unique in the annals of Jewish history? Who is the "real" Maimonides amidst all the competing models of him presented by the many diverse and opposing schools within Judaism?

Maimonides' political thought holds the key to understanding his life work.[7] A summary of Maimonides' view of political philosophy is contained in the only treatise he wrote in his long and illustrious career that he would label as "philosophic"—the *Treatise on Logic*.[8] This treatise is fairly short. It is devoted to defining the technical terms and concepts of Aristotelian philosophy. The treatise apparently is also one of his earliest.[9] It is divided into fourteen chapters—a number that was to play a prominent role in Maimonides' subsequent writings, and serves as a type of leitmotif.[10] In the final chapter of this treatise, Maimonides explains the term "philosophy." He presents a summary of the various branches of Aristotelian philosophy, both the theoretical and practical ones. Theoretical philosophy begins with the "learning sciences" (arithmetic, geometry, astronomy and music), advances to natural science, and culminates in metaphysics. Practical philosophy, also termed "political" and "human" philosophy, consists of the areas of self-government (ethics), the government of a household (economics), the government of a city-state (politics), and the government of a great nation or nations.[11]

There is little, if anything, that is novel in Maimonides' treatise. Nor does he regard it as more than a synopsis. In writing this treatise, Maimonides bases himself on the Islamic Aristotelian tradition, particularly on the works of Alfarabi. The most significant aspect of the treatise is Maimonides' concluding remarks defining the practical philosophy of the governance of the city:

> As for the governance of the city, it is a science that provides its inhabitants with knowledge of true happiness and the way of striving to attain it . . . and with training their moral qualities to abandon things that are presumed to be happiness. . . . It likewise prescribes for them rules of justice by means of which their associations are well ordered. The learned men of bygone nations used to posit governances and rules in accordance with the perfection of each individual among them, by means of which their kings governed subjects. They called them *nomoi*. The nations were governed by these *nomoi*. The philosophers have many books concerning all these things that have been translated into Arabic. What has not been translated may even be more extensive. But in these times all of this has been dispensed with—I mean, the regimes and the nomoi—for people are governed by the divine commands.[12]

Maimonides maintains, in the name of the Aristotelian tradition, that politics ideally consists of the following components: knowledge of what is true happiness and what is not, the way of attaining it, training in the moral qualities, and finally, rules of justice for the ordering of society. In this context Maimonides does not spell out what is true happiness. Nor does he indicate the relation between his discussion here and his discussion of the Aristotelian four causes in chapter 9. There he posits the attainment of intelligibles as the purpose of human life, its final cause. Even without a knowledge of Aristotelian philosophy, one is tempted to conclude that true human happiness and the attainment of the final cause are closely related, if not identical. A study of Aristotelian philosophy and Maimonides' own writings confirms that this is the case. True human happiness lies in active contemplation of the unchanging verities of the world. The higher on the chain of being is the object of apprehension, the greater the felicity experienced. The apprehension of God to the extent of human ability results in the highest level of felicity.

Politics thus is ultimately concerned with the attainment of the human beings' final end—the apprehension of the intelligibles contained in the theoretical sciences. Its goal is the creation of a social environment most conducive to the individual's pursuit of perfection. Insofar as it does not deal with the actual knowledge possessed by the one who attains the final end, but with the *process* by which the final end is attained, it is a practical rather than a theoretical science. Noteworthy is the fact that politics does not consist only of laws or rules but also teachings—that is, what is true happiness and how to attain it. Moreover, it is concerned with the individual's moral qualities in addition to just laws—qualities that are necessary for the pursuit of intellectual perfection as well as social well being.

Maimonides ends his treatise on a personal note. He maintains that the divine commands make all human *nomoi* superfluous. While scholars have debated the precise meaning of Maimonides' remark,[13] at least certain points appear to be clear. The quality of the legislations of bygone nations—the *nomoi*—was directly related to the perfection of their legislators. The implication is that divine legislation is the most perfect, its source being the perfect legislator. This makes all human legislations superfluous, regardless of how close to perfection they may be. They can never equal the perfection of the divine legislation.[14]

Does this make also the books of the philosophers on political philosophy dispensable? The primary purpose of the books of the philosophers, as viewed by Maimonides, is in providing a blueprint for ideal legislations—ones that contain not only laws, but also teachings indispensable for the attainment of true happiness. Mosaic Law, Maimonides constantly reiterates, contains true teachings in metaphysics and the prescription to learn the sciences, as well as just laws ordering society and bringing about moral virtues. From this perspective, this would make philosophic works on politics dispensable, in contrast to their works in the theoretical sciences, or even the practical philosophy of ethics.

Yet Maimonides is careful not to make the claim that these books are no longer of any value. The fact remains that he was deeply indebted to philosophic works on politics, particularly those of Alfarabi, in developing his own political thought. In a letter to the Hebrew translator of the *Guide*, Samuel Ibn Tibbon, Maimonides goes so far as to single out Alfarabi's *Political Regime* as a work that is completely "pure grain."[15] The value of such works for Maimonides is in the key they hold for properly understanding Mosaic legislation—its underlying goals and the strategies it employs to accomplish them. The importance of the insights they contain does not belong solely to the realm of theory. They are crucial for the task of adapting the ancient Mosaic legislation to changing conditions.

Why did Maimonides abandon philosophy after writing the *Treatise on Logic*—not the study of philosophy in which he was passionately engaged his entire life, but the writing of philosophy? The answer is that he devoted his literary life to politics. His concern was not in teaching political philosophy per se, but in teaching Mosaic Law as the ideal expression of political philosophy. Maimonides' goal was to reorient Mosaic legislation to direct its adherents to true happiness.[16] His life work may be characterized as the practical implementation of political philosophy in Jewish society. In this essay I present a few examples from the vast mosaic of Maimonides' thought to illustrate the multifaceted nature of this task.

II

While Aristotelian political philosophy is labeled a "practical science" as we have seen, its foundation is to be found in the theoretical sciences. It is rooted in the study of the nature of human beings, their final end, and the role of society in relation to human existence. All theoretical philosophic investigations ultimately lead to a discussion of the nature of God and God's relation to the world. From this perspective, medieval Islamic Aristotelian philosophy is exceptionally "holistic" in nature. Before turning to a study of Maimonides' adaptation of Aristotelian political philosophy to a Jewish context, we must first take a brief look at his view of Aristotelian theoretical philosophy.

The Jewish tradition and the Aristotelian tradition present two fundamentally opposing conceptions of the world. The Torah depicts God in anthropomorphic terms, and the sages of the Talmud continue to depict God in the same manner. More important, God is seen as the creator of the world in its entirety, who exercises never ceasing personal providence over the world. All human deeds are observed. God intervenes in history, performing miracles subverting the order of nature. God is the immediate author of the Law, which was revealed to Moses. Reward and punishment are meted out in accordance with obedience or disobedience to the divine commands. The Jews are regarded as God's elect, but the principles of reward and punishment are universal. Non-Jews are also rewarded or punished on the basis of their deeds. One has free will to obey or disobey, but not to determine what is binding or not.

The Islamic Aristotelian God, on the other hand, is the First Cause and Prime Mover of an eternal world. God is the incorporeal One, the Self-Intellecting Intellect. God gives existence and "governs" the world through the impersonal emanation of the hierarchy of beings. God does not know individuals *qua* individuals, does not keep a record of people's deeds, does not perform miracles, and is not the immediate cause of anything that touches upon the human condition. All that happens results either from the impersonal workings of nature, or from human volitional activity. Nature is constant and will never change. Everything that exists or occurs is ultimately traced to God, but only as the remote Cause. The purpose of any species is integrally bound up with its essence. The perfection of human beings *qua* human beings belongs to them by nature. It is discovered by rational investigation, not created. One may choose to pursue perfection or not, but one cannot choose what perfection is.

Each species has two goals: to perpetuate itself, and to produce the perfect specimen. The latter is an exceptionally rare occurrence. In the context of human beings, the perpetuation of the species requires society. "Man is a political animal," Aristotle maintains.[17] Society in turn requires leaders who can overcome the conflicting temperaments of people and organize them to function peacefully and efficiently together to provide for their needs. Human perfection, however, lies not in the collective but in the individual—in the perfection of the intellect. Few are equipped by nature to attain this goal. Even fewer engage in the necessary preparations to reach the final destination. These preparations involve not only a continuous in-depth study of the sciences, but also living a strictly moral life. One cannot totally commit oneself to the contemplative life while being a slave to one's physical passions, which are responsible for the evils one commits against others and against oneself. Maimonides himself, in the introduction to his *Commentary on the Mishnah,* notes in the name of Aristotle that one cannot be a true philosopher without curbing one's desires for physical gratification. Yet morality primarily serves as a means to intellection in the case of the elite. In the medieval Islamic Aristotelian tradition, most viewed the immortality of the intellect as dependent upon the attainment of final perfection—the apprehension of incorporeal existence.[18] The end of the rest of humanity, whether righteous or wicked, is the same as it is for the members of all earthly species—degeneration and death. There is no "injustice" in this state of affairs. This is simply the way of the world. Of course the philosopher does not go and teach these matters publicly to the masses. Discretion is not only the better part of valor, but also the philosophically more responsible course. The masses are taught those beliefs or myths that insure their proper behavior and contribute to the welfare of society.

One can easily understand why from a traditional perspective it is so difficult to accept the notion that one of Judaism's all-time leading legal authorities would accept the philosophic picture of the world. Given the fact that Maimonides devotes most of his efforts to legal matters, explicitly labels many of the Aristotelian doctrines as heretical, upholds God's creation of the world, God's dictation of the Torah word for word to Moses, miracles, individual providence and the resurrection of the dead—it is tempting to conclude that any interpretation that sees Maimonides as an Aristotelian in Jewish guise reflects the depraved imagination of the interpreter. Yet a careful reading of Maimonides' writings, not only the *Guide*, lends a great deal of support to the conclusion that he embraced the philosophic worldview.[19]

More than in the case of any other medieval Jewish philosopher, the effort to understand Maimonides relies on the fine art of reading.[20] While most philosophers may at times be very obtuse in their presentation, they tend to write with the sole purpose of revealing their positions. Once one understands the argument being presented, the question: "But does the author *really* think that this is the case?" is generally out of place. Maimonides, on the other hand, is interested in concealing his views from many of his readers, at the same time he imparts them to some. His points often appear to the quick and careless reader deceptively simple, and deliberately so. One thus must slow up and start examining his discussions word by word not only in order to understand the nuances of the points he presents, but also to determine his commitment to them. What makes the *Guide* such an exciting and complex work is not simply the philosophic subtlety of the arguments themselves, though from a philosophic perspective many of them hold much value in their own right. The great fascination the treatise holds for the reader lies also in its style of presentation. In his attempt to communicate his thoughts only to the elite reader, and not to any reader who may lay hands on the treatise, Maimonides deliberately obfuscates his views on certain religiously sensitive issues. In the introduction to the *Guide*, he explicitly indicates that this is his writing strategy. This position lays the foundation for the search for Maimonides' esoteric views, a search that was to preoccupy the attention of Maimonides' earliest commentators, and continues up to his present-day interpreters. The act of reading the *Guide* was intended by Maimonides to be an intellectual adventure of the highest order. It was not primarily fear of persecution that led Maimonides to resort to the art of esoteric writing, but fear of the social destruction that would result if he did not.

Philosophic arguments in Maimonides' treatise are subservient to the doctrine that he wishes to communicate in a particular discussion. Not all of the doctrines necessarily reflect his own belief. This casts a different light on how we are to understand and evaluate the arguments he advances. The issue on which Maimonides presents his most extensive and penetrating philosophic argumentation—creation—is one on which a sharp debate continues to exist among scholars as to his true view on the subject. If Maimonides in fact believed in the eternity *a parte ante* of the world as a number of "hints" scattered throughout the *Guide* intimate, his arguments against the philosophers' proofs for eternity, as well as the proofs he presents for creation, must have been viewed by him as far less persuasive than he suggests. At the very least, Maimonides' philosophic arguments were designed to support doctrines that he regarded as important to impart to the average reader in order to preserve and strengthen one's commitment to Judaism.

To arrive at Maimonides' view, it is crucial to surrender one's preconceptions of what "must" be the case. Instead the reader must take a very close look at what exactly is being said by Maimonides, and other authors whose works he read, particularly those he cites or praises.[21] Furthermore, the reader must constantly keep in mind the wider context of the discussion and its purpose. What Maimonides holds out to the reader at the end of the journey is enlightenment on those issues that he regarded as the source of perplexity. This enlightenment is to be reserved for those who were bright enough and well grounded enough in philosophy to appreciate its significance. To Maimonides, in the case of this special reader a full appreciation of the meaning and function of the Law as grounded in a proper understanding of reality serves to strengthen the commitment to tradition, together with reinforcing the pursuit of philosophic knowledge. Moreover, the ultimate aim of the Law is to create this type of individual.

Certain points in Maimonides' treatise are not even minimally comprehensible without an examination of their philosophic sources. As I try to show in some of the chapters in the present volume, this is true of some of his discussions in his legal writings as well.[22] The average reader was not to be allowed to see what was below the surface of the text, for such glimpses would only cause him a spiritual crises for which he was not prepared. Students of Maimonides' *Mishneh Torah* have long held the view that a close examination of each word is crucial for the proper appreciation of Maimonides' presentation of Jewish law. This principle is no less applicable in studying those passages in which philosophic conceptions play a prominent role, where one must turn to Maimonides' philosophic sources, and not only rabbinic sources, to understand his formulations. While Maimonides' legal writings do not presuppose the reader's acquaintance with philosophy, the message that the astute reader attains in those discussions is that in order to grasp what Maimonides is saying, and at the same time fulfill one's legal requirements as formulated by Maimonides, one has no choice but to turn to the corpus of Aristotelian writings.

Truth for Maimonides is one. It may be represented by images or presented in an abstract conceptual manner, but there can be no opposing truths. Judaism and philosophy cannot present contradictory doctrines and both be right. Maimonides holds no "double truth" theory. It is highly unlikely that any medieval philosopher ever seriously entertained such a theory.[23] Maimonides was convinced in the truth of the conception of the philosophers and reinterpreted Judaism accordingly. Judaism presented figurative representations of philosophic truths, whether it be in its corporeal descriptions of God or in the manner in which it depicts God's governance of the world. Maimonides made it his life work to teach publicly the truth of the philosophic conception in regard to the doctrine of the incorporeality of God.[24] The truth of their view on the manner in which God relates to the world he presents in a veiled manner. It is precisely the latter view that is far more problematic from a religious perspective.

The one who discovers the truth must return to the cave in Plato's famous allegory.[25] The cave consists of those to whose society one belongs, in whose midst one was born and grew up. I have no doubt that Maimonides was convinced that Judaism from its inception was led by those who had attained intellectual enlightenment. The human masses in whatever society they are born are condemned by nature to remain in darkness. A leader who understands the truth of the world must still guide others by means of images of reality. The difference between the images presented by the leader who has attained intellectual enlightenment and those promulgated by one who has not is that the former contain hints to the abstract truths underlying them. They are designed to be closer to the truth, though all "images" of reality are intrinsically false. The masses continue to treat the images as real. The elite gradually learn to see the abstract reality that underlies them.

It is exceptionally hard, if not also dangerous, to break the thought patterns of the masses. For them the corporeal and imaginable are more real than the incorporeal and intellectually apprehensible. The supernatural is more awe inspiring than the natural. No leader who has seen the light of the sun can afford to blind oneself to this fact when returning to the cave. There is simply no way to turn all of the masses of society around and march them out of the cave where they can see the world in the full light of the sun. The need of the philosophically enlightened leader to compromise with social reality is inevitable. In the case of the unenlightened leaders, no abstract truths are intended to underlie the images presented by them. They share with the masses the same false view that the images are reality. Not knowing what is the true goal that society is to pursue, they posit false goals instead—for example, the pursuit of wealth, honor, conquest. The images promote the pursuit of these false goals, distancing society ever further from the attainment of perfection.

If Maimonides felt that many of the teachings of Judaism consist of myths and other figurative representations of the truth, and that God is not the corporeal "personal" deity depicted in Jewish law, then one is tempted to rashly conclude that he could not have viewed Jewish law as really being divine. Why would he remain loyal to such a law? Why would he continue to observe, study, and codify all the commandments if he did not trace them to the immediate will of God, or think that divine reward and punishment followed in the wake of observance and disobedience? The answer that emerges from Maimonides' writings is that the person asking such questions does not have a proper understanding of what is "divine" or the true nature of "reward and punishment." To this person we continue to teach that God reveals the Law word by word and checks carefully our level of observance.

The person possessing a true understanding of reality will have a different view of the meaning of these notions. The "divine" is not opposed to what we call "natural," or even what many of us would regard as "human." The medieval Aristotelian philosophers posit a difference between divine and natural on the basis of the incorporeal and corporeal. The forces that belong to the world of matter are "natural," while "divine" is used to characterize the metaphysical world. "Human" is applied to those areas in which an individual's deliberation and choice are involved. The world of the Separate Intellects is considered "divine." Nevertheless, it operates in a fixed impersonal manner that in today's parlance we would call "natural." In the philosophic view, all events in our physical world, whether "natural" or tied to human volition, ultimately can be traced to a "divine" origin. None, however, has God as its immediate agent.

Implicit in this conceptual approach is the view that from the standpoint of "origins," human law is no less divine than divine law, and divine law is no less human than human law. If a categorical distinction is to be drawn between them, a different definition of "divinity" must be introduced. Maimonides' doctrine of prophecy, adopted from his Islamic philosophic sources, provides the basis for such definition.[26] Maimonides defines prophecy as an "emanation" from God to the Active Intellect, and from there to the rational faculty and to the imagination of the individual (*Guide* 2:36). This "emanation" is to be distinguished from the emanation that reaches the rational faculty alone and results in the apprehension of intelligibles, and from the one that reaches the imagination alone and results in divination or in the ability to govern. The prophetic "emanation" is received only by one possessing a good physical disposition and perfect imagination, who has acquired the virtuous character traits and intellectual perfection. Proper potential and training thus are necessary (and it appears also sufficient) conditions for attaining prophecy.

The "divine speech" is a figurative way of depicting this special type of "emanation." God does not "pick" a particular individual, formulate a particular "message" and send the individual on a specific mission. The "message" results from the "contact" of the mind of the perfect individual with the impersonal force emanating from a "divine" intellect. Those lacking the necessary intellectual and moral prerequisites cannot attain revelation. This emanation strengthens the individual's apprehension, allowing the individual to reach a higher level of enlightenment. The individual attains a more profound understanding of metaphysical truths, grasps rules of governance, and is also able to learn the future. Prophecy, in short, is a natural attainment. This naturalistic approach, it should be noted, also contains the criteria for validating who is a true prophet. One lacking any of the criteria necessary for the attainment of prophecy cannot possibly be a true prophet, despite the individual's claim to the contrary. Many of the Islamic philosophers added an ontological dimension to this phenomenon. They described it in terms of "conjunction" between the human intellect and the Active Intellect in which a quasi identity between the two is achieved.[27]

Moses, in Maimonides' view, reached the highest level of prophecy possible, one in which the imagination was no longer required to play a role. This level enabled Moses to "receive" in his prophetic experience a law that alone deserves the label "divine." Only one who achieves ultimate perfection can receive a revelation allowing the recipient to lay down a perfect legislation that best promotes the guidance of others to true happiness. In several passages Maimonides hints to Moses' authorship of the Law, but in exceptionally veiled terms as appropriate to this most religiously sensitive of subjects: "After we have spoken of the quiddity of prophecy, have made known its true reality, and have made it clear that the prophecy of Moses our Master is different from that of the others, we shall say that the call to the Law followed necessarily from that apprehension alone" (*Guide* 2:39.378).[28]

The "divinity" of the Law is brought to light, according to Maimonides, by its unique perfection, the "equibalance" of its commands in which there is "no burden or excess." The Law strives to create morally and intellectually perfect individuals: "If you find a Law all of whose ordinances are due to attention being paid . . . to the soundness of the circumstances pertaining to the body and also to the soundness of belief . . . and desires to make man wise, to give understanding, and to awaken his attention, so that he should know the whole of that which exists in its true form—you must know that this guidance comes from Him, may He be exalted, and that this Law is divine" (2:40.384). Other legislators also lay down laws as a result of an "emanation," but ones in which their imaginations are primarily involved. As a result, their legislations are seriously flawed. They neither achieve a perfect equibalance in moral matters—as a close examination of their commands reveals—nor do they attempt to direct their adherents to intellectual perfection. These legislations are termed, "human."[29]

People of limited understanding would say that this position entails that the divine law is really an excellent human law, with Moses being its immediate author. The philosopher would respond that the divinity of the law stems from the fact that it is derived from the "contact" between the Active Intellect and a perfect human intellect, resulting in a perfect legislation. Maimonides was committed to a reconstruction of history in which the prophets are to be viewed as those who received revelation on the basis of their perfection in the natural and metaphysical sciences. Moses attained the highest level of perfection and revelation possible. A law that comes about in this manner is no less divine than one in which a personal deity speaks each of the commandments.

Similarly, "reward" and "punishment" are not extrinsic to the natural order of the world. They are not meted out directly by God. They are not the product of particular acts of divine volition. Rather, they are the natural consequence, "impressed" by God upon the order of the world, of the type of life one leads. Goodness is its own reward, evil its own punishment. Since the masses cannot possibly appreciate this point, it is crucial to continue to present to them the "traditional" picture. If the notion that living a life that is truly "human"—one that provides the individual with the most true happiness and is closest to being "divine"—does not provide people with sufficient motive to observe the commandments laid down in the Law, then the picture of rewards and punishments in the "next" life, coupled with the belief in the resurrection of the dead, must be presented to them instead.[30]

The relation between Maimonides' metaphysical and political thought is multifaceted. Political activity is not an alternative to metaphysical speculation but rooted in it and an extension of it. It does not result from the inability to apprehend God and the turning to the next best activity available to humanity. Rather, it flows from the highest level of apprehension. I will deal in detail with Maimonides' approach to *imitatio Dei* in chapter 4, but a few words on the subject are appropriate here. Maimonides adopted an extreme version of negative theology which maintained that nothing positive can be known about God's essence.[31] God can only be known by the attributes to be negated of the divine essence. This view of God's essence to which Maimonides was driven by philosophical considerations does not hold much promise as a goal or as a model for human striving. While Maimonides argues that progress in this type of apprehension is possible (*Guide* 1:59–60), it can never result in actually knowing God. The importance of this approach to knowledge of God lies in preserving the notion of God's absolute unity and transcendence.

The ontological, and not only epistemological implications, of this approach are profound. In medieval Aristotelian thought, knowledge lies in the intellect's apprehension or grasping of a thing as it "is." The thinking mind is the intelligible it apprehends. For many Aristotelians, the immortality of the intellect is rooted in grasping the incorporeal essence. Knowledge of what an object "is not" cannot be equated with the apprehension of the object. The former type of knowledge leaves no room for attaining some type of unity with God. It appears to close the door on the possibility of achieving immortality. Moreover, it gives little direction for human endeavors. No matter how high an individual climbs on this ladder of knowledge, he still is left only with knowledge that is negative in character.

For Maimonides, however, there is another type of knowledge of God that overcomes these problems by providing positive content. This is the knowledge of God's attributes of "action" (*Guide* 1:54). These attributes are the entire realm of existence "under" God, for which God serves as the First Cause. We can never grasp anything positive about God's essence, but we can apprehend God's governance of what exists. Knowledge of God's "actions," or the whole of existence, includes even the Separate Intellects. This leaves open the possibility of grasping and conjoining with the Active Intellect, thereby achieving immortality. The knowledge of God's attributes of action also provides a model for imitating God in our practical activity. All that exists and the interrelation between all things are treated by Maimonides as the product of God's "emanating perfection" (2:12). The notion of "emanating perfection" is crucial for Maimonides not only in that it provides an Archimedean point on which to establish some type of "resemblance" between the perfection of God and the human ideal, but also a way to establish a continuum linking the divine domain and its activity with the human. The Separate Intellects, the spheres and the ideal human beings are all the products of God's emanating perfection. Each possesses the intellectual perfection that characterizes its level of existence. They all imitate and extend God's perfection by emanating their perfection to that which is "below" them. The knowledge attained by the perfect human being results from the emanating perfection of the Active Intellect. The ultimate expression of emanating human perfection, in turn, assumes the form of the ideal governance of others.

The significance of the knowledge of God's attributes is highlighted by Maimonides' interpretation of God's revelation to Moses at Sinai in *Guide* 1:54. The knowledge attained by Moses represents the absolute limits of human capacity in Maimonides' view. Moses asks to see God's "face" but is denied this request. He is given only a glimpse of God's "back." In the opening section of the *Mishneh Torah*, the *Laws of the Principles of the Torah* 1:10, Maimonides interprets "face" to indicate God's essence, while "back refers to the manner God is distinct from other beings"—an allusion to the doctrine of negative attributes. He continues to present the same interpretation of "face" in the *Guide* but interprets "back" in a different manner. This apprehension is equated with knowledge of God's "ways," or all of God's "goodness," as represented by the "thirteen characteristics":

> Scripture has restricted itself to mentioning only those *thirteen characteristics*, although [Moses] apprehended *all His goodness*—I mean to say all His actions—because these are the actions proceeding from Him, may He be exalted, in respect of giving existence to the Adamites and governing them. This was [Moses'] ultimate object in his demand, the conclusion of what he says being: *That I may know Thee, to the end that I may find grace in Thy sight and consider that this nation is Thy people* (Exod. 33:13)—that is, a people for the government of which I need to perform actions that I must seek to make similar to Thy actions in governing them. (Pp. 124–25)

In this passage too Maimonides alludes to the view that the legislation of the Law is the product of Moses' "translation" of the theoretical knowledge of all of existence into a system of ideal rule in the human context. He is adamant on the point that God's "characteristics" are not affections of the soul. They represent the activity resulting in ideal cosmic order, described in terms of human emotions. The ideal human ruler must also govern solely on the basis of rational considerations free from all passions. Anger, or any other emotion, should never be experienced since it would inevitably cloud one's rational judgment on what is the best course to adopt. The ruler may at times have *to feign* anger to insure obedience, Maimonides agrees, but this is a far different matter than *experiencing* anger. The ruler may also have to teach that God is angry with the disobedient in order to accomplish the desired end.

Even the notion that God purposefully destroys the wicked by way of natural catastrophes that overtake them, or by way of defeat in wars and the like, is a form of myth designed to improve people's conduct. Maimonides is careful to conceal this point in *Guide* 1:54 as well as in his discussion of providence in 3:17. Yet it emerges when one ties together his various discussions in the treatise, as he urges his readers to do. All natural evils are regarded by him as the necessary consequence of the process of generation and corruption characterizing sublunar existence. They are not brought about directly and willfully by God. God cannot give existence to the sublunar world without their occurring, as Maimonides' approach to the problem of evil clarifies (3:12). The order is designed to operate in an optimal manner in general. This does not mean that individuals will not at times be inadvertently harmed by what occurs in nature. Nature cannot be designed to pay attention to the isolated, exceptional cases (3:34). Nor does God have an immediate hand in any of the evils that humans inflict upon each other. They are the product of our own poor choices based on the privation of knowledge of what is the true good. Still, Maimonides regards it as crucial that people believe that God acts willfully in bringing evils upon the disobedient when this occurs, and these evils do not occur by accident, just as it is important that people should think that God "bends" nature to reward the righteous when they attain natural benefits.[32] It is evident from Maimonides' discussions that the "translation" of divine governance to human governance is not a straightforward one. Yet all ideal human governance is ultimately rooted in the theoretical knowledge that one attains.

III

Maimonides establishes as a principle of Judaism, as laid down in Mosaic Law itself, that no legislation will ever come to replace it (*Guide* 2:39). He endeavors to show that none of the prophets before or after Moses in biblical tradition sought to lay down laws governing a polity (1:63; 2:39). He insists that even in messianic times no new legislation, or even formal changes in Mosaic legislation, will come about (*Laws of Kings* 11:3). Moreover, Maimonides rules that any claimant to prophecy who attempts to do so is automatically to be regarded as a false prophet (*Laws of the Principles of the Torah* 9:1). The role of all the prophets after Moses, and the talmudic sages who followed them, is seen as implementing and adapting Mosaic Law to their historical period. This will be true also of the king-messiah. Maimonides takes as his model Alfarabi's description of the "princes of the law," while breaking with Alfarabi's view on the possibility of successive divine legislations. The "princes of the law" are sufficiently well versed in the ancient laws and their purpose to enable them to adapt and implement the old legislation. Yet due to their inferior level of perfection in comparison to the ideal ruler, they lack authority to introduce a new legislation.[33]

Inasmuch as Mosaic Law, in being the ideal legislation, is concerned with one's knowledge and moral qualities, in addition to the just ordering of society, the activities of the subsequent rulers focus on the same areas. This is the key to understanding their literary output in Maimonides' view. The sages, for example, were jurists who had the ability to decree new enactments, though not of the same legal status as Mosaic commandments, in addition to interpreting the Mosaic Law. The Mishnah and Talmud in particular reflect the legal side of their activity. The Talmud, however, also contains many homilies or midrashim. Separate collections of midrashim also were collated by the sages. Maimonides maintains that these homilies, when examined closely, are parables containing the philosophic truths of the natural sciences and metaphysics. The homily is a literary device, addressed to society at large, for teaching philosophy. The sages showed their concern also for an individual's ethical qualities in such works as the tractate *Avot*.

The same concerns explain the nature of Maimonides' literary output in his attempt to adapt Mosaic Law to his own period. His *Commentary on the Mishnah* contains all the main elements of the ideal legislation—strict legal matters, an ethical tract, and philosophic teachings. These elements reemerge in Maimonides' subsequent major works, but in different ways in accordance with the nature of the work. The *Mishneh Torah* is essentially Maimonides' reformulation of the Mishnah and legal material in the Talmud while the *Guide of the Perplexed* is his reformulation of the midrash.

The *Mishneh Torah* is Maimonides' crowning achievement, the practical adaptation of theoretical political philosophy to Jewish law. In respect to the form of this legal composition, it is highly innovative. As opposed to the *Mishnah*, it is designed to be all inclusive. The entirety of Jewish law is organized topically by book and section, with Maimonides determining the structure and order of classification. Every law is carefully and concisely formulated. No dissenting opinions are presented that may lead to a conflicting view of what is the proper practice. No references are cited that would lengthen the work and make it more cumbersome. In the attempt to preserve the Law, Maimonides set out to compose a work that is accessible to all. One no longer needed to devote years of intricate study of the rabbinic sources to learn what the Law is, or spend a great deal of time researching particular questions.[34]

In keeping with the objectives of this work, Maimonides for the most part adopts a conservative stance in the content of his rulings. Only on rare occasion does he appear to reinterpret the Law in accordance with his personal views—ones that can be discerned in the *Guide* for example—when they stand in opposition to the weight of the Jewish legal tradition.[35] Maimonides makes no serious attempt in his reformulation of the Law to introduce extensive changes in the guise of Jewish tradition. For the most part, he rests content in letting his views emerge by subtly modifying the formulations appearing in his sources. He often reveals the significance he attaches to certain laws by where he places them in the code. He brings together laws that are not found together in his sources and separates laws that are brought together in his sources. While the reasons behind Maimonides' classification and organization of the various laws are for the most part clear, this is not always the case. At times a study of his rabbinic sources helps to clarify the reasons. At other times they do not, signaling Maimonides' innovative thinking on the issue. This is the reason why a painstaking study of Maimonides' sources is crucial for understanding his legal thought and its relationship to his philosophy.[36] Only on the most significant issues, those that concern the ultimate ends of the Law in his view—namely, intellectual and moral perfection—does Maimonides introduce his most blatant, far-reaching legal innovations. The far different order and formulation of commandments in the *Mishneh Torah* in comparison to his earlier more succinct legal compendium, the *Book of the Commandments*, gives us a chance to see also in what ways Maimonides chose to change his approach.

Maimonides' effort to continue the process of reformulating the Law of Moses is characterized by a number of competing concerns. The mediation between these concerns, in his view, can be seen in the original legislation. For example, the Law must mediate between the social welfare of Jewish society at large, which is its initial goal, and the intellectual perfection of the elite, which is its ultimate goal. In a crucial sense this is part of a larger conflict—the well-being of the majority versus the well-being of the individual. While Maimonides views the Torah and Talmud as creating a polity that admirably harmonizes these two goals, he is well aware that in certain situations the two goals stand in conflict. Compromises are necessary. The art of governance, unlike the art of medicine, cannot be tailored to the needs of each individual. Law is similar to nature, which brings the most good to the greatest number, but at times inevitably causes some individuals harm (*Guide* 3:34).

Ethics helps to reduce the conflict considerably. The attainment of ethical traits, Maimonides insists against opposing conceptions, is a legal obligation. It is the object of the command to "walk in God's ways" (*Laws of Character Traits* 1–3). Yet the crucial difference between this commandment and most others is clear. Ethical regimen can be modified in accordance with the circumstances of the individuals. There is enough flexibility in the actions required to attain the ethical traits (or even in the determination of what is the proper ethical trait in certain circumstances) so that the activities of different individuals pursuing this goal may differ considerably.[37] This type of flexibility is certainly not true of other areas of Jewish law. As is the case with the governance of the Jewish community in general, here too the sage plays a dominant role. It is the sage who acts as the "physician of the soul" determining what are the activities most appropriate for the morally sick individual (*Eight Chapters* 3).

There is yet another set of competing concerns in Maimonides' writings. Maimonides follows rabbinic tradition in insisting that Mosaic Law was revealed together with its oral explanations, which are those presented by the sages of the Talmud. No changes can be introduced in the legal definitions of the commandments as laid down in the Oral Law. For example, the conditions laid down in the Oral Law for the construction of a *sukkah* (booth) to fulfill the commandment of sitting in a *sukkah* on the *Festival of Sukkot*, or the manner that the commandments of *mezuzah* and *tefillin* are to be fulfilled, can never undergo change.[38] Furthermore, Maimonides takes an exceptionally extreme position in maintaining the inviolability of Mosaic Law in its entirety. He insists on the eternal uniqueness of this legislation. No Mosaic commandment, as opposed to rabbinic enactment, can ever be formally abrogated. No commandment can be formally added to the body of Mosaic commandments. Not all rabbis felt that tradition compelled one to adopt such extreme stance.[39]

The divine legislation is given at a certain point in history, but is from then on treated by Maimonides as ahistorical. On this point too, nature is taken as the paradigm for the divine Law. Like nature, the governance of the divine Law must be absolute and universal (*Guide* 3:34). This position receives a very concrete expression in the *Mishneh Torah.* Maimonides, alone among the great jurists of Judaism, codifies the entire range of Jewish law including sacrifices, Temple Service, and all the laws of ritual purity. No area of law, whether actively practiced in his time or not, is ignored. The Law is presented in its entirety as an absolute, formally unchanging system.

This view appears to ignore the obvious need for changes as social situations change. Maimonides insists that every commandment is designed to promote perfection. He devotes many chapters of the *Guide* to showing how the commandments contribute to the intellectual perfection of the Jews, their ethical traits, and to a just social order. They all have discernible reasons in his view, though not all of them are immediately evident. All are designed solely for the sake of humanity. God is totally unaffected by the fulfillment or transgression of the commandments. Maimonides, however, is not oblivious to the fact that aspects of the human condition do not remain static, even if the components of human perfection never change. Furthermore, his approach to the reasons for the commandments serves to sharpen the problem. Maimonides views many of the commandments as being promulgated to address the specific historical circumstances of the Jews leaving Egypt, certain types of compromise being necessary. The Torah commands sacrifices, Maimonides argues, for this was the way of worship to which the people were accustomed. A failure to command sacrifices would have resulted in the people continuing to offer sacrifices to other gods, being unwilling or unable to surrender this practice. Sacrifice is not in itself a desirable way of worship, in Maimonides' view, but was historically necessary. Maimonides comes close to indicating explicitly that were the Torah to be legislated in his own day, no sacrifices would be commanded (*Guide* 3:32).

The view of the historical obsolescence of many of the commandments, when viewed from the standpoint of the reasons for their legislation, stands in stark contrast to Maimonides' insistence upon the eternal validity or authority of these commandments. Maimonides was certainly aware of this conflict and some of his positions are aimed at resolving it. He sees Mosaic Law itself addressing this issue by limiting the scope of many of the historically relative commandments. Sacrifices, for example, are to be performed only in one place, by a certain class and only when the Sanctuary is in existence. Commandments whose reason is not attached to historical circumstances—prayer, for example—are not governed by the same limitations (*Guide* 3:32).[40] In this practical manner Mosaic Law draws a line distinguishing between different commandments, while treating all of them as eternally valid.

As with all living institutions, Mosaic Law is flexible enough to adapt, survive, and achieve its ultimate purpose to the extent possible in any historical period.[41] Changing social needs can be met by legal mechanisms that are part of the initial Mosaic Law. Rabbinic enactments, and even the right to suspend temporarily Mosaic commandments, are sanctioned by Mosaic Law. So is the institution of a judicial system with the authority to interpret the Law and the manner in which it is to be implemented in the variety of situations that arise. The *procedure* by which law is interpreted and rulings are determined is in itself a Torah commandment that will never undergo change in Maimonides' thought. The novelty of Maimonides' approach in this area is in his treatment of the great legal authorities of the past as great philosophers in addition to jurists. Thus he views their activity in light of the Platonic political tradition.

Maimonides' extreme position in regard to the eternal authority of all the Mosaic laws undergoes modification in still other ways. While he insists, for example, that the Oral Law was revealed together with the written Torah, and is the only legally valid interpretation of it, he adopts an extreme and exceptional position in limiting its scope. Only those legal interpretations in which there were no disagreements between the sages can be considered as part of the Oral Law.[42] This position serves an important function in the rabbinic polemic with the Karaites, for it views the numerous disagreements between the talmudic sages as not being on matters that were "handed down" from Sinai. There was never any break in the chain of transmission, appearances notwithstanding. All the arguments involved rabbinic interpretations of the details of the law. The Karaite claim that even according to rabbinic tradition the Oral Law was forgotten is in this manner dismissed.

The position adopted by Maimonides is also significant from a political/legal standpoint. By removing the status of "Oral Law" from many of the talmudic laws, Maimonides leaves open the possibility of far reaching changes in these laws in the future. The complete inflexibility of the outer structure of the law is balanced by the great flexibility of many of its particulars. Only those with the proper legal authority may work these changes, but Maimonides accords them much latitude in which to work. The messiah and his court of law will not have the authority to change formally Mosaic legislation, but they will be able to make formal changes in all prior rabbinic legislation. Maimonides may have even allowed himself a certain amount of greater flexibility in his own rulings on the basis of his minimalist position of what laws fall under the category of Oral Law, a point that requires further study.[43]

There is a hint in the *Guide of the Perplexed* that Maimonides, like the Karaites, regards the Oral Law itself as a post-Mosaic historical creation. In presenting the reasons for the commandments, for example *lex talionis,* he points to the fact that he is interpreting the commandment in accordance with the literal meaning of the biblical text, and not in accordance with its legal definition (*Guide* 3:41). Insofar as the legal definition is given in the Oral Law, Maimonides' move suggests that some of the commandments were interpreted differently when given to the Jews leaving Egypt.[44] If this in fact is his esoteric view, he would have considered the notion presented by the sages of the Talmud that the Oral Law was given at Sinai to be a rabbinic myth. It was formulated for the purpose of sanctioning their interpretation of Mosaic Law against competing interpretations. Since Maimonides regards the sages as philosopher-jurists whose approach to Mosaic Law was appropriate to the changing circumstances, and the myths they framed serve as an important pedagogical tool, he continues to perpetrate this myth in his legal writings. Indeed he has no choice if he is to uphold rabbinic tradition, and insure the commitment of his coreligionists to this tradition.

The Torah's treatment of God as corporeal is probably the most poignant example of a far-reaching compromise made in Mosaic legislation out of consideration for the situation of the masses (*Guide* 1:46). Maimonides felt the time was ripe to reject this compromise. He insists in all his works that one must hold the opinion that God is incorporeal, with failure to do so constituting heresy (*Commentary on the Mishnah: Introduction to Pereq Ḥeleq,* third principle; *Laws of Repentance* 3:7). He treats knowledge of God and the world as necessary for achieving true love of God, this love constituting a primary legal obligation. In this manner he refines the education of the masses, thereby creating a more conducive environment for the pursuit of intellectual perfection. Maimonides inculcates the notion that the ultimate goal of the Law is intellectual perfection, and that the pursuit of this perfection is the ultimate legal obligation. All the laws are seen as advancing this goal, either directly or indirectly (*Guide* 3:27). His codification of the Law reflects this objective. The message of the first four chapters of the first book of the *Mishneh Torah—Book of Knowledge*—the last chapter of the book, and the last chapter of the entire treatise is that the final purpose of the eternal Law is the attainment of knowledge of God in accordance with human ability.[45]

One may question why Maimonides went out of his way to insist upon the eternal validity of all the laws if he felt that changes were necessary. Why, for example, does he indicate that sacrifices will be reinstituted in messianic times when he no longer saw any historical need for sacrifices? Quite the contrary, from a certain perspective the reintroduction of sacrifices would be a retreat from the purer forms of worship Maimonides advocates. Moreover, what is the basis for Maimonides' confidence that no divine legislation will ever come to replace Mosaic legislation when he himself sees the need for changes, and can envision a legislation more suitable for his own day? Maimonides' desire to protect and preserve Judaism from the various challenges facing it, and his conviction in its superiority over the other religions, are crucial elements in appreciating the positions he adopts. The possibility of formal abrogation of any of the commandments paves the way for an abandonment of Judaism as a whole in favor of the other religions that also claim divine authority. Such compromises as the acceptance of the reinstitution of sacrifices—an issue that had only theoretical rather than practical significance for his own day—was a small price to pay for preserving a law that Maimonides viewed as the most conducive legislation overall for attaining intellectual perfection.

IV

In Jewish legal tradition, the two institutions that were seen as being on the top of the pyramid of political authority were the king and the high court, the Sanhedrin. The authority of the second was not only judicial, but just as important, legislative. While the authority of the king was largely executive, it also extended to the other two areas. To what degree the laws found in the Talmud regarding these two institutions conformed to social reality at any time in history is a problem not germane to our discussion. The important point is that a legal tradition existed, considered as being rooted in Mosaic Law, which at least loosely defined the extent (and limits) of political institutional authority within Judaism. The individuals occupying these offices derived their authority by virtue of the office. The Law sanctioned their authority. Neither the king nor the members of the Sanhedrin stood above the Law, whose authority reigned supreme. As is the case with all areas of Jewish law, whether of practical application in his own time or not, Maimonides devotes parts of the *Mishneh Torah* to the laws governing these two institutions. He culls these laws from a wide range of talmudic sources. In the process of arranging and codifying them, he presents a much clearer picture of the authority of these institutions, a picture that also bears the impress of his own conceptual approach.[46]

There is another institution within Judaism whose authority may be viewed as exceeding that of the other two mentioned—the prophet. In a crucial sense prophecy is not an "institution" at all, though the legal tradition accords the prophet a number of institutional roles such as that of anointing the king. In the case of the other political institutions, the Law defines the manner in which an individual ascents to office and assumes the authority of office. The prophet, on the other hand, is "appointed" directly by God. The Law can only define the manner in which the people are to confirm that God in fact made this appointment. The Law defines the authority of the king and Sanhedrin. The prophet receives the communication from a higher authority, the Giver of the Law. One thus may be led to believe that the prophetic communication overrides the Law. The revelation of the Law and the revelation of prophecy are both immediately traced to the same source. Moses too received the Law by way of prophecy. The miracle confirms the prophetic message just as at Sinai it confirmed the legislation of Moses.

When viewed from the perspective of maintaining the integrity of the Law, such view poses great dangers. It is not always so easy to distinguish "true" prophets from "false" ones, thereby knowing which messages are to be heeded and which not. If left unchecked, the potential damage to Jewish law that the false prophet could bring about is immeasurable. The Torah itself makes the first move to meet this danger by ruling that any message to follow other gods and worship them is not to be obeyed. The prophet is to be put to death despite any "sign" offered (Deut. 13:2–6). The talmudic sages continued this trend by placing severe limitations on the prophet's authority to make changes in the legal tradition. According to one well known story the sages went so far as to refuse to heed a Heavenly Voice in deciding questions of law (*Baba Meṣi'a* 59b). In a paradoxical move it was argued that once the entire Torah was given from heaven, and in it was contained the established process for deciding questions of law, there was no place for divine revelations in these matters. Heaven, as it were, had already exhausted its stock of laws, and was no longer to meddle in legal matters.[47]

Perhaps more than any authority, Maimonides follows this extreme trend of thought. He attempts to tie the prophet's hands in matters falling in the domain of legislative/judicial authority almost completely. He confines prophetic authority to strictly political decisions on which the Law adopts a neutral stance. The extent of authority he grants to the prophet in the domain of law is the right to issue decrees and more significantly, to suspend temporarily Torah laws (with the exception of the laws of idolatry) in exceptional circumstances. The latter area of prophetic authority was already well established in talmudic texts and was based on biblical precedents (*Sanhedrin* 90a). Otherwise, prophets have no right even to *interpret* laws *qua* prophets. Any attempt, no matter how "minor," to rule in matters of law on the basis of revelation is treated as a sure sign that the individual is a false prophet. The authority prophets have in legislative/judicial matters is rooted in their being sages, with the exact same authority accorded any sage. Maimonides discusses this issue at length in the *Introduction to the Commentary on the Mishnah*, returns to it in a later part of his commentary, *Introduction to Pereq Ḥeleq*, reiterates his views in the *Epistle to the Jews of Yemen* and codifies these rulings in *Laws of Principles of the Torah* 9:1–5.

Maimonides had before him too many historical precedents of catastrophes to the Jewish people and to Jewish observance brought about by those who could only be regarded as false prophets from the standpoint of rabbinic tradition. The founders of Christianity and Islam are the most conspicuous, but far from the only examples.[48] When viewed in this light, the measures adopted by Maimonides to limit the danger of false prophets become understandable. His entire legal approach is designed to preserve the authority of the Torah in the face of the manifold challenges facing it. Instead of seeing the great miracles that were performed for Israel as the basis for accepting the Law, a position found in some of his sources, Maimonides argues that our acceptance of Mosaic prophecy is not based on any "sign." Rather, it is based upon the unique Revelation at Sinai. All of Israel served as witnesses: "Our eyes saw and not [those of] another, our ears heard and not [those of] another, the fire, sounds and torches. He [Moses] advanced to the mist and the voice spoke to him. We heard: 'Moses, Moses, go tell them such and such.' So it is said, *Face to face God spoke to you* (Deut. 5:4)" (*Laws of Principles of the Torah* 8:1).

A categorical distinction is drawn by Maimonides between the Revelation at Sinai and the performance of miracles. Miracles are downplayed by Maimonides by being treated as a totally unreliable way of verifying prophecy. Any authority it carries in this matter derives *solely* from the Law in his view. No independent status as a mode of verification is to be ascribed to it.

Maimonides makes no attempt to explain the nature of this "voice" or the other exceptional phenomena accompanying the revelation. His goal is to preserve the notion of the uniqueness of Mosaic prophecy and the inviolability of the product of his prophecy, the Torah. The notion of God's public "speech" to Moses serves to promote this goal.[49] It is not primarily Maimonides' desire to inculcate a more naturalistic worldview that is involved in his approach to miracles here, though this certainly plays an important role. It is the necessity of establishing a criterion for accepting Mosaic law that he could argue was both public and unique. Miracles have no authority to undermine the Law. Only God directly addressing the entire nation carries any weight in this matter.

Even with these precautions designed to preserve commitment to the Law, Maimonides does not rest content. He confines the "sign" to divination of future events, rather than the performance of miracles.[50] While on the surface this appears to make it easier for the prophet to verify his mission, and is more in harmony with a naturalistic worldview, the test as formulated by Maimonides is nonetheless a nigh impossible one to pass. The prophet must successfully predict a *number* of future events, in all their *details* (10:1–2). Even the smallest mistake indicates that the individual is not a true prophet. Maimonides argues that the complete accuracy of the prophet's predictions distinguishes the prophet from soothsayers and magicians (10:3). So central to public prophecy is one's ability in this area that Maimonides describes the prophet's role primarily as a diviner.

The contrast between Maimonides' dual approach to prophecy in the *Laws of Principles of the Torah* is striking. His discussion begins in chapter 7 with a description of prophecy as ultimate intellectual perfection attained after exhaustive preparations. Maimonides essentially transforms prophecy from being conceived primarily as a mission to being conceived primarily as a perfection. To underscore this point he introduces the notion of private prophecy, which is confined to the individual's own intellectual attainment. Public prophecy is described as involving *in addition* a mission. Yet in turning to public prophecy, Maimonides is not at all interested in developing a conception that gives this individual an opportunity for making full use of the prophetic perfection. He is more interested in setting tests that are nigh impossible to pass, severely limiting the authority of even one who passes them, and then treating the individual primarily as a glorified diviner. The conception underlying Maimonides' approach is that the integrity of the Law must be protected as much as possible from the potential havoc wreaked by false prophets even if it means sacrificing some of the benefits a true prophet is capable of bestowing. He was well aware how tempting it is, particularly in times of despair, to heed the call of any charismatic individual who claims to bear the message of God. In the effort to safeguard the Law, the best course is to assign responsibility for the interpretation of law to different institutions—for example, the Sanhedrin. Those who attain perfection were to find expression for their ability within the confines of the authority vested in these human institutions.

Significantly, Maimonides in the introduction to his *Commentary on the Mishnah* treats R. Judah the Prince, the compiler of the *Mishnah,* as a person whose intellectual and moral perfection was exceeded only by that of Moses. In ascribing to him all the qualifications for prophecy, Maimonides essentially indicates that while there were no postbiblical *public* prophets, those possessing prophetic perfection continued to arise on the stage of history. They functioned as great sages. R. Judah the Prince is the model of such a sage. The product of his activity had a singular impact both in preserving and adapting the Law to his period. More than any other postbiblical figure, he served as the model for Maimonides' own activity.

The conception underlying Maimonides' legal approach to public prophecy also stands in contrast to the one underlying his more theoretical approach presented in the *Guide*. Alfarabi had already transformed Plato's philosopher-king to the perfect individual who receives "revelation" *(waḥy)*—an emanation from the Active Intellect to the rational faculty of the individual who had attained complete knowledge of all the sciences—and is best equipped to govern. The *Guide* reflects the extent Maimonides takes over this model. Maimonides continues to insist that the revelation of the divine Law to Moses is a unique occurrence (2:39). Yet it is the prophet who is treated by Maimonides as the political leader *par excellence* by virtue of the revelation received (*Guide* 2:36–37).[51] One is justified in concluding that from the perspective of Maimonides' conception of the nature of the prophetic perfection, the prophet is in fact the one best suited to interpret Mosaic Law. This individual, even more than the sage, fully grasps the nature of existence and the purpose of the Law, and is best capable of adapting it to the social situation. If Maimonides does not draw the practical implications of this view in his legal approach, it is not so much because of the weight of the legal tradition. The goal of preserving Mosaic Law stood foremost in his mind. Private prophecy for him remains the goal of human striving while public prophecy is effectively dismissed. The public prophet is replaced by the great sage, who may at times be an individual who has attained the level of private prophecy.

A few words should be added in this context on Maimonides' view of the king-messiah.[52] Certainly no figure better lends itself to being described in terms of the philosophic model of the ideal ruler than that of the messiah. Maimonides discusses the messiah in *Laws of Kings* 11:1–12:5, a section whose significance is underscored by the fact that it marks the conclusion of his great legal compendium. The messiah is depicted as an exceptional human being, rather than a quasi-supernatural one. Maimonides insists that the order of nature will not change at all in the messianic period, and that the Law *in its entirety* will continue to be in effect. The picture drawn by Maimonides is one of an ideal *historical* period, in which obedience to the Law, world peace and prosperity, and the universal pursuit of knowledge of God will reign supreme. He attempts to eliminate all supernaturalistic elements from the picture of the messianic period.[53] He expressly wants his readers to regard the intellectual perfection of the individual and its "reward"—eternal incorporeal existence in the world to come—as the goal of human striving, not the benefits of the messianic age (12:4; cf. *Laws of Repentance* 8:1–9:2).

A question that immediately comes to mind is whether the messiah must also be a prophet in Maimonides' view. The answer is unequivocally in the affirmative (12:3). In the *Laws of Repentance* 9:2 he is even described as close to the prophetic level of Moses. The institutional authority of kingship in his case comes together with the personal attainment of prophecy. Despite this view of the messiah, the criteria laid down by Maimonides in *Laws of Kings* for authenticating who is the true messiah is different in some crucial respects from the criteria for verifying who is a true prophet. Bar-Kokhba, Maimonides points out, was regarded as the messiah by the leading sage of the generation Rabbi Akiva. He was not asked by any of the sages for a "sign" (11:3). Maimonides goes on to maintain that a learned and observant king from the House of David who enforces the Law and liberates Israel should be regarded as the messiah. If the individual is completely successful in his endeavors, builds the sanctuary and brings together all the dispersed Jews, then he is definitely the messiah (11:4). Military and political success of the person with the appropriate lineage and commitment to Jewish law, rather than exceptional divinatory ability, is the test. By painting the messiah in this manner, Maimonides not only inculcates a naturalistic conception of the "end of time," which is clearly an important objective in his description. He also best preserves the integrity of the Law. The messiah is not treated as a public prophet, whose dual authority and special ability might place him beyond the strictures of the Law in the view of the masses. He remains bound by the Law, and his enforcement of the Law is one of the criteria by which he is judged. If the messiah were seen as a quasi-supernatural figure of unique authority who ushers in a period in which the order of nature changes, then it is only natural to think that the Law too has run its course.

In contrast to his discussion of public prophecy in *Laws of the Principles of the Torah*, Maimonides' presentation in *Laws of Kings* does not appear to be overly concerned with the problem of protecting Judaism from false claimants to the title of messiah. No formal procedure is laid out for verifying the claim. The focus of Maimonides' presentation is dictated by other considerations. Thus it is interesting to see how Maimonides relates to the issue of false messiahs when it assumes central stage in his discussion. This in fact is the case in his earlier *Epistle to the Jews of Yemen.* In the actual case addressed by Maimonides in the epistle, he challenges a person's claim to be the messiah precisely by pointing to the criteria for verifying who is a prophet. Maimonides argues that all the conditions that apply to prophecy must apply to the messiah. He must be an individual of exceptional wisdom whose "signs" are proven true. An ignorant person who possesses none of the qualifications for prophecy, offers no signs, and proceeds to issue foolish commands—as was the case in Yemen as reported to Maimonides—clearly is a false messiah.[54] Maimonides' approach to the conditions for prophecy in this context serves to meet a severe social-religious challenge. The epistle provides us with an instructive example of how the change in the focus of Maimonides' discussion of a topic in different contexts affects how he formulates his position.

V

If the ultimate idea for Maimonides is the monotheistic idea, then the ultimate threat is idolatry. The two figures in Jewish history who played the most decisive role in promoting the monotheistic idea and combating idolatry were Abraham and Moses. This view is hardly a new one in Judaism. As is the case with all of the "traditional views" presented by Maimonides, it is important to see the ways he develops them and integrates them into his thought. Maimonides often employs ideas and motifs derived from non-Jewish sources in his interpretations. The "traditional view" is given a whole different meaning, one that is in harmony with Maimonides' conceptual approach or educational objectives. A careful glance at the strategies he ascribes to Abraham and Moses in accomplishing their historical roles helps us to understand better Maimonides' own. In light of Maimonides' reconstruction of history, a number of his positions become clearer. Others become more perplexing. A study of Maimonides' views not only leads to a better understanding of the issues one is interested in exploring. Often it also brings to the surface problems that were not immediately evident on a cursory reading of his discussions.

Maimonides opens his *Commentary on the Mishnah,* his *Book of the Commandments*, each book of the *Mishneh Torah* and each section of the *Guide of the Perplexed* with the verse that describes Abraham's call: *In the name of God, Lord of the World* (Genesis 21:33). The constant repetition of this verse indicates that Maimonides sees in it his own "calling." The significance of this verse is explained by Maimonides in *Guide* 2:13, 2:30 and 3:29, as well as in the *Mishneh Torah: Laws of Idolatry* 1:3. It refers to Abraham's public teaching of the existence and unity of God, who is neither a body nor a force in a body, as well as God's creation of the entire world. The latter teaching is clarified by the verse, *Maker of Heaven and Earth* (Genesis 14.22).[55]

The "discovery" of the treatise known as the *Nabatean Agriculture*—a treatise that purportedly belonged to the ancient pagans, the Sabians, and described their beliefs and practices[56]—provided Maimonides with much of the foundation upon which he built his reconstruction of early biblical history. Moreover, it had a dominant influence on his approach to the reasons for many of the commandments.[57] According to Maimonides, Abraham grew up in a period when the universal belief was that of the Sabians. They taught that the only deities were the stars. Consequently, the stars, or objects believed to act as their intermediaries, were the objects of worship. Abraham's preaching served as the turning point in history, stemming the spiritual-intellectual degeneration of humanity. So great was Abraham's ultimate victory in this matter that: "His activity has resulted, as we see today, in the consensus of the greater part of the population of the earth in glorifying him and considering themselves as blessed through his memory. . . . No one is antagonistic to him or ignorant of his greatness except the remnants of this religious community that has perished. . . . These are the remnants of the religious community of the Sabians, for this was a religious community that extended over the whole earth" (*Guide* 3:29.515).

In utilizing Gen. 21:33 as the leitmotif of all of his major works, Maimonides implies that he views his task as continuing Abraham's mission to proclaim God's unity. In Abraham's day the main challenge to this teaching was posed by the belief that the planets were the deity. For Maimonides, the belief in God's corporeality now comprised the main stumbling block to the attainment of a true conception of God.[58]

Both in the *Laws of Idolatry* and in the *Guide* Maimonides refers to the necessity for Abraham to flee his native land. The authorities were far from pleased by the success of his teaching. Eventually Abraham makes his way to the land of Canaan (*Laws of Idolatry* 1:3; *Guide* 3:29). Maimonides does not discuss the revelation to Abraham to settle in Canaan, except to indicate in a different context that the divine speech came via an "angel" (*Guide* 2:41). Given Maimonides' naturalistic approach to revelation, the "command" to Abraham to settle in Canaan should not be viewed as a direct communication from God. It alludes to the prophetic enlightenment attained by Abraham, as a result of the emanation from the Active Intellect. One may hypothesize that as a result of this enlightenment, Abraham grasped that the conditions in Canaan were more conducive for the propagation of the monotheistic idea. While idolatry was rampant also in Canaan, no strong central authority existed there that would try to put a stop to Abraham's teachings. The "choiceness" of the land lies in the social and physical environment it provided for the flourishing of Abraham's progeny and their beliefs. It should be noted that Maimonides in his legal discussions regarding Israel does not treat the "holiness" of the land as reflecting some special "metaphysical" state. He formulates his discussion in a manner that places greater emphasis on the study of the Law even outside of Israel than settlement in Israel. The special "nature" of the land lies in its being the place where Jews can develop a polity best designed to practice the divine Law and achieve its ultimate end.[59]

In light of Maimonides' estimation of Abraham, and his viewing him as the role model for his own pedagogical efforts, it is somewhat surprising that in the same passage in 3:29 Maimonides presents the following position: "We have already made it clear in our great compilation, *Mishneh Torah*, that Abraham our Father began to refute these opinions by means of arguments and feeble [*da'if*][60] preaching, conciliating people and drawing them to obedience by means of benefits" (p. 517). Maimonides' characterization of Abraham's preaching as "feeble" should not be construed as an evaluation of Abraham's arguments from an intellectual or even a rhetorical point of view. In 2:39, Maimonides refers to Abraham's speeches as "eloquent" [or "fine"—*ḥasan*]. The feebleness in Abraham's preaching is characteristic of the weakness of rational argumentation in general to attain its objective. Abraham himself was aware of the inherent deficiency in turning people to proper belief in God by means of argumentation alone. He complemented his efforts by bestowing "benefits." The need for material benefits as an incentive to learning the truth is described by Maimonides in detail in *Introduction to Pereq Ḥeleq*. While the goal is to wean the individual gradually to the point that one learns the truth for its own sake, the educator must recognize what is possible to accomplish at each step and how best to accomplish it. One cannot prove to be an effective educator by skipping steps in the process.

The passage in the *Mishneh Torah* to which *Guide* 3:29 refers (*Laws of Idolatry* 1:3), makes no mention of the weakness in Abraham's use of argumentation. Stress is placed on Abraham's tremendous success in the pursuit of his goal by virtue of his argumentation: "till thousands and tens of thousands gathered to him, and they are the members of the house of Abraham." Abraham's pedagogical skills are underscored by his ability to vary his argumentation, teaching each person, "in accordance with his intellectual ability, till he returned him to the way of truth." This is the very same method Maimonides insists upon adopting in teaching the multitude that God is incorporeal (*Guide* 1:35). Yet even in this discussion, the shortcomings in the use of argumentation alone implicitly emerge. From the outset, Abraham's activity, in Maimonides' description, is not confined to preaching. Abraham engages in the physical destruction of the idols. He understood that arguments will not suffice if the idols remain. Moreover, his initial victory was not long lived according to Maimonides. The nation that sprang up from the progeny of Abraham lapsed into idolatry as a result of the influences of the idolatrous practices of the Egyptians. In the social clash between beliefs not supported by practices, and beliefs supported by practices, the latter are sure to emerge victorious. In a short period, "the principle which Abraham had planted was uprooted, and the children of Jacob returned to the error of the nations and their going astray" (*Laws of Idolatry* 1:3).

It is only with the laying down of a law designed to combat the practices of idolatry that the monotheistic belief was able to emerge victorious: "From God's love of us and in keeping with the promise to Abraham our father, He made Moses our Master the master of all the prophets and sent him. Since Moses our Master prophesied and God chose Israel as a portion, He crowned them with the commandments and informed them the way to worship Him, what is to be the law concerning idolatry and those who go astray after it" (*Laws of Idolatry* 1:3). In 3:29, too, Maimonides continues his discussion of Abraham by contrasting his approach with that of Moses: "Then the Master of the prophets received prophetic inspiration; thereupon he perfected the purpose in that he commanded killing these people, wiping out their traces, and tearing out their roots . . . and forbade following those ways of theirs in anything . . . The first intention of the Law as a whole is to put an end to idolatry, to wipe out its traces and all that is bound up with it, even its memory as well as all that leads to any of its works" (p. 517).

Moses' superiority in the eyes of Maimonides lies in the fact that his prophetic mission assumed the form of political governance and commands, not just teachings. His was a unique mission for it alone resulted in laying down a legislation for governing a polity (*Guide* 1:63; 2:39). Laws governing a polity are far more efficacious than the teachings of an individual for molding the beliefs of society, even when the teachings are bolstered by additional activities. Law is the ultimate pedagogical tool in Maimonides' philosophy. This view is rooted in the integral relationship between beliefs and practices. Just as beliefs can give rise to and reinforce certain practices, practices can give rise to and reinforce certain beliefs. Law institutionalizes both the beliefs and the practices. Abraham too laid down for his household certain practices in order to bind them together in their faith—the command of circumcision being the most notable example (*Guide* 2:39).[61] Yet this was still a far cry from the legislation of a complete code of law that was in large measure designed to preserve certain beliefs.

The dynamic relation between beliefs and practices underlies Maimonides' description of the rise of polytheism. The beginning of history, in Maimonides' reconstruction, is marked by a universal monotheism. Based on rabbinic sources, Maimonides traces the introduction of idolatry to Enosh and his generation.[62] He ascribes this turning point to a critical error—more a fundamental error in judgment than an error in theoretical speculation. Since God created the planets as intermediaries for governing the world, it was reasoned, they too are worthy of honor. This is the will of God, just as it is the will of a human king that the people pay honor to his officials (*Laws of Idolatry* 1:1). What begins as the worship of the planets as God's intermediaries, according to Maimonides, ends with an elaborate system of *institutionalized* worship of the planets alone as deities. The true God was eventually forgotten by all but a handful of individuals. Thus the belief in the planets as intermediaries—in itself a true belief—step by step gives rise to the ultimate false belief—namely, that they are the deity. The worship of the stars, supported first by the sages of the nations, and then by false prophets who claimed to receive revelation from the planets, eventually completely replaced the worship of God.

The "logic" of the historical process outlined by Maimonides emerges clearly from his thought. Star worship ultimately proved dominant since the stars are both more immediate than God and are visible. People tend to pay greater heed to the rulers who are in closer proximity. In other contexts Maimonides indicates that the masses are prone to believe in the existence only of that which they can visualize (*Guide* 1:46; 1:49). With the worship of the stars and *their* intermediaries—for example, talismans—the belief in the one God beyond the visible heavens, a belief that is hard to grasp, inevitably vanished. Polytheism resulted from the lack of appreciation on the part of the monotheists of the dire consequences in counseling the worship of anything in addition to God.

The monotheistic idea and idolatry are not logically contradictory. Idolatry lies in the *act* of worship. Contradictions exist between propositions. There can be no *logical* contradiction between a belief and an action, only with the belief normally associated or underlying the performance of a certain act. The belief underlying a given action may vary among those who perform it. It may also change over time. This is in fact the case with idolatry in Maimonides' reconstruction of history. The belief underlying idolatry did not initially reflect a rejection of God. The object of worship was worshipped as an intermediary rather than as the deity. The main lesson in history, however, is that idolatry leads to polytheism and strengthens this belief. For this reason one who worships idols is said to "reject the fundamental principle"—that is, God (*Laws of Idolatry* 2:6). Thus the elimination of idolatry assumes such high priority. It is, Maimonides maintains, the foundation of the Law (*Guide* 3:29–30).[63]

The Law employs a myriad of strategies to combat idolatry. For example, it promulgates opinions designed to discourage idolatrous practices or directly combat polytheistic beliefs. It teaches that God's wrath is directed against idolaters. It holds out the threat that idolatrous practices will ensure all forms of calamity as divine punishment—for example, famine, pestilence (*Guide* 3:30). Most of the strategies employed by the Law deal with the realm of practice. It enjoins the physical elimination of idolaters.[64] It forbids the idolatrous practices of the Sabians or practices that lend support to their polytheistic beliefs. Practices that the Law cannot forbid without dire consequences, such as sacrifices, it transfers to the worship of God (*Guide* 3:32). At the same time, it minimizes the extent of these practices and modifies their details.

What light can this view of history shed on Maimonides' activities and teachings? Maimonides' concentration on legal matters, as opposed to a discussion of philosophical-theological issues, becomes more understandable. The *Mishneh Torah* takes Moses' activity as it primary model. Law is a more effective tool than rational argumentation for educating society. The *Guide of the Perplexed*, in being a work of rational argumentation, follows the path of Abraham. Maimonides in a sense "reverses" history. In history, the teaching of the monotheistic idea by means of rational arguments precedes the law. A nation must come into existence before a law may be legislated. Till that point, however, the idea rests on a shaky foundation. Maimonides concentrates on the Law since it provides a far more solid foundation for Jewish education. He turns to rational argumentation only after writing his great legal work, the *Mishneh Torah*. The *Guide,* unlike the *Mishneh Torah*, is not directed to Jewish society at large. Rational argumentation is not appropriate for everyone. It is directed to a group who have been raised in the practice of the law and its beliefs, started studying philosophy, and must now be addressed through the medium of reason.

VI

In light of my argument that Maimonides sees as his task the preservation and adaptation of the Law, his insistence that the primary purpose of the Law is the eradication of idolatry, though well anchored in traditional sources, is somewhat surprising. By stressing in the *Guide* that many of the commandments serve to combat idolatry, he appears to undermine in part the rationale for obedience. Maimonides himself points to the nigh eradication of the idolatrous religion of old, attesting to the singular victory of Abraham and Moses. The reasons for many of the commandments were forgotten, according to Maimonides, as a result of this victory (*Guide* 3:49). The Law thus appears to be dated. If the commandments nevertheless remain binding, and must continue to be practiced, it is because their authority is not derived from the reasons for their promulgation. Nevertheless, it is difficult to encourage observance of laws that no longer serve an apparent purpose. This problem was not lost on some of Maimonides' medieval followers. They preferred to offer nonhistorically obsolete reasons, such as symbolic ones, for many of the same commandments that Maimonides explains along historical-anthropological lines, such as the sacrifices.[65]

One can only speculate why Maimonides did not follow the same path. In his discussion of the reasons for the commandments in the *Guide*, Maimonides' cardinal principle is that no commandment was designed arbitrarily. All were designed to further the Law's end, which is the end of all human society. There is no room in Maimonides' thought for any magical or quasi-magical explanation of laws. He also appears to show little tolerance for symbolic explanations in understanding why certain laws were promulgated, and uses them sparingly. Maimonides brings a symbolic reason for sin-offerings and the scapegoat ritual on the Day of Atonement: "No one has any doubt that sins are not bodies that may be transported from the back of one individual to that of another. But all these actions are parables serving to bring forth a form in the soul so that a passion toward repentance should result: We have freed ourselves from all our previous actions, cast them behind our backs, and removed them to an extreme distance" (3:46.591). The ethical significance of Maimonides' explanation is clear. Yet it is noteworthy that he brings this type of explanation precisely to commandments that in the eyes of the casual observer appear to be magical practices reminiscent of, rather than a rejection of, those belonging to the idolaters. The symbolic explanation serves to combat this dangerous view.[66]

Maimonides' approach to the reasons of the commandments is marked by competing considerations. One must try to understand what was his dominant consideration in formulating his views in any given discussion. The historical explanation best illuminates the wisdom of all the commandments in a manner that is harmonious with Maimonides' conception of the purpose of the Law from the perspective of the Lawgiver, and in accordance with the initial promulgation. This is the view he is interested to communicate to the philosophic reader of the *Guide.* Perhaps he was of the opinion that other types of explanation could not adequately explain the rationale for legislating the specific content of these laws. The problem this view raises regarding the contemporary "relevance" of those commandments designed to combat idolatry was for Maimonides a secondary consideration in this context. Significantly, he explains some of the commandments in the *Guide* according to their literal meaning, and not according to the Oral Law, as I indicated above. He alludes to his esoteric view that in this manner these commandments were meant to be understood by the Israelites when they first received the Law. Maimonides also includes in his explanation commandments that were only incumbent upon the generation leaving Egypt, and not subsequent generations, such as sprinkling the blood of the Paschal offering on the door posts (3:46).

While the use of historical explanations for the commandments are extensive and explicit in the *Guide*, they do not play a prominent role in his earlier *Mishneh Torah.*[67] Maimonides adopts a different approach in his code of law. *Laws of Idolatry* is an exceptional section precisely because of the fact that it begins with a reconstruction of history, thereby at least implying that the prohibitions that follow should be understood in light of historical circumstances. The practices of the ancient idolaters play no evident role in the explanation of the laws found in the other sections of the code. In the *Mishneh Torah,* Maimonides prefers to show the ethical-spiritual significance of laws to which subsequently in the *Guide* he gives a historical explanation. This is in keeping with the primary intention of both works. The explanations in the *Mishneh Torah* are predominantly concerned with their practical implications for observance.

A good example of this point is Maimonides' discussion of the laws of ritual purity.[68] In the *Guide* Maimonides lists four reasons for this category of law: "One of them is keep men away from disgusting things. The second is to safeguard the Sanctuary. The third is to protect what is generally accepted and customary, for, as you will hear presently, unpleasant things were imposed on the Sabians in cases of uncleanness. The fourth is to ease unpleasant restrictions and to order things in such a manner that questions of uncleanness and cleanness should not prevent a man from engaging in any of the occupations" (3:47.594). The last reason too, Maimonides indicates, combats accepted Sabian practice, the remnant of which could still be detected in his own time.

How different is Maimonides' stance in the *Mishneh Torah: Laws of Ritual Baths* 11:12:

> It is clear and manifest that impurity and purity are decrees of Scripture. They are not among the things to which human reason inclines, but are among the divine statutes *(ḥuqqim).* Similarly, the immersion [that purifies] one from impurity is a divine statute. Impurity is not mud or excrement that is removed by water. It is a decree of Scripture dependent upon the intention of the heart. For this reason the sages said: "If a person immerses not for the purpose [of purifying himself], it is as though he has not immersed at all." Nevertheless, there is a "hint" in this matter that just as one who has the intention to be purified by immersion thereby becomes pure, even though nothing new has befallen his body, so too one who has the intention to purify his soul from its impurities—i.e., wrongful thoughts and evil character traits *(de'ot ra'ot)*[69]—becomes pure when he assents in his heart to detach himself from these counsels and he brings his soul to the waters of reason.

Even Maimonides' treatment of idolatry in the *Laws of Idolatry* reflects how he subtly imparts to this subject a more relevant focal point for his own period. He begins his formal legal discussion of idolatry in chapter 2 by defining idolatry as the worship of any of the created things. At this point one would have expected Maimonides to continue his discussion by defining the notion "worship." Instead, he introduces three other commandments: not to turn to idolatry in one's thoughts; not to entertain any thoughts that might lead to rejecting one of the principles of Judaism; not to curse God. The first two commandments primarily concern mental acts. Though reading the works of the idolaters and even looking at idols is included in this prohibition, the emphasis is on controlling one's thoughts. The second and third commandments do not deal with idolatry at all, but are included in this section by "association." Just as one should not have any thoughts that may lead to idolatry, so one should not entertain any thoughts that carry dire consequences for one's beliefs. Maimonides offers as examples doubting the existence of God, the truth of prophecy, and the divine origin of the Torah. He includes the prohibition against blasphemy among the laws of idolatry since one who simply acknowledges the truth of idolatry, even without actually worshipping other entities, is guilty of blaspheming God. Both the blasphemer and the idolater are described as "renouncing the fundamental principle" (*Laws of Idolatry* 2:6).

Idolatry thus is seen as part of a larger topic that deals with one's thoughts. One's mental state is treated as being just as important, if not more so, than one's physical activities. One may argue that Maimonides begins the section with mental acts since they are prior to physical acts and lead to them. The stress nevertheless is on the physical act of worship. Punishment after all, it may be further asserted, is meted out only to one who commits a physical act. In response, it should be noted that the whole tenor of his discussion here, as in *Laws of the Principles of the Torah,* indicates that the mental act is primary. The goal of the prohibitions regarding idolatry is to reinforce certain beliefs, not vice versa.

One has only to contrast the order and formulation of the commandments here and in the earlier *Book of the Commandments* to appreciate the extent to which Maimonides deliberately changes the focus of the discussion. The mental act, which includes also studying the works of idolaters, is downplayed in the *Book of the Commandments* (negative commandment 10). It appears only after Maimonides lists the prohibitions against making and worshipping idols. This commandment is immediately followed by the prohibition not to make a monument to be used for the public worship of God. The reason for this prohibition, Maimonides explains, is that the worship of God should not be similar to the worship of idols. The distinct impression one attains from Maimonides' order here is that the commandments following the prohibition against worshipping idols are designed to safeguard the people from committing this grievous sin. In his presentation of the commandment not to think about idolatry, Maimonides in fact indicates: "Deliberating about these matters and learning these vain imaginings lead the foolish one to seek them out and worship them." The emphasis is clearly on the act of worship.

The point that thinking about idolatry leads to worship is not absent in the *Laws of Idolatry*. Maimonides' constant refrain in this section, however, is not to turn to idolatry in any way. His change in the order of the commandments is significant. By beginning with the prohibition against mental acts, whether they lead to accepting the truth of idolatry or they cast doubt on any of Judaism's principles, Maimonides highlights the severity of this type of transgression. One of his statements in the *Guide of the Perplexed* gives concrete expression to this idea, though not in the context of a discussion of idolatry:

> You know what they say (*Yoma* 29a): "Thoughts about sin are worse than the sin." In order to explain this, I have a very extraordinary interpretation, which is as follows: A man committing an act of disobedience does it only, as I made clear, because of the accidents consequent upon his matter; I mean to say that he commits an act of disobedience through his bestiality. But thought is one of the properties of a human being that are consequent upon his form. Consequently if he gives his thought free scope in respect to disobedience, he commits an act of disobedience through the nobler of his two parts. Now the sin of him who does an injustice through making an ignorant slave serve him is not like the sin of him who makes a free man who is excellent serve him. (*Guide* 3:8.434–35)

It should not be inferred from what has been said that Maimonides felt that the threat of idol worship had vanished. This is not the case. Idolatry had assumed in his view new, more subtle forms. Christianity is regarded by Maimonides not only as a defective imitation of Judaism, but also as an idolatrous religion. The belief in the Trinity, with a human being regarded as the Son of God, is a form of polytheism in his view. Christian worship is thus considered by him to be idolatry in a technical legal sense.[70] It should be added that this view stands in sharp contrast to his appraisal of Islam. Islam too is considered to be a defective imitation of Judaism, but nevertheless is a monotheistic religion. Maimonides goes so far as to refrain from labeling Moslem worship at the Kaaba as idolatrous. He views the worship as being directed not to the stone itself but to the one true God.[71] In the attempt to point out Islam's faults, Maimonides turns to other areas—particularly its views regarding the Torah and some of the extreme practices enjoined by Moslem law.[72]

The threat posed by idolatry does not come only from the direction of Christianity. The human tendency to think that only the corporeal is real, and to prefer to worship what can in principle be sensed, makes the possibility of the reemergence of even the grosser forms of idolatry a real one. In Maimonides' reconstruction of the early history of humanity, twice the monotheistic idea loses out to polytheism: once in the period prior to Abraham, and later when the Jews were enslaved in Egypt. Subsequent history reflects the constant struggle between monotheism and polytheism. Maimonides' reconstruction shows that he was well aware that the effort to promote a more refined conception of God carried with it the constant risk of the monotheists resorting to the worship of "tangible" intermediaries. Subsequent history was to prove the truth of this point. Moreover, while the Sabian religion was almost completely stamped out, remnants remain in his view. Even some of their practices continue to be popular. Thus the peril that this ancient religion posed was not entirely eliminated.[73]

Maimonides' formulation of Jewish dogma in his *Commentary on the Mishnah* already reflects his effort to meet the threat of idolatry while inculcating the philosophic view of God's incorporeality.[74] Of the thirteen principles he presents, the first four convey what is essentially the philosophic conception of God. In this manner he makes an acceptance of the philosophic conception incumbent upon everyone. The fifth principle bridges those involving the divine essence and those dealing with prophecy and the divine Law. It states that God alone, and no other existent thing or object, is to be worshipped and exalted. Maimonides adds: "One should not make them intermediaries in order to reach God. One should direct all thoughts to God, while leaving aside everything else." The same stance reappears in Maimonides' description of different types of heretical positions in *Laws of Repentance* 3:7–8.[75]

In *Laws of Idolatry* 2:1 too Maimonides focuses on the worship of the stars as intermediaries. This threat was far more immediate in his period than the threat of the worship of the stars as deities. For this reason, he is interested in repeatedly emphasizing the former motive for star worship in his writings, an emphasis not found in his rabbinic sources.[76] No monotheist should be deluded into thinking that as long as one does not worship the intermediary as a deity, the person is not guilty of idolatry. History for Maimonides shows that directing the focus of one's attention to the intermediaries *qua* intermediaries, leads to a situation in which the one incorporeal deity is forgotten. This threat must be met at the earliest stages of the process.

By stressing that one who worships certain objects as intermediaries is still guilty of the sin of idolatry, Maimonides at the same time highlights how abominable are false beliefs about God. If one who accepts the existence of one God still may be guilty of this cardinal sin, one who does not acknowledge the one God in the proper manner should be treated as even more guilty. This point is central for Maimonides' strategy in inculcating a philosophically more refined conception of God:

> Now you know that whoever performs idolatrous worship does not do it on the assumption that there is no deity except the idol. . . . Rather is it worshipped in respect of its being an image of a thing that is an intermediary between ourselves and God. . . . However, in spite of the fact that those infidels believe in the existence of the deity, their idolatrous worship entails their destruction; for the reason that their infidelity bears upon a prerogative reserved to God alone, may He be exalted—I mean the prerogative of being worshipped and magnified. . . . This is so ordained in order that God's existence may be firmly established in the belief of the multitude. Now the idolaters thought that this prerogative belonged to that which was other than God; and this led to the disappearance of the belief in His existence, may He be exalted, from among the multitude. For the multitude grasp only the actions of worship, not their meanings or the true reality of the Being worshipped through them. . . . What then should be the state of him whose infidelity bears upon His essence, may He be exalted, and consists in believing Him to be different from what He really is? I mean to say that he does not believe that He exists; or believes that there are two gods, or that He is a body, or that he is other. Such a man is indubitably more blameworthy than a worshipper of idols who regards the latter as intermediaries or as having the power to do good or ill. (*Guide* 1:36.83–84)[77]

VII

The danger of idolatry in its leading to polytheism, and ultimately to a negation of the doctrine of a single deity "beyond" the stars, may be important for understanding Maimonides' position on a number of other issues. Any discussion of Maimonides' true view in regard to the issue of creation should take the problem of idolatry and polytheism under consideration. It is not my purpose to enter into a detailed analysis of the issue of creation. Suffice it to say, Maimonides' "formal" position is that neither the creation nor the eternity of the world are demonstrated doctrines. There are better philosophic reasons, he argues, for accepting the doctrine of creation. What ultimately determines our acceptance of the doctrine of creation, however, is the fact that this doctrine was taught by Abraham and Moses. Moreover, it conforms to a literal understanding of the Torah, and there is no valid reason for interpreting the Torah non-literally on this point. Finally, God's performance of miracles and the giving of the Law becomes possible only if one accepts the doctrine of creation. If one accepts the doctrine of eternity as taught by Aristotle, Maimonides indicates, "the Law as a whole would become void, and a shift to other opinions would take place" (*Guide* 2:25.330).[78] In other words, the doctrine of creation is necessary for religious reasons.

Maimonides does not explicitly introduce the issue of polytheism when discussing creation. The relation between the two emerges from other contexts. In this connection it is highly instructive to see how Maimonides describes Abraham's philosophic enlightenment and subsequent teachings. Let us begin with the description in the *Laws of Idolatry* 1:3:

> He started to think day and night, wondering: How is it possible for the sphere to be continuously ruled [*noheg tamid*], without there being a ruler? Who is its mover, for it is impossible that it should move itself? ... He knew that there is a single deity who is the ruler of the [diurnal] sphere, and who created *(bara')* everything. There is no deity among all the existents other than this one. He knew that the entire world erred. What caused them to err was the worship of the stars and the idols [lit.: "forms"], which resulted in their lose of knowledge of the truth. . . . He started to call in a great voice to the entire world and inform them that there is only one deity in the world, and this deity should be worshipped.

The careful reader of the *Mishneh Torah* will immediately associate this description of Abraham's speculation with Maimonides' discussion of knowledge of God in the *Laws of the Principles of the Torah* 1:5: "This existent is the Lord of the world, the master of the entire earth. He rules the sphere with an infinite unceasing power for the sphere is in continuous motion. It is impossible that it move without a mover. He, may He be exalted, is its mover without hand and without body."

The most important difference between these two citations is that Abraham also deduced that God "created everything." While it is understandable how Abraham's speculation would lead him to view God as the Mover of the sphere, it is not at all clear how he concludes from this that God created everything. In the *Laws of the Principles of the Torah* 1:1 God is described using "slightly" different terminology: "The fundamental principle and foundation of all knowledge is to know that there is a First Existent who gives existence *(mamṣi')* to all existents. All the existents in heaven and earth and what is between did not come into existence except by virtue of His true existence."

Any medieval philosophic reader of the *Mishneh Torah* would immediately recognize in Maimonides' formulation the medieval Aristotelian conception of God. God is both the Unmovable Mover and the First Cause of all existence.[79] The proof of God's existence to which Maimonides alludes in *Laws of the Principles of the Torah* 1:5 is based the constant motion of the sphere. As Maimonides subsequently clarifies in *Guide* 2:1, this proof requires the premise that the world is without beginning. What is crucial to stress in this context is that Abraham is depicted by Maimonides as an Aristotelian philosopher. His deduction that God "created" everything, as depicted in *Laws of Idolatry* 1:3, is in reality the Aristotelian view that God is the First Cause of all existence. The nonphilosophic reader will certainly understand this phrase as conveying the notion of God as creator *ex nihilo.* The philosophic reader will grasp the true meaning of this phrase as it is used by Maimonides in this context.

In Maimonides' description of Abraham in the *Guide* a significant change of formulation occurs. No longer is Abraham described as an Aristotelian philosopher. He is treated as one who opposes the Aristotelian view, and teaches the notion of God as creator *ex nihilo* (*Guide* 2:13). Perhaps no point better illustrates the change in Maimonides' approach than the fact that he no longer describes Abraham as discovering God by the Aristotelian proof of eternal motion. Instead Abraham is credited with a proof of God's existence based on the argument of "particularization"—an argument that at the same time furnishes Maimonides with his strongest proof for the creation of the world: "To my mind there is no proof of purpose stronger than the one founded upon the differences between the motions of the spheres and upon the fact that the stars are fixed in the spheres. For this reason you will find that all the prophets used the stars and the spheres as proofs for the deity's existing necessarily. Thus in the traditional story of Abraham, there occurs the tale, which is generally known, about his contemplation of the stars" (*Guide* 2:19.310).[80]

The question of Maimonides' true view on the problem of creation has attracted the attention of many of Maimonides' medieval and modern interpreters. My purpose at present is solely to point out what I regard as an important piece of the puzzle. The doctrine of creation plays a far more prominent role in the *Guide* than it does in the *Laws of the Principles of the Torah*.[81] This at the very least indicates a change in Maimonides' educational strategy. His realization of the importance of belief in creation for upholding belief in God as miracle worker and revealer of the Law, a belief that remains critical in safeguarding the commitment of the masses to Jewish law, would account in large measure for this change. Yet the import of the doctrine of creation in guarding against polytheism and preserving belief in the unity of God may have also played an important role in Maimonides' thinking on the subject.

In his discussion of creation, Maimonides' main "antagonist" is Aristotle. One of Aristotle's arguments for the eternity of the heavens, Maimonides notes, is the fact that this belief was universally affirmed in the past among all the nations. "When they became aware that they were not subject to coming about and passing away, they asserted that they were the dwelling place of God, may He be exalted, and of the spiritual beings" (*Guide* 2:14.289). Maimonides returns to this point in 2:23: "For Aristotle, the prince of the philosophers, in his main writings has likewise used rhetorical speeches in support of his opinion that the world is eternal. . . . If he refers in support of his opinion to the ravings of the Sabians, how can we but refer in support of our opinion to the words of Moses and Abraham and to everything that follows therefrom" (p. 322).

The Sabian opinion to which Aristotle refers was earlier cited by Maimonides in Aristotle's name as follows: "All men explicitly affirm the perpetuity and permanence of the heavens. And when they became aware that they were not subject to coming-about and passing away, they asserted that they were the dwelling place of God, may He be exalted, and of the spiritual beings—he [Aristotle] means to say, of the angels. They attributed the heavens to Him in order to indicate their perpetuity" (2:14.289). This view is reminiscent of the period in which idolatry is first introduced as a way of honoring God's intermediaries, according to Maimonides' reconstruction of history. In describing the Sabian opinion in the third part of the *Guide* a far different view is attributed to them reflecting the later development of their beliefs:

It is well known that Abraham our father, peace be on him, was brought up in the religious community of the Sabians, whose doctrine it is that there is no deity but the stars. . . . They explicitly asserted that the stars are the deity and that the sun is the greatest deity. . . . When Ibrahim, who was brought up in Kutha, disagreed with the community and asserted that there was an agent other than the sun, various arguments were brought forward against him. In these arguments they set forth the clear and manifest activities of the sun in what exists. Thereupon he, they mean Abraham, told them: You are right; it is like an ax in the hands of a carpenter. . . . The utmost attained by the speculation of those who philosophized in those times consisted in imagining that God was the spirit of the sphere and that the sphere and the stars are a body of which the deity, may He be exalted, is its spirit. . . . Therefore all the Sabians believed in the eternity of the world, since in their opinion heaven is the deity. (*Guide* 3:29.514–15)

Maimonides' "antagonist" in this section is no longer Aristotle, a philosopher who proves the existence of a single incorporeal God *based on* the eternity of the world. It is the Sabians whose belief in the eternity of the heavens brings about the subversion of the monotheistic idea. Abraham is no longer described as following Aristotle's lead and proving that God is the First Mover. Rather the world is described as acting in accordance with the divine Will. It becomes much clearer why Maimonides in this chapter defines Abraham's message as being not only that God exists, but also "the creation of the world in time by that deity" (p. 516). What is created cannot be regarded as a deity. After previously linking Aristotle with the Sabian opinion in order to subtly indicate why it is so important to uphold belief in creation, Maimonides now must carefully sever this link. Aristotle, the great monotheist, should in no way be identified as belonging to the Sabian camp. "[The Sabians] tell most ridiculous lies that show a great deficiency of intellect and that they are more remote from philosophy than any other men and are extremely ignorant" (p. 516).

One of the techniques favored by Maimonides in revealing his true views on a subject is by "flashing" them to the reader in a discussion focusing on a different subject. The average reader remains too focused on the main idea to understand the full significance of what Maimonides says. In light of this point, it should come as little surprise that his discussion of the commandments concerning the Sanctuary in 3:45 is one of the most important passages in the *Guide*. Maimonides indicates in passing that even the prophetic mission of Moses "is inaugurated through an angel" (p. 576), leaving the astute reader to digest the full implications of this highly significant statement. While in 2:23 and 2:25 belief in creation is treated by Maimonides as necessary for belief in the Law, in 3:45 he maintains: "Consequently it has been made clear that belief in the existence of angels preceded the belief in prophecy, and the belief in prophecy preceded the belief in the Law" (p. 576). Given the fact that belief in both prophecy and angels is in complete harmony with the philosophic view of a world that is eternal *a parte ante* as Maimonides had clarified in 2:32, one is left to ponder the full import of this statement too. Maimonides immediately goes on to attack the Sabians for being ignorant of the existence of God and believing that the spheres are eternal and they are the deity. From them overflow forces to idols and certain trees, in their view, by means of which prophets receive their revelation. Note well the continuation of Maimonides' remarks:

> Thereupon when the truth became clear to the men of knowledge and it became known by demonstration that there is a being that is neither a body nor a force in a body, who is the true deity, and that He is one; and that there are also other beings that are separate from matter and are not bodies, being toward whom His being, may He be exalted, overflows—namely, the angels as we have explained; and that all these beings are beyond the Sphere and its stars;—it became known with certainty that true prophetic revelation is given to the prophets by the angels, not by the idols and the asheroth. Thus it became clear through what we have stated before that the belief in the existence of angels is consequent upon the belief in the existence of the deity and that thereby prophecy and the Law are established as valid. (P. 577)

In this passage the philosophers are the ones who disprove the Sabian beliefs about God and prophecy. Maimonides indicates that from God *emanate* the "angels"—that is, the Separate Intellects. In accordance with this view, a view that is predicated on the eternity of the world, the Law is established as valid. To reinforce the hint to his esoteric view in this matter, Maimonides continues: "He, may He be exalted, has commanded the image of two angels be made over the ark so that the belief of the multitude in the existence of angels be consolidated; this correct opinion, coming in the second place after the belief in the existence of the deity, constituting the originative principle of belief in prophecy and the Law and refuting idolatry" (p. 577). The less attentive reader sees in this passage the fundamental beliefs in one God, in prophecy, in the Law, and the refutation of idolatry. The attentive reader notices that in no other passage did Maimonides place such emphasis on the belief in the incorporeal angels.[82] Even more striking is the fact that belief in these incorporeal "angels" occupies the same position that belief in creation occupies in other discussions in the *Guide*. Elsewhere, belief in creation is treated as a fundamental principle coming after belief in the unity of God (2:13). This reader sees that Maimonides accepts the validity of the Law on the basis of the philosophic worldview, a view that completely negates Sabian beliefs.

In summary, Maimonides sees the doctrine of creation serving two important pedagogical purposes: (1) reinforcing the masses' belief in the divinity of the Law, which is consequent upon their belief in a miracle-working deity; (2) reinforcing the masses' belief in the monotheistic idea by combating the Sabian belief that the planets are the deity, a belief that is consequent upon the view that the world is eternal. Given the agreement between the Aristotelians and the Sabians on the eternity of the world, Maimonides initially treats Abraham as an anti-Aristotelian philosopher in his discussion of the problem of creation in part 2 of the *Guide.* Abraham proves the creation of the world. This characterization of Abraham stands in sharp contrast to the one presented earlier in the *Laws of the Principles of the Torah* in which Abraham is depicted as a quintessential Aristotelian philosopher in his proof of the existence and incorporeality of God based on the eternity of motion. We subsequently see from Maimonides' discussion of the reasons for the commandments in part 3 of the *Guide* that Abraham's belief in creation served to counter the polytheistic belief of the Sabians with which he grew up. Yet Maimonides goes on to signal that belief both in the monotheistic idea and the divinity of the Law is compatible with belief in the eternity of the world. He severs the connection between Aristotle and the Sabians. Aristotle, after all, is the model of the monotheistic philosopher in his view. Maimonides also treats belief in the Law as consequent upon belief in "angels" and prophecy rather than creation. The existence of "angels" (= Separate Intellects) and prophecy are accepted by the Aristotelian proponents of an eternal world.

The issue of creation is not the only one that must be viewed in the larger context of Maimonides' educational objectives. His discussion of astrology should also be seen in this light.[83] The issue of astrology is closely associated with those of idolatry and polytheism in Maimonides' thought. He deals with the prohibition against astrology in *Laws of Idolatry* 11:8–9. In his *Commentary on the Mishnah*, Maimonides explicitly traces the development of astrology to the Sabians.[84] The connection between astrology and the religion of the Sabians is crucial in evaluating his approach to the subject. While he continuously stresses the falsehood involved in the belief in astrology, it is the greater falsehoods to which it leads that primarily concern him. Maimonides is not adverse to the propagation of misleading beliefs when it serves the cause of ensuring the acceptance of higher truths. He also sees no reason to combat falsehoods that do not concern central philosophical or religious issues.

Maimonides' educational philosophy in this matter is presented in *Guide*

1:36. Beliefs must be evaluated not only from the perspective of their truth, but also their consequences. Maimonides claims that God is only described as "angry," "wrathful," and "jealous" in reference to idolatry:

> Now the books of the prophets only make this strong assertion because it concerns a false opinion attaching to Him, may He be exalted, I refer to idolatrous worship. For the deviation from truth of one who believes that Zayd is standing at a time when he is sitting, is not like the deviation of him who believes that fire is under the air or water under the earth or that the earth is flat and other things of a similar kind. And this second deviation from truth is not like the deviation of him who believes that the sun consists of fire or that the heavenly sphere forms a hemisphere and other things of a similar kind. Again this third deviation from truth is not like the deviation of him who believes that the angels eat and drink and other things of a similar kind. Finally this fourth deviation from truth is not like the deviation of him who believes that a thing other than God ought to be worshipped. For whenever ignorance and infidelity bear upon a great thing, I mean to say upon someone whose rank in what exists is well established, they are of greater consequence than if they bear upon someone who was of a lower rank. By infidelity, I mean belief about a thing that is different from what the thing really is. By ignorance, I mean ignorance of what is possible to know. (*Guide* 1:36.82–83)

A literal belief in God's anger is itself a cardinal falsehood that Maimonides attempts to correct in the continuation of his remarks, as well as elsewhere.[85] It served as a politically necessary belief designed to ensure obedience to the Law. As we see here, it also served to guard against idolatry and its destructive repercussions.[86] Maimonides felt that the positive function of this belief was no longer the dominant consideration in determining which beliefs were to be taught to the masses. Now the true belief that God feels no emotions was the one that was to be publicly taught.

As for astrology, the belief that one can know the future by examining planetary motions is certainly no more false than the belief that the heavenly sphere forms a hemisphere. When viewed independent of its implications, it is a less serious mistake than the view that angels eat and drink. Yet in certain passages Maimonides is far more tolerant of the latter error.[87] He knows that one cannot divorce a belief from its implications. Astrology leads to idolatry—in addition to breeding a fatalistic attitude to life with all the negative consequences that this attitude carries in its wake—and idolatry leads to the rejection of God. Astrology thus must be rejected out of hand with no qualifications permitted.

The task of distancing people from a belief in astrology was made all the more difficult in light of the fact that Maimonides accepted the foundation upon which astrology is based—namely, all events in the sublunar world are traceable to the motions of the spheres (*Guide* 2:1). The belief that the spheres are intermediaries in divine governance by means of the effects of their motions on sublunar matter is a true scientific belief in his view. He treats the spheres as animate beings, possessing an intellect as well as a soul. The science of their motions—astronomy—is a true science. In short, knowledge of the role of the spheres in divine governance is part of the subject matter necessary to attain intellectual perfection. In rejecting astrology, Maimonides tries to posit a sharp distinction between this belief and what he regards as true scientific beliefs. Yet he is well aware that the distance between astrology and astronomy is not always as great as he indicates.[88]

A significant divergence in Maimonides' approach to the nature of the Separate Intellects and the spheres may be explained in light of the relation between astrology and idolatry. In his formulation of the fifth principle of Judaism, Maimonides justifies the view that God alone should be worshipped by the fact that all the other existents (including the Separate Intellects and the spheres): "act in accordance with their nature. They have no governance, nor choice, except for [what is in conformity to] the will of God."[89] How different is the impression left by this formulation than the one that results from Maimonides' discussion of the nature of the Separate Intellects and spheres in *Guide* 2:7: "All this indicates to you that they [the spheres and the intellects] apprehend their acts and have will and free choice with regard to the governance committed to them, just as we have will with regard to that which from the foundation of our existence has been committed to us and given over to our power. Only we sometimes do things that are more defective than other things . . . whereas the intellects and the spheres are not like that, but always do that which is good" (p. 266).

There is no reason to believe that Maimonides underwent any change of opinion on this issue between the writing of these two compositions. His acquaintance with the philosophic literature describing the nature of the activity of the Separate Intellects and spheres was gained by him at an early age. What changes is the context in which these views appear and the objective of his discussion in these two places. Educational considerations are uppermost in his mind. In the fifth principle Maimonides wishes to leave no opening that may be used for justifying the worship of the spheres. In the *Guide*, Maimonides attempts to impart to his readers an understanding of the nature of the existents who occupy a higher rung on the ladder of being than do sublunar existents, including human beings. This in turn leads to an apprehension of the true nature of divine governance.

VIII

Probably no issue better reflects the complexity of Maimonides' approach, the balancing of so many competing concerns, than his treatment of the commandment to sanctify the Name of God. He deals in detail with this commandment, together with the prohibition against the profanation of the Name of God, in several works. A full appreciation of his approach requires a careful study of his rabbinic sources. Maimonides culls material from a wide range of sources, and organizes the material according to his own systems of classification. From a general perspective, he is loyal to his sources in his rulings, and adopts a consistent approach to these commandments in his writings. Only by a close comparison between Maimonides' discussions and his sources, and between the discussions themselves, can one detect many subtle but significant differences. These differences allow us a glimpse of Maimonides' thought on the subject, as well as his modifications of his views, or at least in how he chose to present them, as reflected by his writings.

Maimonides first deals with these commandments in his *Epistle on Martyrdom.*[90] This epistle was written in response to the harsh stance of an anonymous legal authority, who effectively closed the door on those Jews who were forced to convert to Islam but wished to remain Jews. This authority labeled the forced converts heretics, even if they continued to observe the entire Torah in secret. Maimonides issues a lengthy and sharp attack against this stance. He concludes the epistle with a general legal discussion of the laws of sanctification and profanation. The second source in which Maimonides deals with these commandments is the *Book of the Commandments*. The commandment to sanctify God is presented as the ninth positive commandment, while the prohibition against profanation is listed as the sixty-third negative commandment. The most important source is the fifth chapter of the *Laws of the Principles of the Torah* in the *Mishneh Torah*. Maimonides returns to the issue of forced conversions to Islam in his *Epistle to the Jews of Yemen*, written while he was working on the *Mishneh Torah*. If in the former epistle Maimonides primarily seeks to encourage those who succumbed to forced conversion to maintain their loyalty to Judaism, in the latter he attempts to strengthen the spirit of those who have not succumbed. Absent from the *Epistle to the Jews of Yemen*, however, is a detailed legal discussion of the issues involved.

In Maimonides' treatment of these commandments, the most noble expression of sanctifying God is martyrdom—the willingness to lay down one's life in order to uphold the Law. The most loathsome expression of profanation lies in the wanton transgression of the commandments, the violation of the commandments in order to show one's contempt for them. The unique nature of both these commandments is seen from the fact that they do not stand independently. They accompany the performance or transgression of other commandments. One sanctifies God by dying rather than violate a commandment of the Law. One profanes the Name of God by the manner in which one transgresses one of the other commandments.[91]

Between these extremes lie many other manifestations of sanctification and profanation, not all of them involving the performance or transgression of other commandments. A Jewish scholar sanctifies or profanes the Name by how he conducts himself in public and how his behavior is evaluated by others. One whose conduct is deemed meritorious, though no explicit commandment is fulfilled by him, nevertheless is considered to have sanctified the Name. A scholar whose behavior is subject to widespread condemnation profanes the Name, though he may have violated no explicit commandment in his actions. The commandments of sanctification and profanation are multidimensional. They deal with the manner one lives as well as the circumstances under which one must be prepared to die. They vary in the demands they make on the average Jew and those made on the leaders of the community.

It is not my purpose here to analyze Maimonides' approach in detail. Such an analysis would require a lengthy monograph. At present I wish to confine my discussion to a number of points that illustrate the subtlety of Maimonides' approach and its implications for understanding his political thought. More than any of the other commandments, these commandments are designed to sustain Judaism in times of crisis. They involve the most serious challenges faced both by the religion as an institution and by the individual.

"Know that in every man there is necessarily the faculty of courage." With this comment Maimonides opens 2:38 of the *Guide*. This faculty, he proceeds to indicate, varies in strength in individuals. Some have the courage to advance upon a lion while others flee from a mouse. Courage is dependent upon one's natural temperament. It also varies in accordance with the effort directed to its practice, and in accordance with ones' opinions. In other words, certain thoughts and feelings may embolden the individual while others have the opposite affect. The prophets, Maimonides maintains, are endowed with great courage, strengthened by the prophetic overflow they receive. Moses boldly faced Pharaoh alone with only staff in hand in order to save the Israelites from slavery. He experienced no fear in his actions because God informed him that God will be with him.

As in the case of most of the ethical virtues, courage is defined by Maimonides in terms of the doctrine of the mean. It is the mean between recklessness and cowardice. Yet, as Maimonides indicates in *Eight Chapters* 4, people often are mistaken in identifying the proper activities wherein the mean lies. They tend to treat one of the extremes as good. Recklessness, for example, is treated by some as a virtue. Those who are given to endangering their lives, purposefully pursuing dangers which in all probability will lead to their death, are incorrectly deemed to be courageous. Maimonides' message is clear. Courage lies in knowing which dangers one must encounter head on and which dangers one must avoid, or from which one must retreat.

Thus the "mean" for Maimonides, just as for Aristotle, is not easily quantified. It varies in accordance with the circumstances of the individual and the situation the person finds oneself.[92] Determining the "mean" is dependent upon practical wisdom. By means of this wisdom one ascertains when advancing forward is an act of courage, and when such an action is to be deemed recklessness. Alternately, one apprehends when retreating does not signify a lack of courage, and when it should be considered to be an act of cowardice. For Maimonides, much of the task of practical wisdom is assumed by the divine Law. Many of the commandments of the Law are framed from the perspective of acting in accordance with the mean. Yet the interpreter of the Law must also possess a high degree of practical wisdom in knowing how to apply the Law to particular circumstances in accordance with the aims of the Law.

This point enables us to gain greater insight into Maimonides' approach to the sanctification and profanation of the Name. Conflicting values are at stake. At one end is the necessity to uphold the religion, at the other is the necessity of preserving one's own life. Under what circumstances does one need to find the courage to lay down one's life? Under what circumstances does the sacrifice of one's life reflect recklessness deserving condemnation rather than virtuous conduct? How should one regard those who take the cowardly approach, and who fail to show the required courage in situations that demand the extreme sacrifice? How should one regard those who lay down their lives in situations in which the Law makes no such explicit demand?

As indicated above, Maimonides' rulings are rooted in his rabbinic sources. One must look to the subtle points in his approach for appreciating his view. The talmudic sages laid down a series of conditions under which one must lay down one's life rather than violate the law. The dominant view in the Talmud is that one should not commit idolatry under any circumstances, even if threatened with death. Similarly, the prohibitions against forbidden sexual relations (incest or adultery) and murdering an innocent fellow Jew are never to be violated, even if it means the loss of one's own life. In addition, the Talmud specifies the conditions under which the other laws must be observed, though obedience results in one's being put to death. If a gentile forces a Jew to violate any of the laws of the Torah not for personal gain, but simply in order that the law be violated, *and* ten Jews or more are present, then the victim is not to succumb to the death threat. In times of religious persecution, when a gentile forces a Jew to violate the Law not for personal gain, the victim is not to succumb even when ten Jews are not present. The rabbis went so far to include among the laws that are not to be violated in these circumstances even relatively minor customs, such as not changing the color of the shoelaces by which Jews are distinguished from gentiles. Anyone who publicly lays down one's life in these circumstances is said to sanctify the Name of God.[93]

Maimonides' legal "innovation," if it should in fact be considered as such, revolves around two questions. The first one is how are we to treat the one who showed a failure of character in these circumstances. The sages do not address this issue explicitly in their discussions of the circumstances under which a person is required to lay down one's life. Maimonides, on the other hand, does. He adamantly argues that the Law exempts a person from punishment, human or divine, in situations in which the Law was violated under coercion. In the case under consideration, the person is still guilty of violating the commandment involved *and* of profaning the Name. Due to the mitigating circumstances of the crime, however, one is not to cut the person off from the community of Israel.[94] Jewish society must show some tolerance for its weaker members who faced the difficult choice of sure death or succumbing to coercion, even when ultimate values are at stake. The Law in these circumstances demands heroism. Those who died for the sake of the Law are extolled by Maimonides. Yet we see from history, Maimonides attempts to show in his *Epistle on Martyrdom*, how few were capable of acting so courageously when faced with the challenge.[95]

In exempting the person from the obligation of laying down one's life rather than transgress the commandments, the sages interpret the verse: *One should live by them* (the commandments) (Lev. 18:5)—"and not die by means of them" (*B.T. Yoma* 85b). The question remains whether in those situations in which a person is exempted from the obligation of martyrdom, martyrdom remains optional. Can a person decide to adopt a more strict stance than what is demanded by the Law, and choose death instead of violating a commandment? Maimonides answers unequivocally in the negative. In those circumstances in which one is not commanded to die rather than transgress, one is *obligated* to transgress and live. *One should live by them* is interpreted by Maimonides as a divine command, not an optional mode of conduct. Life has religious value. One should not mistakenly think that dying in these circumstances also sanctifies the Name. Such a person is culpable of a heinous crime *(mitḥayev be-nafsho)* in bringing about his death rather than preserving his life. If we translate Maimonides' legal stance to an ethical plane, we would say that such a person is guilty of wrong headed recklessness rather than true courage. Consequently, he deserves condemnation rather than praise, despite the fact that he acted out of devotion to a "good cause."

The competing concerns that enter into the discussion of this issue are illustrated by the differences between Maimonides' treatments of the sanctification of the Name in the *Book of the Commandments* and in the *Laws of the Principles of the Torah*. In the *Book of the Commandments*, he lists this commandment as ninth, but he relates it thematically to the third commandment, love of God. In Maimonides' discussion of the third commandment, Abraham is described as exemplifying the "lover of God." The greatness of Abraham's apprehension and love led him to call upon others to accept belief in God's unity. Maimonides commences his discussion of the ninth commandment by picking up on this notion:

> We are commanded to publicize this true belief [in one God] to the world without fearing harm on the part of any adversary. Even when one seeks to coerce us to deny God, we will not heed him. We will suffer death instead. We will not have him err in thinking that we have denied God, though in our hearts we believe in Him, may He be exalted. This is the commandment of the sanctification of the Name that is binding upon all of Israel—namely, suffering death at the hands of the persecutor out of our love of God and belief in His unity. . . .[96]

The entire discussion here is devoted to martyrdom. In this context Maimonides does not mention the circumstances under which one is not required to lay down one's life. Nor does he bring up the issue of punishment if one fails to observe the command, or how one sanctifies God in day-to-day life. All these points must await his discussion of the prohibition not to profane God's Name. Maimonides remains focused solely on the great love of God expressed by the extremes to which one is prepared to go in order to proclaim publicly God's unity. His constant refrain is not to fear death in these circumstances. From the standpoint of the Law, the command to sanctify God's Name, according to Maimonides, is incumbent upon Jews alone. Unlike the prohibition against idolatry and other noahite commandments, it is not binding upon the gentiles.[97] One may conclude from Maimonides' discussion that this command, more than any other, embodies the Jewish people's role in the world.

In the *Laws of the Principles of the Torah*, the commandments of sanctifying the Name and not profaning the Name immediately follow the commandments to love and fear God. Significantly, the former commandments, together with the commandment not to physically destroy the written Names of God, appear to interrupt the natural "flow" of topics in this opening section of the *Mishneh Torah*. The following topic, prophecy, is directly connected with the ultimate knowledge that characterizes the love of God discussed in the beginning of the section. Moreover, Maimonides employs similar terminology in discussing both topics. Yet despite the thematic affinity that binds the topic of love of God with prophecy, Maimonides chose to separate these topics by a discussion of the sanctification of the Name.[98]

While Maimonides brings the commandments to love and sanctify God into closer "physical" proximity than he does in the *Book of the Commandments*, he also draws a sharper distinction between them. The first four chapters of the *Laws of the Principles of the Torah*, in which the commandments to love and fear God are outlined, are treated as a section in itself. At the end of chapter 4, Maimonides goes so far as to divide the commandments into two categories: those included in the first four chapters, and all the rest. The notion of publicizing belief in God is not mentioned in his discussion of love of God. Love of God, like the other commandments in these chapters, is described solely in terms of intellectual apprehension.[99] Maimonides opens his discussion in the fifth chapter by stressing that "all of the house of Israel are commanded to sanctify this great Name." This formulation stands in striking contrast to his approach to the commandments included in the first four chapters of the *Laws of the Principles of the Torah*. These commandments are both more universal—in that the knowledge involved is scientific knowledge—and more elitist—in that few are capable of attaining this knowledge. "Israel" is not explicitly mentioned until the opening of chapter 5. The sanctification of the Name is a commandment that all Jews in principle are capable of performing, and at the same time apply to the Jewish people alone. Yet even here Maimonides does not explicitly mention the role of the Jewish people to proclaim publicly God's unity in the world. Nor does he stress the notion of love of God involved in the fulfillment of this commandment, certainly not to the extent that he does so in his previous discussions.[100]

Just as striking is the fact that having presented the general commandment to sanctify the Name, Maimonides first defines the circumstances under which it is *not* to be observed (*Laws of the Principles of the Torah* 5:1): "When a gentile comes and coerces an Israelite to transgress one of the commandments of the Torah or be killed—he should transgress and not be killed." Only at this point does he turn to the circumstances under which the commandment is to be fulfilled. These circumstances are formulated as *exceptions* to the rule. The stress is on when one is obligated to choose life rather than die, a stress that is completely absent in the *Book of the Commandments*. Maimonides glorifies those who choose a martyr's death when obligated by the Law to do so. He is equally adamant in condemning those who choose a martyr's death when not obligated to do so, and in insisting that those who transgressed the Law in situations of coercion are exempt from all punishment. Moreover, in the continuation of his presentation Maimonides emphasizes the notion that we sanctify God by the manner in which we live, not just by the circumstances in which we die. One can clearly discern how skillfully he tries to balance his competing concerns in the discussion.

In neither the *Book of the Commandments* nor the *Mishneh Torah* does Maimonides address the specific problem that was involved in his first discussion of the issue—forced conversion to Islam. In the *Epistle on Martyrdom,* Maimonides praises those who chose death rather than formal conversion to Islam. Nevertheless he counsels the latter course, providing one is not coerced into violating an explicit commandment. His ruling in *Laws of the Principles of the Torah* is black and white. If one is not obligated to choose martyrdom, one is to be condemned for making such choice. Maimonides presents this view not only in the *Mishneh Torah*, but in the epistle itself. We are confronted with a problematic position. One who chooses death when not obligated is guilty of sin. In the case under consideration, however, one who chooses death sanctifies the Name, though martyrdom is not considered by Maimonides compulsory or even advisable.

One should not fail to note that the situation being depicted in the *Laws of the Principles of the Torah* is of an unambiguous nature. Such situations call for unambiguous rulings. One is coerced to violate an explicit commandment. Real life situations, however, often come in shades of gray. In his epistle, Maimonides keeps on stressing the point of how exceptional the situation is. The only action required by the forced converts is to acknowledge the mission of Mohammed. In their state of conversion, they are not forced to violate any commandment. They may continue to observe the entire Torah. Maimonides also argues that the absence of any internal conviction on the part of the converts is well known to the Moslems. Thus the words by which one acknowledges the prophecy of Mohammed are essentially meaningless, and the Moslems understand this point.[101] Since Maimonides regards the Moslems as monotheists, though significantly he does not explicitly make this point in the epistle, he implicitly does not consider this conversion to represent a denial of God's existence or unity. Such denial would engender the necessity of choosing death.

On the other hand, Maimonides is well aware that even forced "token" conversions represent a betrayal of the religion. Furthermore, they *inevitably* result, though perhaps not immediately, in the convert violating explicit commandments. Many eventually forsake Judaism completely.[102] The situation Maimonides faces thus is exceptionally delicate. He must give the proper due to those who chose not to betray Judaism, even in this "borderline" situation, while at the same time succor those who chose life. He must encourage the latter to remain loyal to Judaism, and encourage the Jewish community to keep the doors wide open for them without viewing them as heretics. That the martyrs showed true courage and not recklessness in this case does not necessarily mean that those who did not choose martyrdom should be treated as cowardly traitors.

The legal justification Maimonides gives for the act of conversion, and he is well aware that he stands on tenuous grounds from a legal perspective, is designed to keep the converts' tie to Judaism intact.[103] Yet Maimonides also knows how easy it is for the converts to use this justification as an excuse for following the path of least resistance and continue to pose as Moslems. The nature of the situation undergoes continuous change. What begins as an exceptional situation involving coercion becomes an ongoing situation involving new norms of volitional behavior. For this reason

Maimonides goes on to add a stinging condemnation of those who do not quickly make their way to lands where they can again live openly as Jews. They are described as profaning the Name of God in a manner bordering upon the intentional.[104] Whatever justification there may be from the standpoint of Jewish law for choosing conversion to Islam rather than death, there can be no legal justification for not acting immediately to change the situation, notwithstanding the other types of sacrifices that may be involved.

The epistle shows what liberties Maimonides is prepared to take in presenting an interpretation of the law designed to address the "needs of the hour." While his stance in this case is appropriate in dealing with an actual exceptional situation, it has no place in a code of Law. Maimonides' subsequent silence on the issue should be viewed in this light. It would do far more harm than good to the Jewish community if Maimonides' position found its way into a law code, irrespective of the problem of the legal justification for his stance. Inevitably it would weaken one's loyalty to Judaism when facing the challenges posed by Islam, or even Christianity, despite the differences Maimonides draws between the two religions. Perhaps for this reason Maimonides also completely ignores the stance he presents in the *Epistle on Martyrdom* when he later addresses the particular situation of the Jews of Yemen. Knowing what to say and when to say it are crucial for any legal authority. The application of law to different situations is not only a matter of study and strict legal reasoning, but also of practical discernment.

IX

"God exists in the details" the art historian Aby Warburg was quoted as saying. It was a view that the great scholars of Judaica in this century, particularly Gershom Scholem, took as their guiding principle. Following in the footsteps of Maimonides, I would prefer to think that God is the unity beyond all the details, yet the only way to apprehend God is by way of the details. Certainly the only way to appreciate Maimonides is by paying careful attention to the details. I have no doubt that a perspicacious individual can "cut through all the details" and get to the "core" of Maimonides' philosophy in a few short sentences. I also am aware that one at times gets "lost in the details" and fails to see the main ideas underlying them. Nonetheless, no matter how perceptive a summary may be, it cannot convey a real understanding of Maimonides' thought, any more than a synopsis of a great work of literature can impart the essence of the work. It is not in the basic ideas that one finds the essence of his thought, but in the nuances of his formulations, the undercurrents in his discussions.

In the chapters that follow I take a closer look at certain aspects of Maimonides' political thought. In the next chapter, I explore the role the practical intellect plays in ethics, politics and divination, and deal with the issue why Maimonides never mentions this faculty explicitly. Chapter 3 is devoted to a study of the notion "good" in his thought. I challenge the view that Maimonides adopts a relativistic approach, equating "good" with the efficacy of the means independent of the nature of the ends. The relation between intellectual perfection and political activity, and the metaphysical foundation for Maimonides' approach to *imitatio Dei* form the subject matter of the fourth chapter. Maimonides' numerous apparent contradictory positions on ethics, and the possible reason why he presents his views in such a manner, are explored in the fifth chapter. The sixth chapter discusses the role of the law in inculcating knowledge of God and bringing about intellectual perfection. I also explore the question whether Maimonides remained consistent in his view of public education in this area. The final chapter deals with Maimonides' approach to the love and fear of God, his sources, the manner his views leave their imprint on other laws in the *Mishneh Torah*, and how ideas to which he alludes in his legal compendium are subsequently presented more fully in the *Guide*.

Some of the points I touched upon in this essay I develop in more detail in these chapters. I have not, however, tried to tie all the pieces together or even bring all the pieces. Many critical problems are not treated at all. I have made no effort to explore the relation between Maimonides' activities as the head of the Jewish community in Egypt and his political views as they emerge from his writings. The dissonance that can be detected on occasion between how he viewed certain issues when dealing with them in a more "ideal" and "abstract" manner and how he viewed them in the context of concrete everyday situations that he was forced to address is not dealt with in this volume.[105] In the case of concrete situations, one often tends to adopt a more compromising stance. Maimonides is no exception to the rule. I have paid scant attention to Maimonides' public epistles and the way he grapples with specific crisis situations[106]—an issue that is illustrated by my discussion in the previous section. Neither have I made a serious attempt to explore his codification of laws dealing with governance, and see how his formulations are related to his philosophic positions.[107] The problems I have chosen to study belong to the theoretical aspects of his political thought. They concern the foundation and purpose of ethics, the nature of perfection, and different ways in which some of the main themes in Maimonides' philosophy unfold in his legal writings. At the foundation of all my studies lies the problem of how to read Maimonides.

The present volume is the product of years of "listening to" Maimonides. I attempt to impart to the reader some of the things that I feel I have come to understand after much wrestling with Maimonides' thought, and taking a closer look at his views in their literary and intellectual-historical contexts. My purpose in this book is not to engage Maimonides in an active philosophical "dialogue" across time concerning his views, but to try to gain a better understanding of what those views are. More than bring Maimonides into my world, I have tried to enter into his.

There is certainly more than one way to understand a literary work. The reader inevitably brings his or her intellectual baggage to the act of reading. Interpretations are the product of the "meeting" between the words on the page and the mind of the reader. The "academic" reader tends to bring far more baggage than most, and to read with very specific questions in mind. I must certainly plead "guilty" on this point. In an effort to attain Maimonides' answers to the question I pose, I lift different points from diverse discussions and then paste them together in accordance with my own concerns. While Maimonides may have been concentrating on one point in his discussion, I am often more interested in deriving from the discussion his views on a different point. Often I return to a discussion I have already cited with a slightly different question in mind. I offer the reader no running commentary on any of Maimonides' discussions to show how carefully crafted they are. In truth, only such an approach can even begin to convey the measure of this exceptional individual. Instead, I single out those points that are important for my analysis, before proceeding to relate them to other comments in other discussions. While I try to be faithful to the meaning of Maimonides' comments in the contexts in which they appear, and try to avoid posing questions that there is no reason to believe Maimonides seriously considered, I cannot deny the creative dimension of my reconstructions of his thought. Nevertheless, it is the views that Maimonides tried to convey by the written word, the "original intent" of the texts he has bequeathed to us, that I continue to set my goal to discover.

It has become common in some circles to argue not only the lesser value that the critical-scholarly approach to texts holds in comparison to more "engaged" contemporary readings, but the very impossibility of penetrating a past writer's thought.[108] All we have is the written word as it exists in the present. I remain committed to the view that the limitations in attempting to understand a past writer's thought as it finds expression in the written word should not lead to the conclusion that such an attempt is without foundation. Our own understanding inevitably will play a role in what we "hear" the writer saying, and how we interpret his speech. This does not mean that we must rest satisfied with hearing only the voice of our own imagination when reading the great thinkers of the past. If we prepare ourselves enough by a close reading of the gamut of their writings, and examining them in light of their intellectual milieu, we can traverse time and catch an echo of their original voice. Through a careful, informed reading of the written word, we have the opportunity to let the great minds of the past communicate with us. What a stimulating experience this is in its own right.

TWO

THE PRACTICAL INTELLECT

I

The Islamic Aristotelian philosophers ascribed two main functions to the intellect, a theoretical function and a practical one. The theoretical intellect *(al-'aql al-naṣarī)* has as its object the "intelligibles" *(al-ma'aqūlāt)*. They consist of the unchanging essences of existents not dependent upon human volitional activity, their abstract principles and properties.[1] The intelligibles form the subject matter of the theoretical sciences, beginning with mathematics and culminating with metaphysics.[2] The practical intellect *(al-'aql al-'amalī)* has as its object that which is dependent upon human volitional activity. The various crafts, as well as the deliberation upon the means to attaining a desired end, belong to its domain.[3] The practical intellect is responsible for the proper governance of the body, whether it be of the individual or of society. Thus politics and ethics—two interrelated fields in Aristotelian thought—are rooted, for the most part, in the practical intellect.[4] Maimonides' various comments on the intellect are not without their ambiguities. Nonetheless, they are traceable to Aristotelian sources.[5] Moreover, his reason for refraining from presenting a detailed exposition of the topic is due in some measure to the superfluity of such exposition in light of the Aristotelian discussions. In *The Guide of the Perplexed*, Maimonides concludes his sketchy discussion of the relation between the intellect and the object of apprehension with the remark: "This treatise has been composed only for the benefit of those who have philosophized and have acquired knowledge of what has become clear with reference to the soul and its faculties" (1:68.166).

For all of Maimonides' reticence in discussing the intellect, one is still struck by the fact that not once in any of his writings does he mention the term "practical intellect" or "practical rational faculty." Even when he clearly alludes to this faculty, he fails to mention it explicitly. In the first chapter of *Eight Chapters*, for example, he treats the learning of the various crafts, and the deliberation upon a desired end, as practical activities belonging to the rational part *(al-juz' al-nātiq)* of the soul. Maimonides' discussion is based primarily upon Alfarabi's presentation in *Aphorisms of the Statesman.*[6] The "practical intellect" or "practical rational faculty" appears explicitly in a number of passages in Alfarabi's work, as well as in other works that had a profound influence upon Maimonides' thought.[7] Maimonides appears to have purposefully refrained from employing some of Alfarabi's terminology in regard to the intellect, though he essentially follows his view.

It may be argued that Maimonides' silence in regard to the practical intellect stems from a desire to emphasize the unity of the intellect. There do not exist two distinct intellects or rational faculties in human beings. The human intellect is one. The "practical" and "theoretical" designate different functions of the same entity. Thus Maimonides refrains from speaking also of the "theoretical rational faculty" in the first chapter of *Eight Chapters.* Yet for all the merits of this argument, it fails to provide an adequate explanation for the manner in which Maimonides formulates his position. He shows no qualms in using the term "theoretical intellect" in the following chapter of *Eight Chapters.*

A more significant argument is that Maimonides may have wished to disassociate the subject matter belonging to the practical intellect—most notably ethics and politics—from the intellect per se. From a certain perspective this contention is correct. A number of passages in *The Guide of the Perplexed*, as well as in *Eight Chapters*, can be adduced in support of it. Maimonides at times goes so far as to intimate that these areas belong to the domain of the imagination, in distinct contrast to that of the intellect. Political leaders and legislators, for example, are credited by Maimonides with possessing a highly developed imagination and deficient rational faculty (*Guide* 2:37).

This fact notwithstanding, I will try to show that Maimonides regarded ethics, politics, as well as divination, as being essentially rooted in the workings of the practical rational faculty. His deliberate omission of this faculty should not be interpreted as a major departure from the Aristotelian tradition. Rather, Maimonides at times sought to obscure the role of the practical rational faculty in these areas in order to underscore certain more fundamental views of his related to the intellect and the human being's final end. The study of the "practical intellect" (or absence of it) in Maimonides' writings offers an illuminating example of how in communicating his thought, he at times refrained from employing certain terms for pedagogic, rather than purely philosophic, reasons, just as he at times chooses certain terms and formulations primarily for pedagogic reasons. Maimonides is willing to risk that his readers misunderstand him on certain points, and often goes so far as to deliberately mislead his less astute readers. This is not only to conceal his true views on sensitive subjects, but also to impress upon them more important points that he wishes to communicate.

II

Much of the confusion surrounding Maimonides' approach to politics and ethics stems from the failure to distinguish between different forms of human intellect, and their relation to the soul, in his philosophy.[8] In *Eight Chapters* Maimonides treats the intellect both as the "form" of the soul, the soul serving as "matter" for it (chap. 1), and as a virtue of the rational part of the soul (chap. 2). In the latter context, he mentions two types of intellect. The first is the theoretical intellect, consisting of the first intelligibles found in us by nature. The second is the acquired intellect *(al-'aql al-mustafād),* for which no definition is presented. In *The Guide of the Perplexed*, Maimonides offers additional clues to his view of the various forms of intellect. He mentions the hylic intellect (*al-'aql al-hayūlānī*) or potential intellect *(al-'aql bi-l-qūwa)* (1:68; 1:72; 2:4; 2:38); the intellect *in actu (al-'aql bi-l-fi'l)* (1:68; 2:4; 2:38; 3:27); and the acquired intellect (1:72). The first is explicitly identified with the rational faculty of man. Maimonides goes on to indicate that the rational faculty is a faculty, "subsisting in a body, and not separable from it" (1:72.192).[9] As in *Eight Chapters*, Maimonides regards the rational soul as a "predisposition" (1:70). In apprehending an intelligible, the hylic intellect becomes an intellect *in actu*. The latter intellect is identified with the intelligible it apprehends (1:68). The acquired intellect is mentioned by Maimonides in only one context. Unlike the hylic intellect, it is "truly separate from the organic body and overflows toward it" (1:72.193). While Maimonides deals with the relation between the hylic intellect and the intellect *in actu*, he is silent as to the relation between the intellect *in actu* and the acquired intellect.

In discussing the activities of the hylic intellect or rational faculty, Maimonides lists apprehension both of the theoretical sciences and the practical crafts. This is true of the *Guide* (1:53; 1:72) and the *Treatise on Logic* (chap. 14), as well as of *Eight Chapters* (chap. 1). Moreover, it is the rational faculty's practical activities that are highlighted in the discussions in the first part of the *Guide* that focus on this faculty. Significantly, Maimonides omits all reference to the practical crafts when mentioning the intellect *in actu*. In *Guide* 1:68, he adduces an example from the forms of natural objects in illustrating the identity between the intellect *in actu* and the object of intellection. Later on in the treatise, Maimonides defines the ultimate perfection of man as his having an intellect *in actu*, "knowing everything concerning all the beings (*al-maujūdāt*) that it is within the capacity of man to know" (*Guide* 3:27.511). He identifies this knowledge with knowledge of the theoretical sciences (*Guide* 1:34; 3:28). In another passage, he defines human perfection as: "the acquisition of the rational virtues—I refer to the conception of the intelligibles, which teach true opinions concerning the divine things" (*Guide* 3:54.635).[10]

Only the knowledge that involves "being," or provides necessary premises for attaining this knowledge, can be characterized as knowledge of "intelligibles." This is the knowledge contained in the theoretical sciences. The practical crafts do not deal with ontology, but rather with human volitional activity. Therefore Maimonides does not include them among that which is known by a perfect intellect, or that which results in the actualization of the intellect. In a number of discussion he draws a clear distinction between knowledge of the crafts and knowledge of the intelligibles.[11] The hylic intellect or rational faculty is regarded by Maimonides as the faculty of the soul that enables human beings to learn both the theoretical sciences and practical activities necessary for existence. Only knowledge of the unchanging intelligibles contained in the theoretical sciences, however, results in the rational faculty becoming an intellect *in actu*.

Maimonides apparently does not draw any distinction between the acquired intellect, which is the highest form of human intellect, and a perfect intellect *in actu*—that is, an intellect that has apprehended metaphysics to the full extent of human ability. The term intellect *in actu* is used by him even in reference to the Divine Intellect (*Guide* 1:68). Following the view of Alfarabi, Maimonides appears to have regarded the acquired intellect as a substantiated form of intellect, not dependent upon the body for its existence or activity. It is attained by the one who reaches intellectual perfection.[12]

The identity between the intellect *in actu* and its object of apprehension provides the foundation for Maimonides' view of the human being's final end. In achieving some degree of apprehension of the beings or true realities which exist separate from matter—that is, God and the Separate Intellects—one attains a quasi identity with the Active Intellect. Just as these beings are immortal, so is the intellect that apprehends them. Maimonides repeatedly alludes to this view in his legal writings, as well as in the *Guide*.[13] Only the intellect that has attained true metaphysical knowledge is the immortal soul of the human being, in contrast to the rational soul that is corrupted with the corruption of the body. Maimonides points out that "soul" *(nefesh)* is an equivocal term referring to, "the rational soul, I mean the form of man . . . and it is a term denoting the thing that remains of man after death" (*Guide* 1:41.91). He elaborates somewhat upon this notion in a subsequent chapter. "For that which comes into being at the time a man is generated is merely a faculty consisting in preparedness, whereas the thing that after death is separate from matter is the thing that has become actual and not the *soul* that comes into being" (1:70.173–74).

In his earlier *Laws of the Principles of the Torah* 4:9, Maimonides gives his clearest expression of this view:

> The form of this soul *(nefesh)* [the form of the human being of perfect intellect] is not made up of the elements so that it would decompose into its component parts. Nor is it a faculty of the soul *(neshamah),* dependent upon the soul [for its existence]. Therefore, when the body, which is made up of the elements, decomposes, and the soul *(neshamah)* is corrupted since it exists only with the body . . . this form will not undergo corruption. . . . It knows and apprehends the intellects *(de'ot)* that are separate from bodies [the Separate Intellects], and it knows the Creator of all. It remains eternal *('omed le-'olam ūl'olmei 'olamim).*[14]

The theoretical sciences that deal with corporeal beings serve as a necessary prelude to metaphysics. With the apprehension of the corporeal world, however, the intellect does not yet free itself from the body and other faculties of the soul. Consequently, it does not attain an independent existence.

Maimonides' apparently contradictory views pertaining to ethics and politics, treating them at times as belonging to the rational faculty while at other times appearing to deny this view, should be understood in light of his doctrine of the intellect and the human being's final end. Political and ethical knowledge is treated by him as distinct from knowledge of the crafts in some manner.[15] Nonetheless, they share a number of fundamental traits in common. As with knowledge of the crafts, political and ethical knowledge is concerned with voluntary corporeal activities. That this knowledge is regarded by Maimonides as belonging to the rational faculty can be shown on the basis of numerous passages in his writings. In *Treatise on Logic* 14, he deals with ethics and politics in the context of defining the types of knowledge belonging to the rational faculty. The distinction between the pleasant or fine *(al-jamīl* or *al-ḥasan)* and the bad *(al-qabīḥ)*—a distinction that is identified by Maimonides with the subject matter of ethics—is ascribed by him to the rational faculty in *Eight Chapters* 1, and *Treatise on Loḡic* 14.[16]

In several passages in the *Guide of the Perplexed*, he lists the ability to govern oneself and others among the activities rooted in the rational faculty (1:34; 1:53; 1:72; 3:8).[17] He regards the rational faculty's ability to govern to be the basis of the view that the human being, and no other animal, is considered to be like a small world, a *microcosmos* (1:72). Yet insofar as knowledge of these subjects is not an integral part of the perfection of the intellect, whatever their relation may be to the attainment of intellectual perfection, Maimonides sharply distinguishes this knowledge from knowledge of the theoretical sciences or "true realities" (3:27; 3:54).[18] One may even have "an unerring opinion and an excellent way of conducting affairs in political matters," he indicates, while not "understanding an intelligible notion even though it were close to being one of the first intelligibles" (1:34.78). Thus there is no contradiction between Maimonides' repeated insistence that knowledge of the pleasant and bad, or good *(al-k̲air)* and evil *(al-sharr),* does not belong to knowledge of the intelligibles,[19] and his view that this knowledge belongs to the rational faculty. Knowledge of good and evil does not belong to the intellect *in actu*, which is concerned solely with the apprehension of the theoretical sciences. Anyone who equates knowledge of good and evil with knowledge of the intelligibles is guilty of a fundamental mistake in regard to the nature of the intellect *in actu*, its object of apprehension, and its ultimate perfection.

This point holds the key to understanding a number of confusing passages in Maimonides' writings. In *Eight Chapters* 6, he discusses the problem of who is on a higher level—one who feels no impulse to do evil, or one who feels an inclination to do evil but overcomes it?[20] After citing conflicting opinions placing the prophets and philosophers on one side of the divide, and the rabbinic sages on the other,[21] Maimonides reconciles them by dividing the commandments into two categories. It is not my purpose in the present context to analyze Maimonides' approach to these two character types, or the puzzling manner in which he sets up the proponents of the conflicting opinions. Taking his cue from R. Saadiah Gaon, he terms the second category of commandments, "revelatory" (Ar. *al-sam'iyot,* Heb. *shim'iyot*).[22] In the case of these commandments, those who feel the inclination to transgress and overcome their urge are on a higher plane. Maimonides explains why one should continue to desire to perform these acts yet refrain because of the divine command. "If it were not for the Law they would not be evil at all." The first category consists of those evil actions that one should not feel any inclination to perform. These are the evils that are recognized as such by the philosophers and are "well known" or "generally accepted" *(mashhūrāt)* such as murder, theft, harming the innocent or repaying good with evil. Maimonides does not offer his own name for this category but indicates that those who suffered from the "sickness of the Kalam"—a reference to R. Saadiah Gaon—termed them "intellected commandments" (Ar. *al-sharā'i 'al-'aqliyāt,* Heb. *miṣvot sikhliyot*).[23] If Maimonides accepts this category as a valid one, why does he distance himself from the label by which it is commonly known? Why is one who ties this category of commandments to the intellect worthy of censure?

One need not look too far afield for the answer to this problem as some commentators were wont to do. It is not because Maimonides thought that the term introduced a false dichotomy between the laws, implying that the laws belonging to the first category are irrational. To be sure, he was adamant on the point that all laws are rational in the sense of having a noble and discernible purpose (*Guide* 3:25). Yet this interpretation fails to account for the fact that Maimonides, like R. Saadiah before him, is dealing with the laws from the perspective of the epistemological basis for regarding them as obligatory, not from the perspective of viewing their rationale once they are known. The "revelatory laws" are certainly rational, but this does not entail that they are mandated by reason. Nor is his rejection of the label "intellected laws" due to the notion that the rational faculty is incapable of transcending culturally relative considerations of "utility" in mandating law, considerations that fluctuate from society to society. Maimonides agrees with the view that the actions forbidden by these "generally accepted" dictums are in fact universally "evil" and known by the rational faculty as such. What he rejects is the notion that these laws are "intellected"—that is, their source is in the theoretical intellect.

This point helps illumine a number of passages in Maimonides' great legal compendium, the *Mishneh Torah.* The term *da'at* is used by him in the *Mishneh Torah* in a variety of ways, including as a designation for the intellect or for the rational faculty. Maimonides does not employ two distinct terms as he does in his Arabic writings. In two passages, the rational faculty/intellect is said to be the source for moral knowledge. Maimonides discusses the basis for the prohibition to take an innocent life in order to save another. This prohibition, he indicates, is one "to which the rational faculty inclines *(ha-da'at notah)*" (*Laws of Principles of the Torah* 5:7). Maimonides uses the phrase, "inclination of the rational faculty" as a substitute for the term *sevara* (a rational inference or argument) that appears in the rabbinic sources (*Pesaḥim* 25b; *Sanhedrin* 74b). The ambiguous relation between the intellect and this ethical principle comes across very clearly.

Maimonides chooses the term "inclines" but not "necessitates" to show that while reason is its source, it does not have the status of absolute truth.

The second passage is Maimonides' well-known and controversial ruling concerning the seven noahite commandments incumbent upon all non-Jews. One must fulfill them out of the conviction that God commanded these laws in the Torah. The individual who performs them due to the "leanings of the intellect *(hekhre'a ha-da'at)*" (*Laws of Kings* 8:11), according to Maimonides, cannot be accorded the status of a resident alien, or be considered one of the righteous gentiles. This individual belongs to the category of the gentile sages.[24] The noahite laws include idolatry, cursing God, murder, forbidden sexual relations, theft, establishing courts of law, and not eating the limb of a living animal. Given all we have seen till now, there is no basis for the view that Maimonides rejected the notion that these laws are known by the rational faculty, or that a morality not based on revelation is without all foundation. He may be interpreted as saying that one who performs these laws out of purely rational considerations is in fact a philosopher. Many of the actions prohibited by these laws are listed by Maimonides in *Eight Chapters* 6 as those regarded by the philosophers as truly evil. One must rid oneself of all desire to perform these actions in their view, a point on which Maimonides is in full agreement. What he wishes to deny in both these passages is that these laws have the status of truths known by the intellect.

The "practical" implications of Maimonides' ruling is that only gentiles living in Israel who formally accept the noahite laws based on the revelation at Sinai may be accorded the *legal* status of resident aliens. From a theological perspective, they are considered to be righteous gentiles who have a portion in the World to Come. Presumably the gentile philosopher is excluded by Maimonides from those who merit immortality. I will touch upon the issue of the World to Come in Maimonides' thought in later chapters.[25] Suffice to say in the present context that Maimonides does not employ the traditional notion of achieving a portion in the World to Come in order to express his philosophical view as to who attains immortality. For Maimonides, immortality results *only* with the attainment of intellectual perfection, whether the individual be a Jew or a gentile. In his legal writings Maimonides holds out the promise of a portion in the World to Come in order to underline the centrality of certain beliefs and practices that he regards as incumbent upon society to accept (or alternately, to reject).

Maimonides may have inserted here the proviso that the motive for observance must be the acceptance of the revelation of the Torah since he regarded this belief as necessary for nonphilosophers. It provides them with a solid foundation for ethics in which ethical activities are seen as promoting final perfection. Furthermore, Maimonides may have conceived the ideal political situation in Israel as being one in which all inhabitants, including the gentiles, accept the divine origin of the Torah. This helps insulate the inhabitants from negative influences that could weaken their commitment to the Torah. It is also important to note that belief in the existence of God is not explicitly included in the noahite laws. By insisting that these laws be fulfilled based upon an acceptance of revelation, Maimonides essentially makes belief in God's existence legally incumbent upon everybody.[26]

III

Maimonides' allegorical treatment of the Garden of Eden story in *Guide* 1:2 should also be understood in light of his distinction between the theoretical intellect and the practical activities of the rational faculty.[27] In the opening chapter of the *Guide*, he treats the intellect as the faculty by virtue of which Adam is said to have been created in the *image* and *likeness* of God. In this manner Maimonides begins to meet the challenge of reconciling Jewish tradition and Aristotelian philosophy by interpreting Scripture so as to negate from God all corporeal attributes. Simultaneously he imparts his view of wherein lies true human perfection. Chapter 2 picks up where chapter 1 leaves off. Maimonides is well aware that this interpretation is open to a serious objection. He opens the chapter by indicating his having heard it from a "learned man." Adam, according to the biblical account, was forbidden to eat of the Tree of Knowledge of Good and Evil. He gained his intellectual perfection only as a result of his act of disobedience. Maimonides' learned antagonist concludes: "This is like a story told by somebody that a certain man from among the people disobeyed and committed great crimes, and in consequence was made to undergo a metamorphosis becoming a star in heaven" (p. 24).

The objection places Maimonides in a difficult position. It implies that either he is wrong in seeing the perfection of the intellect as the true human perfection insofar as Adam was forbidden to attain it, or even more problematic, the Torah is wrong in not treating the perfection of the intellect as true human perfection, the human being's *telos* in the order of existence. Moreover, God is depicted in the Torah as selfish. God desires to keep this knowledge out of human hands lest they become like God *(elohim),* as the serpent whispers to Eve. When the objection is viewed in this light, nothing less than the belief in the truth and authority of the Torah is at stake.

Given the larger issues involved in this objection, Maimonides' initial response is to vilify his antagonist.

> O you who engage in theoretical speculation using the first notions that may occur to you and come to your mind and who consider withal that you understand a book that is the guide of the first and the last men while glancing through it as you would glance through a historical work or a piece of poetry—when, in some of your hours of leisure, you leave off drinking and copulating: collect yourself and reflect, for things are not as you thought following the first notion that occurred to you. (P. 24)

The inability to appreciate the allegorical nature of the story of the Garden of Eden and the philosophical truths underlying it indicates not only a serious intellectual flaw in the antagonist in not knowing how to read the text of the Torah. It also reveals severe deficiencies in his character. Anyone who attempts to undermine the text that more than any other is designed to guide society at large to perfection must be attacked head on in Maimonides' view. There is no place here for polite discourse, which would leave the dangerous impression that there may be some validity in the objection. The antagonist is after all a "learned man." The most dangerous threat to Judaism is not posed by those who understand the Torah's figurative accounts in a literal manner, and accept them. It is posed by those who understand these accounts in a literal manner and dismiss the truth of the Torah as a result, wreaking havoc on Jewish society as a result.[28] This group must be treated severely.

Rhetoric, however, is no substitute for a substantive response. Maimonides knows that he still must answer the challenge. He provides the key to his answer already at the very beginning of the chapter. The term *elohim*, he maintains, is used not only as a reference to God but may also designate human rulers. In this manner he clearly hints that knowledge of good and evil refers to the knowledge belonging to this group. In laying out his argument, Maimonides builds about this crucial point of scriptural exegesis.

Adam, prior to his act of disobedience, possessed a perfect intellect *in actu*, in Maimonides' view. The fact that Adam was given commands attests to the fact that he was not devoid of intellect. By means of his intellect Adam was able to distinguish between truth *(emet)* and falsehood *(sheqer)*. With his sin he became engaged with distinguishing between fine *(al-ḥasan)* and bad *(al-qabiḥ)* actions. Maimonides equates the latter judgments with generally accepted moral matters that are not cognized by the intellect. His example of a true proposition is that the heaven is spherical, and of a generally accepted dictum that uncovering the genitals is bad.

> When he disobeyed and inclined towards the desires of the imagination and the pleasures of the corporeal senses . . . he was punished by being deprived of that intellectual apprehension. He therefore disobeyed the commandment that was imposed upon him on account of his intellect and, becoming endowed with the faculty of apprehending generally accepted things, he became absorbed in judging things to be bad or fine. Then he knew how great his loss was, and what he had been deprived of, and upon what a state he had entered. (P. 25)

We should interpret Maimonides as maintaining that the command not to eat from the Tree of Knowledge of Good and Evil is in essence a command not to actualize the corporeal passions, and turn away from the metaphysical contemplation in which Adam was engaged. Only with the sin of becoming preoccupied with the corporeal world, and the loss of perfection that resulted thereby, did Adam's rational faculty have to become engaged in distinguishing between good and bad actions. Maimonides treats Adam's initial intellect as an acquired intellect, which, like the Separate Intellects, is divorced from the body and concerned solely with ontology. Some connection to the body nevertheless existed, allowing for Adam's turning away from the contemplation of the divine reality to a preoccupation with the corporeal world. Adam in essence experienced a change of identity. His intellect reverted to the state of a hylic intellect, inseparable from the body and the other faculties of the soul. While the only activity characterizing his identity as pure intellect was that of contemplation, all the activities characterizing the identity of a rational corporeal being belong to him in his "fallen" state.[29] It is at this point that his rational faculty became engaged in value judgments regarding various voluntary corporeal activities. Prior to this point, Adam experienced no passions. Ethical judgments became necessary when the passions began to exert their pernicious influences.

Maimonides refers to the practical intellect in this context, but in a veiled manner.[30] He interprets the verse, *And the eyes of them both were opened and they knew that they were naked* (Gen. 3.7), as the opening of "mental vision" *(baṣira)*. As a result, they considered their nakedness as bad. "Mental vision" refers here to the rational faculty, not to the imaginative. Not only is this interpretation in harmony with Maimonides' position in the *Treatise on*

Logic and *Eight Chapters*, but it emerges also from his description of the role played by the imagination in Adam's fall. It is the imagination that influences the individual to choose the pleasures of the senses.[31] The covering of nakedness serves to combat this inclination. This indicates that it is the product of rational activity. The need to combat the desires of the imagination, however, comes into being only after humans become tempted by corporeal pleasures. For this reason, Adam did not judge nakedness as bad in the state of living a life of pure intellect.

In general, the practical intellect is concerned with change or "becoming" as it relates to volitional activities. The theoretical intellect is concerned with "being." The story of Adam and Eve in Eden and their expulsion is a philosophic allegory symbolizing the state of intellectual perfection and the state of nonperfection. The individual in a state of perfection is not concerned with the *path* to perfection. Furthermore, nakedness in not a distraction to one who is in this state and is completely free from the desire for corporeal pleasures. Only in one's imperfect state, in which one is subject to the influence of the imagination, does one have to apply the rational faculty to mastering and properly channeling one's corporeal passions. Failure to do so both jeopardizes one's physical existence, and makes the attainment of intellectual perfection impossible.

Maimonides' approach may best be understood in light of Avicenna's views in *Theorems and Axioms*. Avicenna too terms these value judgments "generally accepted opinions" *(mashhūrāt)*.[32] While Avicenna regards these judgments as at times false, a view also shared by Maimonides, he treats them as the product of contemplation *(al-naṣra)*.[33] He distinguishes the generally accepted opinions from the primary intelligibles by the fact that the former are unknown to the solitary individual of pure intellect. This is an individual who experiences no passions, and whose natural moral traits do not suggest these opinions to him. It follows from Avicenna's account that the generally accepted opinions in the sphere of morality belong to humans primarily qua social creatures. The very *need* for "generally accepted opinions," not only the content of these opinions, reflects the imperfect human condition. Once passions are obliterated and intellectual perfection attained, a person naturally does not commit any of the actions that result from the passions. Contemplation concerning these matters is unnecessary. Maimonides essentially adopts Avicenna's approach, and alludes to the connection between generally accepted opinions and the workings of the rational faculty in the human being's imperfect state. It should be added that for Maimonides, following the Aristotelian tradition, such judgments form the basis of dialectical syllogisms rather than the irrefutable demonstrative ones or the false sophistical ones (*Treatise on Logic* 8).[34]

In his treatment of the Garden of Eden story, as well as in most of his other discussions in the *Guide,* Maimonides uses the term "intellect" in reference to the apprehension of the theoretical sciences wherein its perfection lies. The intellect *in actu* does not have as its object of apprehension volitional activities, including those very activities that contribute to its attainment of perfection. The "practical intellect" and "practical intelligibles" are terms never employed by Maimonides so as not to blur this point.[35]

IV

From Maimonides' description of the various powers of the rational faculty in *Eight Chapters* 1, the one that appears to be most directly responsible for political and ethical knowledge is the power of deliberation *(al-fikr* or *al-rawīya).*[36] By means of deliberation, one discovers the means by which desired ends may be attained. Ethical and political knowledge is, for the most part, knowledge of the regimen to be adopted by the individual or by society in the pursuit of its well being. It is true that in the following chapter, Maimonides ascribes ethical traits and conduct solely to the appetitive faculty, without including the rational faculty.[37] His concern in that context is to indicate the faculty most directly responsible for the *practice* of ethics, rather than how ethics is known. Aristotle defines moral virtue as: "a state of character concerned with choice, and choice is deliberate desire, therefore both the reasoning must be true and desire right, if the choice is to be good, and the latter must pursue just what the former asserts."[38] It is precisely the element of deliberate choice, to Aristotle, which serves as the basis for distinguishing the practical intellect from the theoretical. Following Aristotle, Maimonides sees ethical behavior and traits as requiring acts of will, thus belonging to the appetitive faculty. The fact that in the first chapter of *Eight Chapters* he ascribes knowledge of the pleasant and bad to the rational faculty, and in the third chapter he treats unethical behavior as a sickness of the soul to be cured by the sage, indicates quite explicitly that he regards the rational faculty as the source of this knowledge.

In at least one of his discussions in the *Guide*, Maimonides suggests that certain ethical knowledge is known intuitively.

In every passage they [the sages] state clearly that for Him, may He be exalted, justice is necessary and obligatory; namely, that an obedient individual receives compensation for all the pious and righteous actions he has accomplished, even if he was not ordered by the prophet to do them, and he is punished for all evil acts committed by him, even if he was not forbidden by a prophet to do them; this being forbidden by an inborn disposition *(al-fiṭra)*—I refer to the prohibition against wrong-doing and injustice. (3:17.470)

Maimonides brings this view in the name of the sages, and appears to be in agreement with it. Yet in his other discussions he leaves little doubt as to the primary role played by deliberation in this area. He explicitly traces the ability to govern oneself and others, as well as knowledge of the various crafts, to the power of deliberation (1:72; 3:17). Maimonides' list of those activities consequent upon the human form consists of, "man's apprehension of his Creator, his mental representation of every intelligible, his control of his desire and his anger, his thought *(fikra)* on what ought to be preferred and what avoided" (*Guide* 3:8.431).

The power of deliberation itself is essentially a neutral power in Maimonides' thought. It is not limited to positive practical activities, and may include thinking how to realize base ends (*Guide* 1:7; 3:8, 3:49). The basic neutrality of the deliberative faculty is a position found in Alfarabi's writings. Maimonides' views in regard to deliberation, both explicit and implicit, are essentially rooted in Alfarabi's approach. For Alfarabi, a virtuous deliberative faculty is one that deliberates about the means to achieve true felicity—that is, perfection of the intellect. It is precisely on this point that the theoretical rational faculty (whose knowledge is equated by Alfarabi with true wisdom) provides the grounds for deliberative virtue (or practical wisdom). The theoretical rational faculty provides humans with knowledge of true felicity. The deliberative faculty then judges how to realize it in actuality.[39] Knowledge of the actions leading to final perfection thus results from the cooperation of both parts of the rational faculty, the theoretical and the practical. In addition, the appetitive faculty must desire to achieve ultimate perfection and implement the judgments of the practical rational faculty. The imagination and senses play their part in assisting the soul to dedicate itself to this end. When all these faculties work in harmony in this manner, Alfarabi concludes, all the individual's activities will be good *(ḵairāt)* and pleasant *(jamilāt)*.[40] The deliberative faculty, on the other hand, may be employed in pursuing base ends. In this case, no "practical virtue" is to be ascribed to it no matter how well it performs its task.[41]

In his studies on the internal senses, H. A. Wolfson traces the history of the power of deliberation in ancient and medieval thought.[42] He shows how deliberation became associated with the imagination, one of whose functions is the combination and separation of sensibilia. This resulted in the positing of a compositive human imagination. The history of the philosophic approach to the power of deliberation supplies us with an important key in understanding a number of Maimonides' views.

V

The connection between deliberation and imagination in part explains Maimonides' position regarding nonprophetic legislators and rulers. In his discussion of prophecy, he classifies them with those possessing a superior imagination, but deficient rational faculty (*Guide* 2:37). Ascribing to them a superior rational faculty would be more consistent with his previously stated positions. Maimonides' classification becomes clearer when one keeps in mind that governance entails dealing primarily with sensibilia. In keeping with his philosophic sources, Maimonides treats the imagination as the faculty responsible for retaining sensibilia, combining and imitating them (2:36).[43] The ruler must continuously use the imagination in viewing all the particular circumstances of the society over which he rules, and in determining his actions accordingly. When viewed in this light, it is understandable why Maimonides chose to trace deliberation concerning political matters to the imaginative faculty.

Yet the fact that Maimonides in the *Guide* alternates between ascribing governance to the rational faculty and ascribing it to the imagination suggests a more complex picture. All governance for him results from the cooperation between the practical rational faculty and the imagination, not from either one alone. Why Maimonides alternately singles out the rational faculty or the imagination depends on the context of the discussion. In his discussions of nonperfect governance, or governance in contrast to theoretical contemplation, the imaginative component of governance is stressed.

Maimonides' treatment of nonprophetic legislators and rulers as those possessing a superior imagination and deficient rational faculty does not have an explicit source in the writings of his philosophic mentors. Given the strong influence of Alfarabi on Maimonides' approach to prophecy and governance, it is tempting to conclude that he extrapolated this notion from Alfarabi's writings. It is clear from Alfarabi's writings that nonvirtuous legislations and governments are the product of deficient theoretical rational faculties. That the imagination plays a dominant role in these cases is also clear from his approach. Nonvirtuous legislators and rulers pursue an end presented by the imagination, as well as employ the imagination in the process of pursuing the end they desire.[44]

In his discussion of prophecy, Maimonides introduces a number of modifications in Alfarabi's approach to governance. The points on which Maimonides differs from Alfarabi, even if the differences are more apparent than real, highlight the points he seeks to stress. The most important modification Maimonides introduces is the omission of the role of the practical rational faculty. He emphasizes instead the role of the imagination. This allows him to fix sharp boundaries between three groups of individuals—those receiving the emanation from the Active Intellect by their rational faculty, but not their imagination; those receiving the emanation by both their rational faculty and imagination; and those receiving it by their imagination alone (*Guide* 2:37). The first class, that of the philosophers, possesses knowledge of the intelligibles. The second class, that of the prophets, combines knowledge of the intelligibles with knowledge of all that relates to the sensibilia. The last class, that of the nonprophetic rulers and legislators, excels only in that which is related to sensibilia.

The prophets thus are those who combine the perfection of the philosophers with the perfection of the rulers. The whole in this case is greater than the sum of its parts. The prophets are superior rulers to nonprophetic rulers due to the perfection of their theoretical intellect. This enables them to guide society to true felicity, and not to a base end. They are also superior to the philosophers in their knowledge of theoretical truths. Maimonides indicates that "the true prophets indubitably grasp speculative matters; by means of his speculation alone, man is unable to grasp the causes from which what a prophet has come to know necessarily follows" (*Guide* 2:38.377). This appears to be due primarily to their possession of a superior rational faculty.[45] Yet their perfect imagination may also in part account for Maimonides' view in this matter. In explaining why the philosophers do not receive an emanation to their imaginative faculty, Maimonides traces the reason to a defect either in their rational faculty, resulting in a "scantiness of the overflow," or in their natural disposition, resulting in an inferior imagination. Maimonides may have regarded the imagination as aiding the prophets to grasp metaphysical matters that rational faculties attached to deficient imaginations are incapable of attaining.[46] A healthy imagination, faithfully serving the rational faculty, is a necessary condition for rising on the ladder of knowledge.[47] The defect in the imagination, in turn, prevents one from attaining intellectual perfection.

For Maimonides to distinguish between the practical and theoretical rational faculties, as Alfarabi does, would complicate his schema. The boundaries between these classes would become partially blurred. A superior practical rational faculty belongs to the groups to whom Maimonides ascribes a superior imagination. The point Maimonides wishes to convey, which is shared by Alfarabi, would stand out less sharply. Perfection of the rational faculty is essentially the perfection of the theoretical rational faculty. When the practical rational faculty does not operate in the service of the theoretical rational faculty, but serves other faculties instead, then it is fundamentally deficient despite its practical capabilities. By subsuming the activity of the practical rational faculty into the activity of the imagination in this context, Maimonides leaves no doubt where the perfection of the rational faculty lies.

VI

While Maimonides subsumes the activity of the practical rational faculty into the activity of the imagination in his characterization of nonprophetic governance and legislation, he adopts an entirely different stance in his characterization of Mosaic prophecy and legislation. Only the rational faculty is mentioned. Maimonides emphasizes the point that the imagination was not involved in Mosaic prophecy. This view of the ideal legislator is exceptional in relation to his philosophic sources. Alfarabi regards a perfect imagination as one of the qualities of the ideal legislator, in addition to a perfect theoretical and practical rational faculty.[48] The ideal legislator not only must deal with sensibilia in framing the particulars of the law, but also in translating intelligibles into images for pedagogic purposes.[49] In molding society to pursue true felicity, the ideal legislator presents figurative representations of theoretical truths since the masses are incapable of grasping and appreciating abstract truths. Alfarabi advances the possibility that several ideal legislators may emerge in the course of history, each laying down an ideal legislation appropriate to the social circumstances.[50]

Had Maimonides followed Alfarabi's approach to the letter, he would have assigned to the prophets a legislative role since they possess all the requisite perfections. Rather, he accepts Alfarabi's approach only to the extent of ascribing to the prophets a political role. While they have the authority to govern society, they may not legislate or even interpret the law in their prophetic capacity.[51] Maimonides emphatically insists that one prophecy alone, that of Moses, culminated or ever will culminate in a divine legislation (*Guide* 2:39).[52] In effect, he thereby posits a fourth category of those receiving the overflow from the Active Intellect. This category is confined to Moses. In common with those of perfect imagination, he shares with them many of the same practical functions. Yet the imagination, which is partially responsible for those functions, is absent from his prophecy.

On one major point Maimonides' disagreement with Alfarabi is less substantive than appears at first glance. Moses is not distinguished from the other prophets and nonprophetic legislators by his lack of a perfect imagination. Maimonides presents the view that Moses' prophecy initially came through the mediation of an "angel"—that is, the imaginative faculty (*Guide* 3:45). Characteristic of his esoteric approach, he advances this view in passing in the midst of a different discussion—the reasons for the commandments, rather than in his discussion of prophecy. Thus all the qualifications belonging to the ideal legislator in Alfarabi's account are ascribed by Maimonides to Moses. Yet Maimonides was also interested in omitting Moses' perfect imagination when he discusses his prophetic perfection.

One may argue that Maimonides posits this unique type of prophecy in order to preserve the uniqueness of the Torah. By ascribing to Moses a purely intellectual overflow in which the imagination played no role, he also implicitly undermines any attempt to interpret the commandments in a figurative manner. All the commands must be taken at "face value" as activities that one is obligated to perform. The imaginative dimension of the prophetic vision provides the basis for allegorical interpretation. One looks for the "inner truths" of the prophetic vision while rejecting a literal acceptance of the contents of the vision. Such an approach could lead to looking for the truths symbolized by many of the commandments, while denying that they were actually meant to be performed.[53]

Maimonides' desire to safeguard Judaism in this manner does not necessarily mean that he regards Mosaic prophecy and the framing of the Divine Law as non-natural events. A naturalistic conception may still underlie his view. Maimonides may be interpreted as maintaining that the imagination of Moses played no part in the prophetic experience itself. The intellectual overflow received by Moses culminated in a perfect theoretical understanding of all the existents, their forces, and their interrelationship. Maimonides equates this knowledge with knowledge of divine governance (*Guide* 1:54; 3:51). He appears to be hinting that on the basis of this theoretical knowledge, Moses' practical rational faculty and imagination framed the Law. The Law includes imaginative representations of the truth, as Maimonides' interpretations indicate. Knowledge of sensibilia necessarily underlie the particulars of the laws. Thus the imaginative and practical deliberative faculties are implicitly involved in its legislation.[54] Only a prophecy in which the imagination is absent from its theoretical component, however, could serve as the foundation of a law which deserves to be labeled divine. Moses' legislation alone perfectly translated (and extended) the principles of divine governance of the world into a system for the governance of human society. This is the highest level of prophetic perfection.

The other prophets did not attain the level of perfection of the theoretical intellect attained by Moses. This is evidenced by the fact that their imagination continued to play a role in the illumination they received of metaphysical reality. The overflow to the imagination was not only important in enabling the prophet to communicate speculative truths to society. It also helped the prophet grasp metaphysical reality in a more unified and penetrating manner than the philosopher, whose knowledge is discursive in character. The prophets, in Maimonides' famous parable in the introduction to the *Guide*, view metaphysical reality directly as though illumined by a flash of lightning at night. The philosophers are inferior to the prophets, insofar as they are like those staring at a polished stone as the lightning flashes, allowing them to see only a reflection. Moses, however, reached such a high level of intellectual perfection that he was able to dispense with the service of the imagination completely in grasping metaphysical truth, and attain a purely intellectual vision.[55] In Maimonides' parable, Moses is the one for whom the lightning flashes continuously, as though he were in daylight. On the basis of this unique apprehension, Moses alone was capable of framing a law deserving to be considered divine. Maimonides could only allude to the view that Moses was the immediate agent of the Law in the most veiled manner. To do otherwise would undermine the masses' belief in the divine nature of the Law. Maimonides' view that Moses' perfection can never again be equaled, as is the case with the perfection of the Divine Law, may have been dictated by religious considerations alone. Maimonides, however, does not present his view as one dictated solely by faith, but offers also a conceptual argument in its defense (*Guide* 2:39). This view serves to preserve the Law from the multiple challenges facing it. It represents an important break with Alfarabi's doctrine of successive ideal lawgivers, each laying down a new law better suited for the time.

The categorical difference between Moses' perfection and that of other lawgivers in Maimonides' philosophy has its counterpart in the categorical difference between the final end aimed at by the Divine Law and that of other legislations. Only the Divine Law ultimately aims at the perfection of the intellect, as well as the perfection of the "body"—that is, a perfect social order and system of ethics (*Guide* 2:40). Insofar as many of the commandments of the Divine Law are designed to promote the perfection of the body, which is regarded by Maimonides as a necessary condition for intellectual perfection, it is not surprising that it shares certain points in common with other legislations. Maimonides emphasizes the Divine Law's ability to direct its adherents to a more perfect social order and ethical life than do other legislations since the latter are framed from the standpoint of aiming at imaginary goods.[56] He does not deny, however, that they may bring about a well-ordered society. In being the product of those lacking intellectual perfection, their main shortcoming lies precisely in the fact that they do not aim at the true end of humanity. The other ends are at best only stepping stones for this end.

Knowledge of good and evil is on the ultimate level knowledge of the path to intellectual perfection.[57] Only one whose intellect has reached the level of perfection in which it knows the true end of humankind can possess this knowledge in full. On this point, the nonprophetic legislators and rulers are to be distinguished from prophetic ones, and the ability to govern is to be distinguished from political philosophy. Political philosophy is not concerned solely with effective social organization, but with the organization of society to pursue true felicity.[58] For Maimonides, it is the ultimate purpose or *telos* of a moral order that determines our evaluation of it. Even two outwardly similar orders are to be evaluated in a far different manner when their *telos* differs.[59]

The distinction between legislations and ethical systems based on their *telos* throws some light on at least one of the passages in the *Guide* in which he refers to "generally accepted opinions" *(al-mashhūrāt)*. Maimonides explains the rabbinic view that Israel heard only the first two commandments from God:

> For these two principles, I mean the existence of the deity and His being one, are knowable by human speculation alone. Now with regard to everything that can be known by demonstration, the status of the prophet and that of everyone else who knows it are equal; there is no superiority of one over the other. . . . As for the other commandments, they belong to the class of generally accepted opinions and those adopted in virtue of tradition, not to the class of the intellecta. (2:33.364)

While this explanation is consistent with Maimonides' exclusion of politics and ethics from the realm of the intelligibles, it remains problematic in a different respect. One would assume that a prophet is hardly needed to reveal generally accepted matters. The social prohibitions are common to all societies. What advantage does a prophet possess over others in these matters? In light of Maimonides' view of the significance of the ultimate *telos* of the system, the answer becomes clear. To Maimonides, the social prohibitions are transformed from "generally accepted opinions" into the products of prophetic revelation when viewed from the perspective of their promoting true knowledge of God as mandated by the first two commandments.

All of Maimonides' examples of "generally accepted opinions" in moral matters are in fact proper—that is, the prohibitions they posit are useful or necessary ones for attaining the "perfection of the body."[60] Prophetic morality and conventional morality in large measure overlap. The maintenance of a just social order is, in the final analysis, a characteristic shared by many human *nomoi*. As is the case with these legislations, the Divine Law includes many of the generally accepted moral opinions for it too aims at the just ordering of social life as its initial, though not ultimate, goal. The main flaw of generally accepted opinions in human nomoi is that the prohibitions they include aim no higher than one's corporeal well-being. They do not aim at promoting intellectual perfection. Thus they are the product of a practical rational faculty that does not serve the theoretical rational faculty. This is the case with the nonprophetic legislators and rulers. In changing the ultimate *telos* of the prohibitions of conventional morality and directing them to the attainment of intellectual perfection, the Divine Law changes the nature of these prohibitions.

VII

Maimonides' implicit view that all forms of governance involve the collaboration between the practical rational faculty and the imagination, with the prophetic forms of governance involving also the theoretical rational faculty, is paralleled by his view of divination. In his tripartite division between philosophers, prophets, and those possessing only a superior imagination, Maimonides places diviners, along with nonprophetic rulers, in the last category (*Guide* 2:37). In the following chapter, Maimonides mentions a different faculty found both in prophets and nonprophets that is responsible for foretelling the future, the faculty of divination *(al-qūwa al-shu'ur)*.[61] This faculty is treated by him as interchangeable with the imaginative faculty. From his usage one may infer that he regards divination as a product of the imagination. Unlike the case of governance, no explicit source can be found in Maimonides' writings in which the ability to divine is linked also to the rational faculty.[62] His description of the faculty of divination, however, suggests such a link:

> It [the faculty of divination] exists especially with regard to things with which a man is greatly concerned and about which his thought *(fikr)* turns. . . . You will find among people a man whose conjecturing *(ḥudsa)* and divination are very strong and habitually hit the mark, so that he hardly imagines that a thing comes to pass without its happening wholly or in part as he imagined it. The causes of this are many—they are various anterior, posterior, and present circumstances. But in virtue of the strength of this divination, the mind goes over all these premises and draws from them conclusions in the shortest time, so that it is thought to happen in no time at all. In virtue of this faculty, certain people give warnings concerning great future events. (2:38.376)

One is struck by the fact that the activity he describes very much appears to be a rational activity, akin to the framing of syllogisms. This point is considerably strengthened by the fact that Maimonides employs the term *ḥudsa* (conjecture) in describing the divinatory activity. The term *ḥads* signifies intuition. It appears in Maimonides' sources, most notably Avicenna, as designating the ability to "intuit" the middle terms in framing syllogisms by means of which one attains theoretical knowledge.[63] Maimonides himself lists a superior *ḥads* among the rational virtues in *Eight Chapters* 2. There he describes this trait as the ability to apprehend matters in "no time at all or almost no time." Maimonides' list leaves little doubt that he is dealing with the intelligibles belonging to the theoretical intellect. This ability is in particularly associated with the prophetic intellect in the context of Avicenna's thought, which is also the subject of Maimonides' discussion in *Guide* 2:38. Those reading this chapter in the Arabic could not fail to see that Maimonides utilizes a term most closely associated with the theoretical rational faculty and its apprehension of intelligibles, though he applies it to the apprehension of the future. In Maimonides' descriptions of the imaginative faculty proper, no similar activity is described. He ascribes to the imagination the preservation of sensibilia, and the act of joining and separating them. The latter activity is treated as an irrational one. In the case of divination, the activity of reason and that of imagination is in some manner combined.[64] While Alfarabi does not mention the faculty of divination, nor does he explicitly link diviners and rulers, his approach to divination may hold the key to understanding Maimonides' view. Alfarabi, in his discussion of visions in *The Opinions of the Inhabitants of the Virtuous City*, describes the imaginative faculty as being attached both to the theoretical and to the practical rational faculties:

> The practical [rational faculty] is that whose nature is to know the particulars of present and future matters. . . . The imaginative faculty is attached to two types of rational faculty. Consequently, that which the rational faculty obtains from the Active Intellect—namely, that which is like light in relation to sight—may emanate from it to the imaginative faculty. The Active Intellect thereby exercises a certain activity *vis-à-vis* the imaginative faculty. Occasionally it bestows upon it the intelligibles that by nature belong to the theoretical rational faculty, and occasionally the sensible particulars that by nature belong to the practical rational faculty. It [the imaginative faculty] receives the intelligibles by means of the sensibilia that imitate them, and which it combines. It receives the particulars—i.e., those that by nature are created by the practical rational faculty by deliberation *(rawīya)*—occasionally by imagining them as they are, and occasionally by imitating them by means of other sensibilia. Some of them [the particulars] are in the present and some of them exist in the future. All that occurs in the imaginative faculty is without the mediation of deliberation. For this reason, the things occur in it after being discovered by deliberation. The particulars that the Active Intellect bestows upon the imaginative faculty are by way of true dreams and visions. It bestows upon it the intelligibles, which it [the imaginative faculty] receives by adopting imitations in their place, by way of divinations of divine things. All this may occur in sleep, and it may occur in wakefulness.[65]

By tracing the knowledge of future particulars to the practical rational faculty's power of deliberation, Alfarabi shows that he regards divination as essentially a rational ability. Yet his position is ambiguous as to the precise relation between the Active Intellect and the imagination in this matter. Is the activity of the Active Intellect vis-à-vis the imagination a substitute for deliberation—that is, the Active Intellect possesses knowledge of future particulars that it bestows directly upon the imagination? Or does the imagination receive the future particulars most immediately from the practical rational faculty after the deliberative process has been completed? The first possibility is more in harmony with the simple sense of the text.[66] Yet it stands in opposition to Alfarabi's view that the Active Intellect does not know sensible particulars. Moreover, Alfarabi depicts the imagination as being connected to the rational faculty and receiving from it the emanation from the Active Intellect. The activity of the Active Intellect is compared to the activity of light enabling a person to see—that is, the Active Intellect bestows the ability to apprehend rather than the actual knowledge. This supports the position that while Alfarabi views the activity of the Active Intellect as strengthening the imagination and enabling it to act, he regards the actual information the imagination receives of the future as coming from the practical rational faculty.[67]

If the practical rational faculty already possesses this knowledge by way of deliberation, the advantage conferred by the activity of the imagination is not immediately evident. Alfarabi may have thought that the imagination adds nothing to the individual's perception in these matters. On the other hand, he may have held the view that the imagination helps clarify to the individual the information possessed by the rational faculty. In discussing the various types of revelation received by the imaginative faculty, Alfarabi explicitly indicates that, "all this is of assistance to the rational faculty."[68] This point would be particularly true of diviners, who do not appear to deliberate about the future in a conscious manner.

Maimonides adopted Alfarabi's view of the relationship between the Active Intellect, the theoretical rational faculty and the imagination. He made it the cornerstone upon which he built his theory of prophecy. Furthermore, Alfarabi's linking of present and future particulars may well be the basis for Maimonides' juxtaposition of rulers with diviners. The significant difference between the two approaches lies in Maimonides' omission of the practical rational faculty. It nevertheless is lurking beneath the surface of his discussion. From Maimonides' description of divination, this "faculty" is nothing more than the practical rational faculty deliberating in conjunction with the imagination to draw conclusions about the future. Maimonides may have regarded this deliberative activity, which involves only particulars, as confined to the imagination. As in the case of Alfarabi, at times he appears to posit a direct link between the Active Intellect and the imagination in regard to knowledge of the future.[69] The connection he draws between rulers and diviners, however, suggests that the imagination operates in conjunction with the practical rational faculty in the latter group, just as it does in the former. The emanation from the Active Intellect to the imagination is always via the rational faculty.

Just as the perfection of the theoretical rational faculty distinguishes prophetic governance from nonprophetic, so does it distinguish prophetic divination from nonprophetic. Maimonides insists that prophetic divination is inevitably correct, while diviners inevitably err. In the *Laws of Principles of the Torah* 10:1–3, this point serves as the basis for his legal ruling that the claimant to public prophecy must be tested *repeatedly*, and prove infallible in all the details of his predictions. By treating prophecy as a naturalistic phenomenon, Maimonides denies the non-naturalistic conception of God's governance that is most compatible with this position.[70] He may have insisted on the infallibility of prophetic predictions for religious/political reasons. Prophetic infallibility suggests God's exercise of personal providence in this matter, a belief that Maimonides wishes to soften but not undermine completely in his writings. Viewed from a social perspective, he creates for the aspirant to public prophecy a nigh impossible test in a world operating in accordance with natural law. His legal ruling appears to be designed to combat the dangers posed by false prophets in postbiblical times. Public prophecy was no longer essential for Jewish political leadership. There was no danger to the survival of the Jewish community in presenting insurmountable obstacles for the aspirant to overcome. It was far more important to protect the Jewish community from false public prophecy whose effects are completely negative.

This is not to say that Maimonides' position lacks all conceptual basis in light of his naturalistic approach. It can be traced in part to the role played by the *theoretical rational faculty* in divination. In knowing all the universal laws of nature, the prophets divine about individual matters based on their all-encompassing theoretical knowledge of nature.[71] This at least ensures a high level of accuracy in their predictions.[72] Diviners lack this knowledge. Their divination is based on a knowledge of particulars, which cannot be all encompassing, and inevitably leads to numerous errors.[73] Significantly, Maimonides maintains in the course of discussing prophetic divination and intuition about theoretical matters: "The overflow of the Active Intellect goes in its true reality only to it [that is, to the rational faculty], causing it to pass from potentiality to actuality. It is from the rational faculty that the overflow comes to the imaginative faculty" (*Guide* 2:38.377). Maimonides intimates that it is the overflow from the theoretical rational faculty that forms the basis for prophetic prediction. In the case of nonprophetic divination this overflow is lacking, but a superior deliberative power to draw conclusions from particulars underlies this phenomenon.

VIII

The question still remains whether Maimonides in fact excludes all ethical propositions from the realm of the theoretical intellect. I have argued that an analysis of the relevant passages in his writings reveals that he regards the rational faculty, but not the theoretical intellect, as the source of ethical knowledge. One must be careful to distinguish between commandments that according to Maimonides are known by the rational faculty and those that are not only known by it but whose *performance* is restricted to this faculty alone. The latter commandments are fulfilled by holding certain true opinions. In *Eight Chapters* 2, Maimonides broaches the issue whether there are commandments that belong to the rational faculty. He answers in the affirmative without elaboration. From his subsequent writings one obtains a clear view of what commandments he has in mind: knowledge of the existence of God, that there are no other gods, God's unity, and the intellectual love and awe of God. This point emerges from *Book of Commandments*, ninth principle; *Laws of the Principles of the Torah*, chapters 1–4; and *Guide of the Perplexed* 3:27–28. The knowledge required to fulfill these commandments are the most noble verities belonging to the theoretical intellect.

Are there physical actions whose content may be known in the same manner? As I have shown above, Maimonides denies this to be the case when dealing with the most well-known social laws. Yet his remarks in a number of passages suggest a different conclusion. In his *Introduction to the Commentary on the Mishnah*, he treats the message of the false prophet to worship other gods as negated by the intellect *('aql)*. This indicates that he regards the prohibition against idolatry, a physical act, as rooted in the theoretical intellect. Maimonides appears to retreat from this position in the *Mishneh Torah*. In the beginning of the *Laws of Idolatry* he maintains that the origins of idolatry can be traced to rational considerations. The situation then quickly degenerated to the point that the people forgot the existence of God. Psychological and historical reasons assume the place occupied in his earlier work by propositions belonging to the intellect.[74]

Another proposition ascribed by Maimonides to the intellect in the *Introduction to the Commentary on the Mishnah* concerns the pursuit of physical gratification:

> In the [process of] conceiving the intelligibles it is necessary to reject immoderation in physical pleasures. Apprehending that the corruption of the soul is in the

welfare of the body and the welfare of the soul in the corruption of the body is a first intelligible. If a human being seeks to satisfy desires, favors the objects of one's senses, and subjugates the intellect to one's desire, he is like the beasts and grazing animals who only think of [lit., imagine] eating, drinking and sexual intercourse. Then the divine faculty—i.e., the intellect—will not emerge. The individual will consist of matter disconnected [from intellect], swimming in a sea of hyle.[75]

Maimonides does not maintain that one should ignore one's physical needs altogether. His subsequent remarks make it clear that one should satisfy those needs that are necessary for survival. Any pursuit of physical gratification above and beyond that point is what is detrimental to the soul. Maimonides treats knowledge of the inverse relation between body and soul as a "first intelligible." Together with the proposition that human perfection lies in the perfection of the soul, this proposition becomes the basis for abstaining from any activity that is designed to gratify the body aside from its minimal requirements. Abstinence from pleasures thus may be traced to the theoretical intellect according to Maimonides' view.

One should not ignore some of the obvious problems with this "first intelligible." Does Maimonides wish to maintain that the welfare of the body inevitably involves the destruction of the soul and vice versa? This is hardly the case, even in the context of his philosophy. What kind of "first intelligible" then is this? Perhaps Maimonides has in mind a "voluntary intelligible"—a notion contained in Alfarabi's writings. According to Alfarabi, this type of "intelligible" is not contained in the theoretical sciences. It concerns things that are brought about by human will. Knowledge of "voluntary intelligibles" belongs to the deliberative faculty, the faculty responsible for knowledge of the rational ethical behavior aimed at the pursuit of perfection.[76]

One passage in the *Guide* appears to demand the stronger conclusion—that is, that the theoretical intellect is the source of certain ethical propositions. Maimonides distinguishes between generally accepted prohibitions and ones mandated by the *intellect* based on their content. Uncovering the genitals is an example of the former while "gatherings with a view to drinking intoxicants" is an example of the latter. The reason given by Maimonides is: "the corruption of the intellect and of the body is shunned by the intellect *('aql)*" (*Guide* 3:8.434). The intellect, according to this view, prohibits the individual from any activity that has adverse effects on one's intellectual or corporeal state.

One is justified in arguing that there is no inherent contradiction between

Maimonides' position here and the "first intelligible" he presents in *Introduction to the Commentary on the Mishnah.* The difference in formulation is nevertheless striking. Maimonides no longer speaks in terms of the necessity for the corruption of the body to insure the welfare of the soul, but stresses the need to avoid its corruption. Moreover, he speaks of the activity of the intellect in terms of practical judgments—"shunning"—rather than "grasping," which would be more appropriate for describing the activity of attaining theoretical knowledge.

The use of the term "intellect" in this context is puzzling for yet other reasons. The particular prohibition discussed by Maimonides is not expressly contained in the Divine Law (with the exception of the case of the nazirite), despite it being the ideal legislation. On Purim there is even a rabbinic command to get drunk. Maimonides includes this commandment in his *Mishneh Torah,* though from a legal perspective he has little choice in the matter (*Laws of Megillah* 2:15).[77] Nevertheless, one would hardly expect this to be the case if Maimonides seriously regarded this prohibition as belonging to the theoretical intellect. One would have to conclude from the view that he voices in *Guide* 3:8 that participating in drinking parties, insofar as it is harmful to the individual himself, is worse than murder, theft, adultery, and so on. The manner in which Maimonides distinguishes the participation in drinking parties and the uncovering of the genitals is also problematic:

> As for gatherings with a view to drinking intoxicants, you should regard them as more shameful than gatherings of naked people with uncovered private parts who excrete in daylight sitting together. The explanation of this is as follows: Excreting is a necessary thing that man cannot refrain from by any device whatever, whereas being drunk is an act committed by a bad man in virtue of free choice. (P. 434)

Is public nudity basically an involuntary act? May it not lead to a greater preoccupation with sexual matters, a preoccupation that Maimonides himself constantly reiterates is destructive both of body and intellect? Significantly, he concludes the chapter with a paean to the Hebrew language for having no word that designates according to its primary meaning: "the male or the female organ of copulation" (p. 435). It is clear from this passage that Maimonides was interested in strongly condemning certain social practices prevalent in his time, and formulates his position accordingly.[78] He conveys this point by contrasting a popular practice that he wishes to combat with one whose condemnation is accepted by all. There is a rhetorical quality to his argument. Maimonides chose his "generally accepted" dictum carefully.

He brings as an example of the uncovering of private bodily parts one in which the sexual dimension is absent. Would he have assumed the same stance if asked about nudist beaches? It is doubtful that this is the case. One would be rash to draw from this passage the conclusion that he regards intoxication as worse than other "generally accepted" prohibitions such as murder, or that he is alluding here to a system of ethics known by the theoretical intellect.[79]

I do not wish to deny that Maimonides distinguishes the morality characterizing the social and private life of the perfect individual from moralities belonging to humans *qua* imperfect social creatures (including the morality contained in the Divine Law). This distinction underlies his discussion of the final end of humankind in the closing chapter of the *Guide*. There he presents as the end the practice of loving-kindness, judgment, and righteousness *following* the attainment of the perfection of the intellect.[80] Maimonides also distinguishes between the morality of one who strives for perfection and the morality of one who does not aim at this goal, though outwardly the two may appear to be identical. My argument is that none of these types of morality belong to the realm of the intelligibles, which are concerned with the eternal truths of science. This is true even of the type of morality most firmly related to and grounded in a perfect theoretical intellect.

In conclusion, the practical intellect is a faculty never explicitly mentioned by Maimonides. It would be a mistake to conclude, however, that he parts company with the Aristotelian tradition on this matter. In his various enumerations of the activities belonging to the rational faculty, he includes types of practical knowledge as well as theoretical knowledge. Political and ethical knowledge clearly depend upon the activity of the practical intellect for Maimonides. Yet it is not simply his reticence in matters pertaining to the intellect that accounts for the omission of this faculty. In the very discussions in which Maimonides borrows heavily from Alfarabi, most notably his discussion of prophecy, he conspicuously leaves out this faculty. By failing to mention this faculty in any of his writings, Maimonides implicitly stresses a fundamental point of his philosophy—the intellect proper is the theoretical intellect. It is this intellect that is the actualized form of intellect, and attains an identity different from the hylic intellect or rational faculty. The perfection of this intellect by means of the study of the sciences, culminating in the study of metaphysics, is the final end of humankind, and the key to immortality.

In essence, the practical "intellect" is not an intellect at all. It is a capacity of the rational faculty, which is corrupted with the corruption of the body. Political and ethical knowledge thus do not constitute an integral part of one's true end, however much they may be instrumental in the attainment of that end. By avoiding even the term "practical rational faculty," Maimonides further underscores the fact that the rational faculty's perfection lies in the perfection of its theoretical function.

The final end of humankind presented by Maimonides in the conclusion of the *Guide*—the practice of loving-kindness, judgment, and righteousness—suggests that the perfection of the practical intellect is in fact the ultimate perfection, with the perfection of the theoretical intellect serving as a stepping-stone. Maimonides, however, is not in truth radically altering his view. He is reformulating the prophetic ideal. Perfect practical activity is the natural complement of perfect theoretical apprehension, rather than its end. It is the product of the translation of theoretical knowledge, characterizing one's life as intellect, into a blueprint for social action, characterizing one's life as physical being. Maimonides characterizes this activity as the product of the "emanating" perfection of the prophetic intellect. By means of this overflow, the individual governs oneself and others in the most perfect manner.[81]

The practical intellect is omitted even in this context, despite the fact that it is the faculty most directly responsible for translating metaphysical knowledge into a system of perfect governance. Its role is secondary in comparison to that of the theoretical intellect. To Maimonides, the perfection of the theoretical intellect constitutes not only the true perfection of the individual, but the ultimate source for perfecting all with which its emanation is in contact. The "practical intellect"—in the sense of the rational faculty's deliberation concerning voluntary activities or future particulars—remains a faculty consigned to remain in the shadows of the theoretical intellect, or relegated to the imaginative faculty, in order to highlight more fundamental points in his philosophy.

THREE

THE CONCEPT "GOOD"

I

What does "good" mean? One's answer ultimately depends upon the place of this notion in one's conceptual scheme. For some, underlying the term "good" is the view of a world with built in values or purpose. Others treat it as an emotive term indicating one's personal preferences in a relativistic world in which no absolutes reign. "Good" may also be interpreted in a strictly utilitarian sense to indicate the accomplishment of any given objective. It refers to the efficacy of the "means" rather than the quality of the "ends." Not only is one's perception of morality the issue, but also one's perception of reality. By exploring how a thinker uses the term "good" one attains a better perspective for viewing how he perceives these areas.

In the case of Maimonides, his approach to the notion "good" offers no clear conclusion as to what that perception is. It is one of the more puzzling topics in his thought. He does not deal with this topic in an organized, detailed manner. His approach must be construed from a number of brief comments, scattered among discussions covering a variety of issues. One must carefully examine the manner in which Maimonides uses the various terms in Arabic for "good" in the course of these discussions. More crucially, one must see how he interprets verses in which the Hebrew term for good—*tov*—appears. An appreciation of Maimonides' approach to this notion has far-reaching implications for understanding his philosophy in general.

Two contemporary scholars, Warren Zev Harvey and Sara Klein-Braslavy, have shed a great deal of light on Maimonides' approach to this topic.[1] They have dealt with the problem of the concepts "good" and "evil" in his thought from a range of perspectives. Both researchers have presented penetrating theses to explain and bridge the various uses of "good" in Maimonides' writings. As they have shown, Maimonides uses "good" to characterize: the ultimate end of the individual—that is, the perfection of the intellect in its apprehension of God, and its attainment of immortality (*Guide* 1:18; 1:42; 3:27); the actions by means of which one attains the virtues and the ultimate end (*Eight Chapters* 3, 4, 8; *Treatise on Logic* 14); the activity of God in the creation of all the existents (*Guide* 3:10; 3:12); God (*Guide* 3:12); and the "generally accepted" moral dictums that were attained by Adam as a result of his sin, and were not known by him when he possessed a perfect intellect (*Guide* 1:2). In other words, "good" designates: ultimate perfection and the ethical characteristics of those pursuing perfection; all of existence including the existence of God; and finally, inferior conventional morality. In addition, "good" can be used as a noun designating those things human beings value and desire to attain (*Guide* 3:12; 3:16; 3:53). In his writings, the vast majority of them written in Arabic, Maimonides does not employ a single Arabic term for "good." At times he brings the Hebrew word for good—*tov*—without a translation.

Though these two researchers differ on a number of fundamental points, they are united in their view that the subjective definition Maimonides offers for the concept "good" in *Guide* 3:13 lies at the foundation of the various uses. Maimonides writes, "Good *(tov)* is an expression applied by us to what conforms to our purpose" (p. 453). "Good" does not designate the attainment of a specific goal, but the attainment of any goal one desires. "Good" also designates those means that are instrumental for attaining a desired goal.

In accordance with this definition, Klein-Braslavy argues that Maimonides uses the subjective notion "good" to designate the realization of God's goal. This goal consists of the bestowal of existence upon all the existents. It also includes the determination that the ultimate end of the human being is the perfection of the intellect. It is not the case, according to this interpretation, that existence is intrinsically "good" and hence God chose to actualize it. Existence is "good" *because* God chose to actualize it and succeeded in doing so. By the same token, God could have chosen not to act in this manner. The concept "good" does not tell us anything about the nature of the goal itself, only about its actualization. God's purpose, however, provides the basis for "good" in the realm of ethics. When human purpose is in accord with God's purpose and the individual pursues intellectual perfection, the individual is guided by the intellect and does what is absolutely good in the ethical realm. When human purpose differs from God's purpose, the individual is guided by the imagination and pursues relative "good," which in effect is absolute evil. This was the situation of Adam after his sin. Maimonides thus treats the knowledge of "good" negatively when he deals with human goals that are not in accordance with the natural goal of human beings. For this reason he equates Adam's knowledge of "good and evil," acquired by his act of disobedience, with the "well-known" ethical dictums unknown to him when he still possessed intellectual perfection. This type of ethical knowledge results from the activity of the practical intellect when it is in the service of the imagination in pursuing an imaginary end.[2]

In Harvey's reconstruction of Maimonides' approach, imagination presents the individual with several possible ends. "Good" as: "what conforms to our purpose," is rooted in the notion that the individual is free to determine one's goals. The view that different goals are open to the individual, and that there is not a single true goal, is the product of the imagination. In order to attain its goals, the imagination employs the intellect to determine the appropriate means. In essence, the imagination is the faculty that knows "good and evil." The intellect in itself knows only the "true"—that which is necessary. For pedagogical reasons, Maimonides employs the subjective concept "good" even in those contexts in which the objective concept "true" is more appropriate. He wants to encourage the nonperfect individual, who lives under the illusion of the imagination that he can choose between different goals, to actualize the natural, necessary end—the perfection of the intellect. For the perfect individual, who knows only the "true," there is no room for choice at all. Similarly, God does not *choose* the "good." The term "choice" is anthropomorphic. God acts in accordance with necessity, which is to actualize existence. The term "purpose" is an amphibolous one. There is absolutely no relation between its use in reference to God and its use in reference to human beings. The connection between knowledge and existence in Maimonides' thought (truth corresponds to reality) leads him to employ the subjective notion "good" to designate not only the human end and all that contributes to its attainment, but also all that is known to the perfect individual—namely, all the existents.[3]

While I agree with many of the points in these two analyses of the concept "good" in Maimonides' thought, the foundation upon which they are built is highly debatable in my view. Is Maimonides being essentially a subjectivist in the definition he offers of "good" in *Guide* 3:13? Is the view that the utility of the means, but not the quality of the ends, the starting point for his approach to the concept "good"? Would Maimonides agree that according to his definition the concept "good" can be applied to the actualization of any goal or desire? Is the "good," when used in reference to ends, simply a matter of taste? Both Klein-Braslavy and Harvey rightly stress the fact that Maimonides does not regard the "good" in the realm of voluntary human activity as a matter of personal taste. According to his worldview, human beings have a natural end, as is the case with all creatures.

"Good" is what contributes to the actualization of that end. To escape from the dilemma posed by Maimonides' subjectivist approach to the definition of "good," Harvey distinguishes between "good" on the ethical plane and "good" on the metaethical one. The former is not subjective, at least not when used in reference to ideal morality based on knowledge of the truth. "Good" on the metaethical plane, on the other hand, is subjective and the product of the imagination. It stands in opposition to "truth," which is objective and known by the intellect.

I do not deny that some support can be garnered for this distinction. Nevertheless, it is a difficult one to sustain in light of the philosophic tradition upon which Maimonides was nurtured. There one finds a different distinction between "good" and "true." Avicenna, in his division of the sciences, explains:

> The theoretical part is one whose end is to acquire certainty about the state of things whose existence does not depend on human action. Here the aim is only to acquire an opinion. Examples of it are the science of [God's] unity and astronomy. The practical part is the one whose aim is not merely to acquire certainty about the beings; its aim can be the acquisition of a sound opinion about a matter that exists through man's endeavor, with a view to acquiring by it what is good *(al-k̲air)*. Thus the aim here is not merely to acquire an opinion, but rather to acquire an opinion for the sake of action. Therefore, the end of the theoretical part is truth *(al-ḥaq)*, and the end of the practical is the good *(al-k̲air)*.[4]

In the continuation of his remarks, Avicenna divides practical science into the governance of oneself (ethics), the governance of the household (economics), and the governance of the state (politics).

Avicenna's distinction between "good" and "true" is not between the subjective and the objective. It is between *praxis* and *theoria*. Avicenna aptly defines the difference between these two realms. The object of theoretical knowledge is the natural world and God. This knowledge has as its focus everything whose existence is not dependent upon human activity. The object of practical knowledge, on the other hand, is that which is dependent upon human activity. This includes knowledge of ethics on all of its various levels.

Avicenna's distinction between the theoretical and practical is based on Aristotle. Aristotle too incorporated the notions "true" and "good" in the context of this distinction.[5] Alfarabi is yet another philosopher who profoundly shaped Maimonides' thought and who presents this distinction.[6] Avicenna in the above-cited passage does not define the "good." Yet he certainly does not appear to regard it as a subjective notion that is the product of the imagination. On this point Alfarabi is even more explicit. "Good" refers to the human end and all the activities that lead to it or flow from it, with the rational faculty being the source of this knowledge.

Happiness is the good *(al-ḵair)* without qualification. Everything useful for the achievement of happiness or by which it is attained, is good too, not for its own sake, however, but because it is useful with respect to happiness; and everything that obstructs the way to happiness in any fashion is unqualified evil *(al-sharr)*. The good that is useful for the achievement of happiness may be something that exists by nature or that comes into being by the will. . . . As to voluntary good and evil, which are the noble *(al-jamil)* and base *(al-qabiḥ)* respectively, they have their origin specifically in man. Now there is only one way in which the voluntary good can come into being. That is because the faculties of the human soul are five: the theoretical-rational, the practical-rational, the appetitive, the imaginative, and the sensitive. Happiness, which only man can know and perceive, is known by the theoretical-rational faculty and by none of the remaining faculties. Man knows it when he makes use of the first principles and the primary knowledge given to him by the Active Intellect. When he knows happiness, desires it by the appetitive faculty, deliberates by the practical-rational faculty upon what he ought to do in order to attain it, uses the instruments of the appetitive faculty to do the actions he has discovered by deliberation, and the imaginative and sensitive faculties assist and obey the rational . . . then everything that originates from man will be good. It is only in this way that the voluntary good comes into being.[7]

This position can be traced back to Aristotle, who in the opening section of *Nicomachean Ethics* identifies the "good" with the ultimate felicity of the soul and the final goal of human existence. "Human good," Aristotle concludes, "turns out to be an activity of soul in conformity with excellence, and if there are more than one excellence, in conformity with the best and most complete" (1.7.1098a).[8]

The human will is the cornerstone in the Aristotelian tradition upon which the distinction between "good" and "truth" rests, but not because of the subjectivity in the desires of the will. "Good" is different from "truth" in that it designates something about which knowledge alone is insufficient. One must also act to attain it. In other words, its attainment is dependent upon human volitional activity. The individual, however, does not determine what is "good." The individual discovers it. Not only is the "good" basically objective when it characterizes ends, but in large measure also when it is used to characterize means. In every craft there are effective means to attain a given end, while other means are ineffective. The effectiveness or ineffectiveness of the means is determined independently of the subjective thinking of the agent. The attainment of the "good" is similar. Human choice in this area is confined to the decision to pursue the good and engage in the proper activity necessary for realizing it, not for arbitrarily deciding what that activity is.

According to this view, "good" as a subjective notion does not exist on the metaethical plane but on the imaginary one. On the metaethical plane, "good" refers to the human *telos* or to the essence that belongs to humans by nature. This is not a derived usage of the concept, but the primary one. On the ethical plane, "good" refers to those voluntary activities that lead to the goal of human existence or flow from one's rational essence.

In light of the Aristotelian tradition, there is room to question whether Maimonides approaches the concept "good" in such a fundamentally different manner. He adopts the conclusions of that tradition in regard to the end of humankind. He also accepts the Aristotelian distinction between the theoretical and the practical (*Treatise on Logic* 14; *Eight Chapters* 1),[9] though without introducing the concepts "true" and "good" in the contexts in which this distinction is brought by him. In no passage does Maimonides explicitly state that the imagination invents the concept "good," or that it is the source of knowledge of "good and evil." In some passages he ascribes the knowledge of "good and evil" to the rational faculty without so much as a hint to the view that the imagination plays a primary role in this matter.[10]

How then are we to understand Maimonides' definition of the "good" as: "an expression applied by us to what conforms to our purpose"? One should pay attention to the context in which this definition appears. Maimonides deals with the problem of the *telos* of existence as a whole. In his view, the recurring phrase in the first chapter of the Torah, *God saw that it was good*, indicates that the existents conform to God's purpose. One should not look for any other goal. By maintaining that the Torah is employing here the nonphilosophic language of the masses, Maimonides "solves" the problem of the purpose for which God created the world. According to the definition he brings, "good" tells us nothing about the divine purpose itself, only about its realization.

The subjective nature of the concept "good" follows from this point. One can objectively determine if something conforms to its agent's purpose, providing one knows what that purpose is. Maimonides appears to be arguing here that the concept "good" is not a value term that applies to ends. The term can be used indifferently in reference to the attainment of any end. One should not deduce from this argument that every purpose is considered to be "good." The concept "good" simply does not apply in this matter. If my purpose is to become rich, it is not the purpose itself which is either "good" or "bad." The actual attainment of wealth is what is good in this case. One may define the "good" as the correspondence between reality and desire, just as the "true" is the correspondence between reality and knowledge.

What about the purpose itself? Does Maimonides really think that the concept "good" does not apply to ends, and there is no criteria by which goals are to be judged? Is knowledge of the "good" essentially limited to knowledge of the effective means to attain any given goal? In other passages of his writings, this is certainly not the case. Maimonides does not use the various terms for "good" to designate the effectiveness of the means irrespective of the goal at which they aim. "Good" is used only in reference to an end that is treated as a positive one. In *Guide* 3:25 Maimonides defines a good *(jud ḥasan)* activity as: "that accomplished by an agent aiming at a noble end (*ghāya sharīfa*), I mean one that is necessary or useful, and achieves that end" (p. 503). This definition of "good" applies also to divine activity. It is designed to explain how we are to view God's motive in giving us the commandments. According to this definition, two conditions characterize an activity that is *jud ḥasan*. One, that the end is a noble one, in contradistinction to a "insignificant end" to which a "frivolous action" aims. Second, the activity contributes to the realization of the end. Maimonides does not appear to regard the "nobility" of an end as a subjective judgment. He treats it as something that characterizes the nature of the end.

If Maimonides does not use "good" as a concept that is neutral in regard to goals, the "subjectivity" of his definition in 3:13 becomes empty of all content. One must look for the starting point to his approach to "good" in a different direction. There are, however, at least two passages in the *Guide* that may be adduced as contradicting my claim. Both of them have already been mentioned as figuring prominently in the analyses of Klein-Braslavy and Harvey. The first is Maimonides' approach to knowledge of good and evil in his discussion of Adam's sin in *Guide* 1:2.[11] In his discussion he adopts an exceptionally negative attitude to this knowledge. He equates it with knowledge of conventional morality. He associates this knowledge with the fallen state of Adam, after he inclined in the direction of his imagination and lost his intellectual perfection. Knowledge of the "good" in this context may be interpreted as serving goals presented to the individual by the imagination. The second passage is the starting point of their analyses—Maimonides' discussion of the purpose of the world in *Guide* 3:13, where he defines "good" as "what conforms to our purpose." One is left with the impression that Maimonides sees God's purpose in bringing the world into existence as neutral in character, with no inherent value. The world is "good" solely in that it conforms to God's purpose that it exist. In the case of both these passages I will advance a different line of interpretation. Good is always equated by Maimonides with the actualization of a "noble end."

II

In Maimonides' discussion of Adam's sin in the second chapter of the *Guide*, he grapples with a difficult challenge. As I already indicated in the previous chapter, this challenge focuses on a fundamental problem with the Torah's account of Adam in the Garden of Eden. Maimonides had presented the view that human perfection lies in the perfection of the intellect in the opening chapter. According to Maimonides, by virtue of a perfect intellect Adam is said to be created in the "image of God." The challenger, on the other hand, interprets the Torah as indicating that Adam acquired intellectual perfection as a result of his sin. Prior to that point, he was like the other animals, "devoid of intellect *('aql)*, of thought, and of the capacity to distinguish between good *(al-ḵair)* and evil (*al-sharr*)" (p. 23). Underlying the challenge of Maimonides' antagonist, is the notion that the Torah is based on false conceptions. In his view, Maimonides is wrong in ascribing to the Torah the philosophically correct view that intellectual perfection is the final perfection of humankind. Otherwise the Torah would not present the view that God forbade Adam from eating from the Tree of Knowledge of Good and Evil and that intellectual perfection came in the wake of disobedience of the divine command.

Nothing less than the acceptance of the truth of Judaism is at stake here. For this reason Maimonides begins by vilifying the challenger, while arguing that he is incapable of reading the Torah in accordance with its intended meaning. In Maimonides' interpretation, Adam is said to possess a perfect intellect prior to his sin. By virtue of the intellect the individual distinguishes truth from falsehood.

> Fine *(al-ḥasan)* and bad *(al-qabiḥ),* on the other hand, belong to the things generally accepted as known *(al-mashhūrāt),* not to those cognized by the intellect. For one does not say: it is fine that heaven is spherical, and it is bad that the earth is flat;

rather one says true and false with regard to these assertions. Similarly one expresses in our language the notions of truth and falsehood by means of the terms *emet* and *sheqer*, and those of fine and bad by means of the terms *tov* and *ra'*. (*Guide* 1:2.24–25)

Maimonides' example of something that is "generally accepted" is that uncovering the genitals is bad.

The story of Adam in the Garden of Eden is treated by Maimonides as a philosophic parable. It does not describe the natural state of any human who ever lived, but comes to teach us what is the true perfection of humans and what characterizes their imperfect state, which is their natural state. Maimonides ascribes knowledge of the "generally accepted" to judges and rulers. According to his view in *Guide* 2:36, these individuals are characterized by an emanation from the Active Intellect to the imagination, and not to the rational faculty. Maimonides treats the imagination as the source for the sins of humans. He goes so far as to identify this faculty with the evil inclination (*Guide* 2:11). Those who receive the emanation by their imagination alone are not perfect, nor is it in their power to lead others to perfection. In drawing a connection between Adam's sin, knowledge of the "generally accepted," political leaders, and the imaginative faculty as the source of sin and the beneficiary of the emanation from the Active Intellect in the case of political leaders, Maimonides appears to be saying that knowledge of the "generally accepted" is connected to the imagination. Essentially, this knowledge is what causes us to fail to attain the goal that belongs to us *qua* human beings. It is the negative consequence of Adam's sin, if not the sin itself.

This conclusion raises some fundamental problems. According to Maimonides' view, should we regard the uncovering of the genitals, which he labels "most manifestly bad," with indifference or even as something positive? It is highly unlikely that Maimonides would assent to this view. Maimonides was an outspoken critic of all activities that stimulate the sense of touch, especially in the sexual realm (*Guide* 2:36; 3:8; 3:33). The importance of other "generally accepted" moral maxims, such as the prohibition to steal or murder, is even more apparent.[12] Not only are these prohibitions generally known since they are crucial to the existence of human society. The Torah, which directs its adherents to perfection, also includes them. The prohibitions included in the "generally accepted" moral dictums thus are treated positively and do not prevent the attainment of perfection. The question remains: What is the essential difference between the "intelligibles" and what is "generally accepted," or between the "true" and the "good"?

Maimonides maintains, "with regard to what is of necessity, there is no good *(tov)* or evil *(ra')* at all, but only the false *(sheqer)* and the true *(emet)*" (*Guide* 1:2.25). Maimonides' examples of the false and the true are all derived from the scientific realm. Though he does not explicitly bring Avicenna's distinction between the "true" and the "good," it appears that this distinction underlies his stance. The "necessary" are those matters that do not change and over which humans have no control. These are the matters contained in the theoretical sciences listed by Maimonides in *Treatise on Logic* 14. All human volitional activities, including moral activities that deal with self governance, should be judged according to the notions of "good" and "bad," not "true" and "false."[13] As I have argued in the previous chapter, Maimonides posits a distinction between the rational faculty and the intellect *in actu*. The intellect knows only the theoretical sciences, while the rational faculty knows also the practical matters. Hence knowledge of morality in general, and the "generally accepted" moral dictums in particular, belongs to the rational faculty. Its source is not the imagination, nor is it the intellect per se.

That knowledge of the "good" is not knowledge of the "necessary" does not entail that it is essentially subjective. Knowledge of the "generally accepted" does not have the same certainty as knowledge of the "intelligibles," but neither for the most part is it false. In Maimonides' summary of Aristotelian philosophy in his *Treatise on Logic* 8, the syllogism based on well-known moral propositions is treated as a dialectical one, not sophistical.[14] Knowledge of morality does not fall under the category of knowledge of the "necessary" for several reasons. Its subject matter is human activity. Moral knowledge is connected to the changing physical life of the individual. It is also not relevant in every situation. In the medieval Aristotelian tradition, the perfect individual who is cut off from all society feels no desires for physical pleasures and thus is naturally "moral."[15] An individual of this description has no need for knowledge of morality. Moreover, this knowledge in part changes in accordance with changes in the situation. From this perspective, moral knowledge is analogous to medical knowledge. Not every sick person must undergo the same treatment to attain health. Much of the treatment is based on knowledge attained by experience rather than theoretical speculation. Similarly, not every individual or society stands in need of same exact activities in the realm of ethics. Self-governance and the restraint of one's desires must take under consideration one's situation, even if one's behavior should conform to certain general principles. For this reason, there is a measure of subjectivity in judging the moral "good." Nevertheless, there are specific criteria by which one judges if an activity is good. Moreover, there is no subjectivity in determining to what goals the activity should aim.

In *Eight Chapters* 4, Maimonides explains the verse, *Love truth and peace* (Zech. 8:19): "Know that *truth* refers to the rational virtues of the intellect, since they are the unchanging truths as we have mentioned in the second chapter. *Peace* refers to the moral virtues, by means of which there is peace in the world."[16] One can detect here the same distinction that exists between "truth" and "good." The first objective of morality is well ordered human relations. Maimonides terms this objective, "the welfare of the body" in *Guide* 3:27. It includes two matters: abolition of wrongdoing (many of the "generally accepted" moral dictums belong to this category) and the acquisition of moral virtues "that are useful for life in society so that the affairs of the city may be well ordered" (p. 510). The final perfection is the perfection of the soul :

> I mean to have an intellect in actu *('aql b'il-f'il);* this would consist in his knowing everything concerning all the beings *(maujūdāt)* that it is within the capacity of man to know in accordance with his ultimate perfection. It is clear that to this ultimate perfection there do not belong either actions or moral qualities and that it consists only of opinions toward which speculation has led and that investigation has rendered compulsory. (P. 511)

The same distinction between the moral virtues and the rational virtues reappears in *Guide* 3:54. We may conclude that the final perfection of the soul falls under the category of "truth." This consists of the rational virtues and the "intelligibles." Knowledge of the intelligibles is knowledge of the "unchanging" and "necessary" truths, or knowledge of the natural existents. The sciences dealing with "truth" are the theoretical ones, especially physics and metaphysics. "Peace" belongs to the "good," which is identified with the "welfare of the body." This consists of the "generally accepted" moral dictums and the moral virtues. Knowledge of the "good" is the subject matter of practical philosophy, dealing with the various types of governance—self-governance (ethics), governance of the household (economics), and governance of society (politics). The theoretical intellect does not know practical philosophy, but neither does the imagination. This knowledge belongs to the rational faculty.

In light of this distinction we should view Maimonides' approach to Adam's sin. Adam prior to his sin possessed no moral knowledge. He knew only the theoretical sciences. Maimonides adopts a negative attitude to the generally known moral dictums in this case since he is not dealing with an imperfect individual. He is dealing with an individual of perfect intellect who gained knowledge of the generally known moral dictums as a result of the loss of his perfection. Nakedness has no significance for the perfect individual who lives in the world of the intelligibles. Corporeal matters are of no concern to him. Only when he turns his attention to the pleasures of the body, suggested to him by the imagination, does the state of the body leave its imprint on the soul. Then he must distinguish between the "fine" and the "bad" in order to protect himself from his corporeal desires. Other generally known moral dictums—for example, murder and theft are bad—are also not known by him prior to this point. They belong to a social context that has no relevance for him. One can also say that the perfect individual does not *judge* these activities as bad, but naturally would not engage in them. These activities result from the evil inclination. The perfect individual possesses a pure intellect, detached from the body and its inclinations. Its activity is uninterrupted contemplation of the truths of ontology. The "emanation" from this intellect to the body leads it to behave in a perfect manner.[17] There is no need for the rational faculty to judge between the fine and the bad in reference to volitional activities. The situation of imperfection is one in which a person is concerned with matters pertaining to the body, is tempted by the imagination, and feels corporeal desires. This is the situation that necessitates framing moral dictums.

After Adam lost the perfection of the intellect and had to start judging between the "fine" and the "bad"—"then he knew how great his loss was, and what he had been deprived of, and upon what a state he had entered" (1:2.25). Adam understood that his previous situation was the final end to which he must now struggle to reattain. Maimonides is not describing in this context subjective knowledge of morality taking the place of objective knowledge of morality. He is describing knowledge dealing with practical philosophy, with *praxis*, taking the place of knowledge dealing with theoretical science, with *theoria*. The expulsion of Adam from the Garden of Eden, the struggle to attain physical necessities, and the comparable nature of Adam's state and that of the beasts, signify the corporeal life of an individual. In this state, however, the generally known moral dictums play a very positive role.

God's command to Adam not to eat of the Tree of Knowledge should not be seen as a contradiction to the claim that Adam had no knowledge of morality in his initial state. God's "command" is to contemplate the intelligibles— represented in the parable by the other trees in the Garden whose fruits are permitted—without turning one's attention to bodily matters. This "turning" is what brings in its wake the necessity of judging between "good" and "bad." Adam should not place himself in a state that demands the use of the practical rational faculty to determine his physical activities.

Maimonides writes in reference to God's command: "It was likewise on account of it [the intellect] that he was addressed by God and given commandments . . . for commandments are not given to beasts and beings devoid of intellect" (1:2.24). His intent is to indicate that commands are given only to one who possesses intellectual apprehension. Even the Separate Intellects, according to Maimonides, "apprehend their acts and have will and free choice with regard to the governance committed to them" (2:7.266). Their activity is the continuous, uninterrupted contemplation through which the world is governed. They too heed the divine "command" by fulfilling the purpose characterizing their existence. As in the case with human beings, they act from a state of intellectual discernment. On this point they differ from nonrational beings or from the forces of nature. In contradistinction to human beings whose activity is characterized by privation or imperfection, they "always do that which is good *(al-ḵair)*" (2:7.266). The "command" to Adam essentially is the same "command" to the Separate Intellects. Since some connection remained between Adam's intellect and his body, the possibility remained for him to transgress this "command." He could stop behaving in accordance with his final end, which is the continuous, uninterrupted contemplation of the intelligibles.[18] God's "command" does not involve moral knowledge, which is not an integral part of final perfection.

One should not conclude from Maimonides' discussion that no distinctions are to be drawn between moral systems. His position that Adam prior to his sin possessed no knowledge of morality, and that the distinction between the theoretical and practical is what underlies his approach to Adam's state "before" and "after," still leaves room to distinguish between moral systems by their content and the end to which they aim. According to Maimonides, there are fundamental differences between the moral system of those seeking intellectual perfection and one not designed to guide individuals to this end.[19] The generally known moral dictums usually are found in societies that do not recognize that true human perfection is the perfection of the intellect. In these instances the dictums are not directly related to final perfection.[20] Nonetheless, they allow for the physical existence of human beings in society, and social order for Maimonides is "good."

One of the ends of human beings is the preservation of the species in Maimonides' view (*Guide* 1:72; 2:40; 3:13). This end is shared by humans with the other living creatures. Yet it is not an "imaginary" end, lacking all value in itself. It is an end implanted in nature in accordance with God's purpose. Maimonides regards society as necessary for the survival of the human species (2:40).[21] Judging between "good" and "bad" in reference to physical activities is essentially the judgment between what contributes to human existence and what does not contribute. In most societies this judgment takes place in the shadow of pursuing false ends presented by the imagination—for example, wealth, honor, and the like. For Maimonides, however, what determines whether an activity is "good" is not its efficacy in attaining any end that humans desire, without any reference to the nature of the end. The activity must contribute to the continued existence of humankind. From this perspective, the end to which the generally known moral dictums aim is a noble one. As is the case with rational judgments in other areas, what is "generally accepted" may be mistaken.[22] Maimonides recognizes the fact that humans often employ their reason in the pursuit of frivolous or harmful ends. Yet he never labels the activities that are instrumental in attaining these ends, "good" or "fine."[23] Despite the positive role of moral knowledge in society, Maimonides' negative approach to this knowledge in his discussion of Adam's sin is understandable. He is dealing with a case in which the individual started concentrating on matters pertaining to physical existence instead of preserving the final perfection of the intellect.

Maimonides' complex approach to the well-known moral dictums parallels his approach to those who are said to know good and bad—the nonprophetic rulers and legislators. As shown in the previous chapter, the ability to govern belongs to the rational faculty. Maimonides attaches extreme importance to this ability. When he speaks of the special nature of the rational faculty in *Guide* 1:72, he stresses the ability to govern among the examples he brings. All of his examples belong to the realm of practical activities that facilitate the physical existence of humankind. On the other hand, when Maimonides compares rulers with prophets, he stresses the defect in the rational faculty of the former, and the superiority of their imagination (*Guide* 2:37). These positions raise in their wake the problem: Which faculty is responsible for the ability to govern, the rational faculty or the imagination? The answer is that both faculties work in conjunction in this matter. The positive aspect of the ability to govern—namely, knowledge of the means that are instrumental for the perpetuation of the species—belongs primarily to the practical rational faculty. The negative aspect—namely, the pursuit of ends having no value—belongs to the imaginative faculty that is not tied to a perfect theoretical rational faculty.

The negative aspect of nonprophetic governance and legislation is highlighted in Maimonides' discussion of prophecy. Only one who attains complete understanding of the world and the human being's place in the hierarchy of existence is in a position to translate one's knowledge into a perfect system of governance in the social sphere. It is clear that this system differs from the system legislated by nonprophets (who are not philosophers), who have themselves not attained perfection or even appreciate where true human perfection lies. Yet the positive aspect of rulers and legislators can also be detected in Maimonides' discussion of prophecy. After establishing the necessity of society for human beings, Maimonides continues: "It is part of the wisdom of the deity with regard to the permanence of this species of which He has willed the existence, that He put into its nature that individuals belonging to it should have the faculty of ruling. Among them there is the one to whom the regimen mentioned has been revealed by prophecy directly; he is the prophet or the bringer of the nomos" (2:40.382).[24]

The legislator, like the prophet, is part of the system of divine providence in that he promotes the existence of the human species. The phenomena of nonprophetic rulers and *nomoi*, together with the well-known moral dictums incorporated into them, fall far short of ideal governance. Despite their inferiority to the phenomena of prophets and divine legislation, they are positive. Without knowledge of the "fine" and the "bad," the physical existence of humankind is impossible. This existence conforms to the divine purpose. Any activity that is detrimental to human existence is neither "good" nor "fine," according to Maimonides, though it may be instrumental in attaining the objective desired by its agent.

Despite the fundamental differences in the various systems of governance and moral systems, all of them have as their immediate source the practical rational faculty. None of them have the epistemological status of the "intelligibles" belonging to the theoretical intellect. In light of Maimonides' acceptance of the Aristotelian identity of intellect, intellection, and object of intellection, this point has far reaching ontological implications. Moral knowledge belongs neither to the beasts nor to the angels—that is, the Separate Intellects. The perfect human intellect, or the "acquired intellect,"[25] does not grasp moral knowledge. This knowledge remains in the province of the rational faculty to which the perfect intellect "emanates." With the final separation of the immortal acquired intellect from the soul, this knowledge, like everything else that is dependent upon matter for its existence, no longer remains. The immortal intellect contemplates only the nonchanging aspect of reality that exists independent of human activity.

III

The view that all forms of moral knowledge in Maimonides' thought belong to the practical rational faculty, not the theoretical intellect, is open to a number of objections worthy of consideration. Maimonides' use of the term "intellect" in *Guide* 3:8 suggests that there exist moral dictums that are objective and fall under the category of the "true."

> As for gatherings with a view to drinking intoxicants, you should regard them as more shameful than gatherings of naked people with uncovered private parts who excrete in daylight sitting together. The explanation of this is as follows: Excreting is a necessary thing that man cannot refrain from by any device whatever, whereas being drunk is an act committed by a bad man in virtue of free choice. The disapproval of the uncovering of the private parts is a generally accepted opinion, not a thing cognized by the intellect, whereas the corruption of the intellect and of the body is shunned by the intellect *('aql)*. (P. 434)

I have dealt with this passage toward the end of the previous chapter arguing that there is a rhetorical dimension to Maimonides' presentation. One may maintain that he considers all dictums that contribute directly to the preservation of one's intellect and body as mandated by the intellect. Social morality, on the other hand, falls under the category of "generally accepted" dictums. This distinction is significant since it echoes his division of the commandments into the categories of those aiming at the individual's perfection and those whose purpose is social welfare (*Guide* 3:35). Yet Maimonides explicitly rejects the notion that any of the divine commandments are known by the intellect, with the notable exception of those that are fulfilled solely by means of knowledge of God and the world.[26] Given his view of the divine law, one is hardly justified in drawing the conclusion that Maimonides accepts the notion of a morality known by the theoretical intellect based on his comments in regard to drinking parties.

There remains the issue whether the various terms employed by Maimonides for "good" and "bad" all have the exact same meaning. Should not the various terms be viewed as subtle indicators of different types of morality? This hypothesis is strengthened by Maimonides' discussion in *Guide* 1:2. The challenge presented to Maimonides is that Adam prior to his sin was like the rest of the animals, "devoid of intellect *('aql),* of thought *(fikra)* and of the capacity to distinguish between good *(al-ḵair)* and evil *(al-sharr).*" Maimonides responds by stressing that Adam prior to his sin possessed a perfect intellect. By virtue of the intellect, one distinguishes between truth and falsehood. "Fine *(al-ḥasan)* and bad *(al-qabīḥ),* on the other hand, belong to the things generally accepted as known *(al-mashhūrāt),* not to those cognized by the intellect."

Immediately evident is the fact that Maimonides switches the terms employed by the challenger. The challenger argues that Adam did not know the "good" *(al-ḵair)* prior to his sin, while Maimonides indicates that Adam did not know the "fine" *(al-ḥasan).* It is tempting to hypothesize that the change in terminology is highly significant. After all, Maimonides cautions his readers to pay careful attention to all his words in the treatise for none were chosen haphazardly. In the present context, Maimonides may wish to signal his elite readers that knowledge of the "fine" and "bad," which is equated with knowledge of the "generally accepted" moral dictums, was acquired by Adam after the sin. This moral knowledge is represented by the Tree of Knowledge of Good and Evil and is not known by the intellect. Knowledge of good (*al-ḵair*) and evil *(al-sharr),* on the other hand, is the morality known by Adam prior to his sin when he possessed a perfect intellect. This moral knowledge belongs to the intelligibles and falls under the category of "true."

The only problem with the hypothesis that Maimonides draws a distinction between the "good" *(al-ḵair)* and the "fine" *(al-ḥasan),* or between the "evil" *(al-sharr)* and the "bad" *(al-qabīḥ)* is that a study of the gamut of Maimonides' writings lends it no support. In *Eight Chapters* 6, Maimonides uses the term *al-sharr*, not *al-qabīḥ*, in reference to the well-known moral dictums.[27] He treats this knowledge in an exceptionally positive manner, maintaining that the excellent *(al-faḍīla)* soul has rid itself of all desire to perform any of these well-known evils. Yet he does not intimate that the knowledge of the moral dictums belongs to knowledge of the intelligibles.

Maimonides broaches the issue of moral knowledge also in the concluding chapter of *Eight Chapters*. He offers a significant interpretation of the other verse in which "good" *(tov)* and "evil" *(ra')* appear in the story of Adam in the Garden of Eden, *Verily man has become like one of us, knowing good and evil* (Gen. 3:22). This verse records God's speech after Adam's sin. Interestingly, Maimonides does not cite this verse in *Guide* 1:2. In *Eight Chapters*, Maimonides, following Onkelos, reads the verse, *Verily man has become unique, by himself knowing good and evil.*[28] In other words, man has attained the unique ability to distinguish between good and evil by his own capacity. By virtue of this capacity, Maimonides continues to explain, he should now stretch out his hand and eat from the Tree of Life, thereby attaining eternal life. The cherubim with the fiery swords were not placed by God at the entrance to the Garden in order to prevent Adam from entering. Rather they were placed there to point out the way. Maimonides understands the story to signify that moral practice paves the way for attaining intellectual perfection. The cherubim represent the Active Intellect, which is the source of the human intellect and the theoretical knowledge that results in the immortality of the intellect.

In his discussion, Maimonides uses the terms *al-ḵair* and *al-sharr*, not the terms *al-ḥasan* and *al-qabiḥ*, to render *tov* and *ra'*. Maimonides equates the "good" with the moral virtues, yet here too he does not trace this knowledge to the intellect, *'aql*. Moreover, Maimonides' reading of the verse suggests that God and the Separate Intellects do not possess knowledge of "good and evil." Otherwise it is difficult to understand why he does not follow the more conventional way of interpreting the verse—namely, God indicates that Adam has become like "one of us" *(ke-'eḥad memenū)* by virtue of his moral knowledge. This interpretation entails that knowledge of *al-ḵair* and *al-sharr* is knowledge that belongs to the realm of the intelligibles known by the theoretical intellect, hence known also by God. Instead, Maimonides negates this knowledge of God by placing a comma after the term "one," and interpreting this term as meaning "unique." *Memenū* does not mean "of us," in Maimonides' view, but "by himself"—by virtue of his own distinctly human capacity.[29] In summary, despite Maimonides' exceptionally positive evaluation of knowledge of *al-ḵair* and *al-sharr* in *Eight Chapters*, this knowledge includes the "generally accepted" moral dictums and does not belong to knowledge of the intelligibles. This parallels his view of *al-ḥasan* and *al-qabiḥ* in *Guide* 1:2, with the notable difference that there he adopts a negative evaluation of the well-known moral dictums.

In *Treatise on Logic* 8, Maimonides employs the terms *al-jamīl* (the beautiful) and *al-qabīḥ* (the bad or ugly) in reference to the well-known moral dictums.[30] In this work he is summarizing the position of the Aristotelian philosophers. Here too he cites the prohibition of the uncovering of the genitals as an example of a generally accepted moral dictum. The ability to distinguish between the beautiful and the bad belongs to the rational faculty according to Maimonides' presentation in chapter 14. The latter view and terminology is brought by Maimonides in his own name in *Eight Chapters* 1. In his discussion of the activity of the rational faculty in this chapter,

Maimonides does not employ the terms *al-k̲air* and *al-sharr*. This fact only serves to strengthen the hypothesis that Maimonides draws no distinction between "good" as *al-jamīl* or *al-ḥasan* and "good" as *al-k̲air*. From his subsequent discussions in *Eight Chapters* in which the terms *al-k̲air* and *al-sharr* appear, it is clear that the ability to distinguish between these two categories belongs to the rational faculty, certainly not to the imaginative. Nor does it belong to the intellect, as we have seen. Thus we must trace this knowledge to the practical activity of the rational faculty. If Maimonides does not explicitly mention knowledge of *al-k̲air* and *al-sharr* in chapter 1 in the course of dealing with the rational faculty, the most evident explanation is that he identifies this knowledge with knowledge of *al-jamīl* and *al-qabīḥ*. It should be added that in *Treatise on Logic* 14, Maimonides also does not appear to draw any distinction between these terms. There he indicates that from the "fine" (*al-ḥasan*) virtues come the "good activities" (*al-k̲airāt*). Both these terms have an exceptionally positive connotation, with the "distinction" between them consisting of moral character traits versus moral actions.

In one passage in *Eight Chapters* 3, Maimonides enumerates the various terms for good and evil. He defines a healthy soul as one whose characteristics is such that one frequently performs, "the good *(al-k̲airāt),* the fine *(al-ḥasanāt)* and the beautiful acts *(al-af'al al-jamīlā)*." The diseased soul, on the other hand, is one whose characteristics result in one frequently performing, "evil *(al-shurūr)*, vile *(al-sayyi'āt)* and bad acts *(al-af'al al-k̲airāt)*."[31] These formulations might be interpreted as indicating that Maimonides sees some type of distinction between the terms. Otherwise, why should he list them separately? Nonetheless, if Maimonides was of the opinion that these terms are distinct, it is difficult to see from the context what that distinction might be. His entire discussion focuses on the health of a soul from the perspective of moral traits. Maimonides does not present any distinction between various forms of good or of evil in this context.

One may argue that Maimonides was far more precise in his terminology when writing the *Guide*. One should confine one's investigations of the issue under discussion to this text alone. Most of the time Maimonides employs the terms *al-k̲air* and *al-sharr* when speaking of good and evil. When he wishes to characterize God's activity in giving existence to the world and governing it, or the activity of the celestial entities, he uses the term *al-k̲air* (*Guide* 2:4; 2:7; 3:7; 3:10; 3:12; 3:13; 3:25). *Al-sharr* is used to refer to evil, which Maimonides equates with privation (*Guide* 3:10). The evils that befall the individual—whether from nature, others, or those one brings upon oneself—are also termed *al-shurūr* (3:11-12). As for the moral virtues, Maimonides most of the time employs the term *al-faḍā'il*. Evil characteristics are referred to as *al-raḍā'il* (*Guide* 3:8; 3:27; 3:54).[32] When Maimonides speaks of human acts that are good from a moral perspective he also tends to use the term *al-ḵair* (2:45; 3:19). The term *al-ḥasan,* however, is not entirely absent from the *Guide*. It too is used to refer to the moral virtues (3:35).[33] The term *al-qabīḥ*, in addition to *al-sharr* and *al-radī'*, characterizes the evil acts that are to be repudiated since they prevent the attainment of perfection (3:33).[34] As we have already seen, Maimonides terms a good activity *jud ḥasan*, and defines it as one that is "accomplished by an agent aiming at a noble end (*ghāya sharīfa*), I mean one that is necessary or useful, and achieves that end" (3:25.503). An activity thus is not considered *ḥasan* if it does not aim at a noble end. Maimonides does not use the term *ḥasan* to refer to corporeal pleasures, but employs the term *al-laḍḍa*—a term that is used to refer to the pleasure of intellection as well.[35] He also does not use the term *ḥasan* when he defines good as "what conforms to our purpose," but employs only the Hebrew term *tov*. Thus despite Maimonides' "hint" in *Guide* 1:2 that there is a distinction between good as *al-ḵair* and good as *al-ḥasan*, he *consistently* employs these two terms in a manner that suggests that he regards them as interchangeable.

In this area, as in so many others, the profound influence of Alfarabi's writings on Maimonides' discussions is discernible. Alfarabi uses the term *al-ḵair* to characterize the absolute good—namely, the final end of humanity and true felicity[36]—the means to true felicity,[37] the virtues,[38] and the First Cause together with the chain of existence that emanates from God.[39] *Al-jamīl* is a less general term that is used by Alfarabi in reference to human voluntaristic activities that contribute to true felicity,[40] or are associated with the moral virtues.[41] In some of his discussions, he employs both terms and he too appears to treat them as interchangeable. The term *al-ḥasan* also appears in some passages as the antonym of *al-qabīḥ*.[42] In all his writings, the terms have an exceptionally positive connotation, with the exception of those places in which Alfarabi explicitly distinguishes between true good and that which people imagine to be good. Despite the fact that the term *al-jamīl* is used to characterize means rather than ends, Alfarabi never employs it to refer to means that succeed in achieving an "imaginary good." He is explicit in his rejection of the view that the imagination is the source of knowledge of *al-jamīl* and *al-qabīḥ*.[43] "If the means discovered are the most useful for a virtuous end," Alfarabi indicates, "then they are noble and fair. If the ends are evil, then the means discovered by the deliberative faculty are also evil, base and bad."[44]

The use of terms in the realm of morality that are borrowed primarily from the realm of aesthetics—for instance, *jamīl*, *ḥasan*—leads to a further crucial point. Beauty and goodness are intrinsically linked. Actions that are immoral are ugly. A moral human being is essentially a beautiful human being.

IV

The relation between the concept "good" and God's activity in giving existence to the world appears in the context of the problem of the purpose of the world. Maimonides cautions his readers not to seek a final purpose to the world. God's view of the world as "good" does not refer to the world's realizing some final end. The term "good" simply indicates that the world came about just as God intended. Existence is "good" since it conforms to God's purpose to create the world (*Guide* 3:13). This view would appear to support the position that God could have decided just as easily not to create the world.[45] "Good" in this context is a neutral concept that offers no evaluation of the final end itself. The state in which there is an existent world is no "better" or "worse" than the state in which no world exists.

Numerous difficulties are entailed by this view. Especially problematic is the question of the relation between divine will and wisdom.[46] Are we dealing here with a case in which the two possibilities—the existence of the world and the world's non-existence—are completely equal from the standpoint of divine wisdom and the divine will must mediate between them? This problem is raised by Alghazali in his *Incoherence of Philosophy*. The manner in which we interpret Maimonides' approach to "good" in reference to the divine activity hinges directly upon the answer to this problem.

Alghazali's proof that there exists a choice that is neutral from the standpoint of wisdom is based on the argument that it exists even among humans. Taking a cue from Avicenna, he argues that a person desirous of dates, and before whom are placed two basketfuls with no characteristic that make one preferable to the other—not quality, distance, difficulty to acquire, and so forth—is still capable of choosing one. This individual will not die of starvation, while remaining standing in his place paralyzed by wisdom's incapacity to indicate which he should choose. Will alone determines the choice.[47] One finds also in nature accidents whose actualization is not superior to other possibilities. For example, if the planets moved in the opposite direction to their present orbit, the situation would still be the same. There is no difference from the standpoint of wisdom if their orbit is from east to west or west to east. The divine will alone is responsible for the choice between these two possibilities. Alghazali's conclusion is that there is no necessity to posit that the world is without beginning because of the argument that God cannot discriminate between the infinite number of equal possibilities when to create the world. God has the power to perform willful acts that are not dependent upon the ability of wisdom to discriminate between the possibilities involved.[48]

One may interpret Maimonides as agreeing that there are acts of divine will that are not dependent upon divine wisdom. The creation of the world in its entirety, not just certain details in nature, falls under this category. Maimonides' position would then be that the world's existence has no more immanent value than its nonexistence. Existence is no "better" than the state of absolute privation. The choice to create the world from a state of absolute privation is dependent solely upon the divine will, which is capable of discriminating between these two possibilities. Both possibilities are equal from the standpoint of divine wisdom. Existence is said to be "good" only because it conforms to the divine will, not because the will chooses the "good" or "better" possibility. In those contexts in which Maimonides stresses the idea of God's free will, in contrast to the idea that God is completely bound by necessity, he appears to be arguing this position.[49] The task of divine wisdom in these cases is to determine the most effective way for God to actualize what God chooses.

Opposed to this interpretation is the one that maintains that Maimonides did not accept the notion that there exists choices between things that are completely equal from the standpoint of wisdom. There are no "neutral" choices.[50] In those contexts that Maimonides stresses the idea of divine wisdom, he appears to advance this position.[51] Wisdom not only determines how to actualize what is chosen, but also what the divine will should choose. Thus God gives existence to the world since its existence is better than its privation from the standpoint of God's wisdom.

These two opposing interpretations can look to support from Maimonides' explications of the verse, *And God saw everything that He had made and behold it was very good* (Gen. 1:31). In his explications, Maimonides draws a connection between existence and the "good," but in entirely different ways. In *Guide* 1:54 Maimonides cites the verse to prove that *all My goodness* (Exod. 33:19) that was shown by God to Moses refers to all of the existents. From this context one cannot deduce the roles of divine wisdom and divine will in giving existence to the world. Is "good" equivalent to existence because God chose it to be so, or is "good" equivalent to existence hence God chose to give existence to the world?

Maimonides appears to answer this question in *Guide* 3:10. He cites Genesis 1:31 to show: "Accordingly the true reality of the act of God in its entirety is the good *(k̲air)* for the good is being. . . . Even the existence of this inferior matter, whose manner of being it is to be a concomitant of privation entailing death and all evils, all this is also *good (tov)* in view of the perpetuity of generation and the permanence of being through succession" (p. 440). Maimonides' discussion suggests that the divine will is not what imparts value to existence, but existence has an inherent value which is the reason behind the divine choice. He concludes 3:12 by stressing: "For His bringing us into existence is absolutely the great good" (p. 448).

The same approach can be detected in other passages in which Maimonides deals with God's activity. However, the import of some of his remarks is not without ambiguity. As we have seen, in 3:25 Maimonides defines a good (*jud ḥasan*) activity as "that accomplished by an agent aiming at a noble end (*ghāya sharīfa*), I mean one that is necessary or useful, and achieves that end" (p. 503). The verse cited by Maimonides to confirm this point is Genesis 1:31. It appears that giving existence to the world is regarded by Maimonides as a "noble end," thus God judges the product of the divine activity as "very good." This interpretation is strengthened by Maimonides' subsequent comment:

> Know that the majority of false imaginings that call forth perplexity in the quest for the end of the existence of the world as a whole or the end of every part of it have as their root an error of man about himself and his imagining that all that exists exists because of himself alone, as well as ignorance of the nature of inferior matter and ignorance of what is primarily intended—namely the bringing into being of everything whose existence is possible, existence being indubitably a good *(k̲air)*. It is because of this error and of the ignorance of these two notions that the doubts and the perplexity arise, so that some of God's actions are imagined to be frivolous, others futile, and others vain. (P. 506)

The existence of the world does not result from an arbitrary act of the divine will. Existence has intrinsic value hence divine wisdom favors giving existence to the world. In this discussion Maimonides emphasizes the role of divine wisdom in all of God's activities. He concludes the chapter by again citing Gen. 1:31, together with Deut. 32:4 *(The Rock, His work is perfect),* to prove that everything flows from the divine wisdom.

Yet in the very same chapter Maimonides also blurs the distinction between ends and means. The examples he brings of God's activities show: "Everything that He, may He be exalted, has done for the sake of a thing is necessary for the existence of the thing aimed at or is very useful" (p. 503). Maimonides does not refer to the quality of the end itself. When he discusses the divine wisdom at the end of the chapter, it is not completely clear whether he has in mind solely the wisdom reflected by the particulars of creation—which fall under the category of effective means—or also the wisdom reflected by the very act of the creation of the world—which falls under the category of noble ends. Furthermore, his comment that creation itself is the final end since existence is "good" is not without its problems. On the surface it contradicts his insistence that one should not seek the final end of the world. Despite these difficulties, on the basis of his discussion in 3:25 it does not appear that he holds a subjective view of "good." Maimonides identifies the "good" with existence.

Opposed to this approach to the "good" stands Maimonides' definition of the good as: "what conforms to our purpose" (*Guide* 3:13). In this chapter too he cites Genesis 1:31 and explains the verse in conformity with his definition. Maimonides stresses the role of divine will and cautions against ascribing any other purpose to creation. The subjective definition of "good" suggests that the divine act of creation is an arbitrary one. Yet Maimonides' concluding comment in the very same chapter raises a difficulty for this view: "For when man knows his own soul . . . and understands every being according to what it is, he becomes calm and his thoughts are not troubled by seeking a final end for what has not that final end; or by seeking any final end for what has no final end except its own existence, which depends on the divine will—if you prefer you can also say: on the divine wisdom" (p. 456).

In the middle of the chapter too Maimonides indicates that the answer to the problem of the final end of the world is, "God has wished it so, or: His wisdom has required this to be so" (p. 452). One should keep in mind that Maimonides' main intent in rejecting the search for a final end of the world is to negate the view that humanity is the end, a view that can be found in some thinkers prior to Maimonides, such as R. Saadiah.[52] In negating the view that humanity is the purpose of creation, Maimonides offers yet another solution to the problem: "All the other beings too have been intended for their own sakes and not for the sake of something else" (p. 452).

Maimonides thereby offers three answers to the problem of the purpose of creation which are in effect one: divine will, divine wisdom and existence itself.

Maimonides grapples with the problem of the "good" also in 2:30.[53] The difficulty he addresses is why the phrase, *And God saw that it was good* does not appear in conjunction with the second day, when God created the firmament. Maimonides offers two explanations. The first one is based on the connection between "good" and existence: "For whenever it mentions a thing among those that exist, having been produced in time and subsisting in durable, perpetual and permanent fashion, it says with reference to it *that it was good*" (p. 353). The second explanation suggests a different view of the "good":

> There is something hidden . . . with regard to the *firmament* and the thing above it, which is called *water*. For if the matter is considered according to its external meaning and with a recourse only to superficial speculation, it does not exist at all. For between us and the lowest heaven, there exists no body except the elements, and there is no water above the air. . . . If, on the other hand, the matter is considered according to its inner meaning and to what was truly intended, it is most hidden. For in that case it was necessary for it to be one of the concealed secrets so that the vulgar should not know it. How then could it be proper to say of such a matter *that it was good*? For the meaning of the words, *that it was good*, is that the thing in question is of externally visible and manifest utility for the existence and permanence of that which exists. But in a matter whose meaning is hidden and that, understood in its external meaning, does not exist in such a way as to appear useful, what utility externally visible to the people at large could there be so that the words, *that it was good*, could be said with reference to it? (Pp. 353–54)

In the latter explanation, Maimonides treats the "good" as the useful. The Torah employs the term "good" in the story of creation to indicate what is useful for the perpetuation of existence. The phrase, *that it was good*, does not appear by the firmament since the masses are unaware of its true existence and utility, and this point must be withheld from them. When viewed from this perspective, there is no point for the Torah to label the firmament "good."

Maimonides' concludes his discussion of the firmament with a further explanation, quite obscure in character: "The thing in question, though it represents a very great part of the existents, does not constitute the purposed end for the permanence of that which exists; and therefore the words, *that it was good*, could not be said with reference to it. This could rather occur with reference to a compelling necessity that the earth be uncovered. Understand this" (p. 354). He appears to be saying that "good" in the context of creation is used only in reference to those existents that were intended primarily for their own sake and not to serve as an instrument for the existence of something else.[54] The existence of the firmament was not primarily intended for its own sake but for the purpose of allowing the earth to be uncovered. In this matter it serves as an intermediary for the existence of things that were intended for their own sake, such as humanity. According to this interpretation, here too Maimonides equates the "good" with existence, but only with that part that is not primarily a means but an end in itself.[55]

Maimonides' position can be summarized as follows: "Good" is what conforms to one's purpose. God's purpose is to give existence to the world. This purpose, however, is not grounded in an arbitrary act of will. It is rooted in the divine wisdom. Wisdom determines not only the particulars that are necessary for the optimal realization of God's intent to give existence to the world. It determines the very intent. There are many things whose existence is an end in itself. According to divine wisdom, the state of existence is better than the state of nonexistence. There is no point for Maimonides to introduce the notion of divine wisdom in this context if we are not dealing with a choice between things that are not equal in value. When Maimonides negates the notion of final end in reference to the world or what is in it, his intent is to combat the view the there is a final end beyond their existence.[56] In particular, Maimonides wishes to show that humans are not the goal of creation. Consequently, existence is "good" so God chose to give existence to the world. Since the totality of existents is a perfect expression of God's choice, it is said of the world that *God saw that it was very good.*

From the identity of God's wisdom, will and essence,[57] together with the view that the purpose of existence is existence itself, the conclusion follows that the existence of the world is necessary from the perspective of divine activity (though it remains contingent from the perspective of its own nature).[58] If existence is "good," and God acts in accordance with the divine wisdom/essence, there is no real possibility for God not to give existence to the world. Maimonides continuously stresses the idea of God's freedom of will, but in the final analysis he leaves no room for volitional activity that is not dependent upon wisdom. The choice not to give existence to the world stands in opposition to divine wisdom, hence it is not a real possibility.

For the Islamic philosophers, this point necessitates the eternity *a parte ante* of the world since divine wisdom is without beginning (*Guide* 2:14). Maimonides attacks the philosophers' view precisely because it leads to the conclusion that God has no choice in the matter of giving existence to the world. Nor is God capable of introducing even the smallest change in the world according to this view. Everything follows from natural necessity (*Guide* 2:22). The impossibility of miracles follows from the philosophers' premise. Maimonides argues that in creating the world, God can work outside the operative natural law and can freely choose whether to give existence to a thing or to demolish it (2:25; 2:27).[59]

There are signs, however, that Maimonides' esoteric view agrees with that of the philosophers. God acts only within the framework of nature. Maimonides indicates that the world is without end and that no permanent changes are introduced into nature once the laws of nature are established (2:27–29). After criticizing the philosophers' position for treating God as impotent to lengthen a fly's wing or shorten a worm's foot, Maimonides himself comes to their defense. "But Aristotle will say that He would not wish it and that it is impossible for Him to will something different from what is; that it would not add to His perfection but would perhaps from a certain point of view be a deficiency" (2:22.319). Maimonides lets this rejoinder stand, signaling his essential agreement with it. He also introduces certain remarks that may be construed as hints to the view that the world is eternal *a parte ante*.[60] He is very careful to keep this opinion hidden because of the danger it poses to the naive faith of the masses.

In the final analysis, it is difficult to discern the distinction between Maimonides' view that God "can" choose between different possibilities but always actualizes only that possibility which is in accordance with wisdom, and the view of the philosophers that the existence of the world is necessary. Maimonides criticizes the philosophers who maintain that the world is without beginning but God still exercises choice. Of them he says that they, "have altered the term "necessity" but have let its meaning remain" (2:21.315). Yet Maimonides himself sees no contradiction between the idea of freedom of choice and the idea of a constant activity that at no point undergoes any change due to the nature of the agent. He ascribes this type of "choice" to the Separate Intellects (2:4; 2:7). Though their choice remains constant, their activity is considered by Maimonides volitional since they act out of awareness. Whether the agent can realize other possibilities does not enter Maimonides' discussion of this issue.[61]

The world may be said to be possible for Maimonides, taking his cue from Avicenna's view of necessary and possible, from the perspective of its nature. Its essence does not necessitate its existence hence its existence is "possible" and requires an external agent to actualize it.[62] Thus the act of giving the world existence is a act of "loving-kindness" when seen from the standpoint of the recipient. From the divine standpoint, on the other hand, wisdom dictates the existence of the world hence there is in effect no possibility for God not to act accordingly. Since God's existence is in no way rooted in external causes, it is considered to be a necessary existence. The world's existence, on the other hand, is of contingent nature for it is not necessitated by its essence. Yet this kaleidoscope of perspectives should not make us lose sight of the conclusion to which these views lead. God's essence necessitates not only God's existence, but the existence of the world.

In reference to the divine activity the term "good" is used by Maimonides since the activity is the product of volition,[63] even though God's essence leaves no room for actualizing other possibilities. When speaking of God's essence itself, Maimonides normally uses the term "truth" *(emet)*.[64] Truth signifies unchanging reality. God is absolutely unchanging reality. The relation between "good" and existence in Maimonides' thought leads him to refer to God also as "the absolute good" (*Guide* 3:12). This is not only because, "all His acts are an absolute good for He only produces being and all being is good" (3:10.440). It is primarily because God's existence is absolute, necessary existence, which is the reason for God's activity in producing only being. The "adherents of the truth," Maimonides indicates, regard "His being the absolute good *(al-k̲air al-mahd)*," and "all that proceeds from Him being indubitably an absolute good" (3:12.442). "Good" and "truth" are identical when characterizing the existence of God. All that flows from the divine being is also both good and true.

V

The line connecting the ways the notion "good" as employed by Maimonides, and the various terms he uses to express this notion, is not immediately evident. If "good" signifies that which "conforms to our purpose," what is the meaning of Maimonides' insistence that the criterion for judging whether any activity is good, including divine activity, is that it aims at a "noble end"? If the notion "good" is rooted in the notion of volitional activity, how can God's existence be termed "absolute good"? If good is identical to existence, why is knowledge of the "good" specifically knowledge of the generally accepted moral dictums, while knowledge of the "truth" is equated with knowledge of reality? It is clear that if a link is to be found between all these different uses, it will not be an immediate connection. One must seek the primary meaning, and see how the other uses are derived from it, or from each other.

This is the path traveled by both Warren Harvey and Sarah Klein-Braslavy. Despite a number of disagreements between them, the basic point that they have in common is that the definition of "good" as "what conforms to our purpose" is the primary one in Maimonides' thought. The view I have been arguing is that the definition of "good" as that which is necessary or instrumental in achieving a "noble end" is the more important one for appreciating Maimonides' approach. Maimonides regards existence as a "noble end" since he sees it as having inherent value. Consequently, every volitional activity that contributes to existence, whether it be divine activity or human, is "good." Because of the value of existence, existence itself is labeled good. God, who is absolute or necessary existence, is absolute good. In Maimonides' discussion of Adam's sin, one should interpret his position as follows: constant contemplation of the intelligibles is preferable to volitional activities in the realm of the human being's physical life, though these activities contribute to one's existence *qua* physical creature. In other words, *theoria*, which is the human being's final end or absolute good, is preferable to *praxis*. In *Guide* 1:42 Maimonides identifies the "good" *(tov)* with life (on the basis of Deut. 30:15), which he in turn identifies with the acquisition of true opinions. This identification becomes all the more clear in light of the view to which Maimonides frequently alludes. By virtue of intellectual perfection one attains the immortality of the intellect.[65]

Maimonides' remark that one does not say: "it is fine that heaven is spherical, and it is bad that the earth is flat; rather one says true and false with regard to these assertions" (1:2.24–25) is from the perspective of humanity. Nature is not an object of human activity, hence the notions of "true and false," rather than "fine and bad," apply to statements concerning it. "Fine and bad" apply to human volitional activities. In the human realm, Maimonides distinguishes "good" and "truth" in accordance with the limitations of human action. What humans are capable of contributing to their existence, or to the existence of others, falls under the category of "good." What is solely the object of knowledge, rather than activity, falls under the category of "truth."[66] In the divine realm there is no room for this distinction. All existence is the product of divine volition, and necessary for achieving a "noble end"—namely, the chain of existence itself—hence it is "good." All existence is also the object of divine intellection, hence "true." There is no discrepancy between God's Self-knowledge as the agent of all existence, and the existence of which God is the agent. God's being too is both "true"—absolutely necessary existence—and "good"—the final end of all existence.

One additional matter is worthy of investigation in this context. In his definition of the "good" as what "conforms to our purpose," Maimonides opens with the comment:

> If you consider that book which guides all those who seek guidance toward what is correct and therefore is called *Torah*, the notion that we have in view will become manifest to you. . . . For with reference to none of them is the statement made in any way that it exists for the sake of some other thing. He only says that He brought every part of the world into existence and its existence conformed to its purpose. This is the meaning of his saying: *And God saw that it was good.* For you know what we have explained with regard to their saying: *The Torah speaketh in the language of the sons of man.*[67] And *good* is an expression applied by us to what conforms to our purpose. (3:13.453)

The use of the saying, *The Torah speaketh in the language of the sons of man* is puzzling. Maimonides generally employs this saying to negate the simple sense of the attributes that are applied to God in the Torah.[68] He explains that it was necessary for the Torah to ascribe to God corporeal attributes, or attributes that entail corporeality, as a concession to the populace. Following their imagination, they view these attributes as necessary for existence or positive ones. Thus they help reinforce the masses' belief in God. Maimonides insists that in truth we must interpret these attributes in a figurative sense when they are used in reference to God. In the case of "good," however, we are not dealing with a corporeal description of God that Maimonides seeks to negate. Moreover, we are not dealing here with a description of God at all. The term "good"—*tov*—in Genesis 1 does not refer to God but to the product of the divine activity, the world. There is no other case in which Maimonides cites the saying, *The Torah speaketh in the language of the sons of man* that does not deal with an essential or accidental attribute that is applied to God. Even more perplexing is the fact that he cites this saying in the present context at the same time pointing out that the *simple sense* of Scripture supports his view of the good.

One solution to this dilemma is to interpret Maimonides as indicating that the notion "purpose," which is intrinsically connected to the notion "good," should be interpreted figuratively when used in reference to God.

God's view of the world as "good" leads the reader of the Torah to conclude that God possesses will, and the decision to give existence to the world is realized completely in accordance with God's intent. Maimonides regards this reading as based on a fundamental error. Is Maimonides hinting by citing the rabbinic dictum that one should not ascribe "purpose" to God at all, and everything in fact follows from necessity? This is precisely the doctrine that he continuously criticizes the philosophers for maintaining. Are we to conclude that in this passage Maimonides subtly signals his agreement with the philosophers' view?

A less extreme interpretation of Maimonides' position is also possible. Maimonides approaches the philosophers' position, but he does not wish to negate the notion of divine "purpose" entirely. What he wishes to negate is any similarity between divine purpose and human purpose. This is analogous to Maimonides' treatment of divine knowledge. Maimonides does not reject the notion that God "knows," only that there is a relation between divine knowledge and human knowledge. In the same chapter that Maimonides deals with the distinction between God's knowledge and the knowledge possessed by human beings, he concludes: "Similarly the word 'purpose' *(al-qaṣd)* is used equivocally when applied to what is purposed by us and to what is said to be His purpose" (3:20.483).

In contradistinction to the issue of divine knowledge, Maimonides does not enter into detail concerning the issue of divine purpose. Nevertheless, it is not difficult to ascertain the differences he draws between human intent and divine. Human being's intent is influenced by external causes and aims at obtaining something for the agent that the agent feels is lacking. God's purpose is not influenced by any external factors, nor does it aim at making up some deficiency in God. The purpose of human activity is not always a "noble end" while God's purpose is always to realize such an end. Finally, there is a gap between what humans intend and reality. Not everything that a person intends is capable of being realized, or even when realized fulfills all the expectations. It is precisely the gap between intent and reality that gives significance to the notion "good" in the human sphere. By God there is no gap between intention and reality. Such a gap is impossible by the very nature of things. God always intends to produce being, and being as God intended always exists. In a similar vein, God's knowledge of Self as the source of all existents, God's knowledge of the divine activity as giving existence to all existents, and God's knowledge of all existents as conforming to the divine intent, are one. For this reason when the Torah uses "good" to indicate conformity with the divine purpose, *The Torah speaketh in the language of the sons of man*. There is no possibility of failed intentions in the case of God. One should not interpret Maimonides as maintaining that "good" is essentially a subjective notion. There is no "good" where a "noble end" is not involved, and every "noble end" is intrinsically bound up with existence.

FOUR

IMITATIO DEI

I

Probably no topic in Maimonides' philosophy has been more thoroughly explored than that of human perfection. Many studies deal explicitly with the notion of *imitatio Dei*. Maimonides' approach to ultimate perfection has been alternatively interpreted as primarily intellectual, political, ethical, or within the confines of religious observance (halakhic).[1] Many have viewed Maimonides as positing a harmonious combination of the contemplative life and the life of socially oriented activity—*bios praktikos*—despite the evident tension between the two.[2] Others have explained the apparent inconsistency in Maimonides' approach in terms of the distinction between exoteric and esoteric doctrines.[3] The appropriate texts in Maimonides' writings have been analyzed in detail and the sources at his disposal have been discussed at length. The challenge facing the student of Maimonides' thought lies not only in explicating the individual texts that deal in a direct manner with the topic. One must also identify all the issues and texts that are relevant to the topic, their sources, and how they are related.

The position I shall argue in this chapter is that Maimonides' view of human perfection as it emerges from *The Guide of the Perplexed*, and his approach to *imitatio Dei* in the context of this topic, is in fact a harmonious combination, at least in its essential features, of intellectual perfection and *bios praktikos*. Moreover, it is integrally rooted in Maimonides' metaphysical views concerning God and the Separate Intellects, as well as his doctrine concerning the movement of the spheres. The key to understanding his view is his notion of "emanation" or "overflow" (Ar. *faiḍ*, Heb. *shefa'*). This notion is presented by Maimonides not only in relation to the activity of God and the supernal world, but also the prophets.[4]

This is not to say that all the inconsistencies in Maimonides' approach are more apparent than real. Maimonides purposefully introduced inconsistencies into his treatise due to the religious sensitivity of the subject in question or for pedagogical reasons, as his introductory remarks in the *Guide* indicate. Yet not all the inconsistencies in his approach, if not outright contradictions, should be explained in this manner—his view to the contrary notwithstanding.[5] It is important to reiterate that the *Guide* is not intended to be a philosophical work devoted to an exposition of physics and metaphysics, as well as the nature of the human soul. Nor is it designed to serve as a substitute for these works. Maimonides repeatedly refers his readers to the extensive philosophic literature on these subjects. He treats this literature as mandatory reading for those striving to attain perfection. The *Guide* is a theological-exegetical work devoted to a solution to the dilemmas that arise from a broad comparison between Jewish tradition and Islamic Aristotelian philosophy (*Guide* 1:Introduction; 2:2). Maimonides nowhere presents his own worldview in full. It is at least questionable whether he ever sought to develop his own philosophy in a systematic manner.

Maimonides certainly accepts the Aristotelian approach to understanding existence in most of its essentials. This point is already discernible from his earliest writings.[6] He wavers, however, between different individual philosophers in formulating his approach to particular issues, not always committing himself to a specific view. In some issues he appears to mediate between the philosophers' approach and traditional Jewish views—for example, the problem of miracles and nature (*Guide* 2:29). At the same time he leaves certain critical questions unanswered—such as, what is God's precise role vis-à-vis specific miracles.[7] He fails to address these problems explicitly perhaps for reasons of esotericism, or perhaps because he had not answered them fully to his own satisfaction. Even where it appears that Maimonides rejects outright the philosophers' views, most notably the view of a primordial universe, his presentation is far from unequivocal. Certainly the fact that Maimonides subsequently answers in a manner compatible with belief in eternity many of the questions he raises in *Guide* 2:25, where he claims that their answer is compatible only with a belief in creation, suggests that he has an esoteric view on this subject.[8] Yet here too we should not dismiss the possibility that Maimonides never arrived at a final conclusion despite his realization of the philosophical-theological "stakes" involved.[9]

In general, Maimonides provides a basic framework for a solution to the issues with which he deals. He probably sensed many of the remaining problems, whose details he had not fully worked out. His work has a jigsaw puzzle quality. Yet even after leaving out all the "extraneous" pieces—those not reflecting Maimonides' true views—all the others do not necessarily fit smoothly together. The *Guide* should be viewed as the product of an author in the process of thinking and rethinking some of the important issues he discusses, even while writing his work. In developing his conception of God, the world, and humanity, Maimonides read his philosophical predecessors and wrestled with their views. He often reinterpreted traditional Jewish sources to agree with his conclusions. He chose between alternative conceptions, incorporating certain views while rejecting others. The precise relation between the views adopted by Maimonides is not always immediately evident, nor are they all easily reconcilable. Though he introduces certain inconsistencies on purpose, it appears that at times he only realizes in the course of writing his work there are certain inconsistencies between some of his views and he seeks to offer a solution. At other times certain inconsistencies appear to escape his notice altogether, or he is not convinced of the final answer.

Plato's *Republic*, Aristotle's *De Anima* and *Nicomachean Ethics*, together with the works of some of his commentators such as Alexander of Aphrodisias, and an abridged version of Plotinus' *Enneads, The Theology of Aristotle*, entered into the Islamic world,[10] and had a decisive influence on the conceptions of human perfection found in the various schools of thought—theological and mystical as well as philosophical. This in turn influenced the Jewish thinkers. The philosophy of Alfarabi, followed by that of Avicenna and Ibn Bajja, made a particularly sharp impress upon Maimonides' thought.[11] Any attempt to develop a conception of human perfection and *imitatio Dei* drawing upon the Greek and Islamic philosophical sources had to address a range of questions concerning God and the essence of the human soul, questions on which these sources were hardly unanimous or unequivocal in their answers. What does it mean for the individual to assimilate himself to God? Is God to be conceived as Intellect or as the wholly Unfathomable One? What is God's relation to the world? Is union with God, or with any of the beings of the metaphysical realm, possible? If so, what is the nature of this union? Under what conditions does it occur? What is the nature of the human soul? Is the soul immortal, or can it at least attain immortality? If so, what characterizes its immortal state? What level of intellection is the individual capable of attaining? What is the implication of this for evaluating his ontological status? What is the relation between intellection and the practical virtues in regard to the individual's ultimate perfection and happiness? Is the perfect individual a ruler, or one who isolates oneself from humankind as much as possible? What is prophecy and how is it related to human perfection? The medieval philosophers, while sharing certain fundamental conceptions in common, differ among themselves on the answers to these questions. Furthermore, in the context of their own philosophy not always do their answers to individual issues combine to form a clear and coherent picture of human perfection and the individual's relation to God.

Any attempt to understand the notion of *imitatio Dei* in Maimonides' philosophy can hardly ignore the various issues to which this notion is integrally related. Maimonides also had to grapple with biblical pronouncements bearing on this topic, together with their rabbinic interpretations, such as God's demand to be holy just as He is holy (Lev. 11:44; 19:2). I have already indicated that there is a fundamental coherence in the picture of human perfection that underlies Maimonides' philosophy, but that not all the inconsistencies in his approach can be easily reconciled or should be. Maimonides understood that the fundamental set of problems underlying human perfection is the nature of intellect and its relation to the human soul and body on one hand, and its relation to God and the Active Intellect on the other. Yet it is precisely to this set of problems that Maimonides presents a tentative solution at best.[12]

II

God in Maimonides' thought is the completely simple and unfathomable One to whom no positive attribute may be attributed (1:56-60). Yet God at the same time is defined as Self-intellecting Intellect (*Guide* 1:68). He is also both Wisdom and Will, which are treated as identical with His essence (1:69). He is the wholly transcendent God, not dependent upon any other existent nor even related to any other existent (1:52). He nevertheless is the Cause—efficient, formal, and final—of all existence (1:69). All the problems emerging from this paradoxical conception of God are ultimately resolved by the complete "otherness" of His existence, which can only be known by what He is not or by what He does.[13]

How can a human being "imitate" the totally other? Maimonides was not the first to wrestle with the problem. Plotinus dealt with the question explicitly in *Enneads* I.2, though his probing discussion does not appear to have been known to the Islamic philosophers.[14] So did a number of Maimonides' medieval Jewish philosophic predecessors, such as Joseph Ibn Ṣaddik.[15] A similar question is found in some of Maimonides' rabbinic sources. There is little reason to think, however, that the conception with which the sages grappled was that of a completely transcendent God as understood by the philosophers. The rabbinic answer suggests that God can be imitated only by His attributes.

> *To walk in all His ways* (Deut. 11:22)—These are the ways of God (lit.: the Place): *The Lord! a God compassionate and gracious* . . . (Exod. 34:6).[16] And it is written: *Whoever shall call [read: be called] by the name of the Lord shall escape* (Joel 3:5).[17] How is it possible for man to be called by the name of God? Rather, just as God is called *compassionate* so should you be compassionate; just as the Holy One, blessed be He, is called *gracious*, so should you be gracious . . . and give free gifts to all . . . (*Sifre, 'Ekev* 49)[18]

> Abba Saul says: *Ve-'anvehu* [*And adorn Him*] (Exod. 15:2)—be like *(domeh)* Him.[19] Just as He is gracious and compassionate, so you shall be gracious and compassionate. (*B.T. Shabbat* 133b)

Both in the *Book of the Commandments*: Positive Commandment no. 8, and in *Mishneh Torah: Laws of Character Traits* 1:6, Maimonides refers to the source in the *Sifre* in interpreting the commandment to *walk in God's ways* (Deut. 28:9). For Maimonides, to walk in His ways means nothing less than "to resemble (*le- hiddamot*) Him to the extent of our capacity." One's imitation of God assumes the form of perfecting one's character traits and ethical activity.[20] Maimonides, however, does not elaborate how these attributes are related to God. His discussion goes so far as to suggest that they are not related to God in any way. They are ascribed by the prophets to God in a figurative manner simply to indicate that these are the attributes that man should acquire.[21] In his *Laws of the Principles of the Torah* 1:11, Maimonides explicitly rejects the notion that God possesses character traits, together with any other attribute characterizing corporeal entities. His interpretation of the revelation granted Moses (1:10) suggests that Moses learnt God's negative attributes—that is, all the attributes characterizing other existents which are to be negated of God. Yet there is no indication how the content of this revelation serves as a model for human activity and perfection.

The notion of imitating God occurs in still other passages of *Mishneh Torah*. Notable is the reference in *Laws of Megillah*, 2:17. Maimonides rules that it is preferable on Purim to spend more on gifts to the poor than on the meal and presents to friends, "for he who gladdens the hearts of these unfortunates imitates the Divine Presence." In this context, one imitates divine activity by a human activity improving the state of those who are lacking and require assistance. In performing this command, one in a sense is imitating divine governance of that which is below God. This notion foreshadows an essential aspect of Maimonides' approach to *imitatio Dei* in the *Guide*.[22]

Maimonides' crucial discussion of *imitatio Dei* in *Guide* 1:54, also refers to the source in the *Sifre*, but with several significant additions. In this passage he treats the attributes as pertaining to God, but as attributes of action. Maimonides explains that Moses was denied any knowledge of God's essence, a position in keeping with his negative theology, but was granted knowledge of His actions. God's actions refer to the totality of existence of which God is the Cause, and to the divine governance of the world. Maimonides goes on to indicate:

> Scripture has restricted itself to mentioning only those *thirteen characteristics*, although [Moses] apprehended *all His goodness*—I mean to say all His actions—because these are the actions proceeding from Him, may He be exalted, in respect of giving existence to the Adamites and governing them. This was [Moses'] ultimate object in his demand, the conclusion of what he says being: *That I may know Thee, to the end that I may find grace in Thy sight and consider that this nation is Thy people* (Exod. 33:13)—that is, a people for the government of which I need to perform actions that I must seek to make similar to Thy actions in governing them. (Pp. 124–25)

Maimonides' answer suggests that perfect political leadership, a leadership "translating" knowledge of physics and metaphysics into a set of rules and directives for human society, is the ultimate human expression of *imitatio Dei*.[23] The perfection of the intellect is regarded by Maimonides as a necessary condition. A thorough understanding of reality is required for directing society to pursue humanity's true good. It is not, however, the end in itself. Maimonides does not refer here, in contrast to his legal writings, to the individual's own ethical perfection.[24] He certainly regards this as a necessary condition for achieving intellectual perfection, as well as integral to perfect leadership. A person who is a slave to his passions can hardly attain intellectual perfection or lead others to their perfection.[25] Yet in this context he focuses upon the realm of political leadership. While Maimonides deals with Moses, he is quite explicit in treating Moses as a paradigm case, rather than the exception to the rule.[26] Moses' characteristics serve as the model for every prophetic ruler—governance in accord with reason freed from all feelings of emotion. This is Maimonides' characterization of God's governance. Nonprophets too must attempt to approach this ideal in their social setting, and in accordance with their ability.

Maimonides' concluding remarks in *Guide* 3:54 refer to the same ideal, as his reference there to 1:54 indicates. After positing the perfection of the intellect as the ultimate human perfection, and explicating Jer. 9:22–23 accordingly,[27] Maimonides adds:

For when explaining in this verse the noblest ends, he does not limit them only to the apprehension of Him. . . . But he says that one should glory in the apprehension of Myself and in the knowledge of My attributes, by which he means His actions. . . . In this verse he makes it clear to us that those actions that ought to be known and imitated are *loving-kindness, judgment and righteousness*. He adds another corroborative notion through saying, *in the earth*—this being a pivot of the Law. . . . Then he completes the notion by saying: *For in these things I delight saith the Lord.* He means that it is My purpose that there should come from you *loving-kindness, righteousness, and judgment in the earth* in the way we have explained with regard to the *thirteen attributes*: namely, that the purpose should be assimilation *(tashabbuh)* to them and that this should be our way of life. (P. 637)

This is one part of the picture of human perfection. It corresponds to one aspect of Maimonides' conception of God. God, however, is not only the Necessary Existent who through an act of will gives existence to what is other than He. God not only is the wise ruler who organizes the order of existence in a flawless manner—*imitatio Dei* consequently lying in the perfection of our own activities and the virtues underlying them, particularly in the realm of politics. God's essence is intellect. Maimonides, for all his insistence on the equivocality of the term "intellect," and his doctrine of negative attributes, never frees himself from this basic Aristotelian conception, neither in the *Guide* nor in his legal writings.[28] Intellection for Maimonides, no less than for Aristotle, is what characterizes divinity. To the degree that humans engage in intellection, they approach divinity. Maimonides himself explains the notion of approaching God as: "union *(ittiṣāl)* in knowledge and drawing near through apprehension" (*Guide* 1:18.44). He reiterates this notion in 1:54. Thus despite the unbridgeable chasm between God's intellect and the human intellect, it is intellect which provides the point of resemblance and "contact."

In *Guide* 1:1 Maimonides already develops this point.[29] In explicating the term *demūt* (likeness) as it appears in Gen. 1:26 *(Let us make man in our image, after our likeness)*, Maimonides comments:

As for the term *likeness*, it is a noun derived from the verb *damoh* [to be like], and it too signifies likeness in respect of a notion. . . . Now man possesses as his proprium something in him that is very strange as it is not found in anything else that exists under the sphere of the moon, namely, intellectual apprehension. In the exercise of this, no sense, no part of the body, none of the extremities are used; and therefore this apprehension was likened unto the apprehension of the deity, which does not require an instrument, although in reality it is not like the latter apprehension, but only appears so to the first stirrings of opinion. It was because of this something, I mean because of the divine intellect conjoined with man, that it is said of the latter that he is *in the image of God and in His likeness*, not that God, may He be exalted, is a body and possesses a shape. (Pp. 22–23)

Many of the tensions in Maimonides' conception of God, as well as in his view of *imitatio Dei*, emerge from this passage. God is said to possess apprehension, though totally unlike human apprehension.[30] By means of intellectual apprehension human beings in some way resemble God, though they can never resemble God at all. I do not think that Maimonides ever fully resolved this tension. Yet he leaves no doubt in this passage that the intellect is in some significant sense "divine."

I have already argued that the intellect to which Maimonides is referring is the theoretical intellect. By means of this intellect, Maimonides goes on to explain in the following chapter, humans distinguish between truth and falsehood—that is, attain knowledge of the sciences culminating in the knowledge of God. He treats the possession of this intellect in full as Adam's "ultimate perfection." On account of this it is said that Adam was created, *in the image of God and in His likeness*.[31] The treatment of ultimate perfection as the perfection of the theoretical intellect reemerges in several critical passages in the *Guide* (3:8; 3:27; 3:51; 3:54).[32] Maimonides presents this position also in some of his legal writings, most notably in *Mishneh Torah: Laws of the Principles of the Torah* 3:8–13.[33] Moreover, in both his legal writings and in the *Guide*, he treats immortality and eternal felicity as consequent upon the attainment of intellectual perfection.[34] It would be very strange for Maimonides to maintain that ultimate perfection is political activity while at the same time immortality and eternal felicity is consequent solely upon theoretical perfection. Yet it is precisely between these two approaches to perfection, both of which are rooted in his conception of God, that Maimonides appears to waver in the *Guide*.

III

The immediate question that arises is: Why should these two approaches to perfection be regarded as inconsistent? No one disagrees that perfect political activity for Maimonides requires a perfect theoretical as well as practical intellect, in keeping with the Platonic tradition of the philosopher-king. Even those who interpret Maimonides as positing a different form of practical activity as the ultimate perfection (e.g., ethical, halakhic) stress the importance of theoretical knowledge in guiding the individual not only to the performance of the proper activity, but also to the proper state of consciousness or intent with which this activity is to be performed.[35] Maimonides' view that practical perfection is necessary for theoretical perfection causes no difficulties in itself, any more than his view that theoretical perfection is necessary for practical. Intellection requires a conducive "environment," whether it be one's social environment or the disposition of one's own soul. It may be argued that far from being mutually exclusive, these two perfections are integrally related to each other. They are in fact two sides of the same coin, the attainment of either one dependent upon the attainment of the other.

For all the validity of this argument, a basic tension exists between these two types of perfection nonetheless. The life of contemplation is in a crucial sense opposed to a life of practical activity. Both often make competing demands on one's time and effort. More important, intellectual perfection for Maimonides does not lie simply in the attainment of a certain level of knowledge, leaving open the possibility of a subsequent turning to other pursuits. He treats intellectual perfection as dynamic in nature. It entails a life of continuous uninterrupted intellection. One's felicity *(al-sa'āda),* termed also "pleasure" *(al-laḍḍa),* is dependent upon active intellection, and is proportionate to the level of intellection. Maimonides explains that this type of pleasure is totally unlike the pleasures associated with one's corporeal faculties. It is purely intellectual in nature, with no connection to any of the soul's other faculties. This pleasure is experienced by all intellects *in actu*, including the Separate Intellects, in their contemplation of the incorporeal world. Continuous intellection, and the felicity integrally bound up with it, is how the state of immortality itself is conceived.[36] Moreover, it is how God's eternal Self-intellection is conceived (*Guide* 1:68).

Given the equivocal relation between the human intellect and body, the diversion of one's attention to matters pertaining to corporeal existence deflects from one's intellection of the higher realities. Thus it appears that any form of practical activity cannot but bring about a loss of perfection, an interruption in the contemplative life. Why should a person who has achieved a perfect theoretical intellect choose the practical life at all if one's end is theoretical perfection? Why should this individual not seek isolation from others to the extent possible, and devote all endeavors solely to intellection?

Maimonides is certainly aware of this problem. He indicates that Adam lost his intellectual perfection by turning to matters pertaining to the corporeal world (*Guide* 1:2).[37] He describes the perfect individual as living in solitude so as to avoid disturbing influences (2:36; cf. 1:35). He terms the prophet's attainment of theoretical perfection as "ascent" and the leadership and education of others as "descent" (1:15). If political perfection is the ultimate one, why should it be viewed as a "descent"? On the other hand, if the contemplative ideal is ultimate, why should the prophet descend at all, disturbing his state of precious isolation, in order to assume an active role in society? This is the very problem which disturbed Plato in his Myth of the Cave, and which he "solved" by subjugating the individual's own good to the good of society.[38]

The key to understanding Maimonides' basic solution to the problem lies in the notion of "overflow" or "emanation." Maimonides offers the most extensive discussion of this notion in *Guide* 2:11–12 in reference to the activity of God, the Separate Intellects, and the spheres.

> It is further to show that governance overflows from the deity, may He be exalted, to the intellects according to their rank; that from the benefits received by the intellects, good things and lights overflow to the bodies of the spheres; and that from the spheres—because of the greatness of the benefits they have received from their principles—forces and good things overflow to this body subject to generation and corruption. . . . In effect a thing that is perfect in some kind of perfection sometimes possesses this perfection within such limits that it perfects the thing itself; perfection does not, however, pass over from it to something else. Sometimes its perfection is within such limits that a residue of perfection is left over from it for something else. . . . The case of being is similar. For the overflow coming from Him, may He be exalted, for the bringing into being of separate intellects, overflows likewise from these intellects, so that one of them brings another one into being and this continues up to the Active Intellect. (2:11.275)

The notion of "overflow," Maimonides continues in 2:12, primarily characterizes the activity of the incorporeal beings. They do not act by physical contact, and their activity is constant and received by all that are prepared to receive it. It is also used to describe the forces flowing from the spheres to the sublunar world, though the spheres are bodies and distance is a factor in their activity upon the matter of the sublunar world. None of these entities experience any change of essence—their essence being intellect—or loss of perfection as a result of their activity vis-à-vis others. God never ceases

Self-contemplation as the Principle of all existence, as the order of existence emanates from God. The Separate Intellects engage in uninterrupted intellection of God and themselves, and from this intellection emanates the chain of Separate Intellects and spheres. The spheres engage in uninterrupted intellection of the immaterial world, and their movement, together with the forces overflowing from their movement, is the consequence.

There are a number of passages in the *Guide* that indicate that Maimonides maintained this model also in understanding human perfection. The notion of "overflow" enters into the very definition he gives to prophecy, a phenomenon equated with human perfection or at least contingent upon it: "Know that the true reality and quiddity of prophecy consist in its being an overflow overflowing from God . . . through the intermediation of the Active Intellect, toward the rational faculty in the first place and thereafter toward the imaginative faculty" (2:36.369).

Not only do God and the Active Intellect not experience any loss of perfection as a result of the overflow, but neither does the rational faculty in its overflow to the imagination. Moreover, Maimonides distinguishes between two types of prophets (as well as philosophers)—those who do not take an active public role and those who do: "Sometimes the prophetic revelation that comes to the prophet only renders him perfect and has no other effect. And sometimes the prophetic revelation that comes to him compels him to address a call to the people, teach them, and let his own perfection overflow toward them" (2:37.375).

Ultimate human perfection thus may be seen as "overflowing" perfection. The rational faculty maintains its own perfection while affecting that which is beneath it, whether it be the imagination and the rest of the soul in the case of private prophecy, or in addition, other individuals in the case of public prophecy. The political-pedagogical role assumed by the public prophet results from an internal feeling of compulsion to perfect others in accordance with the level of one's own perfection. This is analogous to the "overflow" from the higher entities. Due to the strength of the overflow from the intellect, the prophets necessarily possess a strong faculty of courage that enables them, indeed compels them, to perform their task (2:38). No one who attains perfection "willingly" seeks to assume a leadership role. The desire to rule is a spurious desire in Maimonides' view. The perfect person desires solitude to the highest degree possible. This individual feels, however, that there is no choice but to govern, whatever one's individual preferences may be. In this manner Maimonides hints how one should understand the biblical accounts of Moses' and Jeremiah's initial refusal to accept their prophetic missions. Their "dialogue" with God represents the tension they felt in their own souls, with their personal preference being to maintain their isolation. God's "command" is the internal compulsion experienced by them to undertake the mission of leading society.[39] It is not only the ability to govern—an ability belonging both to the intellectually perfect and nonperfect (2:40)—that is a natural one. The internal need felt by some of the perfect to govern is also part of the natural order. The perfection of the individual nevertheless remains the perfection of the intellect, the "overflow" being the practical consequence of this perfection.

IV

What, however, does the notion of "overflow" mean in the context of human experience? When all is said and done, one may live a life that strikes an admirable "balance" between contemplation and practical activity, but one form of activity still appears to come at the expense of the other. It is precisely to this problem that Maimonides turns toward the end of the *Guide*. He maintains that the prophets are those who "direct all the acts of their intellect toward an examination of the beings with a view to drawing from them proof with regard to Him, so as to know His governance of them in whatever way it is possible" (3:51.620).

While Maimonides hints at the political role of the prophets, the knowledge he stresses is that of God's governance—that is, knowledge of the totality of existence. He continues to stress that "total devotion to Him and the employment of intellectual thought in constantly loving Him . . . mostly this is achieved in solitude and isolation" (p. 621). Yet the subsequent discussion in the chapter is devoted to outlining a regimen, revolving around the performance of the commandments, that gradually brings about a separation of the intellect from the corporeal faculties. One may contemplate God while *simultaneously* engaging in physical activity: "And there may be a human individual who, through his apprehension of the true realities and his joy in what he has apprehended, achieves a state in which he talks with people and is occupied with his bodily necessities while his intellect is wholly turned toward Him, may He be exalted, so that in his heart he is always in His presence, may He be exalted, while outwardly he is with people" (p. 623)

This type of perfection is ascribed by Maimonides to Moses and the

Patriarchs. It entails living on two plains at the same time. One exists as an intellect engaged in constant contemplation and as a corporeal entity engaged in corporeal acts. Maimonides continues his discussion by tying divine providence to this state of continuous contemplation. The conclusion to which the reader is drawn is that the individual who attains the identity of an intellect separate from matter no longer feels the afflictions that continue to accompany the corporeal dimension of his existence. This individual experiences neither suffering, even while continuing to exist also as a corporeal entity, nor death, insofar as he has attained immortality.[40]

To reinforce this point, Maimonides ends the chapter with a description of the death of the perfect individual while in the state of contemplation: "When a perfect man is stricken with years and approaches death, this apprehension increases very powerfully, joy over this apprehension and a great love for the object of apprehension become stronger, until the soul is separated from the body at that moment in this state of pleasure" (p. 627). Maimonides brings as examples Moses, Aaron, and Miriam, who died by the "kiss of God"—that is, in contemplative ecstasy. Their death in this state is in reality "salvation from death" in his view: "After having reached this condition of enduring permanence, that intellect remains in one and the same state, the impediment that sometimes screened him off having been removed. And he will remain permanently in that state of intense pleasure, which does not belong to the genus of bodily pleasures" (p. 628).

The relation between the individual's perfect intellect and the rest of the soul and the body, during the period in which the individual exists also as a corporeal creature, is not discussed by Maimonides. A hint of his view on this matter is presented in an earlier chapter. In *Guide* 1:72, he treats the world as a *macroanthropos* and the human being as a *microcosmos*. This comparison is based on the fact that humans possesses a rational faculty that rules them, just as the world is ruled by a rational principle—God. It is reason, Maimonides stresses, that distinguishes humans from all other sublunar creatures and allows for drawing an analogy between them and the world. Here too his view suggests that by virtue of reason, though he deals in this context primarily with practical reason, we are in some way like God. Maimonides, however, presents three points on which the analogy between humans and the world breaks down. The third point is that the rational faculty subsists in the body and is inseparable from it. God, on the other hand, does not subsist in the body of the world and is completely separate from it. Maimonides continues: "Know that it behooved us to compare the relation obtaining between God, may He be exalted, and the world to that obtaining beneath the acquired intellect *(al-'aql al-mustafād)* and man; this intellect is not a faculty in the body but is truly separate from the organic body and overflows toward it" (p. 193).

The notion of the "acquired intellect" is found in the writings of the Islamic Aristotelians, and has its source in the Arabic translation of Alexander.[41] In his *Letter on the Intellect*, Alfarabi treats the acquired intellect as an immortal entity. It requires the body neither for its function nor for its subsistence. The acquired intellect is attained at the stage that the individual, having intellected the forms inhering in matter, turns inward and apprehends its intelligibles as separate from matter. With the attainment of the acquired intellect, the individual can apprehend the forms not inhering in matter—that is, the Separate Intellects. The Active Intellect becomes the "form" of the acquired intellect—a clear allusion to conjunction. Alfarabi maintains, however, that the acquired intellect is below the level of the Active Intellect.[42] In his earlier work, *The Political Regime*, Alfarabi enters into fewer details regarding the acquired intellect. One of the primary points that emerges from his treatment of the topic there is that conjunction with the Active Intellect follows the attainment of the acquired intellect.[43] Avicenna and Ibn Bajja adopt much of Alfarabi's approach, though they all differ on a number of salient details.[44]

Maimonides skirts the issue of the differences of opinion between the philosophers. He maintains in the chapter under discussion that the proofs regarding the Separate Intellects, the intellects of the spheres and the acquired intellect are well hidden though correct. The implication of his brief statement on the matter is that the individual may continue to exist as a corporeal entity even with the attainment of the acquired intellect. This view is found also in his Islamic philosophic sources. The emanation from the acquired intellect sustains and guides the rest of the soul and body, while it is no longer dependent on the soul and body.

Maimonides seldom mentions the acquired intellect in any of his writings. Nevertheless, the positing of this form of intellect appears to serve as the basis for his views relating to immortality and prophecy in a number of his legal writings, most notably *Mishneh Torah: Laws of the Principles of the Torah*. A clear allusion to the acquired intellect is to be found in his comment on the verse, *Let us make man in our image after our likeness* (Gen. 1:26). The human form to which the verse refers is the "form which knows and apprehends the intellects *(ha-de'ot)* that have no body—for example, the angels (= Separate Intellects) that are form without body—until he is similar *(yidmeh)* to them" (4:8). Maimonides terms this form, "the form of the soul." His subsequent remarks in the next paragraph *(halakhah)* serve to confirm the identification of this "form" with the acquired intellect. He maintains that this form is not a faculty of the soul that is dependent upon the body and destroyed with the disintegration of the body. Rather, it is independent of the soul, knows the Separate Intellects and continues to exist eternally.[45]

The view of prophecy presented in *The Laws of the Principles of the Torah* also alludes to the attainment of the acquired intellect and conjunction with the Active Intellect. Maimonides describes prophecy as a state in which the holy spirit descends upon the individual who has attained knowledge of all existence, particularly the "holy, pure forms" (= Separate Intellects). At this point, "the soul of the individual conjoins *(tit'arev)*[46] with the degree of angels called *'ishim* (= Active Intellect),[47] and he is transformed into a different individual.[48] He understands with his intellect which no longer is as it previously was" (7:1).[49] A similar description of prophecy can be found in the sixth principle presented in *Introduction to Pereq Ḥeleq*: "Their souls are prepared to receive the 'form' of the intellect [= the acquired intellect]. The human intellect conjoins *(yattaṣilu)* with the Active Intellect and there overflows to them a noble overflow. These are the prophets" (p. 212).

Maimonides' views in a number of passages in the *Guide*, most notably 3:51, may best be understood in light of the doctrine of the acquired intellect. In his description of the level attained by Moses and the Patriarchs—one in which they acted solely with their limbs while their intellects were constantly focused on God—Maimonides also mentions, "the union *(ittiḥād)* of their intellects through apprehension *(idrāk)* of Him" (p. 623). This is an apparent reference to the state of conjunction resulting from the apprehension of the Separate Intellect. Maimonides' view of their "permanent state of extreme perfection" adds support to this interpretation.[50]

A description of the state Maimonides may have had in mind can be found in Judah Halevi's *Kuzari*, a work with which Maimonides appears to be acquainted.[51] In the speech of the "philosopher" at the beginning of the work, Halevi offers the following description of human perfection:

> There conjoins with the perfect individual a light of a divine sort, called Active Intellect. His passive intellect conjoins with it to form a complete unity [lit.: a conjunction of unity, *ittiṣāl ittiḥād*]. The individual sees that he is the Active Intellect, there is no difference between them. The organs—that is, the limbs—of that individual reach

the point where they perform only the perfect activities at the most appropriate times and in the most excellent manner. It is as if they were organs of the Active Intellect, not of the passive hylic intellect which employed them beforehand. . . . This degree is the final one to which the perfect individual may aspire to attain. . . . The soul of the perfect individual becomes one with that Intellect. He is not concerned about the decay of the body and its organs.[52]

Imitatio Dei thus assumes two aspects. On the ultimate level the tension between them is surmounted, and they serve to complement each other. When Maimonides speaks of "assimilation" to God as an end, he refers to the realm of action or character traits. This is the perfection that one attains as a corporeal creature ruling oneself and others in the best possible manner. A similar usage occurs also in Alfarabi's writings.[53] Significantly, Maimonides refrains from employing the phrase "assimilation to God" when positing the perfection of the intellect as the final end, though he mentions assimilation to the Separate Intellects in this context. He wished to preserve the unbridgeable chasm separating the divine essence and the human essence. One can imitate God's actions but not essence. Nevertheless, Maimonides cannot escape seeing some point of similarity between God and human beings. It is by virtue of the theoretical intellect that the human being is said to be created in God's "likeness." This aspect of perfection, the one that deals directly with the essence of the individual and results in immortality, comes with the apprehension of the immaterial world and conjunction with the Active Intellect.

The perfect individual lives according to both perfections simultaneously. This individual's "separate" intellect continuously contemplates the totality of existence. At the same time, the emanation from it to the rational faculty rules the soul in the best possible manner. The soul in turn practices the most perfect actions of which it is capable, whether in the area of ethics (self-governance) or politics (the governance of others). Political leadership is for Maimonides the highest level of practical perfection.[54] Yet the individual's imitation of the divine attributes—the practice of justice, righteousness, and loving-kindness as outlined at the conclusion of the *Guide*—need not take only that form. The perfect individual will behave in the most noble manner in all dealings vis-à-vis oneself and others. One's behavior will no longer stem from certain affections of the soul (mercy, anger, etc.), which are in themselves corporeal attributes. It will follow from purely rational considerations rooted in, or "flowing" from, theoretical knowledge.[55] To what degree this individual will feel compelled to guide others to perfection, and the capacity for doing so, will depend on the level of perfection of the intellect and the corporeal faculties. It will also depend upon the social situation.

V

The concepts of emanation, acquired intellect and conjunction provide the key to harmonizing the two types of perfection presented by Maimonides. Certain aspects of his discussion, however, raise the question whether he accepted the position here outlined. It is unclear what is the connection in Maimonides' thought between one's apprehension of the Active Intellect and one's knowledge of God, the latter being treated as the pinnacle of knowledge. According to Maimonides, one cannot attain any positive knowledge of God, but can know only God's "negative" attributes.[56] How such knowledge, which is not the apprehension of being and identification with the object of apprehension, can lead to the immortality of the intellect, or even contribute to it, calls for an explanation. Maimonides, however, makes no attempt to provide one. In the *Guide*, Maimonides cites from Alfarabi's lost commentary on Aristotle's *Nicomachean Ethics*, a work in which he apparently retracted his position on the possibility of conjunction with the Active Intellect and the attainment of immortality. This may have led Maimonides to doubt the basis for accepting Alfarabi's earlier views. Moreover, Maimonides' views on the limits of knowledge—even in areas such as physics and astronomy, let alone metaphysics—suggest that he may have in fact accepted Alfarabi's later view.[57]

In *Guide* 2:36, Maimonides does not introduce the notion of acquired intellect nor that of conjunction in his description of prophecy. This position not only reflects a break with Alfarabi's earlier treatments of the subject,[58] but Maimonides' own description of prophecy in *Laws of the Principles of the Torah* 7:1. He nowhere in the *Guide* explicitly ascribes the attainment of the acquired intellect to any historical personage, including Moses who is the ultimate paradigm of human perfection. The equivocation in his various writings on the issue whether Moses' intellect remained tied to the body,[59] appears to indicate that Maimonides at least questioned whether Moses in fact did. His position that practical affairs interfered with Moses' prophecy, as in the incident of the spies (*Guide* 2:36), serves to reinforce this interpretation. How much more so would the failure to attain the acquired intellect and achieve conjunction with the Active Intellect be true of the other prophets. The imagination, a corporeal faculty of the soul, is treated by Maimonides as integral to their prophecy. Maimonides' failure in the *Guide* to discuss the issue of the intellect, indicating that the philosophers have already treated this subject, can only be regarded as disingenuous in light of the many differences of opinion that existed among the philosophers themselves. This point would certainly not be lost on his philosophically versed readers. He appears to be hiding something. His rejection of human immortality, an achievement that he apparently concedes is only possible with the apprehension of the existents separate from matter and the attainment of the acquired intellect, may be his esoteric doctrine. Even the notion that immortality is limited to the intellectually perfect would then be an "exoteric" doctrine designed for some of his philosophically versed readers.

Yet Maimonides' views need not be interpreted in this manner.[60] In the final analysis, human immortality and the limits of perfection of the intellect belong to the domain of philosophical issues that are not known demonstratively. As Maimonides himself cautions, one cannot hold conclusions in nondemonstrative matters with complete certainty. One must nevertheless favor those views bolstered by the strongest arguments and subject to the least significant doubts (*Guide* 2:22). Maimonides does not appear to have undergone any change of mind in regard to his earlier held view on the immortality of the perfect intellect, or to its being an entity distinct from the rational soul.[61] In the *Guide*, however, he appears to show greater awareness of some of the problems involved, particularly in light of the limits of human knowledge. The critical question is what level of knowledge suffices for a person to attain the "acquired intellect" and achieve immortality. This problem troubled philosophers in the Aristotelian tradition not only prior to Maimonides but also well after him.[62] More specifically, is the apprehension of the Active Intellect a *sine qua non* for attaining immortality?

The tie between the attainment of the acquired intellect, the apprehension of, and conjunction with, the Active Intellect, and immortality lies at the foundation of the approach of Alexander, Alfarabi (his early writings) and Ibn Bajja. For all the important differences between them, they share the view that only by apprehending existents separate from matter does one become an existent separate from matter. One conjoins with the object of apprehension, the Active Intellect, and remains in that state permanently, matter being the cause of corruption. This follows from the well-known principle extrapolated from the writings of Aristotle, and accepted by Maimonides, on the identity between intellect, the intellectually cognizing subject, and the intellectually cognized object.[63] Not all philosophers adopted this view of the immortality of the intellect. Avicenna, for example, considered the rational soul generated but immortal. It is only the degree of one's eternal felicity that is depended upon the level of intellection attained.[64] Maimonides, in consistently alluding to the view that the nonperfect rational soul is corruptible, is unambiguous in his rejection of Avicenna's position in this matter.[65] The limits Maimonides places on human knowledge on one hand, and his acceptance of immortality on the other, may be interpreted as suggesting that he had a different view of the level of knowledge necessary for immortality than the level envisioned by his predecessors. The conclusion I would argue, however, is that he continued to posit, though in a somewhat tentative manner, the apprehension of the Active Intellect as a necessary condition for immortality.[66]

The possibility of apprehending the Active Intellect, as well as the tie between this apprehension and immortality, is quite explicit in *Laws of the Principles of the Torah* 4:8, as we have seen above.[67] In the *Commentary on the Mishnah* and in the *Mishneh Torah* Maimonides often speaks of the apprehension of what is separate from matter in the more lofty terms of apprehending God. Yet he leaves little doubt that it is precisely in the transition from the apprehension of the material world to the apprehension of the incorporeal world that immortality is attained. In the *Introduction to Pereq Ḥeleq,* Maimonides mentions only the apprehension of God, but adds:

> There [the World to Come] our souls apprehend the knowledge of God, similar to the apprehension possessed by the spheres or greater. . . . The existence of the soul is in the existence of its intelligible. They are one as maintained by the most expert philosophers. . . . These souls take pleasure in what they apprehend of the existence of the Creator just as the Holy Beasts and other levels of angels [= Separate Intellects] take pleasure in what they apprehend of His existence. . . . The existence of the soul, as we have explained, is eternal, just as the existence of the Creator Who is the cause of its existence, inasmuch as it [the soul] apprehends Him. (Pp. 204–5)

Maimonides clearly intimates that the apprehension of the immortal intellect is similar (though not necessarily identical) to that of the Separate Intellects. His mention of the "expert philosophers" in this context certainly includes Alfarabi and Ibn Bajja.[68] In the *Commentary on Avot* 5:15, the principle that immortality is attained by apprehending incorporeal existence is formulated in terms of love of God. Maimonides presents this principle as follows:

> All love that is dependent on a thing that terminates—when the thing terminates, the love terminates. When the love is not dependent upon a thing that terminates—the love does not terminate forever. You know that all material causes terminate and vanish. Consequently the effect vanishes when its cause vanishes. Thus when the cause of the love is a divine thing—namely, the true science—then this love cannot vanish forever since its cause is necessarily existent.[69]

Maimonides does not abandon this position in the *Guide*. While he mentions the difficulty in apprehending the Active Intellect in chapters 1:43 and 1:49, his discussion in both places suggests that this apprehension is attained by the perfect after they have completed their training. In 1:62 Maimonides indicates: "It has been made clear in the books that have been composed concerning divine science that it is impossible to forget this science; I mean thereby the apprehension *(idrāk)* of the Active Intellect" (p. 152). This statement is a clear echo of Ibn Bajja's position concerning the acquired intellect.[70] The conclusion of 2:12 also contains a reference to the apprehension of the Active Intellect. Maimonides returns to the individual's efforts to apprehend the incorporeal world in the third part of the *Guide*. His remark that, "matter is a strong veil preventing the apprehension *(idrāk)* of that which is separate from matter as it truly is" (3:9.436) does not necessarily negate his previously stated view. The attainment of the acquired intellect reflects the stage in which the intellect frees itself from matter in a significant sense.[71]

Maimonides shows his awareness of the fact that not everyone accepted the possibility of the apprehension of the Separate Intellects. His interpretation in 1:37 of Onkelos' view that God's "face," hidden even from Moses, refers to the Separate Intellects, may well be an allusion to Alfarabi's later view. Significantly, this is not Maimonides' own interpretation. In 1:54, Maimonides interprets the "face" as referring to the divine essence. God's "back," which was apprehended by Moses, refers to all the existents. This knowledge is identified with knowledge of God's attributes of action, and presumably includes apprehension of the Separate Intellects.[72]

In the *Guide*, Maimonides also at times alludes to the possibility of conjunction with the Active Intellect, a notion that is explicit in his earlier legal writings.[73] In several passages, he incorporates the very terms used for conjunction *(ittiṣāl, ittiḥād)*. While he does not have in mind complete union and identity with the Active Intellect, he is certainly referring to a special ontological state. It is true that the term *ittiṣāl* has several meanings in Islamic philosophy. The notion plays different roles in different epistemologies. In addition to some form of ontological union with the Active Intellect resulting from the apprehension of this Separate Intellect, *ittiṣāl* may refer to the apprehension of any intelligible. This usage is found by Avicenna, for whom every intelligible is received by direct "contact" with the Active Intellect.[74] In some of the passages in which Maimonides employs the term, he may have had this meaning in mind, though this is far from conclusive.[75]

Avicenna himself describes a form of "conjunction" characterizing the prophetic intellect in which all intelligibles are received nearly at once from the Active Intellect. This is due to the strength of the prophet's intellectual "intuition."[76] Certain views Maimonides voices about prophecy clearly reflect Avicenna's influence in this matter. Maimonides' use of *ittiṣāl* in his discussion of prophetic visions at the end of 2:45 hardly refers to the regular process of discursive reasoning, as Maimonides' remarks make clear: "In a vision of prophecy only parables and intellectual unifications are apprehended that give actual cognition of scientific matters similar to those, knowledge of which is obtained through speculation as we have explained" (p. 403). Underlying his description is Avicenna's notion of the special intuition possessed by the prophetic intellect.[77] Maimonides' concluding remark refers to his description of prophecy in 2:38, a chapter in which the impress of Avicenna's views concerning prophetic intuition is evident. Maimonides' view in 3:51 on the "union" of the Patriarchs' intellects with God also suggests conjunction with the Active Intellect after their apprehension of the metaphysical world, rather than their apprehension of intelligibles in general. His description of passionate love *(ḥesheq)* at the end of the chapter—a description that I cited in part above, and is reminiscent of philosophic-mystical accounts of ecstasy in the Neoplatonic tradition—also appears to refer to conjunction.

Maimonides' use of *ittiṣāl* in 3:8 in reference to the perfect individuals should be interpreted in a similar vein: "[They] seek a state of perpetual permanence according to what is required by their noble form. They only reflect on the mental representation of an intelligible, on the grasp of true opinion regarding everything, and on union *(ittiṣāl)* with the divine intellect, which lets overflow toward them that through which that form exists" (p. 432). "Union" or "conjunction" in this passage does not refer to the point at which one attains a "mental representation of an intelligible." It refers to the end result of the process of attaining *all* the intelligibles, or "true opinion regarding everything." "That through which that form exists" is a reference to the emanation of the rational faculty, or perhaps the acquired intellect, from the Active Intellect, labeled "the divine intellect."[78] "Perpetual permanence" is achieved when conjunction with the Active Intellect takes place.

Another source that appears to have left a sharp imprint upon some of Maimonides' views of apprehension of, and conjunction with, the Active Intellect is Avicenna's treatment of perfection toward the end of *Theorems and Axioms*. Avicenna does not employ there any of the terms for "conjunction." However, he likens the intellectual illumination of the divine world, and resulting ecstasy experienced by the "knower" (gnostic), to lightning flashes. Even at this level, progress can be made in the frequency of the flashes and illumination which results. At the end of the process, illumination is experienced as a constant flame. The "knower" finds all knowledge within the self, and achieves some form of identity with the Truth.[79] Avicenna's view suggests a notion of conjunction that builds upon, but goes beyond, the description of the prophetic intellect found in his *De Anima*. Ibn Tufayl, in *Hayy ben Yaqdhan*, understands the final stage described by Avicenna as one of conjunction.[80] In all probability this passage from Avicenna is the one that Maimonides had in mind in framing his parable of the lightning flashes in the introduction to the *Guide*. The prophets are those who experience illumination of the metaphysical world in such a manner. Maimonides, like Avicenna, does not mention "conjunction" explicitly, but clearly alludes to this state.[81]

Maimonides' views on the limits of reason, even in regard to corporeal matters, do not hint at any esoteric doctrines on this issue. Neither do his views that even Moses' intellect remained tied to matter, and that the prophets required the use of their imaginative faculty. Intellectual perfection for Maimonides is intrinsically tied to the apprehension of essences. This leaves open the possibility that one may apprehend the essence of corporeal entities, such as the spheres, without necessarily apprehending all their accidents. For this reason Maimonides continues to accept Aristotelian physics and to regard Aristotle as the philosopher *par excellence*, though he knows that scientific progress has proven Aristotle wrong on many of the details of his system.[82] The apprehension of essences also appears to go beyond knowledge of propositions in Maimonides' thought. One grasps the "form" itself and not only propositions about the form. This view may help explain the superiority he accords the prophets over the philosophers even in theoretical matters.[83]

One cannot deny that the view presented by Maimonides on the tie of

Moses' intellect to matter entails a certain ambiguity in his position in regard to the perfect intellect. This ambiguity can be detected already in his legal writings. Moreover, this ambiguity is found also in Alfarabi's description of the acquired intellect. In his *Letter on the Intellect*, Alfarabi treats the acquired intellect as a self subsisting, immortal substance. It does not inhere in matter, and is of the same species as the Active Intellect. At the same time, he maintains that the acquired intellect is below the realm of the immaterial existents and related to matter. He compares it to the intellect of the heavenly bodies.[84] In other words, it is an intellect that is separate from matter, but not completely separate. Even in Alfarabi's earlier writings, where he explicitly mentions conjunction between the acquired intellect and the Active Intellect, and that no intermediary exists between them, he does not appear to posit their complete identity.[85] Thus Alfarabi may never have entertained the possibility of completely apprehending the Active Intellect. Maimonides essentially remains loyal to Alfarabi's earlier views in their very ambiguity. He does not, however, introduce Alfarabi's view of the stage in which the intellect apprehends itself. Furthermore, he goes beyond Alfarabi's view, approaching that of Ibn Bajja, in his description of the acquired intellect in 1:72.

When we combine all of Maimonides' views on perfection, the picture that emerges is not without its problems. His treatment of perfection in *Laws of the Principles of the Torah* shows that he regards perfection as involving apprehension of the metaphysical realm, conjunction with the Active Intellect, and a permanent transformation of the intellect in its attainment of an immortal form (4:8–9; 7:1). At the same time, he treats the resulting "illumination" in terms of transitory experiences that are not purely intellectual in nature (7:2–4). In the *Guide*, Maimonides does not abandon his previous positions. Some of them, however, he appears to hold in a more tentative manner. He also places greater emphasis on the limits of human knowledge. Nevertheless, he continues to allude to the view that it is with the apprehension of the existents separate from matter that the acquired intellect and immortality are attained. His remark that one who apprehends the Active Intellect never forgets this knowledge shows that he regards the transformation as a permanent one. At the same time, he views the actual experience of prophecy, a phenomenon he equates with human perfection, as a transitory one involving intellectual illumination (1:Introduction). He also stresses that the imagination, and not just the intellect, is integrally involved in the prophetic experience (2:36).

The fact that there is a certain lack of clarity in the picture that Maimonides draws is hardly surprising. The topic of human perfection involves a host of issues—for example, the rational soul, prophecy, the Law. He deals with them in different contexts, drawing upon different views in the course of his discussion. In a crucial sense this is not unlike the case of his philosophic predecessors, most notably Alfarabi and Avicenna. At times Maimonides seeks to impress upon his readers different points, which may vary from discussion to discussion. The primary purpose of the discussion influences the views he chooses to stress. This tendency is clearly reflected by his discussions of prophecy. Maimonides alternates between stressing the role of the imagination and stressing that of the intellect in accordance with the main point he wishes to convey. The different contexts and purposes of his discussions also help explain why he sometimes describes Moses alone in terms suggesting conjunction, while at other times he depicts classes of individuals in such terms. Still other times his views suggest that conjunction is not possible for anyone. In dealing with the issue of perfection from different perspectives, Maimonides on occasion presents views whose relation is not readily discernible, even in the course of the same discussion. Some of his remarks in 3:51, for example, indicate that conjunction is possible during the course of one's life. The end of the chapter, on the other hand, suggests that it is possible only at the moment of "death"—that is, the final separation from the body.[86]

Maimonides' failure to harmonize between all his views does not necessarily mean that the inconsistencies always allude to an esoteric doctrine. The esoteric-exoteric distinction is far from an adequate key to solve all the problems involved. While many inconsistencies should be interpreted as signaling the existence of an esoteric doctrine, this does not exhaust all the possibilities. At times Maimonides' emphasis of different aspects of his overall view may have given rise to apparent inconsistencies. At other times they may well be a result of an equivocation in his thought on the subject.

In a crucial sense, the *Guide*, like all great philosophic works (though Maimonides did not regard his work as such in the strict sense of the term as I have argued) should be regarded as a work "in progress." That equivocation and inadvertent inconsistencies characterize some of Maimonides' views hardly detract from the depth of his thought and the grandeur of his achievement, any more than they detract from the achievement of his great philosophical predecessors of whom this point is equally true. Maimonides creates the conceptual framework for understanding Judaism in light of an

Aristotelian worldview. Within this framework he approaches the problem of human perfection. His work reflects a profound synthesis between views involving a myriad of topics. Yet given the nature of the work, it does not even attempt to pull together all the elements of this synthesis in a thorough manner.

There are indications that Maimonides conceived of perfection in terms of "degrees." One can attain a "quasi" separate existence in this life in the form of the "acquired intellect," and "quasi" conjunction with the Active Intellect as a result of "quasi" apprehension. The level of conjunction is greater or lesser depending upon the level of intellectual perfection in theoretical matters that is attained. Even for the perfect, progress is possible. The individual can approach greater unity with the Active Intellect, though never complete oneness. One may gradually free the intellect from corporeality while maintaining a corporeal existence. During one's corporeal lifetime, however, one cannot do so completely. Hence "illumination" comes in flashes. Even for Moses corporeal matters continued to interfere with the level of intellection. Only with the acquired intellect's final separation from the body does its apprehension, and the conjunction that results, remain unimpeded and constant. The intellect is no longer hindered by the body in any way. Toward the end of the *Guide*, Maimonides holds out the possibility of individual immortality in accordance with the level of perfection achieved, a possibility that he rejects in an earlier chapter.[87] He only alludes to these notions revolving around the idea of levels of intellectual perfection. He does not attempt to work them out in detail, and may in fact have felt that he is missing the tools to do so. Maimonides' metaphysical views provide at least partial support for such approach. He distinguishes between the perfection of the intellection even of the Separate Intellects, despite the fact that each apprehends the incorporeal world and in itself is incorporeal.[88]

The notion of the emanating perfection of the intellect provides a model of perfection that can never be attained in full, but can be approached. Action and contemplation will inevitably conflict, but the level of conflict can be minimized. The person who attains intellectual perfection and strives to maintain it will almost instinctively avoid all wrongdoing. This individual will have freed the self from the pursuit of imaginary goods and the subjugation to corporeal desires that are at the root of evil actions. The corporeal actions performed will inevitably be the most noble ones. Yet the perfect individual's existence as a "separate" intellect will never be complete until the acquired intellect's final separation from the body and the latter's corruption.

VI

The notion of *imitatio Dei* appears in a number of other contexts in the *Guide* that do not deal exclusively with human beings. Maimonides explains the term "back" as having among its meanings, "following and imitating the conduct of some individual with respect to the conduct of life" (*Guide* 1:38.87).[89] He continues by interpreting the verse, *And thou shalt see My back* (Exod. 33:23): "Thou shall apprehend what follows Me, has come to be like *(tashabbaha)* Me, and follows necessarily from My will—that is, all the things created by Me."

The meaning of the phrase, "has come to be like me," when used in reference to the existents in their entirety, receives further elucidation in a subsequent passage. In 1:69, Maimonides discusses the notion of God as the cause—efficient, formal and final—of the world. "Consequently He, may He be exalted, is the ultimate end of everything; and the end of the universe (lit. all—*al-kal*) is similarly a seeking to be like *(al-tashabbuh)* unto His perfection as far as in its capacity" (p. 170). In this passage Maimonides presents his fundamental view of *imitatio Dei.* God is conceived as perfect existence. Each existent is characterized by its particular perfection or final end. The attainment of its perfection thus is an attainment of a likeness to God, though there be nothing in common between their respective perfections.[90]

The idea of imitating God through the achievement of one's final perfection also underlies a passage dealing with the motion of the spheres.

> Furthermore, it follows necessarily from this that the sphere has a desire for that which it represents to itself and which is the beloved object: namely, the deity, may His name be exalted. He says that it is in this manner that the deity causes the sphere to move, I mean to say through the fact that the sphere desires to come to be like *(al-tashabbuhu)* that which it apprehends, which is the notion represented—a notion that is most exceedingly simple, in which there is no change and no coming-about of a new state, and from which good always overflows. This is impossible for the sphere qua body unless its activity be a circular motion and nothing else. For this is the final perfection of what is possible for a body to have as its perpetual activity. For it is the simplest of motions that a body may have; and no change occurs be-

cause of it in the essence of the body or in the overflow of good effects resulting necessarily from the motion of the body. (*Guide* 2:4.256)

Though Maimonides brings this position in the name of Aristotle, his subsequent remarks indicate that he agrees with it (2:5; 2:7; 2:10–12). In certain fundamental respects, human perfection is closest to that of the spheres in Maimonides' worldview. He in fact indicates that the relation between the human being's rational faculty and the rest of the soul and body is most similar to the relation between the intellect of the spheres and their body (1:72). Both are composite existents, whose perfection touches their intellectual and corporeal aspects—intellection of the incorporeal world simultaneous with the most perfect physical activity of which they are capable. The perfection of the spheres, as Maimonides points out, is even superior to that of the human being in both aspects.[91]

The intellect of the spheres, like the human rational faculty, adheres in matter. This leads Maimonides to reject the state of the spheres as the ultimate model for human perfection. Instead he draws a model of human perfection in which the intellect eventually frees itself from all matter.[92] The relation between God and the world (and between the Separate Intellects and the spheres) is treated by him as the appropriate paradigm. This corresponds to the relation between the acquired intellect and the rest of the human soul, including the rational faculty, and body. Thus while *imitatio Dei* characterizes the final perfection of every existent in Maimonides' view, he comes close to maintaining that the intellect of the perfect individual, similar to the Separate Intellects and in contradistinction to every other entity including the spheres, bears a critical point of resemblance to God.

VII

The divine injunction to be holy for God is holy (Lev. 11:44; 19:2) raises the question of how Maimonides views the notion of holiness. What is the meaning of the term Scripture presents to characterize divine being and the goal of human striving? What is the relation between holiness and *imitatio Dei* in Maimonides' thought?[93]

Maimonides deals with holiness in several passages in his writings, each time in a succinct manner. At times he sees holiness as the product of observance, citing the rabbinic dictum that one sanctifies oneself by means of the commandments.[94] This usage hardly explains the precise meaning of holiness in reference to human beings, let alone its meaning in reference to God. Nor does it elucidate its meaning when applied to other areas, such as the Sanctuary and the Sabbath. A perusal of the gamut of Maimonides' writings reveals that he ties the notion of *imitatio Dei* with the notion of holiness only in passing. Despite the prominence the Torah accords the connection between the two, Maimonides has little to say on the matter. Nonetheless, a fairly complete picture of holiness and *imitatio Dei* emerges from Maimonides' scattered remarks.

In Maimonides' abbreviated citation of *Sifre, 'Ekev* 49 ("He is called gracious so you shall be gracious . . .") in *Book of the Commandments*: positive commandment no. 8, there is no mention of holiness. In *Laws of Character Traits* 1:6, on the other hand, Maimonides adds: "He is called holy, so you shall be holy," without mentioning his source explicitly.[95] This citation suggests that Maimonides regards holiness as a character trait. He does not say anything more about the subject at this point, leaving open the question of what type of trait is "holiness." Inasmuch as his discussion is marked by a general ambiguity as to the connection between God and the attributes that we are commanded to attain, we are also left wondering what "holiness" may mean in reference to God.

The connection between "holiness" and character traits is drawn in still other passages in the *Book of Knowledge*. In the *Laws of the Principles of the Torah* 7:7, Maimonides indicates that the aspirant to prophecy must walk in the ways of holiness and separation *(perishut)*. In linking separation and holiness, Maimonides is echoing rabbinic literature. "As I am separate, so you be separate. As I am holy, so you be holy," God is described as saying in *Leviticus Rabbah* 24:4. These two characteristics are thus treated in this source as the paradigm ones for *imitatio Dei*. The term, *perishut* refers to both physical separation and the separation of oneself from the less than laudatory practices of the masses.[96] In a subsequent discussion of some of the practices that the sage is to avoid, Maimonides employs the term *holiness*. He maintains that the sage should "conduct himself in a holy manner and should not be found by his wife [for purposes of sexual intercourse] like a rooster, but only from Sabbath night to Sabbath night, and providing he has strength" (*Laws of Character Traits* 5:4). "Holiness" in this context is explicitly connected to sexual restraint, a connection that Maimonides accentuates in later discussions. He goes on in 5:5 to link the notions of "holiness," "purity," and the improvement of one's character traits.

That "holiness" in reference to humanity is connected with character traits in Maimonides' thought is further confirmed by other passages in the *Mishneh Torah*. In the conclusion to *Laws of Impure Foods* (16:12), he writes: "Separation [from contact with other people and eating and drinking with them] brings about the purity of the body from evil acts. The purity of the body brings about the holiness of the soul from evil traits *(de'ot ra'ot)*. The holiness of the soul causes assimilation *(le-hiddamot)* to the Indwelling, as it is written: *You shall sanctify yourself and you shall be holy for I am holy* (Lev. 11:44)."[97] Holiness in this context does not refer to a particular trait, but to the totality of noble traits. It is significant that Maimonides does not view holiness as distinct from the realm of ethics. That *de'ot* refers here to traits and not intelligibles can be shown on the basis of Maimonides' usage of the phrase *de'ot ra'ot* in the *Mishneh Torah*.[98]

It is not accidental that Maimonides brings the idea of holiness at the conclusion to a section dealing with food. The connection between food and holiness is already found in the biblical source cited by Maimonides in Leviticus.[99] The integral connection posited by him between holiness and food emerges from an earlier part of the *Mishneh Torah*: *The Book of Holiness*. All the subjects appearing in that book concern eating, drinking, and intercourse. Moreover, in the conclusion to two sections of this book, the *Laws of Forbidden Intercourse* (22:19), and the *Laws of Forbidden Foods* (17:22), Maimonides explicitly attributes holiness to all who restrain themselves in matters pertaining to intercourse, or to all who are diligent in the observance of the laws pertaining to eating and drinking. The rationale offered by Maimonides for the inclusion of these two topics in a book devoted to holiness is found in the introduction to the *Mishneh Torah*: "In these two matters of forbidden relations and forbidden foods God sanctified us and separated us *(hivdilanū)* from the idolaters. Of both it is said, *That I separated you from the nations* (Lev. 20:24); *I will separate you from the nations* (Lev. 20:27)."

The prohibitions in the areas of eating, drinking, and intercourse not only serve to distinguish Israel from the practices of the other nations, thereby preserving their national identity. They contribute directly to the individual's perfection. Maimonides lists these three activities as impeding intellection in the introduction to his *Commentary on the Mishnah*. This point is later echoed in his discussions in the *Guide*.[100] While he ties holiness to the noble character traits in general, it appears that it is most closely connected to the restraint of one's corporeal desires.

Maimonides presents the idea of "holiness" in several discussions in the *Guide*. The connection between holiness and the attainment of noble character traits appears in the conclusion to 1:54:

> For the utmost virtue of man is to become like unto Him, may He be exalted, as far as he is able; which means that we should make our actions like unto His, as the Sages made clear when interpreting the verse, *You shall be holy* (Lev. 19:2). They said: *He is gracious, so be you also gracious; He is merciful, so be you also merciful.* The purpose of all this is to show that the attributes ascribed to Him are attributes of His actions and that they do not mean that He possesses qualities. (P. 128)

Insofar as the "traits" ascribed to God are attributes of action, we may conclude that holiness is a notion characterizing the perfection of the totality of divine activity. Holiness in reference to human beings thus characterizes the perfection of human activity. Maimonides intimates that he is not dealing with emotional states, but with a state of the soul that always expresses itself in ideal action.

The specific connection between holiness and the restraint of the corporeal desires emerges from the third part of the *Guide*. Maimonides introduces his discussion of the problem of evil in 3:8 with a description of the relation between matter and form. He traces all the various types of evil to matter. The individual requires matter for existence, but must rule over it and quell its impulses. Maimonides praises those who regard all the impulses of matter as shameful and deficiencies. Following Aristotle, he singles out those associated with the sense of touch—eating, drinking and copulating.[101] The perfect individual is one who practices these things as little as possible—that is, only what is indispensable for existence—and a feeling of sorrow accompanies the practice of them. The quelling of the corporeal impulses is regarded by Maimonides as necessary in order to apprehend the metaphysical realm. This is the true human end. The ignorant, who are separated from God, are those who turn away from the contemplation of the intelligibles. They take instead as their end those impulses associated with the sense of touch.

The idea of "holy" occurs several times in this chapter. All of the occurrences are in relation to the quelling of the impulses of matter, particularly the desire for intercourse. One should not even think of these matters in Maimonides' view. He cites the opinion that Elisha was called holy for never having a venereal dream,[102] since he never thought about intercourse at all. Maimonides goes on to maintain that it is inappropriate for us, by virtue of our being a *holy nation* (Exod. 19:6), to follow the practices of the gentiles in speaking and reciting poems about matters concerning the sense of touch, particularly drinking and copulation. Moreover, Hebrew is known as the holy language for it has no word to designate either the male or female organ of copulation.

This approach to holiness is reiterated in 3:33, in the section devoted to the reasons for the commandments. Maimonides posits as one of the purposes of the Law the restraint of corporeal desires as much as possible. Again he singles out eating, drinking, and intercourse. He continues: "Similarly one of the intentions of the Law is purity and sanctification; I mean by this renouncing and avoiding sexual intercourse and causing it to be infrequent as possible. . . . Consequently He states clearly that *sanctity* consists in renouncing sexual intercourse,[103] just as He also states explicitly that the giving-up of the drinking of wine constitutes *sanctity*, in what He says about the *Nazarite: He shall be holy*" (p. 533).[104] Maimonides cites the rabbinic view that "holiness" is attained by means of the commandments. Yet his entire discussion leaves no doubt that the connection between observance of the commandments and holiness resides in the purpose of the commandments to restrain corporeal desires.[105]

Holiness is mentioned by Maimonides also in 3:47, in the context of the discussion of the commandments concerning purity. Holiness is said to be opposed to impurity in the three different senses in which the latter notion is used: disobedience to the commandments concerning action or opinion; dirt and filth; "fancied notions" (carrying certain things or being under the same roof with certain things). Maimonides does not enter into detail concerning the precise way "holiness" is opposed to "impurity" according to the second or third senses. From his discussion it appears that the holiness of the sanctuary is also a "fancied notion." As Maimonides explains in 3:35 in regard to the laws of purity: "The purpose of all of them is in general to make people avoid entering the Sanctuary, so that it should be considered as great by the soul and feared and venerated" (p. 537). The fear of the sanctuary, he elaborates in 3:45, brings about a feeling of submission and servitude to God. "Holiness" in this sense does not refer directly to any human attribute, let alone divine attribute, but is an imaginary concept designed ultimately to strengthen the individual's obedience to God.

While Maimonides in his discussions of *imitatio Dei* connects holiness with God's attributes of action, his view of holiness in the context of human beings implies an even closer connection to God's "negative" attributes. This view is already suggested by the rabbinic view of "holy" as "separate."

The dominant motif characterizing Maimonides' discussions of God is the negation of corporeality. His view of holiness as lying in the ethical virtues in general, and restraint of corporeal desires in particular, connects this notion with the negation of one's own corporeality. One must particularly negate that which is associated with the most corporeal of our senses. God's being as the simple One, or as pure Intellect, stands opposed to any form of corporeality, including affections of the soul. In pursuing the goal of becoming pure intellect and joining the incorporeal world, one thus must gradually free (or "purify") oneself from one's corporeal nature. This includes all affections of the soul. This motif characterizes Neoplatonic philosophy in general, and lies at the foundation of Maimonides' approach to perfection.[106] In describing Moses in the *Laws of the Principles of the Torah* 7:6, Maimonides writes: "Therefore he permanently separated himself from his wife, and from all that is similar to her [i.e., 'corporeal needs']. His intellect was tied to the Rock of Eternity . . . and he was sanctified like the angels."[107] Yet despite the connection that can be detected in Maimonides' thought between the incorporeality of God's "being" and the human being's "becoming," Maimonides never explicitly makes this point in his comments on holiness. Overall, he shows little interest in the notion of "holiness" in reference to God.

VIII

By rooting his approach to *imitatio Dei* in his metaphysical views, specifically the view of emanation, Maimonides is able to reconcile between the practical and theoretical aspects of human perfection. Ethics and human perfection become inseparably bound to the activity of God and the structure of the world. Yet this interpretation raises the question of the philosophic relevance of Maimonides' conception of *imitatio Dei* for the modern reader. It would appear that his approach can serve as a viable model only for those who accept his worldview. The fundamental changes in the conception of the world from Maimonides' time undermine the approach to human perfection developed by him. We may regard with favor a model of human perfection that combines theoretical studies with ethical and social activity. Maimonides' philosophy, however, can no longer provide us with a justification for adopting such a model.

This argument does not entail that Maimonides' approach is solely of historical value. Nor does it necessitate that we seek new paths of interpretation, more consonant with modern thinking, in order to "revitalize" his approach. Maimonides' approach remains a vital one, but more as a challenge to modern ethical philosophy than as a substitute for it. His implicit claim, reflecting the classical Greek and Islamic philosophic traditions, is that the philosophic enterprise must be "holistic." "Practical" philosophy—that is, ethics and politics—is inseparable from theoretical philosophy—that is, physics and metaphysics. The topics of ethics, human perfection, the individual's place in the world and the nature of God and the world order are necessarily intertwined. Maimonides' approach to *imitatio Dei* and human perfection, for all the problems it raises, is profound for the manner in which it integrates these topics. It forces us to rethink the question, recently raised in the philosophic literature, whether we can develop viable approaches to ethics and human perfection that are not part of a "holistic" worldview.[108] Must philosophic ethics swing between intuitive approaches, grounded solely in our "natural" sense of right and wrong, and relativistic approaches, which deny any absolutes while often attempting to avoid the unfortunate consequences of the logic of this view? The classical Greek, and to an even greater degree the medieval philosophic traditions, offer a compelling alternative. While they tend to incorporate an intuitive approach to ethics, they anchor it in a vast conceptual structure that at the same time addresses the central questions of human existence and its relation to God and the world order.

We can no longer return to the worldview of Plato, Aristotle, Plotinus, Alfarabi, or Maimonides while remaining intellectually honest. Modern science has destroyed much of the foundation upon which these views are based. Moreover, we have become justifiably skeptical about philosophy's ability to offer a complete conceptual model for understanding reality. We can continue to study the philosophers for the significant questions they ask (the "perennial" questions of philosophy), and for our effort to understand the history of human thought. This enterprise is of immense intellectual and spiritual value in its own right. We can reinterpret the views of the great thinkers of the past in light of the changes in our understanding of reality, as has often been done. In so doing, however, we tend to recast these thinkers in our own image. We can also wrestle with the philosophies of old in order to think anew our own positions. We can let the great voices of the past help us gain a better perspective for evaluating (or framing) our own approaches.

Maimonides offers us an imposing model for approaching the problem of human perfection, just as he provides us with a majestic model for confronting the age old conflict between religion and philosophy. Perhaps part of the attraction of the former model is due to the sense of dissatisfaction shared by many on how foundationless modern approaches to ethics appear to be, and the longing for a more holistic approach to philosophy.[109] We are thus left with the choice of continuing to approach ethics with certain implicit or explicit metaphysical assumptions, but independent of a metaphysical system, or accept the challenge to develop new systems—holistic philosophies—on which to anchor our approaches to ethics. While many have become justifiably skeptical about the latter course, many will continue to find their inspiration in Maimonides' thought precisely because of the intellectual (and spiritual) appeal such a course holds.

FIVE

THE PROBLEM OF CONTRADICTIONS IN MAIMONIDES' APPROACH TO ETHICS

I

Ethics in the Aristotelian tradition forms the branch of practical philosophy dealing with the problem of how one should comport or rule over oneself. The question addressed by ethics is what character traits and actions are good. It also deals with the regimen required for attaining the good character traits—the moral virtues—and performing the good actions.[1] For the Aristotelians, the answer is in large part discernible by reason. From Aristotle on, however, there is a certain ambiguity about the precise role of reason in this matter.[2] In general, the Aristotelians identify the "good" in ethics with the "mean" between any two contrary traits. Here too there is ambiguity in determining where the "mean" lies.[3]

From a broad perspective, Maimonides develops his ethical thought on the basis of the Aristotelian tradition. Nor does he make any secret of the fact that he draws from Aristotelian sources.[4] The Aristotelian approach to ethics is based upon both the dichotomy and the relation between body and soul, as well as between different faculties of the soul. Voluntary actions (that is, physical activity which is a product of a deliberate act of will)[5] and character traits (that is, firmly established dispositions of the appetitive powers of the soul) are closely related in Aristotelian thought. A given character trait gives rise to a certain type of activity or mode of conduct. Certain activities reinforce a specific character trait. It is not *solely* the internal sensation that determines the possession of a character trait. Sensations must be translated into habitual activity. Training enables one to attain not only those traits to which one has a natural inclination, but also those that run counter to it. The natural inclination of the soul in itself results from the physical temperament of the body (*Eight Chapters* Introduction), which varies from individual to individual. It also undergoes change in different periods of a person's life, and is affected by one's activities and traits (*Guide* 1:34, 3:12, 3:51). The importance Maimonides attaches to the attainment of moral qualities is evident by his repeated discussions of this topic. He insists that sin lies not only in the realm of physical *activity* but more important, in the realm of bad character traits: "These transgressions are more severe than those that involve a certain action. When they engulf an individual, it is difficult to extricate himself from them" (*Laws of Repentance* 7:3). Maimonides regards the inculcation of good traits as one of the purposes of the Law (*Guide* 3:27).

Maimonides' approach to ethics has made a profound impression on Jewish ethical thought to the present day. Yet the careful reader of Maimonides' works cannot help but be struck by the maze of ostensible contradictions that characterizes his discussions on this topic. Some of these contradictions can be discerned also in the writings of his Aristotelian predecessors. Others appear to be unique to him. In most of his discussions, Maimonides adopts a teleological approach to ethics. He treats it as a means, albeit a necessary one, to the ultimate end of human beings—that is, the perfection of the intellect.[6] In other passages of his writings he appears to adopt a deontological approach. Certain activities and character traits are meritorious in their own right, independent of their outcome.[7] The conclusion of the *Guide of the Perplexed* suggests that ethical activity—most notably the practice of justice, righteousness, and loving-kindness—is the ultimate end.

Even in those passages in which Maimonides clearly regards ethics as a means, he hardly adopts a consistent approach. At times he sees the domain of ethics as standing in immediate relation to the quest for intellectual perfection. One cannot properly contemplate the verities of metaphysics without following a certain mode of ethical behavior and acquiring the appropriate character traits. One who fails to overcome the passion for corporeal pleasures, for example, cannot devote to oneself to a life of intellection (*Guide* 1:34). At other times, Maimonides posits a less immediate relation. The attainment of intellectual perfection requires the support of society, at the very least to supply the material necessities that allow for physical existence and well-being. The existence of society, in turn, is impossible if the rulers do not make certain ethical activity legally mandatory. They also must attempt to bring about in the citizens ethical character traits that contribute to social harmony. In other words, one cannot pursue a life of contemplation while in a constant state of hunger or suffering from other physical discomforts. Thus one stands in need of society to supply food, clothing and health care. Society in turn requires ethical rules (for example, do not murder or steal) and the inculcation of certain virtues (for instance, mercy, generosity, even-temperament) to enable people to live together (*Guide* 3:27). This point underlies the second contradiction in regard to ethics that can be detected in Maimonides' writings. At times he appears to maintain that the whole domain of ethics is irrelevant outside of a social context. In other passages his remarks suggest that even the solitary individual is bound by certain ethical considerations and traits in the quest for perfection.

Maimonides presents a less than coherent picture also on the question of what constitutes ethical activity and character traits. In most discussions he adopts the Aristotelian doctrine of the mean as his frame of reference both in regard to character traits and to the activities to which they give rise. For example, one should not be a slave to one's passions for food, drink, and sex, nor should one be devoid of all passion altogether. One should experience some degree of passion and indulge it, but only to the extent necessary to preserve the health of the body (*Eight Chapters* 4). At times in the same context Maimonides posits exceptions to the doctrine of the mean. He advocates an extremist approach in regard to the trait of humility and the trait opposed to anger.

These exceptions to the rule of the mean may require explanation, but in themselves they do not involve any self contradiction. Maimonides' discussion in *Laws of Character Traits (Hilkhot De'ot)* chapters 1–2, however, leaves the reader baffled how one should behave in these areas. He presents a contradictory position on the question whether one should be extremely humble and never feel anger at all, or should be moderately humble and maintain some sentiment of anger. He labels the mean as the "right" and "good path," the "path of the wise" and the "path of God." He *explicitly* includes the mean involving the traits of anger and humility in his discussion. At the same time he goes on to label one who distances oneself to the extreme opposite of haughtiness (that is, one who acts with extreme humility) as righteous *(ḥasid)*. This individual is described as acting beyond the requirements of the strict letter of the law *(lifnim me-shurat ha-din)*, a notion that always has a positive connotation. Maimonides continues his discussion by maintaining that we are forbidden by law to follow the mean in regard to the traits of humility and anger. We must adopt the extreme, this being the good path. In short, the person who is extremely humble possesses a trait which in not good (1:1; 1:3), is a righteous person who acts beyond the strict letter of the Law (1:5), while acting in a way mandated by the Law (2:3). One who is moderately humble follows the good path (1:1; 1:4), is wise (1:4–5), is commanded to do so (1:6), and follows the path of God (1:7). At the same time this individual follows a path that is not good, and is forbidden to do so (2:3). The same confusion surrounds the trait involving the avoidance of anger.[8]

Maimonides' position on some of the other character traits—for example. those involving a passion for corporeal things—is also equivocal. The same is true of his approach to ascetic activities. At times Maimonides forcefully advocates the enjoyment of legally permitted pleasures, while at other times he lauds those who abstain from them. The Nazarite, for example, is alternately treated by him as a "sinner" for depriving himself of wine and as "holy" for doing so.[9] The issue of social isolation is yet another one marked by a similar apparent inconsistency.

How ethics is known is still another question on which Maimonides presents an inconsistent position. In many of his discussions he treats the rational faculty as the source of ethical knowledge. Certain things are good, others are bad, and reason has the power to discriminate between them. Maimonides' discussion of the Garden of Eden story in the *Guide* 1:2, however, suggests that ethics is not a subject known by the intellect at all. It belongs to the realm of those matters which are "well known" *(mashhhurat),* a notion often used to describe accepted social conventions. This position is reiterated in Maimonides' discussion of the revelation at Sinai (*Guide* 2:33). The commandments involving generally accepted ethical dictums are known by prophetic revelation. Intellection is pointedly excluded by Maimonides as a source for knowing them.

A further ostensible contradiction in Maimonides' approach to ethics involves the issue of the possibility of achieving ethical perfection. Maimonides at times maintains that training can always overcome evil inclinations resulting from a bad natural temperament. Ethical perfection is a realistic goal for all individuals. In other discussions Maimonides treats individuals possessing bad temperaments as incapable of attaining certain moral virtues irrespective of how much training they undergo.

In summary, at least five major contradictions emerge from Maimonides' discussions of ethics:

1. Ethics as a means vs. ethics as an end in itself if not the ultimate end.

2. Ethics as a purely social institution that is applicable only in social contexts versus ethics as a domain pertaining to the individual *qua* individual and necessary for perfection even when in a state of isolation.

3. Ethics defined in terms of the doctrine of the mean versus ethics defined in terms of extremism.

4. Ethics as known by reason versus ethics as established solely by social convention or laid down by revelation.

5. All individuals being capable in principle of attaining ethical perfec-

tion versus many individual barred by nature from ever attaining this perfection.

It is only natural for a thinker to change his mind over the course of time in regard to certain questions. This could explain some of the contradictory stances on ethics that Maimonides adopts in different works. Most of the contradictions in his approach, however, defy such a facile solution to the problem. Often they can be detected in the same work, at times even in the same discussion. Nor can many of them be resolved by maintaining that Maimonides in fact deals with different issues in each instance. He at times adopts a contradictory stance while discussing the very same issue as we have seen above in regard to the traits of humility and anger.

The context of the discussions in which the conflicting positions appear is certainly a critical factor for appreciating Maimonides' approach. This point emerges clearly when considering the last contradiction I enumerated. In his popular ethical work, *Eight Chapters*—a work that serves as the introduction to his commentary on tractate *Avot*—Maimonides argues that training can always overcome natural inclinations (chap. 8). The purpose of his discussion in this context is to deter people from thinking that their actions are determined. Maimonides seeks to instill in his readers greater motivation and confidence in their striving for perfection. A similar consideration marks Maimonides' legal discourse in *Laws of Repentance* (5:2).[10] In the Guide 1:34, on the other hand, he reveals his true thoughts on the matter. Certain temperaments cannot be made to acquire specific virtues no matter how much training the individual undergoes.[11]

Certain pedagogical considerations lie at the foundation of the other contradictions as well. These considerations, however, are not quite as evident. Some of the contradictions in Maimonides' approach to ethics have received a fair amount of attention in modern scholarship. I have dealt with two of them—whether Maimonides regards ethics as a means or as an end and whether it is known by reason or not—in the three previous chapters in this volume. I would like to turn now to the study of one of the other apparent contradictions: ethics as necessary only in a social context versus ethics as necessary for the perfection of the individual *qua* individual. This contradiction has received less attention in the scholarly literature than the others.[12] From my conclusions on this issue, I will draw some implications for understanding Maimonides' ethical thought as a whole.

Maimonides does not alternate between fundamentally different approaches to ethics, but between different perspectives for viewing ethics.[13]

The apparent inconsistency in his approach results from his desire to stress different points in various discussions, at times even in the same discussion. This leads him to exaggerate a point by treating it as the whole picture, while ignoring the other perspectives. There is no logical inconsistency between the view that the purpose of ethics is communal welfare and the view that ethics is necessary in the quest for individual perfection independent of any social dimension. The inconsistency arises only when Maimonides appears to maintain that the *sole* purpose of ethics is communal welfare. What is true of this apparent contradiction is no less true of the other ones in his approach to ethics. Maimonides' conflicting attitudes to the doctrine of the mean, particularly in regard to the practice of asceticism, follow from his different perspectives for viewing the purpose of ethics. Together his views form a coherent picture of ethics, but one that is blurred because of his alternating perspectives. This leads to the question why Maimonides chose to present his views on ethics in a manner that suggests an inconsistent approach rather than a unified picture. I will argue that the reason is to signal to the attentive reader that the perspective by which ethics is viewed must constantly be altered to understand the full picture. The nonperceptive reader, on the other hand, remains with the perspective most appropriate for this reader's understanding.

II

Maimonides adopts a consistent position in his legal writings in treating the ethical character traits as necessary to the individual's own perfection. In the introduction to his *Commentary on the Mishnah* he posits as the human being's goal the attainment of intellectual perfection and the moral traits. Overindulging in corporeal pleasures is regarded by Maimonides as destructive of the rational soul. One should satisfy one's corporeal appetites only to the extent required for the existence of the body.[14] In the introduction to the tenth chapter of the tractate *Sanhedrin (Pereq Ḥeleq),* Maimonides labels all the traits that contribute to perfection as virtues, and those traits that prevent perfection as vices.[15] He appears to have in mind the moral virtues in addition to the virtues characterizing the intellect. *Eight Chapters* contains a detailed discussion of the moral virtues. Maimonides treats them as the traits of a healthy soul. Together with the intellectual virtues they are necessary for achieving the final end, the apprehension of God according to human ability (chaps. 3–5). Every moral vice is regarded by Maimonides as a veil separating the human being from the apprehension of God (chap. 7). The attainment of prophecy, a phenomenon related to human perfection in Maimonides' thought, is also dependent upon the moral virtues in his view (chap. 7). In his *Commentary on Avot*, he reiterates his position that the ideal individual is one who possesses the moral as well as intellectual virtues (5:6). He follows the philosophers in labeling the one who possesses all the virtues, "divine" (5:12).[16]

The *Mishneh Torah*, Maimonides' primary legal work, reflects the same trend of thought in this matter. His discussion in *Laws of Character Traits* treats the moral virtues as intrinsic to the path to individual perfection. In 2:1, Maimonides describes the sick soul as one characterized by a desire for the evil traits. That at least some of the moral traits are relevant even to the solitary individual emerges clearly from the opening section of the *Mishneh Torah, Laws of the Principles of the Torah*. Prophecy is attained only by one possessing the moral virtues, and who separates oneself from the ways of the masses (7:1).[17] Certain traits, such as sadness and laziness, interfere with its reception (7:4). The traits Maimonides singles out as necessary for prophecy can well exist outside any social context. Even a trait such as extreme humility *(shiflut ruaḥ)* does not exist only in a social context. Consider, for example, his description of the commandments to love and fear God:

> When one contemplates these matters [physics and metaphysics], becomes acquainted with all the creatures—angel [= Separate Intellect], sphere, human being etc.—and sees God's wisdom in all creatures and created things, one's love for God increases. . . . When one compares oneself to one of these great, holy bodies [= spheres], all the more so to the pure forms that are separate from bodies and are not attached to a body at all [= Separate Intellects], one's humility *(shifluto),* indigence, and lowliness fill one with awe and fear. (*Laws of the Principles of the Torah* 4:12)[18]

From this description it follows that fear of God and extreme humility are intrinsically related. They result from a true understanding of the human being's position on the chain of existence.[19]

The connection between the moral virtues and individual perfection underlies a number of Maimonides' discussions also in the *Guide of the Perplexed*. His treatment of the Garden of Eden story in 1:2 suggests that corporeal desires led to Adam's loss of intellectual perfection. Adam symbolizes the solitary perfect individual.[20] This point emerges more explicitly from Maimonides' enumeration of the causes that prevent the apprehension of the science of metaphysics. Among the causes he lists is one's natural aptitude: "For it has been explained, or rather demonstrated, that the moral virtues are a preparation for the rational virtues, it being impossible to achieve true, rational acts—I mean perfect rationality—unless it be a man thoroughly trained with respect to his morals and endowed with the qualities of tranquility and quiet" (1:34.76–77). The traits Maimonides singles out in this context are anger and a strong sexual drive. He connects these traits to the natural temperament of the individual. This suggests that their acquisition does not necessarily depend upon living in society, though society offers more opportunities for giving expression to these traits and reinforcing them.

In 2:39 Maimonides discusses the issue of the divine Law and human perfection. While the Law is concerned with society at large in his view, its aim is the perfection of the individual. Here too he describes individual perfection in terms of one's moral habits, particularly in the distancing of oneself from greed and corporeal appetites.

Maimonides returns to the trait of controlling ones' corporeal desires and anger in the introduction to his discussion of the problem of evil (*Guide* 3:8). He reiterates his position that these traits characterize the perfect individual. The vice of pursuing corporeal pleasures is viewed by Maimonides in 3:12 as the source of the evils that one brings upon oneself. It results in changes in the individual's physical temperament. This in turn brings about diseases in the soul, inasmuch as: "the moral qualities of the soul are consequent upon the temperament of the body" (p. 445).

III

A different view of ethics emerges from Maimonides' discussion in *Guide* 2:40. Humans are political animals requiring society for existence.[21] On the other hand, they are not suited for life in society. The great differences in the temperaments possessed by individuals prevent them from living together in harmony. Maimonides concludes: "It is by no means possible that his society should be perfected except—and this is necessarily so—through a ruler who gages the actions of the individuals, perfecting that which is deficient and reducing that which is excessive, and who prescribes actions and moral habits that all of them must always practice in the same way, so that the natural diversity is hidden through the multiple points of conventional accord and so that the community becomes well ordered" (p. 382).

The concern of the ruler is primarily the welfare of society as a whole rather than individual welfare. Ethics is required for the perfection, and very existence, of society. Maimonides' position in 2:40 opens up an additional perspective for evaluating the significance of ethics. This position certainly does not contradict the view that ethics plays an important role in the perfection of the individual as an individual. The fact that Maimonides continues to view ethics in this light is clear from the continuation of the chapter. He indicates that in determining the legitimacy of the claimant to prophecy, one must examine the actions and way of life of the individual. In particular, one must check the renunciation of corporeal pleasures. Only such an individual is prepared to attain prophecy.

Allusions to the social perspective for viewing ethics can be detected already in his earlier writings. In *Eight Chapters* 4, Maimonides interprets the verse—*Love Truth and Peace* (Zech. 8:19)—as referring to the intellectual virtues and moral virtues respectively. He explains that "peace" refers to the moral virtues inasmuch as they bring about peace between humankind.[22] A hint of the social role of ethics can also be found at the end of chapter four of the *Laws of the Principles of the Torah*. The first four chapters of this section, the opening section of the *Mishneh Torah*, are devoted to a discussion of those commandments involving the knowledge of God and the world. These commandments essentially mandate the attainment of intellectual perfection. Maimonides concludes with a brief description of the purpose of all the other commandments of the Law. They are necessary, he maintains, in order to bring about tranquility of mind in the individual. This state must precede the quest for knowledge of physics and metaphysics (= *pardes*).[23] In addition, the commandments make civilization possible. It is not coincidental that the two purposes ascribed to these commandments—that is, individual perfection and communal welfare—are precisely those of ethics. Maimonides posits an intrinsic connection between the commandments and ethics. The Torah, in his view, is the ideal legislation for advancing ethical perfection. This idea appears in his *Treatise on Logic* 14. It is also found in *Eight Chapters* 4, *Laws of Character Traits* chapters 1–3, as well as the *Guide* 2:39–40. Maimonides' passing remarks in his legal writings connecting the purpose of ethics with the welfare of society, however, do not approach the clear exposition of this idea contained in *Guide* 2:40.

Maimonides continues his discussion in 2:40 with the idea that the Torah does not rest content with the attempt to bring about ethical perfection. It is concerned also with true beliefs and in directing its adherents to the pursuit of intellectual perfection. It is precisely by the latter goal that the divinity of the Torah can be discerned according to Maimonides. This goal distinguishes it from nondivine legislations. The idea that the perfection of the intellect is the ultimate end of the Law is an idea presented by Maimonides both explicitly and implicitly in previous writings, including all the writings mentioned above. It lies at the very heart of *Laws of the Principles of the Torah.*

With this in mind we can turn to 3:27, a chapter that forms part of the introduction to Maimonides' discussion of the reasons for the commandments. Essentially, he develops the same ideas pertaining to the Law presented in 2:40.[24] Nonetheless, this chapter contains a number of surprising comments. Maimonides posits two goals for the Law, or more accurately, two sets of goals for the Law. The first he calls "the welfare of the soul" and the other "the welfare of the body." The first "consists in the multitude's acquiring correct opinions corresponding to their respective capacity." The second "comes about by the improvement of their [the multitude's] ways of living one with another." The Law adopts two strategies for accomplishing the second goal: "One of them is the abolition of their wronging each other. . . . The second thing consists in the acquisition by every human individual of moral qualities that are useful for life in society so that the affairs of the city may be ordered" (p. 510). Again we see morality being approached from the perspective of society at large. Maimonides also clarifies that the first goal of the Law—the welfare of the soul—is the nobler one. It comes later in time than the other goal, and can only be achieved after the latter is achieved. In other words, correct opinions cannot be inculcated until a well-ordered society has already come into existence. It is important to note that the "welfare of the soul" refers to the beliefs and opinions of society, and not its morals. Ethics belongs to the "welfare of the body."

Maimonides immediately switches from the social perspective to the individual perspective. The individual too has two goals or perfections—the perfection of the body, and the ultimate perfection, the perfection of the soul.[25] That there is a close relation between the goals of the Law and the perfection of the individual is immediately evident. The manner in which Maimonides develops this idea is of some interest. The perfection of the soul of the individual lies in the perfection of the intellect—"knowing everything concerning all the beings that it is within the capacity of man to know" (p. 511). This perfection corresponds to the Law's aim of inculcating correct opinions in society. In some measure it also results from the Law's efforts in this area. The perfection of the body, on the other hand, is defined as: "being healthy and in the very best bodily state, and this is only possible through his finding the things necessary for him whenever he seeks them. These are his food and all the other things needed for the governance of his body, such as a shelter, bathing and so forth."

The "body" to which Maimonides refers is the physical body of the individual. It corresponds to the "body politic." The relation between the two perfections of the individual corresponds to the relation between the two types of welfare that constitute the aim of the Law. The perfection of the soul is the nobler one. It follows the perfection of the body, "for a man cannot represent to himself an intelligible . . . if he is in pain or is very hungry or is thirsty or is hot or is very cold" (p. 511). Absent is any explicit mention or even suggestion of the ethical perfection of the individual as part of the "perfection of the body." This is not simply an oversight on Maimonides' part. The relation he draws between the individual's "perfection of the body" and the Law's aim of the "welfare of the body" shows he is well aware that in his discussion he confines ethics only to the latter. Maimonides reiterates the position he presented in 2:40 that the individual requires society for his material needs. Morality, as we have seen, is the glue that holds society together. It allows society to meets its members' needs, and in the case of the Torah, to inculcate correct opinions instrumental for attaining intellectual perfection.

We may mistakenly think that Maimonides does not mention ethical traits as part of the individual's "perfection of the body" because they belong in fact to his soul. This is the position he adopts in most of his discussions. Maimonides quickly moves to disabuse us from this interpretation. He indicates in regard to the perfection of the soul, "It is clear that to this ultimate perfection there do not belong either actions or moral qualities" (p. 511). Morality in this chapter, in contrast to 2:40, is construed as having significance only in the context of society. Certainly, without morality the individual cannot achieve the perfection of the body or perfection of the soul, both perfections being dependent on the existence of society. Nevertheless, morality forms no intrinsic part of either perfection. This position stands in direct opposition to all of Maimonides' prior treatments of the subject.

The question immediately arises whether any other passage exists that echoes the same idea. Perhaps the interpretation offered here of 3:27 is too extreme. There is in fact another passage giving voice to the same idea, one that is found in the last chapter of the *Guide* (3:54). Maimonides outlines four perfections belonging to humans according to the philosophers. Ibn Bajja is apparently the philosopher Maimonides has uppermost in his mind.[26] The perfections are in ascending order: possessions (wealth), bodily constitution (for example, athletic prowess), moral virtues, and rational virtues. As for the moral virtues, Maimonides has the following to say:

> But this species of perfection is likewise a preparation for something else and not an end in itself. For all moral habits are concerned with what occurs between a human individual and someone else. The perfection regarding moral habits is, as it were, only the disposition to be useful to people; consequently it is an instrument for someone else. For if you suppose a human individual is alone, acting on no one, you will find that all his moral virtues are in vain and without employment and unneeded, so that they do not perfect the individual in anything; for he only needs them and they again become useful to him in regard to someone else. (P. 635)

Maimonides sums up this point while discussing true human perfection, that of the intellect: "If you consider each of the three perfections mentioned before you, you will find that they pertain to others than you, not to you, even though, according to the generally accepted opinion, they inevitably pertain both to you and to others. This ultimate perfection, however, pertains to you alone, no one else being associated in it with you in any way."[27]

This, however, is not Maimonides' last word on the subject. He continues by exhorting the reader not to neglect his soul by allowing the corporeal faculties to gain control over it. This is an apparent reference for the need to limit corporeal desires in order to attain intellectual perfection. The curbing of desires is consistently treated by him, as we have seen, as belonging to the moral virtues. Maimonides' concluding remarks in the chapter raise even graver problems. He appears to posit a goal beyond even that of intellectual perfection—namely the same goal that he had just rejected as belonging to the individual's own perfection: "He [Jeremiah] means that it is My [God's] purpose that there should come from you loving-kindness, righteousness, and judgment in the earth in the way we have explained with regard to the thirteen attributes: namely, that the purpose should be assimilation to them and that this should be our way of life" (p. 637). This way of life, according to Maimonides, comes after apprehension of God has been achieved. At first glance, it is far from clear how this way of life is distinguished from the one of moral virtue. It is at this point that two contradictions in Maimonides' approach to ethics unite: ethics as part of individual perfection versus ethics as concerned solely with social welfare; ethics as a means versus ethics as the ultimate end.

IV

A possible solution to the problem is to divide the virtues into two categories. One category is directly related to human perfection. The other is important for the welfare of society. Though Maimonides refers to both categories as the moral virtues, his treatment of the moral virtues varies in accordance with the category he has in mind. For example, his view that the virtues are necessary for the perfection of the individual may refer to the curbing of corporeal desires, among other traits. His view that the virtues are necessary for communal welfare, on the other hand, may refer to such virtues as pity.

At least one passage in the *Guide* supports this interpretation. In 3:35 Maimonides divides the commandments into fourteen classes. At the end of the chapter he divides the classes into two categories, in accordance with a well-known rabbinic division of the commandments. Some of the classes are described as dealing with relations between humans. Others are said to deal with the relation between the individual and God.[28] Maimonides offers a novel interpretation of the latter category:

> For every commandment, whether it be a prescription or a prohibition, whose purpose it is to bring about the achievement of a certain moral quality or of an opinion or the rightness of actions, which only concerns the individual himself and his becoming more perfect, is called by them between man and God, even though in reality it sometimes may affect relations between man and his fellow man. But this happens only after many intermediate steps and through comprehensive considerations, and it does not lead from the beginning to harming a fellow man. (P. 538)

That only some of the moral qualities are directly involved in the perfection of the individual may be inferred from other remarks in the chapter. The third class of commandments enumerated by Maimonides are those dealing with moral qualities. He refers his readers to those found in the *Laws of Character Traits*. Maimonides explains that, "it is well known that through fine moral qualities human association and society are perfected, which is necessary for the good order of human circumstances" (pp. 535–36). This is the same approach to the commandments that he presents in 2:40; 3:27 and subsequently in 3:54. Yet in enumerating the classes of the commandments that belong to relations "between man and his fellow man," Maimonides includes only "a portion of the third."[29] This seems to indicate that some of the moral qualities are related to individual perfection, while only "a portion" are concerned with communal welfare.

If this is the case, what further indication are we given of which qualities belong to each of these categories? The curbing or abolishing of desires for things corporeal certainly appears to belong to the category of individual perfection since Maimonides constantly mentions it in his discussions of this issue. He describes the purpose of one of the classes of commandments belonging to the category "between the individual and God"—forbidden foods—as putting an end to the "lusts and licentiousness manifested in seeking what is most pleasurable and the taking the desire for food and drink as an end" (p. 537). The purpose of another class belonging to this category—forbidden sexual unions—is to "diminish the desire for mating as far as possible" (p. 538). This offers further confirmation of the importance Maimonides ascribes to the trait of curbing corporeal appetites for the attainment of the perfection of the individual. The avoidance of anger may be an additional virtue belonging to this group.

One of Maimonides' classes of commandments raises some problems for this approach. His fourth class deals with "alms, lending, bestowal of gifts, and matters that are connected with this" (p. 536). These activities appear specifically directed to communal welfare. Surprisingly, Maimonides treats them as belonging to the category of commandments between the individual and God. In a subsequent discussion of this class in 3:39, he indicates their utility in instilling pity for the weak and giving strength to the poor. He also points out the importance of some of these commandments for instilling the traits of generosity and humility. Both pity and generosity are moral qualities that we would think exist for the sake of society. Maimonides' discussion in 2:40 implies this very point. Yet here he treats them as integral to the individual's own perfection. "Fraternal sentiments"—another trait one would think exists for communal welfare—also is presented in the context of laws dealing with individual perfection (*Guide* 3:43; 3:49). This leaves the reader wondering what qualities are concerned primarily with communal welfare rather than individual perfection.

Another approach to Maimonides' dual classification of the moral virtues is to view them as belonging to both categories simultaneously. This approach has already been suggested by a number of his medieval and modern commentators.[30] In classifying "part" of the class of laws dealing with character traits as communal welfare, Maimonides does not wish to exclude certain moral traits from the category of individual perfection. His point is that from one perspective, this class pertains to communal welfare. From a different perspective, it belongs to individual perfection.

Certain textual support can be brought in favor of this interpretation. In

3:33, for example, Maimonides posits as one of the purposes of the Law the abandonment of desires. The vices involving corporeal appetites are explicitly treated both from the perspective of the individual and that of society. Of lust and licentiousness, for example, he has the following to say: "This is what destroys man's last perfection [of the soul], what harms him also in his first perfection [of the body], and what corrupts most of the circumstances of the citizens and of the people engaged in domestic governance" (p. 533). Yet this interpretation too is not without its problems. If Maimonides regards the moral virtues as belonging to both categories of commandments, he essentially weakens the fundamental distinction he draws between the two categories.

V

Both interpretations of Maimonides' stance still lead to the same basic question. Why does Maimonides at times goes so far as to indicate that moral virtues form no part of the individual's own perfection, while in other passages he treats them as intrinsically bound up with individual perfection? The answer appears to lie in the point that he wishes to make in any given discussion. In other words, the purpose of the discussion determines the perspective Maimonides adopts. There is an overall consistency in his approach to ethics, but each discussion focuses on a different aspect of the total picture. The inconsistencies arise from Maimonides' stress on a certain aspect of the picture to the exclusion of the others, his treatment of it as if it were the whole picture.

Maimonides' discussion in 2:40 deals with the issue of the moral virtues from the standpoint of legislation in general. This is the reason he stresses the role they play in promoting communal welfare. There is an additional consideration that emerges from the continuation of his remarks. The major distinction Maimonides draws between divine and nondivine legislations revolves around the question whether the legislation pays attention to the soundness of beliefs. One evaluates the legislation by seeing whether it encourages its adherents to attain knowledge of all that exists. Nondivine legislations are not concerned with the individual's rational faculty. They are not designed to promote the individual's perfection. Thus even in the realm of morality, Maimonides subtly indicates, legislations in general are concerned with inculcating moral virtues only for the purpose of social welfare. Morality in this case does not form part of a regimen aiming at individual perfection. Only in the divine Law do the moral virtues play this additional role.[31] One further point may also underlie Maimonides' approach to ethics in 2:40. By treating rational perfection as the distinguishing characteristic of the divine Law, he implies that this is its ultimate end. The limiting of the role of morality to the realm of communal welfare serves to highlight the importance of knowledge, rather than moral virtue, for the perfection of the individual.

The last point also explains Maimonides' stance in 3:27, a chapter that deals exclusively with the divine Law. He leaves no doubt that moral virtue is not in any way an integral part of the final perfection by treating it as necessary only for the preservation of society. Other views of his in the chapter further serve to emphasize the inferiority of moral perfection to rational. Morality belongs to the "welfare of the body" while correct opinions belong to the "welfare of the soul."

In most of Maimonides' discussions, the moral virtues are treated as belonging to the soul. His exclusion of morality from both the welfare and perfection of the soul in 3:27 entails no outright contradiction to this stance. "Soul" is an equivocal term in Maimonides' view. In Guide 1:41 he treats "soul" as referring, among other things, to the animal soul, the rational soul, and the soul that remains of the human being after death. For Maimonides, morality deals with how humans should govern themselves. The rational faculty is responsible for determining what are the actions and virtues that should be pursued. In lacking the rational faculty, animals cannot be said to possess moral virtues. At best, they may possess traits that bear an external resemblance to the virtues. While the rational faculty points out the way to the moral virtues, these virtues do not characterize this faculty. They belong specifically to the human soul's appetitive faculty. In 3:27, Maimonides uses "soul" as referring to the theoretical rational faculty, and ultimately to that which remains after death. This is why he includes only beliefs and knowledge when discussing the soul's welfare and perfection respectively. Maimonides' insistence that final perfection does not involve morality in any way, and his limitation of the role of morality to the realm of communal welfare, serves to underscore the perfection of the intellect as the only true perfection of the individual. The perfect intellect in this context is the "soul" that remains after the disintegration of the body.[32]

Maimonides' apparent inconsistencies in the final chapter of the *Guide* are also the result of his approaching the subject of ethics from alternating perspectives. His view that moral virtues subsist in the individual but is "only the disposition to be useful to people" (p. 635), exaggerates the social perspective in order to emphasize the perfection of the intellect as the only true human perfection. His statement that the perfections other than intellectual perfection pertain to "others than you, not to you," is said from the perspective of viewing the intellect as being the essence of the individual. Everything else—whether it be other people or one's body—is in fact "other than you." Maimonides switches perspectives at the end of the chapter. While he now appears to posit moral virtue as the ultimate perfection, he is in fact dealing with the physical activity of the individual who has already attained intellectual perfection. This individual's assimilation to the divine attributes—the practice of loving-kindness, righteousness, and judgment—does not in this context refer to the moral virtues per se. Maimonides is describing the activity that ultimately should be traced to purely rational considerations, rather than the dispositions of the appetitive faculty. This activity involves no emotions at all.[33]

VI

The issue of asceticism offers us another example of how Maimonides' alternating perspectives result in the presentation of ostensibly contradictory positions. This issue is integrally related to the more general problem of whether extremism or the doctrine of the mean should characterize one's moral traits. Maimonides emphasizes the relation between physical activity and moral traits in *Eight Chapters* 4. A particular moral trait is strengthened only by repeated performance of those physical activities normally stemming from it. Asceticism is related to the trait that Maimonides labels as lack of sensation of pleasure *('adam al-iḥsās b'l-laḏḏa*; *he'der hergesh hahana'ah)*. At the other extreme of this trait is lustfulness *(al-shirra; rov hata'avah)*. The mean of these traits is temperance *(al-'iffa; zehirūt)*.[34]

As is the case with most of his discussions of the moral traits, here too Maimonides advocates the doctrine of the mean. Extremism serves as a temporary therapeutic measure. When one suffers from an extreme trait, one should continuously act in accordance with the opposite extreme. One ceases to act in this manner once the trait is broken and one finds oneself possessing the trait that is the mean between both extremes. The commandments of the Torah, in Maimonides' view, are designed to guide their adherents to the middle path, or slightly to the side that is normally against our natural inclinations. By means of the path of the mean, Maimonides maintains, one reaches the highest level of humanity and approaches God.

Given this position, Maimonides favors the rabbinic interpretation that views the sin-offering of the Nazirite as an atonement for the "sin" of depriving himself of wine. According to this view, how much more in need of atonement is the one who deprives oneself of every joy. Maimonides attacks his coreligionists who in the attempt to discipline their souls imitate the extreme practices of the ascetics of other nations. In summary, he states:

> Should anyone, who without doubt be foolish if he did so, practice these commands more rigorously—for example, by prohibiting eating and drinking more than does the Law, or by restricting sexual intercourse to a greater degree . . . he would unwittingly be performing improper acts. He would be following one extreme or the other, completely forsaking the mean. In this connection I have never heard a more remarkable saying than that of the rabbis . . . in which they seriously fault those who bind themselves by oaths and vows till they are fettered like prisoners. Their precise words are: "Said R. Iddai in the name of R. Isaac: Is it not sufficient for you what the Law prohibits that you impose upon yourself additional restrictions?!" (*P.T. Nedarim* 9:1).[35]

A similar stance is adopted by Maimonides in the third chapter of *Laws of Character Traits*. Extremism is rejected, the Nazirite castigated, and the importance of a sound body in attaining knowledge of God is underscored. One who refrains from marriage in order to fight evil moral traits is labeled a sinner. Excessive fasting is condemned. Asceticism is to be limited to the *explicit* commands of the Law. Rather than treat permissible pleasures as forbidden—a position that plays a prominent role in the thought of the earlier Jewish ethicist, R. Baḥya Ibn Paquda[36]—Maimonides condemns those who do not enjoy them at all.

There is another side to Maimonides' approach to the moral virtues that is more extreme. He alternates between a moderate and extreme approach to the traits of humility and lack of anger, as has already been pointed out. While such glaring contradictions do not characterize Maimonides' comments on asceticism, one can nevertheless find a far more receptive attitude to ascetic practices in same passages of his writings. A careful reading of his discussion in *Eight Chapters* 4 reveals this undercurrent in his thought. To illustrate the notion that one should strictly follow the path laid down by the Law, Maimonides brings as an example the commands pertaining to sexual intercourse. He goes on to indicate that the sages added additional prohibitions in this area. Maimonides concludes that God commanded these laws in order to distance us greatly from lust, inclining us slightly to the trait of not experiencing the sensation of physical pleasure. In light of Maimonides' doctrine, the added barriers to sexual intercourse erected by the sages should be regarded as bad, for they destroy the equibalance of the Law. Yet he still treats them positively since they serve to distance us from lust.

The positive evaluation of asceticism is even more pronounced in the *Mishneh Torah.* Maimonides commends those whose vows are intended to combat evil inclinations and to establish good moral traits (*Laws of Vows* 10:4). He praises those who become Nazirites for reasons of sanctity, citing the verse in Amos juxtaposing Nazirites and prophets (*Laws of Nezirut* 10:14). In *Laws of the Study of the Torah* 3:12, Maimonides' goes so far as to suggest the complete abandonment of the doctrine of the mean in certain cases. The words of the Torah, he remarks, abide only in one who is completely dedicated to them and who constantly mortifies the body. In *Laws of Matrimony* 15:3, Maimonides permits one to abstain from marriage because his soul is passionately committed to the study of Torah, and he dedicates himself to this end unremittingly. He cites the example of Ben Azzai, notwithstanding the fact that the sages faulted him for the failure to marry and contribute to the habitation of the world.[37] Significantly, he adds that only one whose sexual inclination does not overpower him need not marry.

Maimonides' most positive views on asceticism are found in the *Guide.* Vows, rather than being rejected for going beyond the requirements of the Law, are treated positively. They serve to restrain one's appetite for food and drink (3:48). The Nazirite is praised for avoiding wine (3:33; 3:48). Underlying these views is Maimonides' consistent refrain condemning the sense of touch, particularly in its relation to eating, drinking and copulation (2:36; 3:8; 3:33). He argues for abolishing the desire for all pleasures associated with this sense (2:36). He maintains that one should reduce the practice of these activities to the extent possible. One should admit only the indispensable. Sanctity, according to him, lies in renouncing sexual intercourse (3:33).[38]

As for physical isolation from society, Maimonides for the most part rejects this course. He cautions that one should adopt it only as temporary therapeutic measure, or when one finds oneself in an evil society (*Eight Chapters* 4). Yet in the course of discussing the intellectual love of God in *Guide* 3:51, he presents the following unqualified position: "This is achieved in solitude and isolation. Hence every excellent man stays frequently in solitude and does not meet anyone unless it is necessary" (p. 621).[39]

Maimonides' dual attitude to asceticism reflects his dual attitude to the body and its relation to the soul. He views the multifaceted relation between body and soul in light of the unique and almost paradoxical position the human being occupies on the chain of being. Humans are by nature corporeal beings. They depend upon the body for their existence. Maimonides views existence as good on all the various levels, including that of corporeal existence.[40] Yet humans, at least the elite of the species, have the potential to become existents divorced from matter. One's corporeal nature acts as a hindrance to the attainment of this state. In the introduction to the *Commentary on the Mishnah*, Maimonides goes so far as to maintain that the destruction of the soul lies in the welfare of the body, and the welfare of the soul in the destruction in the body.[41] In most of his writings, including the *Guide*, he adopts a more moderate stance. One must devote oneself also to the welfare of the body in the quest for intellectual perfection. Yet the *Guide* too contains statements reflecting the inverse relation between body and intellect. In 3:51 Maimonides indicates that the intellect is strengthened when the bodily faculties are weakened. His views on asceticism appear to waver between a moderate and an extreme approach as the most suitable one. The implication of his diverse views may be that different regimen are appropriate for individuals at different stages of development.

To what degree Maimonides accepted this implication is unclear. In regard to the moral virtues there are indications that he accepted a multitiered ethical system, with extremism being subtly recommended to the elite. Given the connection between moral virtues and physical activities in Maimonides' thought, one would expect the same to be true of asceticism. Extreme asceticism is inappropriate for the masses, except as a temporary therapeutic measure. This follows both from Maimonides' legal rulings and overall philosophy. Insofar as they are incapable of intellectual perfection, the path of the mean is the one they must always strive to follow. This is the path that best insures social well-being. For the elite, on the other hand, there is a strong undercurrent in Maimonides' thought that extreme asceticism may serve a crucial role. He condemns both extremes of a trait as bad. Nonetheless, he views lust far more negatively than lack of feeling of physical pleasure, if he regards the latter trait negatively at all. His attitude in the *Mishneh Torah* to Ben Azzai and his remarks on this subject in the *Guide*, a work intended for the intellectual elite, reflect a high degree of appreciation for asceticism. It appears that for Maimonides, extreme asceticism and the corresponding moral trait is part of a process accompanying increasing excellence in the intellectual virtues.

Just as one does not begin one's studies with physics and metaphysics, so one does not begin the training of the soul with an attempt to reach the highest level of moral virtue from the outset. Just as the skipping of steps in climbing the ladder of knowledge may destroy the intellect,[42] so does the skipping of steps in the training of the soul cause it great harm. Solitude and ascetic practices are valuable insofar as they enable the individual to complete the process of freeing the intellect from the body. Engaging in such practices when one is not yet intellectually prepared would have the opposite effect. It would result in the strengthening of bodily passions and weakening of intellection. In the case of this individual, abstention from food, drink, and sexual intercourse would lead to concentrating more upon these matters, harming thereby the more noble part of the soul. Maimonides' view that the rational faculty is the most noble part of the individual leads him to conclude that any thought about disobedience is worse than the physical act of disobedience (*Guide* 3:8). Yet he argues that the perfection of the body must precede intellectual perfection, "for a man cannot represent to himself an intelligible . . . if he is in pain or is very hungry or thirsty" (3:27.511). To the degree that one's intellection is dependent upon one's physical condition, physical needs must be satisfied. There is a subtle indication in Maimonides' discussions in *Eight Chapters* 4 and in *Laws of Character Traits* 3:1 that the asceticism he condemns is the one practiced by those who are not spiritually prepared. He explicitly refers to the practices of the ascetics of other nations, and to the Jews who imitate them. For these individuals, extreme asceticism only serves to corrupt the soul. Ben Azzai's asceticism is approved by Maimonides for it was practiced for the purpose of attaining intellectual perfection after his sexual impulse was already overpowered. For those whose sexual impulse is overpowering, the effect of this asceticism would prove to be negative.[43]

It is significant that the individual to whom Maimonides ascribes more extreme forms of behavior is the *ḥasid* (*al-faḍil*). In the introduction to *Eight Chapters*, Maimonides quotes the famous maxim of Pinhas ben Yair, who treats *ḥasidut* as one degree below prophecy.[44] In the context of Maimonides' philosophy, this suggests that the *ḥasid* is one who is close to the intellectual perfection of the prophet. The positive evaluation of the *ḥasid*, and the view that the *ḥasid* is one who pursues intellectual perfection, emerges also from a number of other passages in Maimonides' writings. The *ḥasid* is exceptionally scrupulous in cultivating ethical traits (*Laws of Character Traits* 1:5). He extinguishes all impulse to do evil (*Eight Chapters* 6).[45] In one well-known philosophic exemplar cited by Maimonides, this individual achieves the highest level of humility, eliminating all vestiges of pride (*Commentary to Avot* 6:6).[46] The *ḥasid* is treated as a sage, but one who has adopted a more extreme stance in regard to ethical traits (*Commentary to Avot* 5:6). In the *Epistle to the Jews of Yemen*, Maimonides speaks of the "pure *faḍīlin* (*ḥasidim*) the pursuers of truth."[47] He expresses a similar view in the *Guide:* "For it is the measure of the overflow of the divine intellect that makes the prophets speak, guides the actions of righteous men, and *perfects the knowledge of the excellent men* (*al-faḍā'il*; *ḥasidim*) in regard to what they know" (3:18.475). In *Guide* 3:51, the *ḥasid* is linked with the prophet in the enjoyment of individual providence and the attainment of the immortality of the intellect. It is hardly surprising that the *ḥasid* is more of an extremist. To further develop the intellect, this individual pursues a far more strenuous ethical regimen.

Extreme asceticism may not be the only course for the elite in Maimonides' thought. He depicts an ideal state in which one's intellect continues to contemplate divine realities even while the individual interacts with others and engages in physical activities. This state characterizes an individual who essentially exists on two different levels—as a "separate" intellect and as a corporeal creature.[48] For such an individual extreme asceticism may no longer be necessary. Yet Maimonides is also aware that even most of the elite have not freed their intellect from their body sufficiently so as not to be distracted by it. Solitude and abstinence remain crucial in the pursuit of perfection. For this reason the claimant to prophecy is judged from the standpoint of his ascetic tendencies, among other criteria. Those who indulge their corporeal desires lack the qualifications that would enable them to receive the prophetic overflow (*Laws of the Principles of the Torah* 7:1; *Guide* 2:40).[49] Moses too, who reached the highest level of perfection according to Maimonides, is treated as an extreme ascetic. Significantly, he separated from his wife and completely refrained from sexual intercourse, specifically *after* the attainment of perfection (*Laws of the Principles of the Torah* 7:6).[50] Thus even the one who has attained the dual state described by Maimonides continues to practice asceticism to preserve this state.

Maimonides' views on asceticism have important implications for understanding his approach to the divine Law. The Law aims at the perfection of society at large to the degree it is capable of perfection. To a large degree, it is framed with an eye to the average individual, who is incapable of ever reaching true human perfection. More important, it is directed to the potential elite at the earlier stages of their development.[51] For this reason it is designed in accordance with the doctrine of the mean. This is the path most appropriate for the majority. The "equibalance" of the Law—that is, it being neither excessive nor deficient in its demands—is stressed by Maimonides not only in his legal writings, but also in *Guide* 2:39. He points to asceticism as a form of excess absent in the Law. He continues his argument by maintaining that the Law should be evaluated with reference to the perfect individual, "for it is the aim of the Law that everyone should be such a man" (p. 381). If one keeps in mind that a law demanding of everyone extreme asceticism would be socially destructive, as well as a hindrance to perfection for those at the earlier stages of training, there is no real contradiction between Maimonides' views on this point.

The Law, Maimonides cautions his readers, pays no attention to the isolated (*Guide* 3:34). Some individuals will be harmed by the Law. "In view of this consideration also, you will not wonder at the fact that, on the contrary, it necessarily follows that there should exist individuals whom the governance of the Law does not make perfect" (p. 534). Maimonides appears to be referring to those with certain types of character deficiencies that are aggravated, or at least not improved, by the regimen of the Law. Nonetheless, the position he enunciates may be seen as applying also to the elite. The elite are exceptional. While the Law does not harm them, it can only meet their needs in the most general manner. The particular demands of the Law must be modified in the direction of extreme asceticism to enable them to achieve the goal of intellectual perfection. The Law allows, and even subtly encourages, this modification in their case.[52]

The doctrine of the mean has no intrinsic value for Maimonides. It is the best "natural" course for most people, given the dual nature of human beings. Ultimately the most appropriate course for any individual is the one which brings that individual to the knowledge of God. To underscore this point, in the same places where Maimonides presents the doctrine of the mean, he continues by stressing the fact that one should evaluate all of one's actions from the standpoint of their contribution to attaining knowledge of God. The doctrine of the mean is presented in *Eight Chapters* 4 as the doctrine that conforms to the Law and results in actions that are good. In the following chapter Maimonides enjoins his readers that all the actions they perform should have as their aim knowledge of God. A similar structure characterizes *Laws of Character Traits.* The doctrine of the mean is presented in the opening two chapters as good in its own right, while in chapter 3 it is made subservient to the goal of knowing God. Maimonides in this manner subtly indicates that the course of one's behavior thus varies according to the circumstances of the individual. For those who live a life of intellect, the doctrine of the mean does not provide the path most suitable to follow. Maimonides' alternation between these two doctrines thus depends on the group he is most interested in addressing in a given discussion.

VII

The other apparent contradictions in Maimonides' approach to ethics can also be resolved if we interpret him as constantly switching the perspective from which he approaches the issue. He sees the health of the soul—that is, the possession of the ethical virtues—as something good in its own right, just as physical health is good in its own right. A naturalistic approach underlies this perspective. Yet nature itself is designed in such a way that everything strives for its end, with certain ends serving as the means for more noble ends. "Nature" and "teleology" are closely related notions in Aristotelian thought. This leads to the view of ethics as a means to achieve the loftier goal of intellectual perfection.

As for Maimonides' view of ethics as rationally known and his view that ethics is not known by the intellect but consists of "generally accepted opinions"—these too are not necessarily contradictory positions. Maimonides perhaps is alternating between two different types of ethics—conventional and rational.[53] A closer look at his epistemology reveals a better way to resolve this apparent contradiction. Maimonides equates the intellect with the theoretical rational faculty by which scientific truths are known. Ethics is not a theoretical science, but a practical one. Thus it is not known by the intellect per se, though it is known by the practical rational faculty. Even the divine commandments concerned with universal moral matters are not known by the intellect according to Maimonides (*Guide* 2:33). This position does not entail that he views ethics as a matter of individual taste. Nor does it mean that the divine command alone serves as a basis for a nonrelativistic approach to ethics. Maimonides distinguishes between different systems of morality. The criterion for determining the rationality of any system is its effectiveness in bringing its adherents to perfection. The superiority of the moral imperatives in the divine Law over the imperatives in the various *nomoi* lies not in their origin but in their content (their greater "equibalance") and in their *telos*. Only in the divine Law do they form part of a system aimed at the true perfection of human beings rather than an imaginary perfection (*Guide* 2:39–40). Here too the perspective to the "generally accepted" moral dictums that Maimonides chooses to adopt varies with the main point he wishes to inculcate in his discussion.[54]

One may well ask why Maimonides chose to present this subject in a manner that suggests an inconsistent approach if there is in fact no fundamental inconsistency at all. At times he appears to go out of his way to present his views in an inconsistent manner. His opposing views of humility and anger in the same discussion in the *Laws of Character Traits*, or his discussion of ethics in the last chapter of the *Guide*, are just two of the most notable examples. In both discussions, the apparent inconsistency could have easily been avoided if Maimonides had formulated his views in a slightly different manner. His formulations leave the reader with the impression that he chose to introduce these inconsistencies on purpose.

All students of the *Guide* are aware that Maimonides introduces contradictions on purpose in this work. He himself testifies to the fact. In his introduction, Maimonides lists seven reasons for contradictions in different works. All the contradictions in the *Guide* are traced by him to one of two reasons. The first is a pedagogical one. In explaining a difficult manner, the teacher must begin with statements that are not completely accurate. When the student is brought to the level in which a more precise explanation may be given, the teacher does so. This often entails contradicting earlier statements. The other reason presented by Maimonides is a more subtle one: "In speaking about very obscure matters it is necessary to conceal some parts and to disclose others. Sometimes in the case of certain dicta this necessity requires that the discussion proceed on the basis of a certain premise, whereas in another place necessity requires that the discussion proceed on the basis of another premise contradicting the first one. In such cases the vulgar must in no way be aware of the contradiction; the author accordingly uses some device to conceal it by all means" (*Guide* 1:Introduction.18).

Maimonides, unfortunately, does not explain what he means here by "necessity." Most of the commentators assume that one of the occurrences of "necessity" refers to the view required by theoretical speculation, while the other refers to a type of "political" necessity. Maimonides must hide his true view because of the religious sensitivity of the issue being discussed. Thus often he presents the "orthodox" view on a given subject. At times he introduces a contradictory view in a veiled manner, or a view based on a premise contradicting the premise underlying some of his other views, this being his true view. This type of contradiction forms the basis of the esoteric/exoteric approach to interpreting the *Guide* adopted by many of Maimonides' most prominent medieval and modern commentators.[55] It is tempting to explain Maimonides' contradictory views on ethics in terms of the latter reason for contradictions. Here too they result from the "necessity" of emphasizing different points in different discussions. That he purposefully introduces contradictions in works prior to the *Guide* should not disturb us. Maimonides appears to have begun experimenting with forms of esoteric writing in his early works.[56]

In the final analysis, however, Maimonides' contradictory positions on ethics differ from the contradictions he introduces in other areas. According to the prevailing view, the type of contradiction Maimonides describes is one in which one of his positions is true and the other is false. This is necessarily the case in issues belonging to the theoretical sciences. The world cannot be both created *ex nihilo* and primordial. God cannot intervene in the bestowal of prophecy while prophecy remains a completely natural phenomenon. This is not the case, however, with ethics. We are not dealing here with speculative "necessity," which leads to truth, versus political "necessity," which results in a false view. Maimonides' apparently contradictory positions in ethics may both be true when examined from different perspectives. This is the point that distinguishes the practical sciences from the theoretical ones. The former deal with voluntary activities in changing situations while the latter deal with eternal verities.

The seventh reason for contradictions discussed by Maimonides in the introduction to the *Guide* concerns theoretical matters. He confines this form of contradiction to "very obscure matters." Nowhere does Maimonides include ethics among these matters. A detailed list of these matters is presented by him in *Guide* 1:35. Maimonides lists divine attributes, creation, God's governance of the world, providence, divine knowledge and will, and prophecy—but not ethics—among the "obscure matters" that are the mysteries of the Torah. These are the matters that he indicates should remain hidden from the masses. Moreover, in Maimonides' description of the contradictions involved in the presentation of these matters, he maintains that the very fact that a contradiction is introduced should remain hidden. Presumably, once the reader becomes aware of the contradiction he realizes that one of the views presented by Maimonides is false while the other is true. In his discussions of ethics, on the other hand, he often makes little attempt to hide his contradictory views. The opposite is the case.

A possible solution to the problem is to posit a different reason for contradictions not explicitly mentioned by Maimonides, but which underlies his discussions of ethics. This is the contradiction that arises precisely from the desire to emphasize different points in different discussions. Each point is true from a certain perspective, but false if generalized to characterize Maimonides' entire view. He introduces these contradictions quite openly to impress upon his more astute readers the view that the role of ethics must be evaluated from different perspectives. Furthermore, ethical conduct may vary in different contexts. He also refrains from presenting the "whole picture" so as not to blunt the point he wishes to convey in any given discussion.

I do not claim that there is no esoteric level to Maimonides' discussion of ethics. He was certainly aware of the fact that some of his views touched on religiously sensitive issues and had to be partially veiled. The relation of observance of the commandments to final perfection and reward and punishment is a good example of an issue of this nature. The same is true of the tension between the actions mandated by the Law and the regimen that the individual may have to adopt in order to attain perfection. Maimonides is also willing to introduce views that are completely false if they serve as a goad to good actions. For example, his view that every individual is by nature capable of complete perfection plays such a role. Yet it is interesting to note that in certain places in his legal writings, Maimonides makes only a minimum effort to veil his views on a number of religiously sensitive subjects. He is quite explicit in emphasizing the perfection of the intellect as the true human perfection and the one that results in immortality. Ethics serves as a means to attain this perfection. The Law is framed to promote this end in the context of society at large. Very few, however, are capable of attaining this end.

Maimonides may well have thought that the average reader is generally an inattentive reader, one who overlooks even blatant contradictions. Furthermore, this type of reader is too lazy to pursue the implications of the contradictions when they are noticed. Only the dominant message, or the one that conforms to one's preconceptions, is remembered. The numerous contradictions serve as a sign to the attentive reader that one must keep on varying the perspective with which this subject is viewed. Only when one puts these perspectives together can one appreciate Maimonides' approach.

VIII

Maimonides' different views on ethics coalesce to form a coherent picture. Human perfection for him is the perfection of the theoretical intellect. Society serves two purposes. The first is to insure the survival of the human species. The second and ultimate goal, Maimonides explicitly maintains, is to produce perfect individuals. The vast majority of the members of society exist in order to serve the physical and social needs of the perfect.[57] In certain cases the attainment of perfection is possible only by physically distancing oneself from society. This is due to the evil nature of ones' society and its pernicious influences. For the most part, perfection is to be achieved within society, though practicing a minimum of social intercourse. Human physical needs, as modest as they may be, are most efficiently met by a social arrangement in which there is a division of labor. This frees up both time and energy to concentrate on the quest for perfection.

The ethical virtues help bring about the most harmonious arrangement in society. At the same time, they are instrumental in producing the requisite tranquility of the soul necessary for attaining intellectual perfection. From the latter perspective, they are necessary whether one is part of society or not. Most people are incapable by nature of attaining intellectual perfection. Moral virtue in their case serves to bring about a healthy soul. The soul in this case refers to the appetitive faculties. Moral virtue also helps insure a healthy body. Overindulgence in any of the corporeal pleasures is simply not good for one's health. Yet the primary function of ethics in the case of the majority is to bring about a healthy society that best serves the needs of those capable of intellectual perfection. The doctrine of the mean is the most suitable approach. It best balances the need for imposing restraints on individuals in a social context with the need for insuring that they actively participate in the cultivation of the physical world. It is for this reason that the Law, which governs society at large, is framed primarily from the standpoint of the mean. Even the pursuit of certain extreme traits which Maimonides at times insists is mandated by the Law—that is, extreme humility and elimination of anger—may be viewed as serving to promote social harmony.

In the case of the potential elite, the primary function of ethics is not social welfare but individual perfection. This goal demands a more extreme approach, at least during the more advanced stages of the quest. One must in particular free oneself from corporeal desires. In the case of the elite they interfere with intellection. In the case of others these desires serve the positive function of insuring the cultivation of society. In *Genesis Rabbah* 9:7, we are informed that if it were not for the evil inclination one would not build a house, marry and procreate. Maimonides equates the evil inclination with the imaginative faculty (*Guide* 2:12), which stimulates the appetitive faculty to engage in these activities. The process of perfecting oneself involves the gradual freeing of oneself from the imagination and the activities associated with it. It is important to stress that according to this approach, it is impossible to be immoral and attain intellectual perfection. One may achieve a certain level of scientific knowledge while being ruled by one's corporeal passions. Maimonides goes so far as to say that this is true even of most of the men of knowledge (*Guide* 2:36). Ultimate perfection, however, demands a state of the soul in which all its energies are turned to intellection. Any control the passions exercise over the soul inevitably entails a lack of perfection. All immorality results either from faulty conceptions, indicating a deficient rational faculty, or from the lack of control of the rational faculty over one's desires.[58]

While in the case of the elite ethics is crucial for the attainment of perfection, it does not form an integral part of perfection itself. Perfection lies in the level of apprehension of the theoretical intellect and its attainment of immortality. Ethics pertains to the faculties of the soul that are integrally related to the body. These faculties vanish with the disintegration of the body. The essence of the perfect individual is pure intellect. It is not characterized by matter, nor by the aspects of the soul that are tied to matter or even rule over matter. Thus even ethical knowledge does not belong to the perfect intellect *qua* intellect, though this knowledge belongs to the practical deliberations of the rational faculty.

Maimonides in the end of the *Guide*, as well as in several other passages, does not contradict this picture but completes it. He regards the perfect individual who subsequently assumes a public role as superior to the intellectually perfect individual who assumes no public role. Plato's philosopher-king becomes in his philosophy the prophet-statesman. The perfection of this individual is termed by Maimonides an "overflowing perfection," a perfection that results in perfecting also others (*Guide* 2:37). As I have already argued, this individual has a dual identity—that of pure intellect constantly contemplating metaphysical truths, and *simultaneously* that of a corporeal being ruled completely by the rational faculty and performing the most perfect physical activities possible for human beings, particularly in the realm of politics.[59] The intellectually perfect individual who maximizes society's perfection, both in the realm of morality and in the realm of knowledge, is superior to one who does not. This individual strives to create a social-intellectual environment in which the potentially perfect can more easily attain ultimate perfection. This "overflowing" perfection is not a matter of individual preference, though individuals may choose to pursue the perfection of which they are capable or not. It is built into the order of the world. From this perspective, ultimate perfection, and the "moral" activity accompanying it, are part of God's providential care of humanity through the order of nature.[60]

The perfect individual serves society, but is not subservient to society. This is comparable to the case of God and the spiritual entities who may be said to serve the sublunar world by caring for it, at the same time that they maintain their superiority in the chain of existence (*Guide* 2:11; 3:13). Society exists to serve the needs of the potentially perfect and help to bring them to perfection. Those societies ruled by perfect individuals in turn are better able to endure and to produce perfect individuals in the future.[61] The perfection of the individual and the perfection of society in this manner complement each other. All the contradictions in Maimonides' views on ethics are ultimately reconciled in this unified picture of the multifaceted role of ethics in his thought.

SIX

INTELLECTUAL PERFECTION, KNOWLEDGE OF GOD, AND THE ROLE OF THE LAW

I

Maimonides views human perfection primarily as the perfection of the intellect. In the *Guide of the Perplexed*, he defines perfection as: "the acquisition of the rational virtues—I refer to the conception of the intelligibles *(ma'aqulāt),* which teach true opinions *(ārā' ṣaḥīḥāt)* concerning the divine things" (3:54.692). This knowledge comes with the mastery of all of the sciences and the apprehension of the whole of existence to the extent of human capacity.[1] It alone leads to human immortality. As I have argued in chapter 4, Maimonides maintains this position throughout all his writings. He does not abandon it despite his apparent awareness of the philosophic problems associated with it.[2] It remained for him the most compelling philosophic view.

From a traditional Jewish standpoint this position raises even more difficulties. Neither the sages of the Talmud nor subsequent religious authorities regarded perfection and immortality as consequent upon intellectual perfection, described in terms of mastery of the sciences. In his profound departure from Jewish sources, Maimonides was motivated by philosophical considerations. His approach to the Torah derives from his Aristotelian conception of human perfection. He has no doubt that the ultimate end of the Torah is to direct its adherents to the same end shared by all human beings. The Jewish People for him do not constitute a separate species, as they did for Halevi before him and many of the mystics after him.[3] Furthermore, the road to intellectual perfection is the same for all humans, and that is by way of study of the sciences. Given these assumptions, the problem with which Maimonides grapples is how does observance of the Torah contribute to the attainment of this end, in addition to the end of a well-organized society that is common to all legislations.

In his description of the purpose of the Law, Maimonides states: "The Law as a whole aims at two things: the welfare of the soul and the welfare of the body. As for the welfare of the soul, it consists in the multitude's acquiring correct opinions *(ārā' ṣaḥiḥā)* corresponding to their respective capacity. Therefore some of them are set forth explicitly and some of them are set forth in parables. For it is not within the nature of the common multitude that its capacity should suffice for apprehending *(idrāk)* the subject matter as is" (*Guide* 3:27.510). As I have already pointed out, Maimonides distinguishes between the "welfare of the soul" that applies to society as a whole, and the "perfection of the soul" that applies to the elite individual.[4] The perfection of the soul is defined as having: "an intellect in actu *('aql bi-l-fi'l);* this would consist in his knowing everything concerning all the beings that it is within the capacity of man to know in accordance with his ultimate perfection" (p. 511).

The connection between "welfare" and "perfection" is summarized by Maimonides in the continuation of his remarks. He describes the role of the Torah as imparting "sound beliefs" *(salāḥ al-'itiqādāt)* and "correct opinions through which ultimate perfection is achieved." The Torah directs its adherents to perfection by transmitting correct opinions in a nonscientific manner in order that they be understood by all. Perfection, however, is attained only after intellectually grasping the whole of existence in a scientific manner. Maimonides is explicit on the point that it is the attainment of ultimate perfection which is, "the only cause of permanent preservation" (p. 511). In the following chapter, he indicates that the Torah communicates correct opinions in a sketchy and general manner. A detailed apprehension of these opinions requires knowledge of all of the theoretical sciences.

His attempt to bridge the gap between the correct opinions imparted by the Torah, and the knowledge that leads to ultimate perfection underscores the depth of this gap in Maimonides' thought. There is a profound difference between the acquisition of correct opinions in parable form and the intellectual apprehension of all that they denote. Thus the opinions taught by the Torah and the precepts it commands do not in themselves confer perfection upon the individual. At best they create the ideal environment—both from a social, and more important, an intellectual standpoint—in which the capable individual can strive for perfection. They also help inculcate in the individual those moral traits without which intellectual perfection is unattainable. Maimonides further attempts to bridge the gap between the Torah and perfection by incorporating knowledge of the natural sciences and metaphysics into one's religious obligations.[5] This knowledge forms an integral part of the commandments to know the existence of God, that there is no other deity, to unify God, to love God and to be in awe of God. Maimonides rules that the last two commandments are observed only by contemplating God's activities and creatures—that is, all the existents.[6]

The role of the Torah and its limits are graphically illustrated by Maimonides in his parable of the king in his palace:[7]

> The ruler is in his palace, and all his subjects are partly within the city and partly outside the city. Of those who are within the city, some have turned their backs upon the ruler's habitation, their faces being turned another way. Others seek to reach the ruler's habitation, turn toward it, and desire to enter it and to stand before him, but up to now they have not yet seen the wall of the habitation. Some of those who seek to reach it have come up to the habitation and walk around it searching for its gate. Some of them have entered the inner court of the habitation and have come to be with the king, in one and the same place with him, namely, in the ruler's habitation. But their having come into the inner part of the habitation does not mean that they see the ruler or speak to him. For after their coming into the inner part of the habitation, it is indispensable that they should make another effort; then they will be in the presence of the ruler, see him from afar or from nearby, or hear the ruler's speech or speak to him. (*Guide* 3:51.618)

Maimonides immediately proceeds to explain the parable lest there be a misunderstanding about the groups he has in mind. The final group he describes are the prophets, whose "overflowing perfection" I have analyzed in chapter 4. I would like in the present context to turn to the other groups. One who holds an incorrect opinion either because of "faulty speculation" or an "erroneous tradition"—and from Maimonides' examples it is clear that he is dealing with fundamental errors in beliefs pertaining to the Deity, such as polytheism—is within the *polis*, but with his back to the palace. The masses of Jews, on the other hand, face the palace but are so far away that they do not even catch a glimpse of it. Maimonides indicates that they observe the Torah, but he does not mention anything in regard to their opinions. Those who circle the palace and search for the gate are the scholars "who believe true opinions *(ārā' ṣaḥīḥāt)* on the basis of traditional authority and study the Torah concerning the practices of divine service, but do not engage in speculation *(naṣra)* concerning the fundamental principles of religion and make no inquiry whatever regarding the rectification of belief *(taṣḥīḥ al-'itiqād)*" (p. 619). Only speculation concerning the principles of religion,[8] according to Maimonides, gains a person entrance to the antechambers. Only knowledge of all that humans are capable of attaining in physical and metaphysical matters allows the individual to enter the inner court. The role of the Torah, in this parable, is confined to turning its adherents in the right direction, and at best directing them to the outer wall of the palace. Scientific knowledge, however, is the key to the gate.

Maimonides reinforces this point in the second explanation he gives to the parable: those engaged in studying mathematics and logic are still searching for the gate of the ruler's habitation; those who understand the natural sciences are walking in the antechambers; those who have perfected their knowledge in the natural sciences and understand metaphysics are with the ruler in the inner court. Maimonides may be hinting at an alternative path to God. The latter one is that by which non-Jewish philosophers such as Aristotle have reached perfection, and does not require observance of the Law. More likely, Maimonides presents two explanations of the parable in order to indicate to his Jewish readers that for them both these paths are necessary, complementary, and ultimately converge. At the same time he was interesting in sidestepping the problem where he locates the Aristotelian philosophers, who were not obligated by the demands of the Law. One may infer from his examples of those with their back to the ruler's habitation that he does not include them in this group, but he avoids indicating exactly where they stand in relation to the ruler. Even though he may well have felt that they came close to human perfection, he was careful not to make this claim openly lest he undermine the value of the commandments. The stress in the chapter is on the way that a Jew must attain perfection, though the nature of the perfection and much of the path to it are the same for all humanity. At any rate, Maimonides is clear on the point that one should in no way equate adherence to correct opinions on the basis of tradition with the acquisition of intellectual perfection.

In the concluding chapter of the *Guide*, Maimonides distinguishes between knowledge of the Torah and knowledge of "wisdom" (or philosophy). Knowledge of the Torah is knowledge of correct opinions on the basis of tradition, while knowledge of philosophy is knowledge of the proofs of the correct opinions on the basis of speculative reasoning. The latter knowledge is treated as far superior to the former, though one must acquire knowledge of the Torah prior to engaging in speculation. While Maimonides uses the phrase "correct opinions" *(ārā' ṣaḥīḥāt)* to characterize the knowledge of the masses, the scholars and the perfect, he leaves no doubt as to the difference between possessing these opinions in a nonscientific manner in accordance with the masses' limited capacity, or based solely on tradition, and intellectually apprehending these opinions based on a thorough scientific knowledge of all that exists. The parable of the king and the palace not only underscores the limits of the Torah's capacity to guide its adherents to perfection, but how far the vast majority of its adherents remain from perfection. In most cases the Torah succeeds only in turning them in the right direction, and little more.

II

Maimonides' view that the acceptance of belief solely on the basis of tradition is of limited epistemic value is even more extreme than appears at first glance. It is not only the case that in matters directly pertaining to the theoretical intellect, most notably metaphysics, belief held solely on the basis of tradition is not to be equated with intellectual perfection. From a philosophical standpoint, such belief is generally false due to the improper way in which it is grasped. The belief in the unity of God serves as a good example of this point. In *Guide* 1:50, Maimonides maintains: "If someone believes that He is one, but possesses a certain number of essential attributes, he says in his words that He is one, but believes Him in his thought to be many" (p. 111). The chapter opens with a definition of belief *('itiqād):* "Belief is not the notion that is uttered, but the notion that is represented in the soul when it has been averred of it that it is in fact just as it has been represented."[9]

The conclusion presented in the continuation of Maimonides' discussion of divine attributes in *Guide* 1:60 is exceptionally far-reaching: "I shall not say that he who affirms that God, may He be exalted, has positive attributes either falls short of apprehending Him or is an associator or has an apprehension of Him that is different from what He really is, but I shall say that he has abolished his belief in the existence of the deity without being aware of it" (p. 145). Implicit in these remarks is the notion that anyone who ascribes to God anger, mercy, or any of the other emotions, in a positive manner, essentially denies the existence of God.[10] Such an individual believes in something that does not exist in reality—an emotional deity—while the real deity is not the object of belief. Superfluous to say, the same is the case with one who ascribes to God any corporeal attribute. Maimonides' stance leads to the conclusion that from a philosophical perspective, most Jews deny the existence of God. While many may affirm God's noncorporeality, few conceive of God as lacking all emotions, and fewer still do not conceive of God as possessing knowledge and will as diverse essential attributes. Only through an apprehension of the sciences can one properly represent to oneself correct notions about God, which is the basis for true belief. Without this apprehension, one's representations of God inevitably fall far short of the truth.

Maimonides' view of the Torah's pedagogical role, yet its being severely limited by nature in the extent of its effectiveness, is a fundamental point for understanding his philosophy. The final end of the Torah is the perfection of the intellect. The Torah at best, however, can inculcate true beliefs only in a popular manner to society at large—beliefs that the vast majority will improperly grasp—while it encourages those with the proper potential to strive for final perfection. The fact that the Torah was framed for a community at a certain point of historical development made the challenge all the more acute. It had to address the masses leaving Egypt in the idiom that they were capable of understanding and willing to accept, at the same time that it subtly pointed out to the elite of that generation, and all subsequent generations, the direction that they were to follow.

Insofar as the Torah is concerned with the *process* of bringing people closer to the truth, after insuring their social welfare, it evaluates beliefs in a different way than does theoretical philosophy. The Torah must take into consideration what are the beliefs to which people are accustomed and what are the beliefs closer to the truth that they can be persuaded to accept; which false beliefs are more harmful than others; what are the influences of specific beliefs on people's actions; and how do specific activities influence their beliefs. The method whereby the beliefs of the various strata of society are molded so that benefit accrues to each member is a primary concern of the Torah.[11] Such an approach to belief must be dynamic, changing in accordance with the circumstances. The question of truth and falsity is not in itself sufficient to determine how a belief is to be evaluated. Given the natural limitations of the masses to grasp properly the truth, the Torah must often rest content with formal allegiance being paid to a certain belief even though it is grasped in an inaccurate manner.

How these considerations lie at the foundation of Maimonides' approach to the Torah is illustrated by his treatment of the belief in the corporeality of God. The negation of the corporeality of God is brought by him as one of the principles of Judaism (*Introduction to Pereq Ḥeleq*, principle 3). His attack on the belief in a corporeal deity occurs frequently in his writings and is severe to the extreme.[12] What motivated Maimonides to adopt this stance, and what if any halakhic sources support it, are crucial problems which his position raises. Yet equally significant is the question of Maimonides' approach to the relation between the belief in a corporeal deity and the Torah.

He is well aware that the text of the Torah itself, when read literally, teaches the belief in a corporeal deity. In other words, the Torah, whose primary intent is the inculcation of true beliefs, conveys a false belief in the most important area of knowledge. In a crucial sense the Torah conveys a belief that according to Maimonides stands opposed to one of the principles of the Torah.

From the standpoint of Maimonides' philosophy, this fact demands an explanation. Why does the Torah not teach in a literal manner that God is incorporeal, instead of misleading its followers? Maimonides addresses this problem, but his answer is far from being the one that we anticipate hearing. He does not claim that there existed an exoteric tradition how to understand the corporeal descriptions of God, a tradition that was lost with the dispersion of the Jews. Such an explanation, based on the integral connection between the written text and the oral tradition, would have allowed him to maintain that the Torah always taught true beliefs. False beliefs were never taught intentionally, but came about as a result of a historical tragedy. Maimonides at times employs such an explanation in accounting for the lack of perfection among his contemporaries. The loss of a national homeland, and the accompanying catastrophes, account for the nonappearance of prophecy and the loss of knowledge of the esoteric tradition among the Jewish people (*Guide* 1:71; 2:32; 2:36). He adopts a far different stance when dealing with the problem posed by the Torah's corporeal descriptions of God:

> A similar thing has occurred with regard to the knowledge of God . . . given to the multitude in the books of the prophets and also in the Torah. For necessity required that all of them be given guidance to the belief in the existence of God . . . and in His possessing all the perfections. . . . The minds of the multitude were accordingly guided to the belief that He exists by imagining that He is corporeal, and to the belief that He is living by imagining that He is capable of motion. For the multitude perceive nothing other than bodies as having a firmly established existence and as being indubitably true . . . That, however, which is neither a body nor in a body is not an existent thing in any respect, according to man's initial representation, particularly from the point of view of the imagination. (*Guide* 1:46.98)[13]

It follows from Maimonides' remarks that the Torah deliberately misleads the people in the matter of the corporeality of God. The Torah could either educate the masses to believe in a single, corporeal deity, or educate them to believe in a single, incorporeal deity. If the latter course had been chosen, the result would have been a complete rejection in the belief in

God. The masses were incapable of accepting the existence of such a deity. Consequently, they would have accepted the belief in many gods, such as the belief that the celestial bodies are gods. According to Maimonides, this was the prevailing belief in the period of the Giving of the Torah (*Laws of Idolatry* 1:1-2; *Guide* 3:29). From a conceptual standpoint, belief in a single, corporeal deity is equivalent to the belief in the nonexistence of God, just as is the case with a belief in many corporeal gods. From a pedagogical standpoint, there is a profound difference between these two beliefs. One who believes in a single, corporeal deity is closer to the true belief than one who believes in many gods. It is precisely with the belief in a single deity, as opposed to the belief in many gods or in no god, that one turns to the direction of the palace in Maimonides' parable of the king.

There was no choice but to compromise with reality in order that the Torah should educate the people effectively. For the elite, it can offer only hints that God is in fact incorporeal, and that the descriptions should not be interpreted in a literal manner. Maimonides indicates that the sages of the Talmud understood how to interpret the corporeal descriptions. Yet they continued to employ them in their own parables due to necessity of addressing the masses in a manner that would enable them to form a representation of God (*Guide* 1:46; 1:59). Judaism at times teaches certain beliefs to improve the moral behavior of the masses and insure their loyalty to the Law. Maimonides terms them "necessary beliefs" (*Guide* 3:28). His example is the belief that God gets angry at those who disobey the divine commands—a false belief when understood literally. By teaching the notion that God is corporeal, the Torah, Maimonides hints, also teaches false beliefs in order to inculcate true beliefs in a preliminary manner. The truth that is possible to convey to the masses must be conveyed in stages. In this manner, the beliefs of the masses are refined, without precipitating a regression. From a conceptual standpoint, there is no belief in the existence of God without the belief in God's absolute unity. There is no belief in absolute unity without belief in God's incorporeality.[14] From a pedagogical standpoint, these beliefs must be divided and transmitted one at a time.

III

Those who express a belief in a single, but corporeal, deity, are labeled by Maimonides "heretics," incurring all the legal consequences such a designation entails.[15] In light of his comments in the *Guide*, it is clear that he is well aware of the innovation he introduces in doing so. Not only does Maimonides lack any clear basis in Jewish law for his ruling, as was pointed out by a leading critic in his lifetime,[16] but it negates the stance of the Torah. The Torah intentionally chose to describe God as corporeal. The question raised by this point is why was Maimonides so insistent that Judaism reverse its pedagogical strategy in the area of beliefs about God to the point that he employed all the legal arsenal at his disposal to accomplish this end. Why risk disturbing the naive faith of the masses. Even from a political philosophical perspective, this move was highly debatable. Such luminous Islamic philosophers such as Alfarabi, Avicenna, and Averroes advised against it. The notion of an incorporeal deity should be left to those who were intellectually prepared. The masses were to be taught only the figurative representations of the truth.[17]

One is justified in concluding that Maimonides adopts this position since he felt that the historical circumstances had radically changed. The situation in his period permitted the further refinement of the beliefs of the masses. The greatest change was the decisive victory of the belief in a single God versus the belief in many gods. In the period of Abraham, as well as Moses, the beliefs of the Sabians, according to Maimonides, were dominant. The Sabians worshipped the stars, recognizing no deity beyond the celestial bodies. Abraham began to challenge this belief. He taught that there is a single deity who is the Lord of the world. The Law of Moses continued in the path of Abraham. It employed an even more effective pedagogical device in conveying the belief in a single deity to the masses—that is, commandments rather than rational arguments. The fact that the vast majority of the world now glorify Abraham, and very few remnants remain of the Sabians and their beliefs and practices, attests to the extent of his victory (*Guide* 3:29).[18]

With the victory of the belief in a single deity, there is no longer any danger in publicly teaching the belief in an incorporeal deity. In the period of the Exodus, this teaching would have resulted in the acceptance of many corporeal gods. People would have rejected the belief in a deity that they could not see or imagine. Their reaction would have been an immediate retreat back to the prevalent belief that the stars are deities. After a lengthy historical process, this belief no longer exists.[19] The danger once posed by this state of affairs no longer had to be taken under consideration. There was no reason not to emphasize in public that which the Torah could only hint. The time was ripe to transfer the teaching of the incorporeality of God out of the category of the "secrets of the Torah" that needed to be conveyed in the form of parables, and hidden from the understanding of the masses. It now could be presented, indeed must be presented in Maimonides' view, as a teaching that was to be conveyed to all. The masses must be habituated to think of God in a more profound manner. The corporeal descriptions of God served by Maimonides' time more as a stumbling block to the welfare of the soul rather than an aid. To Alexander of Aphrodisias' list of causes of disagreement and error, Maimonides adds "habit and upbringing." It is both significant and surprising that he brings as an example the multitude's belief in the corporeality of God on the basis of a literal reading of Scripture (*Guide* 1:31). Maimonides' intention is to break this habit. It no longer serves any positive purpose, though it did so in the past. The corporeal descriptions should now be treated for what they really are—figurative representations of God that are not to be interpreted literally.[20]

The spread of Islam, with its proclamation of the incorporeality of God, made the public teaching of this belief within Judaism both easier and more incumbent. Maimonides rules that the Moslems are not idolaters, and moreover, believe in a correct manner in the unity of God.[21] The prevalent belief in Maimonides' milieu was monotheism. Yet this point may have proved to be somewhat of an embarrassment for him as well. Maimonides distinguishes the divine religion from the others by the fact that it inculcates correct beliefs leading to the welfare of the soul (*Guide* 2:40). Islam, which at best was regarded by him as a poor imitation of Judaism,[22] nonetheless was far more explicit than Judaism in its teaching of the incorporeality of God. Thus on one level, it appears to satisfy better the criteria of a divine religion. Maimonides could not allow Judaism to fall behind Islam in the most important task of religion.

Maimonides was far from being the first Jewish medieval thinker or legal authority to publicly teach belief in an incorporeal deity. He was preceded by a number of the gaonim, most prominently by R. Saadiah, as well as such diverse influential thinkers as R. Baḥya Ibn Paquda and R. Judah Halevi.[23] Belief in the incorporeality of God was the dominant belief among the educated Jews who grew up in an Islamic milieu. Maimonides' view that belief in the oneness of God is one of the 613 commandments of the Torah, and that this belief includes belief in God's incorporeality, already found an expression in R. Ḥefeṣ b. Yaṣliaḥ's *Book of Precepts*.[24] Maimonides, however, went much further than any of his predecessors in making the belief in an incorporeal deity a dominant aspect of Judaism.

The rectification of belief is, in the final analysis, the ultimate purpose of the Torah in Maimonides' view. Thus there is no incongruity between the

Torah's choice to hide the view of God's incorporeality in order to safeguard the view of God's existence and perfection, and Maimonides' insistence that the masses, "should be made to accept on traditional authority the belief that God is not a body" (*Guide* 1:35.158). It is clear that the vast majority will continue to hold beliefs which from a conceptual standpoint entail the corporealization, and hence the nonexistence, of God.[25] Significantly, Maimonides does not include among the heretics those who affirm essential attributes, though such affirmation logically entails the lack of unity. He is sensitive to the degree that a proper belief in divine incorporeality can be impressed upon the masses. Maimonides rests content with incorporating the denial of positive attributes as part of the commandment to unify God (*Laws of the Principles of the Torah* 1:11). In the prolonged process of refining people's beliefs, it is sufficient at this stage of history that the explicit, publicly proclaimed belief in a corporeal deity join the explicit, publicly proclaimed belief in the existence of many gods, and vanish from the world.

Maimonides' treatment of heresy in the *Guide* should be understood in light of this point. He defines infidelity or heresy *(al-kufr)*: "a belief *('itiqād)* about a thing that is different from what the thing really is" (1:36.83). Some of his examples do not belong to the religious sphere—that is, belief that the sun is a circle rather than a sphere—showing that he is not using the term in a strict theological sense. Yet it is ultimately the religious sphere that is Maimonides' concern. He contrasts the idolaters with those who believe in a corporeal deity:

> What then should be the state of him whose infidelity bears upon His essence, may He be exalted, and consists in believing Him to be different from what He really is? I mean to say that he does not believe that He exists; or believes that there are two gods, or that He is a body, or that He is subject to affections; or again that he ascribes to God some deficiency or other. Such man is indubitably more blameworthy than a worshipper of idols who regard the latter as intermediaries or as having the power to do good or ill. . . . If, however, it should occur to you that one who believes in the corporeality of God should be excused because of his having been brought up in this doctrine or because of his ignorance and the shortcoming of his apprehension *(idrāk)*, you ought to hold a similar belief with regard to an idolater; for he only worships idols because of his ignorance or because of his upbringing. . . . If, however, you should say that the external sense of the biblical text causes men to fall into this doubt, you ought to know that an idolater is similarly impelled to his idolatry by imaginings and defective representations. Accordingly there is no excuse for one who does not accept the authority of men who inquire into the truth and are

engaged in speculation if he himself is incapable of engaging in such speculation. I do not consider an infidel one who cannot demonstrate that the corporeality of God should be negated. But I do consider an infidel one who does not believe *(lā yit'aqad)* in its negation; and this particularly in view of the existence of the interpretations of Onqelos and Jonathan ben Uziel. (*Guide* 1:36.84–85)

According to this passage, heresy in the religious sphere lies in affirming false beliefs, not in representing them inaccurately in one's mind. It is sufficient to accept these beliefs on the basis of tradition, even if one is incapable of grasping them properly. Particularly poignant is Maimonides' insistence that the literal interpretation of the texts of the Torah is not a sufficient excuse for believing in the corporeality of God. While this may have been the case in the past, it was no longer to be the situation in the present.

IV

The attempt to rectify people's beliefs, in accordance with the path Maimonides regarded as laid down by the Torah, finds its most blatant expression in the first part of *The Book of Knowledge*, the *Laws of the Principles of the Torah.*[26] With this section he opens his great legal compendium, the *Mishneh Torah*. By design, the *Mishneh Torah* is a multilayered work, taking as its model the Torah. The Torah, as viewed by Maimonides, contains both actions and beliefs directed to social well-being and spiritual well-being. It takes into consideration the needs of the masses and the needs of the elite. Maimonides' code too is intended to be all inclusive, and not just in its presentation of all the commandments whether they be operative in his time or not. It incorporates both true beliefs and socially necessary ones, thereby addressing both the potential elite and the masses.

Given the multiple concerns of the *Mishneh Torah*, Maimonides paid considerable attention to the organization of the work. He draws a clear distinction between the content of the first book, *The Book of Knowledge*, and the subsequent books. This is evident by the very title he gives to the book. Within the first book, Maimonides draws a distinction between the first section, *Laws of the Principles of the Torah*, and the subsequent sections. This too is evident by the title. Within the first section, he draws a sharp distinction between the first four chapters—whose subject matter is identified by him with the ultimate esoteric knowledge, *pardes*—and the subsequent chapters. This point is clearly indicated by him in his concluding remarks in chapter 4. He calls the subject of these four chapters "a great matter," while the rest of his legal compendium deals with what he terms "a small matter" by comparison *(Laws of the Principles of the Torah* 4:13). In the first four chapters we receive probably the clearest exposition of Maimonides' theology contained in any of his works, including *The Guide of the Perplexed.* He barely makes an attempt to conceal his views even on sensitive topics.[27] Moreover, these theological views are given legally binding status. Maimonides begins with an exposition of the commandments to know that God exists, that God is one and that there are no other gods. He follows with the commandments to love and be in awe of God. The fulfillment of all five commandments is dependent solely upon the extent of one's knowledge of God and the world.[28]

Yet it is hard to overlook the problems raised by the manner in which Maimonides formulates these commandments. On one hand, these commandments are incumbent upon everyone. On the other hand, Maimonides indicates: "The things which I have said in these two chapters are like a drop in the ocean compared to what has to be elucidated on this subject. The exposition of all the principles in these two chapters is what is called *ma'aseh merkavah (Account of the Chariot).* . . . The early sages commanded not to expound these matters except to a solitary individual who is wise and understands by means of his own reasoning" (*Laws of Principles of the Torah* 2:11–12).

In light of Maimonides' remarks, the question arises why he treats these commandments as incumbent upon everyone if he identifies their subject matter with the esoteric topic *ma'aseh merkavah (Account of the Chariot)*—a topic that he equates with metaphysics. In outlining the knowledge required to attain love of God, he goes on to include the esoteric topic *ma'aseh bereshit (Account of the Beginning),* which he equates with the natural sciences.[29] Even more puzzling—if Maimonides thinks that the teaching of these topics is to be withheld from the masses, following the ruling of the sages in *Mishnah Ḥagigah* 2:1, why does he open his legal compendium with a detailed outline of them? Maimonides appears to demand from the masses what is not in their capacity to fulfill and at the same time reveals to them matters which he himself indicates that the sages commanded to conceal.

Part of the answer to this problem is found in Maimonides' *Guide.* The commandment "to know *(leida')* that there is a First Existent," which opens the *Laws of the Principles of the Torah,* does not imply detailed scientific knowledge. Rather it refers to the acceptance of correct opinions, rendering the Arabic *'itiqād*.[30] These are precisely the opinions that Maimonides indicates in the *Guide* are to be communicated to everyone. The scientific explication of these principles belongs to the domain of philosophy, and is to be restricted to the elite. Maimonides in fact does not demand from the masses what they are incapable of fulfilling on a simple level, even if they are incapable of apprehending the opinions they affirm. It could be further argued that he also does not reveal what the sages command to conceal. Only the scientific explication of these commandments belongs to the secrets of the Torah.

While this answer resolves the apparent contradiction in Maimonides' stance, it does not explain the enigmatic nature of his formulation. In *Guide* 1:35, Maimonides draws a sharp line between that which is to be taught to the masses, and that which is to remain secret. In his earlier *Laws of the Principles of the Torah*, on the other hand, he deliberately blurs the distinction. He appears to encourage the study of esoteric topics by incorporating them as such into the commandments and providing their salient details. This tendency reemerges in the *Laws of the Study of the Torah* (1:11–12). A Jew is obligated to devote at least a third of his study time to the study of Talmud. As part of this study, Maimonides prominently includes the study of *pardes*—which he treats as a general designation for metaphysics and the natural sciences.[31] His reiteration of the warning of the sages regarding the study of these topics thus appears to run counter to the dominant trend of his entire presentation.

Maimonides' approach becomes clearer if we consider the first chapters of the *Laws of the Principles of the Torah* as primarily intended for the potential elite, rather than for the masses. These are the individuals who have the capability of achieving perfection, but lack knowledge of the proper path. This group is particularly worthy of attention for only through them is the ultimate purpose of Judaism realized. This group is not to be completely identified with the ideal readers of the *Guide*. They are not yet prepared for Maimonides' discourse in the *Guide*, for they have not yet attained philosophic knowledge. The challenge facing Maimonides is to reach these individuals when they are scattered around the world, and when it is not easy to identify them.

The social and political circumstances of the Jews in the period of Maimonides made the political-educational model presented by Alfarabi, and rooted in Plato, in large part inapplicable. No enlightened centralized leadership could organize and implant an educational system that segregated people according to their potential and placed each group in its own learning track.[32] Other aspects of Alfarabi's model, however, were open to adaptation within the context of Jewish society—for example, the formulation of religious "principles," in addition to the use of figurative representations of philosophic truths and the introduction of certain changes in the legislation of the ideal lawgiver in accordance with its ultimately objectives, to direct society toward perfection.[33] The primary means at Maimonides' disposal was the written word. He could only hope that in reaching the largest possible audience through his legal works, he would be able to prod the potential elite in the right direction.

It is for this reason that at times Maimonides' philosophic positions are much more explicit in the *Laws of the Principles of the Torah* than they are in the *Guide*. The *Guide* is intended for a limited audience who is well versed both in Jewish tradition and philosophy. The danger in the writing of the *Guide* is that the work may fall into the hands of those who do not belong to this group. The truth concerning certain topics must be revealed by means of hints which only the ideal reader is capable of understanding. The *Mishneh Torah*, on the other hand, is intended for everyone, especially the potential elite at the beginning of their path. Subtle hints would not prove sufficient in reaching this group. Most of them have not yet attained any philosophic knowledge. They may well have been educated in an environment that was hostile to the study of philosophy. It was incumbent upon Maimonides to reveal his positions in a more explicit manner, and from the very beginning of his work, in order to set this group upon the right path.

The essential message that emerges from Maimonides' discussion of the commandments to know and love God in the first four chapters of the *Laws of the Principles of the Torah* is that one who desires to reach perfection as a Jew—which is in fact human perfection—and to attain immortality, must devote oneself the study of philosophy. By describing God in philosophic terms, Maimonides points to the knowledge that is necessary for the full fulfillment of the first commandment. By presenting an outline of *ma'aseh merkavah* and *ma'aseh bereshit* that is in accordance with the medieval Islamic Aristotelian conception of the natural sciences and metaphysics, he indicates his rejection of other conceptions of these topics, conceptions which may attract the potential elite and lead them astray. By labeling knowledge of *all* the other commandments in his legal compendium, "a small matter"—in comparison to the commandments to know and love God, fulfilled through mastering *ma'aseh merkavah*, which is "a great matter"—Maimonides leaves no doubt to which studies a person must dedicate oneself.[34] The former commandments are described by Maimonides as being open to the knowledge of everyone. They precede the commandments described in the first four chapters, he explains, since they prepare a person to engage in the study of the natural sciences and metaphysics and they provide for the needs of society. His reiteration of the warning of the sages regarding the study of these topics in this context serves more as a stimulus to the potential elite rather than a deterrent. Moreover, his subsequent pointed inclusion of these topics in defining what constitutes the study of Talmud *(Laws of the Study of Torah* 1:12) indicates to the elite how they should primarily fulfill this study obligation.

Maimonides would not have revealed what he did in the *Laws of the Principles of the Torah* if he felt that this would cause damage to the faith of the masses. He judged that they would not appreciate the full significance of his position, and only the elite would understand and turn to the right path in their studies. At any rate, he saw no alternative but to set down these commandments at the beginning of his work, with all the transparent "hints" to his true view on the subject of perfection, despite the dangers involved. Otherwise the Torah would be for naught, since it would not attain its ultimate objective. The purpose of the Torah is not only to provide a conducive environment for those studying science and philosophy but to *encourage* the capable among its adherents to pursue this course.

V

It would be wrong to conclude from all that was argued till now that Maimonides believes in historical progress regarding the most important area—knowledge of God and the world—and that he acts primarily from this optimistic evaluation of the situation. Maimonides certainly discerned progress in popular universal beliefs, and consequently what is possible to teach the masses.[35] He also notes the progress made in knowledge of scientific matters, most notably astronomy (*Guide* 2:24). Yet at the same time he believes there was a great regression in regard to the attainment of intellectual perfection. This regression, perhaps even more than the progress that was made, prodded him to compose his treatises.

The regression was most evident in the Jewish leaders and scholars of his generation, the group that served as the model of perfection for the Jewish community at large. The contempt with which Maimonides holds the scholars of his generation emerges clearly from his writings.[36] He is of the opinion that most of the perfect lived toward the beginning of Jewish history. On the highest level stand Moses and the forefathers. Beneath them stand the prophets, followed by the sages of the Mishnah and Talmud. Significantly, the line separating prophet and sage is at times blurred in Maimonides' discussions. In the *Introduction to the Commentary on the Mishnah*, Maimonides treats R. Judah the Prince, the compiler of the Mishnah, as a person whose intellectual and moral perfection was exceeded only by that of Moses. It was this compilation that served Maimonides as perhaps the most important precedent in Jewish tradition for his own endeavors in the field of law. Maimonides' depiction of R. Judah the Prince follows on the heels of his discussion of prophetic authority. As we have already seen, Maimonides negates almost all judicial-legislative authority from the prophet qua prophet and assigns this authority to the sages.[37] This approach was designed to preserve the integrity of the Law from one of the gravest dangers facing it. In ascribing to the author of the Mishnah all the qualifications for prophecy, Maimonides essentially indicates that while there were no postbiblical *public* prophets, those possessing prophetic perfection continued to arise on the stage of history. They functioned as great sages. R. Judah the Prince is the model of such a sage, the product of his activity having singular impact both in preserving and adapting the Law. R. Yohanan, another of the great sages whose activity was decisive in preserving the Law in a time of extreme crisis, is yet another individual treated by Maimonides in terms reminiscent of prophetic perfection (*Guide* 1:34).

Seen from this perspective, there was a sharp decline in the quality of those leading the Jewish people from Moses' day to Maimonides' own. This is a traditional conception, thus it is hardly surprising that it finds an explicit expression in Maimonides' works. It appears, however, that this is not simply Maimonides' "exoteric" opinion, but his real opinion as well. His approach to the prophetic visions and rabbinic midrashim as philosophic parables should not be regarded as an attempt to create a new myth by means of which he can justify and encourage the study of philosophy. The prophets, followed by the sages, reached the pinnacle of intellectual perfection. Maimonides' characterization of R. Judah the Prince and R. Yohanan also reveals the underlying view that this regression need not be considered constant or irreversible. Great prophets in the guise of sages can continue to arise. The problem is that those who were leading the way in the posttalmudic period were far from being individuals of such caliber.

Certainly, even if Maimonides did not believe that the prophets attained a level of metaphysical knowledge greater than that of the Aristotelian philosophers, and that the sages of the Talmud attained at least the same level, he would have had to express this opinion in order to justify his approach from the standpoint of Jewish tradition.[38] Yet the distinct impression that Maimonides conveys is that he believes in his reconstruction of history. In the case of the sages, he interprets their midrashim as philosophic parables but does not always agree with the view that they are said to express. Philosophic speculation, but not the infallibility of revelation, characterizes their thought. Maimonides did not consciously seek to *redefine* the essence of Judaism in order to make it conform to the philosophic truths that he accepted. Rather, he sought to *rediscover* the essence of Judaism, as intended by the Lawgiver and known to the prophets and sages of old. Truth is one. There can be no contradictory truths, just different ways of representing truth. Judaism in his view conformed to the truth contained in the theoretical and political writings of the philosophers.

For this reason, the ignorance of philosophy displayed by the Jewish scholars of his generation distressed him greatly. In his view, they were educating the generation to view the subordinate as primary, and not to recognize the primary at all. No longer were those who attained intellectual perfection leading the people and guiding the elite to the perfection of which they were capable. This platonic ideal of the philosopher-king in Maimonides' reconstruction of history had been to a large degree the case for the Jewish people in the past. At present, the Jewish people were led by those who shared with the masses the same false conceptions of the truth, and guided them accordingly.[39]

What caused this regression, with a narrowing of the gap between the rabbinic leaders and masses, was the loss of the esoteric oral tradition transmitted by the talmudic sages to the elite of their students. Maimonides opens the third part of the *Guide*, which deals with the *Account of the Chariot*, with the comment:

> They have already made it clear how secret the *Account of the Chariot* was and how foreign to the mind of the multitude. And it has been made clear that even that portion of it that becomes clear to him who has been given access to the understanding of it, is subject to a legal prohibition against its being taught and explained except orally to one man having certain stated qualities, and even to that one only the chapter headings may be mentioned. This is the reason why the knowledge of this matter has ceased to exist in the entire religious community, so that nothing great or small remains of it. (P. 415)

Maimonides' remark should not be treated simply as a typical, and even formalistic, rationale for writing down matters whose transmission is supposed to be in oral form. He sincerely believed that by means of his philosophic studies he had rediscovered a tradition that once belonged to the sages. It was now incumbent upon him to transmit what he had learnt to those capable of grasping it. The exile and dispersal of the Jewish people led to the loss of this knowledge (*Guide* 1:71).[40] Conceptions that were far from the truth in Maimonides' view supplanted the lost tradition. If Judaism was to retain its essential meaning, this regression must be halted. The scholars must be directed to a proper understanding of the noncorporeal world and what constitutes human perfection.

From this evaluation of the situation of the Jewish people, Maimonides acted. In order to reach the perfect *in potentia* and to guide them to perfection, he first had to write works directed to the entire people. He had to refine the beliefs of the masses, thereby raising the intellectual level of society, at the same time that he directed the elite to the proper path. His goal was to mold a new group of scholars, who like the sages of old would be teachers of truth and ideal leaders. With no single center for Jewish learning, and with the potential elite scattered throughout the world, no longer could the esoteric tradition be renewed orally. The written word must supplant face-to-face contact between teacher and student.[41]

Initially Maimonides planned to write two theological-exegetical works—one devoted to prophecy and the other to rabbinic midrash—after writing the *Commentary on the Mishnah*. These works ultimately assumed the form of (or were replaced by) the *Guide of the Perplexed*.[42] It is significant that rather than completing these works immediately, Maimonides turned instead to the writing of his legal treatises. He saw that it was first incumbent upon him to write his great legal compendium, the *Mishneh Torah*, a compendium that opens with a section devoted to the principles of the religion. His earlier *Book on the Commandments* he treats as a preliminary work to the *Mishneh Torah*. Only after writing his works addressed to the entire Jewish people and which assumed the form of law, could Maimonides now turn to those scholars who followed the path he had encouraged, and who had steeped themselves in the study of philosophy. These individuals often found themselves torn by the blatant conflicts between philosophic and Jewish teachings. The *Guide* was written to help them over the hurdle that they were facing by showing that both philosophy and Judaism, when properly understood, were in harmony. In the pursuit of perfection, they must continue their philosophic studies while remaining devout Jews.

In summary, the relation between the pedagogical role of the Torah and Maimonides' compositions on one hand, and the acquisition of metaphysical knowledge and intellectual perfection on the other hand, is complex. A profound gap separates the acceptance of the opinions of the Torah, or the principles formulated by Maimonides, and the apprehension of metaphysical truths. The study of philosophy alone can bridge this gap. In the final analysis, both the Jewish masses and those who hold false conceptions of God are far from grasping the truth. A failure to apprehend that which is separate from matter and to conceive God as noncorporeal characterizes the thought of the masses, no matter how much they may affirm the existence of God and God's unity, or observe the commandments.

For the vast majority of the people, philosophy confers no benefit. They are incapable by nature of attaining perfection. The study of philosophy may even bring harm to their existence in this world by undermining their faith and obedience to the Torah, thereby destroying the fabric of Jewish social life. The study of philosophy must be restricted to the elite. The purpose of the opinions inculcated by the Torah is not to serve as a substitute for the study of philosophy, or even to supplement the scientific knowledge attained by way of philosophy.

It is evident from Maimonides' approach that all of Israel does not have a portion in the World to Come, with the exception of a few individuals. The World to Come, he continuously hints, refers to the immortality of the perfected intellect.[43] The find end of all others will be like that of all creatures of the earth whose soul undergoes corruption with the corruption of the body. The final destiny of those outside the *polis*, those whose back is to the palace of the king, those whose face is in the direction of the palace but do not see it, and those who search for the entrance, is the same. The importance of inculcating in the masses belief in the World to Come is to insure their obedience to the Torah.

Maimonides' dedication to the rectification of Jewish belief, and his view that in this area lies the essential superiority of the Torah over all other legislations, thus do not stem from a conviction that the inculcation of correct opinions guarantees the masses their eternal existence. Nor does it add to the intellectual perfection of those who have mastered all of the sciences. The importance of such instruction lies in the type of society it helps mold. The ideal society is the one that provides the best environment, both physically and spiritually, for those with the potential for attaining perfection. Maimonides is explicit in his view that society exists for the perfect. The rest of humanity exist, he explains, in order to provide the physical and social needs of those select few.[44] The significance of different "official" beliefs lies in their role in molding societies that differ in their intellectual orientation and moral climate. A society in which its inhabitants affirm the unity of God, albeit in accordance with their false conceptions of divine unity, fundamentally differs from a society of idolaters. The former provides an environment far more conducive to the attainment of perfection by the elite than does the latter.

The Torah, in Maimonides' thought, addresses itself to everyone, but it is those who are perfect *in potentia* who are its primary concern. The Torah, however, can address this group directly only by means of hints, in order to avoid bringing harm to the others. The hints also serve as a test to determine who really belong to the elite, at the same time that it guides them in the right direction. Though the precise manner in which beliefs are formulated must be determined in light of the social situation, the goal remains forever the same—to bring to intellectual perfection all those with the proper potential, while at the same time ensure the preservation of society and improve its social fabric. It is important to reiterate that the goal is not simply to create a "breathing space" for philosophers so they will not to be disturbed in their endeavors. It is to create an environment that *actively* encourages all those capable of this pursuit. Maimonides sees himself continuing in the path laid down in the Torah.

Elitism characterized Maimonides' political thought throughout his life. This hardly means that the masses are to be ignored or "exploited." The guiding of the masses to the perfection of which they are capable—that is, moral perfection—is a true and worthy goal. Moreover, the individual's ultimate perfection consists of proper governance of others—directing each to the perfection of which that individual is capable of attaining—in addition to one's own intellectual perfection.[45] Those attaining the highest rungs of perfection are driven to care for the needs of the masses as well as those of the elite. They are not cut off from society. They are socially active, even if their minds are constantly turned "upwards." Yet in the final analysis, Maimonides regards the creation of the perfect individual as the final goal of humanity. This task of balancing the needs of the elite with those of society as a whole, to create a situation in which the masses and the elite contribute to each other's existential situation rather than detract from it, called for an exceptionally subtle pedagogical strategy. This strategy finds its expression in Maimonides' various compositions.

VI

The analysis of Maimonides' philosophy presented here raises the question whether he was entirely consistent throughout his literary career in his pedagogical approach. From a broad perspective, the answer is in the affirmative. His early work, the *Commentary on the Mishnah*, particularly the introduction to the tenth chapter of *Sanhedrin (Pereq Ḥeleq),* already reflects the resolution to inculcate a more philosophic conception of God, and to treat this conception as mandated by Jewish law. Maimonides incorporates God's existence, uniqueness, and incorporeality into the principles to be acknowledged by every Jew in order to be considered part of the Jewish people and to attain a portion in the World to Come. Furthermore, he outlines these principles utilizing philosophic conceptions. In *Book of the Commandments*, Maimonides continues this trend by treating the acknowledgment of the uniqueness of God, in addition to God's existence, as the first two positive obligations incumbent upon all of Israel. In the *Mishneh Torah*, he stresses the legal and eschatological significance of proper philosophic knowledge of God with even greater clarity and force. In the *Guide of the Perplexed,* too, he deals at length with knowledge of God, and touches upon legal and pedagogical concerns. Maimonides maintains the necessity of educating the masses to believe in a unique, incorporeal God from whom all the attributes characterizing material entities are to be negated (1:35). He reiterates the cardinal importance of acknowledging God's incorporeality toward the beginning of his subsequent *Treatise on the Resurrection of the Dead.* Yet together with the overall consistency in Maimonides' various compositions marking his legal-pedagogical approach to knowledge of God, there exists an undercurrent of change. His educational strategy underwent certain modifications, at least in emphasis if not substance. The remainder of this chapter is devoted to an outline of some of the changes that characterize Maimonides' approach in this area.

Toward the end of the introduction to his *Commentary on the Mishnah*, Maimonides discusses the issue of human perfection. He is explicit in treating the apprehension of the intelligibles, culminating with the apprehension of God's unity and all that pertains to this apprehension from the science of metaphysics, as the goal of human beings. Maimonides chose to conclude his *Introduction to Pereq Ḥeleq*, an introduction dealing with the subject of reward and eschatology, with an outline of thirteen principles of the Torah. He maintains that denial of any of these principles constitutes heresy, with all the attendant consequences in this world and next. As I have argued, there can be little doubt that the principles serve a pedagogical-political purpose. The enumeration of the principles was not designed to ensure the immortality of all of the adherents. Maimonides' interest was to secure their allegiance to the Torah, as well as to indicate the direction to the proper conception of God that is necessary for achieving immortality.[46]

The first five principles are most concerned with pedagogy since they focus directly on one's concept of God—God's existence, unity, incorporeality, primordiality and that God alone is worthy of worship (against idolatry).[47] Maimonides apparently roots these principles in the Mishnaic pronouncement that the *'epiqoros* has no portion in the World to Come. The other principles are related to the Mishnaic exclusion from the afterlife of those who reject the divine origin of the Torah (revelation) and the resurrection of the dead (reward). This point, however, is far from clear, and even problematic in light of other statements both in talmudic literature and in Maimonides' own writings regarding the notion of *'epiqoros*.[48]

In the first principle, Maimonides describes God as the cause of all existents. All existents are dependent upon God's existence but God's existence is not dependent upon any other existent—a notion whose formulation is reminiscent of Avicenna's doctrine of God as the Necessary Existent.[49] He also indicates in passing that the angels are the Separate Intellects. In the second principle, Maimonides stresses that the unity of God is not like that of the genus or species. Nor is it like a unity that consists of disparate parts, as in the case of the body. It is in every sense a unique unity. The third principle expands upon the notion contained in the second. God is neither body nor a force in a body. He is not subject to the accidents affecting bodies such as motion and rest—a clear reference to the negation of the Aristotelian categories characterizing corporeal entities. The fourth principle treats of God's existence as absolutely without beginning in contradistinction to every other existent. The fifth principle asserts that God alone is to be worshipped, to the exclusion of any of God's intermediaries in the governance of the world. Maimonides adds that this principle is the basis for most of the commandments. Its purpose is to preserve the belief in one God.

The philosophical manner in which these principles are formulated is all the more striking in light of the omission of those descriptions that one would most likely expect to encounter in a traditional work. God is referred to as Creator, but is described as the Cause of all existents. The world is treated as not absolutely primordial when compared to God's existence, but it is not said to be created *ex nihilo*. Maimonides consciously presents his principles in a manner compatible with the philosophic belief in an eternal world.[50] Yet he goes much further than simply skirting the issue of creation in the formulation of his principles. His principles conform to the philosophic conception of God, a conception that finds little support in biblical or rabbinic texts. Maimonides cites biblical proof texts for each of the principles, at times together with rabbinic texts. This lends them the authority of tradition. These proof texts, however, often appear far-fetched. Closer inspection only serves to strengthen this impression.[51] Maimonides explains the misleading use of corporeal descriptions of God in the Torah by referring to the rabbinic dictum: "The Torah speaks in the language of humankind." The use of this dictum, however, is in itself misleading. It is consistently used in the Talmud with reference to the Torah's repetition of terms, particularly in the formulation of certain laws. It is not employed in the context of discussing general theological matters, such as the corporeal descriptions of God.[52] All this highlights Maimonides' boldness in publicly introducing a philosophic conception of God into Jewish tradition, going so far as to dogmatize it. The stance he adopted already in his early writings was that the corporeal conception of God was to be combated and obliterated with the aid of the weapons of Jewish law.

The philosophical conception of God presented in the *Commentary on the Mishnah* is reiterated in greater detail in the first four chapters of the *Laws of the Principles of the Torah* opening the *Mishneh Torah.* God is depicted as the Prime Existent (1:1) and Mover of the outermost sphere (1:5). Maimonides again draws upon Avicenna's notion of God as Necessary Existent in his description of the Deity (1:3-4). Moreover, he offers an abbreviated proof of God's existence and incorporeality based on the notion of the continuous (infinite) motion of the sphere (1:5; 1:7)—a notion that presupposes a world that is eternal *a parte ante*.[53] He negates ascribing corporeality to God, and all the accidents pertaining to corporeal entities including emotions (1:7; 1:11–12). In discussing Moses' request to see God's *Glory* and God's answer that he may not see the divine *face* but may see the divine *back*, Maimonides explains that Moses was not able to apprehend the divine existence "as it is." Moses apprehended the manner in which God is separate from all other existents (1:11). This is a clear allusion to the doctrine of negative attributes.[54] Following Alfarabi and Avicenna, Maimonides sees God as Self-contemplating Intellect, whose knowledge of everything flows from Self-knowledge as the Principle of everything (2:9–10).[55] As in the case of the *Commentary*, he utilizes the rabbinic dictum that the Torah speaks in human terms in order to harmonize the corporeal descriptions of God found in the Bible with the philosophical view of God's incorporeality. God's role in history finds absolutely no expression in these chapters, despite the fact that Maimonides roots the command to know God in the verse, *I am the God your Lord who brought you out of the Land of Egypt from the house of bondage* (Exod. 20:2). In addition to these points, Maimonides presents in an unambiguous manner the doctrine of the emanation of the Separate Intellects one from another (2:11), a doctrine that normally stands in opposition to creation *ex nihilo* and is treated in a contradictory manner in the Guide.[56]

As already indicated, Maimonides equates the knowledge involved in the commandments to know and love God with the esoteric subjects of the *Account of the Chariot* and the *Account of Creation*, which in turn are equated with metaphysics and natural science. He offers a detailed outline of this knowledge, lest there be any misunderstanding on this matter. Maimonides certainly did not feel that everyone can attain the knowledge he outlines, as evidenced by the fact that he equates it with those subjects that can only be known by the select few (2:12; 4:13). It is clear that he framed these chapters for the intellectually perfect *in potentia*, providing them with not too subtle "pointers" to the road to perfection. While some of the positions presented here find expression also in other parts of the *Mishneh Torah*, in no place does he formulate his legal positions in such restrictive manner that only the philosophically educated elite can properly fulfill. Moreover, all the stress in the first four chapters is on knowledge rather than action. Maimonides leaves no doubt that this knowledge is an end in itself—moreover, *the* end—and not just a prerequisite for a certain activity. He makes a conscious effort not to blur the prevailing Aristotelian view that the perfection of the intellect is the perfection of human beings, physical activity being subordinate to this perfection. Only in chapter 5, where he begins to turn to the rest of the commandments—the "small" matters as they are termed by him—does he begin to deal with physical activity.

Maimonides concludes the *Book of Knowledge* (*Laws of Repentance* 10:6), with an explicit reminder to the elite of his position in the *Laws of the Principles of the Torah*. Love is a function of knowledge of God (to the extent of human ability). This is attained through knowledge of the sciences. The individual's goal is the constant contemplation of God. That knowledge of God is of the ultimate importance is also reiterated in Maimonides' ending to the *Mishneh Torah*, *Laws of Kings and their Wars*: "The preoccupation of the entire world will be to know God. Israel will be great sages, knowing the hidden matters and acquiring knowledge of their Creator to the extent of human ability" (12:5).

By depicting the primary legal obligation of the individual in the opening of the *Mishneh Torah* as the attainment of knowledge of the incorporeal God of nature, and describing the ideal situation in the conclusion of the *Mishneh Torah* as one in which all pursue knowledge of God, Maimonides reveals the ultimate purpose of this composition. It is to mold a society in which all are dedicated to the pursuit of knowledge, though only the elite are capable of the metaphysical knowledge that characterizes human perfection. That the vast majority of the *Mishneh Torah* is devoted to technical legal matters hardly contradicts this point. Maimonides indicates in the *Guide* that the Torah communicates the correct opinions by which final perfection is attained only in a summary manner (3:27–28). The primary intention of the Torah, or Maimonides' *Mishneh Torah*, is not to be measured by the amount of space devoted to a certain subject, but by the nobility of the subject itself. In a crucial sense Maimonides wrote the *Mishneh Torah for* its first four chapters—to direct the elite to the proper studies, and to create a social environment supportive of these studies. The *Mishneh Torah* alleviated long years of legal studies to know the law, thereby freeing the elite to concentrate on the knowledge of physics and metaphysics that is necessary for perfection. As Maimonides notes in the introduction to his legal compendium: "A person reads the Written Law first and then reads this [treatise] and knows the entire Oral Law. He does not need to read any other book between these two."[57] Maimonides' primary concern was in redirecting Jewish law to recognize intellectual perfection as its final goal. He was not interested in introducing numerous innovations into the body of the law based on scientific and philosophic considerations.[58] Therefore it should come to no surprise that he opens his work with his most radical legal innovations and leaves the rest of the legal structure fairly intact, limiting most of his creativity to the area of systematization and the manner in which he formulates his rulings.

Between the writing of his *Commentary on the Mishnah* and the *Mishneh Torah*, Maimonides wrote the *Book of the Commandments*.[59] This book was initially intended to serve as a preparatory work for his great legal compendium. The discussion of the commandments is far more brief in the *Book of the Commandments*, as is to be expected given the nature of the work. For all the innovations contained in this work, it is a more conservative work than his subsequent *Mishneh Torah*. The difference between the two works lies not only in their scope, but also in their approach. Maimonides uses different systems of classification in the two works. In the *Book of the Commandments* he also refers to rabbinic as well as to biblical sources for the commandments.[60]

The combination between innovation and conservatism emerges in Maimonides' presentation of the first four positive commandments—knowledge of God's existence, unity, love and awe of God. He refers to God as Cause and Mover, in addition to Agent of all existents, thereby continuing to utilize philosophical terminology. He stresses the importance of knowledge of God by drawing an intrinsic connection between love of God and apprehension of God. Yet he stops short of developing these points in the manner he does in his *Commentary on the Mishnah*, let alone the bolder manner in which he develops them in his *Mishneh Torah*. There is no allusion to the doctrine of God's incorporeality, and what attributes it entails negating of God, in his presentation of the notion of God's unity (positive commandment, no. 2). This stands in sharp contrast to his clear statements on this issue in the other works. While this point may be explained by the sketchy nature of the presentation of the commandments in general in the *Book of the Commandments*, it appears that the omission was not simply due to considerations of brevity. Maimonides purposefully refrained from developing the more philosophical elements of his approach. In his discussion of the commandment to unify God, for example, he treats God's redemption of Israel from slavery, and the other beneficent acts performed by God on Israel's behalf, as intended to instill in us knowledge of God's unity. God is not described as the Lord of nature, but as the Lord of history. Maimonides' move away from a philosophic approach to knowledge of God can also be clearly discerned from his cursory outline of the commandments to love and fear God. No mention is made in this context of the esoteric topics, *Account of the Chariot* and *Account of Creation*, and there is no allusion to the view that a knowledge of the natural sciences and metaphysics is required in order to fulfill these commandments.[61]

Even a careful reading of the *Book of the Commandments* does not reveal any intrinsic connection between philosophical knowledge and fulfillment of the commandments in the area of knowledge of God. In a similar vein, Maimonides' ethical theory, heavily influenced by his philosophic sources, also finds no expression in the *Book of the Commandments*. The Aristotelian "doctrine of the mean" is presented in detail in *Commentary on the Mishnah* (*Eight Chapters* 4), and in *Mishneh Torah: Laws of Character Traits*, chapters 1–2. In the latter source it is integrated into the commandment to imitate God's ways. Yet in presenting this commandment in the *Book of the Commandments* (positive commandment, no. 8), the "doctrine of the mean" is not even mentioned in passing. Maimonides does not contradict the basic ideas presented earlier in his *Commentary on the Mishnah*. There is no reason to conclude that he abandoned any of them. Yet he formulates these commandments in a manner that is closer to a traditional approach, and that would arouse little theological controversy, nor would it pose a stumbling block for their fulfillment on the part of everyone. The conservative nature of this work is all the more underscored by Maimonides' subsequent approach in the *Mishneh Torah*. It appears that some revision took place in his pedagogical strategy between the writing of these two works.

VIII

While the *Commentary on the Mishnah*, *Book of the Commandments*, and *Mishneh Torah* are works intended for the entire Jewish people, the *Guide* is intended only for those who are well versed both in the legal study of Judaism and in philosophy. The perplexity experienced by these individuals results from the contradictions that they encounter between the terms and parables found in the books of the prophets, when understood according to their literal sense, as well as the teachings of Jewish tradition, and between the teachings of the philosophers. The *Guide*, by alleviating the perplexity in revealing the true meanings of the terms and parables, is the "science of the Law in the true sense" (1:Introduction.5).

As Maimonides indicates, he does not only reveal but also conceals. He purposefully introduces contradictions and offers at times only hints to his true views, thereby separating the ideal reader of his work from the uninitiated reader. The danger felt by Maimonides is that certain views when revealed to the uninitiated reader may cause great harm. It may result in the individual's abandonment of Judaism (1:33). This leads him to offer both a far more explicit and detailed discussion of most doctrines of theological import than what is contained in any of his other writings, and a slightly more veiled disclosure of certain views than what emerges from the beginning of the *Laws of the Principles of the Torah*.

Maimonides' basic view of how God is to be conceived appears to have undergone no major revision from his earlier works. What is presented in a brief manner in the *Commentary on the Mishnah* and in the *Mishneh Torah* is elaborated upon in the *Guide*. Most of the first part is devoted to the topic of God's incorporeality. Maimonides offers a detailed exegesis of the corporeal terms used in reference to God. He deals at length with the doctrine of attributes. He presents in detail the doctrine of negative attributes (1:56–60), a doctrine to which he only alludes in some of his other writings.[62] At the same time, he depicts God as the Self-contemplating Intellect (1:68), echoing his presentation in the *Laws of the Principles of the Torah.* As for his pedagogic approach, Maimonides reaffirms the decision to proclaim God's incorporeality, God's not being subject to affects, and the equivocal meaning of the attributes ascribed to God, as beliefs that are to be taught to one and all, each according to the individual's level of comprehension (1:35). That the commandment to love God is fulfilled only through the apprehension of all that exists is also reiterated by Maimonides, at the same time that he refers the reader to his code (3:28).

The one issue concerning knowledge of God on which Maimonides adopts a much more emphatic stance in the *Guide* is that of creation. At stake in the problem of the creation versus the eternity *a parte ante* of the world, according to him, is the issue of how God's will, and by extension God's relation to the world, is to be conceived (2:18–19; 2:22). The possibility of God's performance of miracles and the revelation of the Law follows from God's ability to create (2:25). Belief in eternity is equated with belief that all exists by virtue of necessity (2:13; 2:19; 2:21; 2:25; 2:29). God has no power to modify the customary course of events, or introduce the smallest change into nature. Belief in creation is treated as a principle of Judaism, second only in rank to belief in God's unity (2:13). A denial of creation destroys the very foundations of the Torah (2:23). This position stands in stark contrast to the omission of creation in his initial formulation of the principles of Judaism in the *Introduction to Pereq Ḥeleq*, as well as in the *Laws of the Principles of the Torah.*

It is not sufficient to argue that this principle is implicitly assumed in Maimonides' legal works, and there was no need to mention it explicitly. The same can be said of many of the principles mentioned explicitly by him. Maimonides was certainly aware of his shift in thinking. He gives one indication why he did not mention creation explicitly in his earlier writings. After writing the *Guide*, Maimonides introduces in the *Introduction to Pereq Ḥeleq* an addendum to the fourth principle—God's absolute eternity *a parte ante*: "Know that the great principle of the Law of Moses is the creation of the world by God and that He created it from absolute privation. As for basing myself upon (literally: seeing me turn upon the matter of) the primordiality [of the world] according to the opinion of the philosophers—

this is in order to establish a demonstrative proof for the existence of God, as I explained in the *Guide*."[63]

Maimonides wished to formulate the principles dealing with God's existence in a manner compatible with the philosophic approach for in this manner the truth of God's existence and unity is acknowledged by all in accordance with rational demonstration. Not only does the belief in creation entail the truth of these principles, but so does the belief that the world is primordial. Consistent with the philosophic position, God's primordiality is presented as primordiality in rank, not time. Insofar as all other existents, even those that are considered by the philosophers to be eternal *a parte ante*, depend upon God for their existence, their being without beginning is not absolute. Only God, whose existence is necessitated by the divine essence, is absolutely without beginning—that is, God alone is uncaused.

Yet this rationale does not adequately explain why Maimonides did not initially present creation as a separate principle, nor why only later in the *Guide* did he emphasize creation as a fundamental principle and decide to add this addendum. The *Guide* reflects his awareness that the belief in the God of history—a willing God capable of suspending the natural order in the performance of miracles—remains a crucial component which is dangerous to omit in any teaching about God. The notion of creation *ex nihilo* provides the foundation for this conception of God, though Maimonides attempts to limit the importance and scope of miracles. Maimonides in no work negates this conception. Many of his thirteen principles are rooted in it. Yet neither does he treat it so prominently. In writing the *Guide*, as is the case with his legal works, Maimonides appreciated the importance of presenting the proper balance between both conceptions—that is, the incorporeal God of nature and the God of miracles. Maimonides' *Treatise on Resurrection*, written subsequent to the *Guide*, continues this trend. While God's incorporeality and governance by means of the order of nature continue to be taught, God's miracle-making powers is even more forcefully stressed, as in keeping with the dual purpose of this work.[64]

Several alternative (though compatible) explanations can be offered for Maimonides' decision to stress the importance of creation in the *Guide*. The first concerns the audience of the work. The *Guide*, in contradistinction to the other works mentioned, was written for an audience versed in philosophy. Maimonides' goal was to inculcate in his readers an appreciation of the harmony that exists between Judaism and philosophy. He was aware, however, that the book may fall into the "wrong hands." Hence it was important to hide certain views behind a maze of contradictions and hints. But whose hands are the wrong ones? Certainly those of the fundamentalists for whom a philosophic understanding of certain topics, particularly those involving God and God's relation to humanity, was looked upon as anathema to revealed religion. Another group from whom Maimonides might have had to hide his true opinions consists of those who would accept his philosophic interpretations but come to the wrong conclusion regarding their significance. As a result they would abandon Judaism. This group consists not only of those belonging to the "masses" who have no philosophic background, but also those who have some background. There is a danger that just as those steeped in philosophy may abandon Judaism for being opposed to philosophy (analogous to the fundamentalists who denounce philosophy for standing opposed to Judaism), they may abandon it for being reduced to philosophy. Why maintain allegiance to the Law if philosophy provides the road to final perfection?

It was thus important, at least on an exoteric level, to emphasize the basic areas of disagreement between philosophy and Judaism, in addition to the many areas of agreement. Maimonides focused on the single most important issue to which the other areas of disagreement can be traced—creation. God's role in history, providential activity as expressed in miracles, God's unique revelation to Moses—in general, the personal God of Jewish tradition—all have their foundation in the principle of God the Creator. Given the nature and audience of the *Guide*, Maimonides provides an extensive philosophic argumentation in defense of this principle.

Maimonides' prior works, on the other hand, were written for the general reader for whom this point was not even open to question. Maimonides continuously employs this belief, or those deriving from it, with no need to place upon it undue stress. It is his novel philosophical views, the ones that pertain to the incorporeal God of nature, that require emphasis, at least in select passages. One may say that while in his prior works Maimonides desires to direct the masses to a more philosophical conception of God, in the *Guide* he wishes to preserve for his readers a nonphilosophic conception that is the basis of revelatory religion.

One may argue that belief in creation is stressed by Maimonides in the *Guide* not only in that it is a central doctrine of Judaism that is rejected by the philosophers. It is also a true doctrine about God. Apprehension of it thus is important in the attainment of intellectual perfection. It is interesting to note, however, that for all the apparent theoretical importance of the question of creation for one's conception of God, Maimonides does not explicitly make this point. He does not include the issue of creation in his outline of natural sciences and metaphysics in the *Laws of the Principles of the Torah*.[65] Not even in the *Guide* does he indicate that acceptance of creation contributes to the true conception of God necessary for the perfection of the intellect.[66]

Maimonides may have believed that creation *ex nihilo* is a true doctrine, though it is questionable whether this is the case.[67] Ultimately it is not the question of the truth of this doctrine that so much concerns him. Creation is a pedagogically necessary doctrine. It is to be accepted because it contributes to belief in a deity who exercises providence. This in turn is the basis for the adherence to the Law on the part of the masses and less astute students of philosophy (2:23). The more mature students of philosophy do not require belief in creation as a basis for their commitment for they appreciate the intrinsic worth of the Law as such (2:39–40).

For many, belief in creation is necessary for the very acceptance of the notion of a single incorporeal deity. Maimonides alludes to this point in the course of his introduction to the proof for the existence of God: "If it [the world] is created in time it undoubtedly has a creator who created it in time. For it is a first intelligible that what has appeared at a certain moment in time has not created itself in time and that its creator is other than itself. Accordingly the creator who created the world in time is the deity" (1:71.181). The proof for the existence of God based on the premise that the world is eternal is a more subtle proof, one that is far more difficult to grasp. Furthermore, Maimonides ascribes belief in the eternity of the world not only to the philosophers but also to the idolaters of old, the Sabians. While the philosophers derive the unity and incorporeality of God from the world's eternity, the Sabians drew an entirely different conclusion from this doctrine. For the Sabians, belief in the eternity of the world was integrally related to belief that the heavens are the deity. They sought to fortify the doctrine of the eternity of the world, Maimonides maintains, "so that it should follow that the stars and the sphere are the deity" (3:29.516). It follows from Maimonides' analysis that to fortify belief in God it was important to promulgate the doctrine of creation. The continuation of his remarks are significant in this regard: "He [Abraham] began to refute their doctrine and to show up their opinions as false; he publicly manifested his disagreement with them and called *in the name of God, Lord of the world*—both the existence of the deity and the creation of the world in time by that deity being comprised in that call."[68]

There is an additional explanation for Maimonides' emphasis on the doctrine of creation in the *Guide*. One can detect in his works a subtle vacillation in the concept of God that he attempts to inculcate. Maimonides assumes a very bold philosophical stance in his *Commentary on the Mishnah*, yet modifies it significantly in his *Book of the Commandments*. He apparently felt that a more conservative stance was called for in a strict legal work. In writing the *Mishneh Torah* he again reversed himself and presents in the opening section of the work his boldest philosophical conception of God and interpretation of Judaism. This clearly reflects his dissatisfaction with the stance he adopted in the *Book of the Commandments*. Perhaps he felt that if this philosophical conception were not clearly and forcefully presented, the ultimate purpose of Judaism as he understood it would be forgotten. This would indeed justify his approach despite the manifold dangers involved. The *Guide*, in its discussions of public education, reiterates this basic stance. Yet the notion of the divine will expressing itself independently of a fixed primordial order, as signified by creation, is given greater emphasis. This notion also underlies Maimonides' addendum to the fourth principle in his *Introduction to Pereq Ḥeleq*. Belief in creation essentially serves to bolster most of the subsequent principles dealing with the divine origin of Torah and divine reward, as well as the masses' belief in an incorporeal deity "beyond" the heavens. Maimonides goes to great lengths to restrain his readers from drawing too many conclusions from the doctrine of creation in regard to God's personal governance. Yet he appreciates the fact that this doctrine is essential for Jewish observance, and must be given its due.

Maimonides' stance in his later works may also reflect his desire to fend off attacks accusing him of the heresy—a point that certainly is important for understanding his *Treatise on Resurrection*.[69] Yet it is not so much his desire to prove his "orthodoxy" that ultimately stands at the root of his defense of creation and miracles. Rather, it is his desire to preserve the "orthodoxy" of others, at the same time that he disturbs this "orthodoxy" by inculcating philosophic conceptions and redefining Judaism accordingly.

One can keenly feel Maimonides' disappointment, almost sense of failure, that emerges from his discussion in the *Treatise on Resurrection*. It is not without bitter irony, of which Maimonides was painfully conscious, that he was forced into a situation in which he had to defend belief in the creator God who works miracles and will restore the dead to their corporeal existence. All his life he devoted his major pedagogical efforts in trying to promote a more philosophical understanding of reality. The notion of a corporeal deity was to be replaced by the notion of an incorporeal one. The view of angels as special heavenly corporeal beings that were created by

God and sent on different missions was to be replaced by the view of angels as the forces of nature, the spheres and the planets, and most important, the incorporeal Separate Intellects. The view of a corporeal afterlife was to be replaced by a view of the immortality of the incorporeal intellect. The view that extols God's governance of the world by means of miraculous acts was to give way to an appreciation of a deity who governs the world by means of the impersonal order of nature. The incorporeal and the natural, instead of the corporeal and the supernatural, were to be the notions that characterize the approach to reality on the part of increasingly growing circles of Jews. Perhaps no passage better captures this point than Maimonides' exclamation in the *Guide* in the course of his discussion of divine governance:

> How great is the blindness of ignorance and how harmful! If you told a man who is one of those who deem themselves *the Sages of Israel* that the deity sends an angel, who enters the womb of a woman and forms the fetus there, he would be pleased with this assertion and would accept it and would regard it as a manifestation of greatness and power on the part of the deity, and also His wisdom may He be exalted. Nevertheless he would also believe at the same time that the *angel* is a body formed of burning fire and that his size is equal to that of a third part of the whole world. He would regard all this as possible with respect to God. But if you tell him that God has placed in the sperm a formative force shaping the limbs and giving them their configuration that this force is the *angel*, or that all the forms derive from the act of the Active Intellect and that the latter is the *angel* and the *prince of the world* constantly mentioned by the *Sages*, the man would shrink from this opinion. For he does not understand the notion of the true greatness and power that consists in the bringing into existence of forces active in a thing, forces that cannot be apprehended by any sense. (2:6.264)

At the end, however, Maimonides had to bow to the reality of the situation. His earlier more optimistic assessment of how far the masses (which from his perspective include the rabbinic scholars of his period) can be weaned away from their preoccupation with corporeal reality and God's miraculous activity proved false. Their resistance to moving in the direction of holding greater esteem for incorporeal reality and God's governance through the order of nature proved too great. Maimonides had to compromise with the belief of the masses far more than he had thought necessary. The time was still far from ripe to cease stressing the corporeal and the miraculous.

Throughout the treatise one sees how Maimonides makes a final effort to change the peoples' thought patterns before surrendering to the demands of the current situation. The World to Come is an incorporeal state of existence, he reiterates, before going on to defend the belief in a physical existence after death that was essential for the masses. Even if they want to think of the World to Come in corporeal terms, let them do so he declares.[70] The angels are incorporeal beings Maimonides reaffirms. Yet if the masses could only believe in angels as corporeal beings, then they should be allowed to continue to hold on to this belief he maintains. Maimonides makes a further attempt to limit in the minds of the masses the scope of God's miraculous activity. He realizes, however, that if the deity of creation and miracles is the foundation for their acceptance of Judaism this doctrine had to be defended with even greater vigor. Only on one issue does he draw the line and refuse to tolerate any compromise. No doctrine that implies that God is corporeal is to be accepted.

The gamut of Maimonides' Jewish writings reveals the constant attempt to balance the desire to inculcate the philosophic conception of God with the need to maintain allegiance to Jewish tradition rooted in the notion of a personal divine will that expresses itself also by way of miracles. The merging and balancing between the two conceptions of God—the incorporeal God of nature and the God of creation and history—in itself says little about Maimonides' own conception of God. The fact that he presents the incorporeal God of nature as the object of knowledge for the one striving for human perfection is of greater significance in determining the relative value of these two conceptions of God in his thought. Maimonides' attempt to balance these two conceptions should be evaluated from a pedagogic standpoint—what conception of God did he wish to inculcate that would best preserve Judaism and enable it to achieve its ultimate goal. It is this consideration that also underlies the subtle changes in his various works of how God is to conceived.

SEVEN

THE LOVE AND FEAR OF GOD

I

It is commanded to love and fear the glorious and awesome Deity as it is stated: *You shall love your Lord God* (Deut. 6:4), and it is stated: *Your Lord God you shall fear* (Deut. 6:13). What is the way to love Him and fear Him? When a person contemplates His wondrous and great works *(ma'asav)* and creatures, and sees through them His infinite wisdom, he immediately loves and extols and experiences a great desire to know the great God, as David said: *My soul thirsts for the Lord, the living Deity* (Psalms 42:3). And when he thinks of these matters themselves, he immediately recoils from fear and terror. He knows he is a small, lowly, dark creature, with an insignificant and limited intellect, who stands before the Perfect Intellect, as David said: *When I behold Your heavens, the work of Your fingers . . . what is humanity that You shall be mindful of them* (Psalms 8:4–5). In accordance with these matters, I will elucidate in general terms upon the works of the Lord of Eternity so that they may provide an opening for the sagacious individual to love God. Our sages have stated in the matter of love [of God] (*Sifre va-Ethanan*, 8): "In this way you become acquainted with the 'One who spoke, and the world was'."

With these words Maimonides opens the second chapter of the *Laws of the Principles of the Torah.*[1] Love is bound with desire. Yet instead of directing it to physical objects, there is a commandment to direct it to God. The only way to experience this love, according to Maimonides, is by means of intellectual apprehension. One can truly love only that with which one is intimately acquainted. Otherwise one loves a figment of one's imagination that has no reality. Since Maimonides regards the essence of God as unfathomable, he treats knowledge of the order of existence of which God is the agent as the way open to humanity to gain the requisite apprehension of God. From this apprehension love inevitably follows. Just as the love of God is unique in Maimonides' view, so is the fear of God. The type of fear depicted by him is an intellectual one. It is the fear one experiences in understanding one's place in the world in comparison to those beings which are above. It is not fear of harm or punishment. Maimonides enumerates the love and fear of God as two separate commandments. At the same time he treats them as two sides of the same coin. They are two states that are intrinsically bound together, with the path to both of them being one.

The commandments to love God and fear God come immediately after the commandments to know that God exists, not to entertain the notion that there is another god, and to know that God is one. Maimonides groups these five commandments together, and devotes to them the first four chapters of his great legal compendium, the *Mishneh Torah*. In these chapters he brings a detailed summary of Aristotelian metaphysics and natural science. He identifies the content of these four chapters with the *Account of the Chariot* and the *Account of the Beginning*, discussed by the sages in the talmudic tractate *Ḥagigah*.[2] The apprehension of these subjects enables a person to grasp God's existence and unity and leads to true love and fear.

The uniqueness of these commandments does not lie only in the special nature of their content. Their uniqueness is also due to the faculty of the soul by means of which they are fulfilled. Only these commandments are fulfilled solely by the activity of the intellect. They involve no physical act at all (or abstention from physical activity), not even speech. The love and fear of God are not analogous to the ethical virtues that are later treated by Maimonides in *Laws of Character Traits*. The ethical virtues belong to the appetitive faculty of the soul, the same faculty that is responsible for one's behavior in general. It should be stressed that Maimonides posits a categorical difference between the love of God as he presents this commandment in the *Laws of the Principles of the Torah*, and the love of one's fellow Jew and of the convert, which are included among the commandments discussed in the *Laws of Character Traits*. He explicitly distinguishes between the commandments concerning the ethical virtues and those involving correct opinions. In the latter category he lists the love and fear of God.[3]

In this chapter I would like to address a number of issues that emerge from Maimonides' view of the love and fear of God. One immediate question that is raised by his radical intellectual stance is whether he was consistent throughout his works on how he views the love and fear of God, or does he present different approaches in different contexts?[4] On this point we shall see that significant changes in his approach to these notions can be detected. These changes raise the further problem why he decided to revise his stance.

Maimonides approaches the love and fear of God not only as concepts that belong to the realm of Jewish thought, but ones that also belong to Jewish law in the strict sense of the term. They are enumerated among the

613 commandments of the Torah. They are given a definition that is presented as a *legal* one, not only a philosophical one. No legal authority ever operates in a vacuum. To attain an appreciation of the Maimonides' achievement, one must strive to gain a clearer view of the inevitable play between the continuity with the past and the forging of new paths that characterizes his approach. His approach must be seen in light of the sources at his disposal. This leads to the problem of what were Maimonides' legal sources for his approach? Was he introducing a far reaching legal innovation or was he essentially continuing in the path of a legal tradition that was already established? Bound up with this problem is the question whether there are sources in Jewish tradition that treat the love and fear of God in a similar manner even from a nonpurely legal perspective.

No less significant is the issue of what traces does Maimonides' approach to love and fear at the beginning of the *Mishneh Torah* leave on his treatment of other, related topics in his legal compendium. In other words, to what degree does he integrate the stance he presents in the first four chapters of *Mishneh Torah* into the rest of his work? By an exploration of these issues one gains a far better perspective for viewing the subtleties of Maimonides' thought precisely in the area in which philosophy and law in his view intertwine.

II

The relation between knowledge of God and love of God is not alien to rabbinic literature. Maimonides refers to the passage in the *Sifre* in the quotation from the *Laws of the Principles of the Torah* cited above. In the *Book of the Commandments*, he brings a longer citation of the passage from the *Sifre* in elucidating upon the commandment to love God: "In the language of the *Sifre*: 'Since it says: *You shall love your Lord God*—do I know how to love God [lit. the Place]? The text teaches us: *And these words that I command you this day shall be in your heart*—in this way you become acquainted with 'The One who spoke and the world was'" (Positive Commandment, no. 3).[5]

As is customary for Maimonides when dealing with topics that are directly related to his core philosophy, he interprets the words of the sages in a manner that is far from literal. A number of researchers have already pointed out the significant difference between his approach in the *Laws of the Principles of the Torah* and the passage in the *Sifre* that serves as his proof text.

The *Sifre* maintains that by knowing the commandments one arrives at a love of God. Maimonides, on the other hand, insists that the way to love God is by contemplation of "His wondrous and great works and creatures"—that is, the order of existence. No explicit mention is made of the commandments in this context. His formulation in the *Book of the Commandments*—a work that served as a preparatory work for the writing of *Mishneh Torah*—is closer to the position presented in the *Sifre:* "The third commandment is that we are commanded to love Him, may He be exalted. We must contemplate and reflect upon his commandments, decrees, and works." Not only does Maimonides explicitly enumerate "commandments and decrees" as objects of contemplation, but he refrains from explicitly mentioning "creatures."[6] Moreover, in this context he does not identify the content of the requisite knowledge with the *Account of the Chariot* and the *Account of the Beginning* as he does in the *Laws of the Principles of the Torah.* The differences between his two works in the formulation of his position indicate that he was conscious of the changes he introduces. In the *Laws of the Principles of the Torah,* Maimonides wishes to stress in no uncertain terms that one fulfills the commandment to love God by means of the apprehension of the sciences, and in no other manner.[7]

Maimonides concludes the fourth chapter of the *Laws of the Principles of the Torah* with a clear presentation of his position. Once again he offers us an illuminative example of his radical exegesis of the position of the sages.

> And the content of these four chapters that deal with these five commandments is what the early sages termed *pardes* [lit., orchard]. . . . And I maintain that it is inappropriate for anyone to stroll in the orchard unless the individual has filled his belly with bread and wine. "Bread and wine" signify knowledge of what is prohibited, permitted, and so forth in regard to the other commandments. The sages termed the latter matters, "a small matter," for they said (*Sukah* 28b): "A great matter—the *Account of the Chariot*; a small matter—the legal disputations of Abbaye and Raba." Nonetheless, it is appropriate to commence with them for they bring about peace of mind *(miyashvim da'ato shel 'adam)* at the outset. Moreover, they are the great good that God bequeathed in order to inhabit this world so that life in the World to Come may be attained. Everyone is capable of knowing them—old and young, male and female, one of broad intelligence and one of narrow intelligence.

Pardes is not treated by Maimonides as a figurative representation for a celestial place—that is, paradise. He regards it as signifying certain areas of knowledge, which he equates with the *Account of the Chariot* and the *Ac-*

count of the Beginning.[8] These subjects, in turn, are identified with Aristotelian metaphysics and natural science. One who reads the sages' explications of the *Account of the Chariot* and the *Account of the Beginning* in the second chapter of tractate *Ḥagigah* would have excusable difficulty in seeing any relation between the descriptions of these subjects and the Aristotelian sciences. Maimonides' reply is that the Torah in the presentation of the *Account of the Beginning*, Ezekiel in the presentation of the *Account of the Chariot,* and the sages in their explications of these two accounts all employ figurative language. The key to understanding these accounts in a nonfigurative manner, in Maimonides' view, is provided by the works of the Aristotelian philosophers.[9]

No less audacious is Maimonides' move to identify all the other commandments of the Torah with the "disputations of Abbaye and Raba." This identification finds no justification from the talmudic text. The text refers to conflicting legal arguments concerning details of the laws, not to knowledge of the basic laws themselves. Maimonides' subtly presented exegesis comes to lend authoritative rabbinic support to the view that the knowledge of the commandments is a "small matter" in comparison to the knowledge of the sciences or *pardes*. The latter knowledge is necessary for the fulfillment of the commandments contained in the first four chapters of the *Laws of the Principles of the Torah.* These commandments essentially involve the perfection of the intellect, the *telos* or final purpose of the individual in Aristotelian thought. All the other commandments are seen by Maimonides as stepping stones to this end.

This point is important for understanding another change that Maimonides introduces in formulating the commandment to love God in the *Laws of the Principles of the Torah* in comparison with his earlier formulation in the *Book of the Commandments*, positive commandment no. 3. In the latter work he writes: "They [the sages] have already indicated that this commandment includes our calling upon all human beings to worship and believe in God." Maimonides' source, the *Sifre*, also emphasizes the practical dimension of the love of God (*Va-Ethanan*, 8): "*And these words that I command you this day shall be in your heart*—in this way you become acquainted with the 'One who spoke, and the world was' and cling to His ways."[10] Maimonides brings an additional quote from the *Sifre:* "In the words of the *Sifre*: *You shall love God*—make Him beloved by the people as did Abraham your father."[11] In Maimonides' description of this commandment in the *Laws of the Principles of the Torah* the mention of any form of external activity is absent. Only the internal, intellectual dimension is present.

He thereby deters his readers from seeing in any external act, no matter how important it may be, a fulfillment of the commandment. This stance should not be seen as reflecting a change in his view that the love of God greatly influences the activity of the individual, especially the public activity. There are many indications both in the *Mishneh Torah* and in the *Guide of the Perplexed* that he continued to hold this view. This is especially true of those places in which he deals with prophetic perfection, in particular the perfection of Abraham.[12] The change in Maimonides' description of the commandment in the *Laws of the Principles of the Torah* stems from pedagogical concerns. There he attempts to underscore the notion that love itself follows solely from intellectual apprehension. No additional idea that may blur this point is included in his formulation of the commandment.

One further difference between Maimonides' approach in the *Laws of the Principles of the Torah* and his approach in the *Book of the Commandments* concerns the commandment to fear God. Maimonides opens the *Book of the Commandments* with fourteen principles for establishing whether a commandment is from the Torah. In his presentation of the ninth principle he lists fear of God among the commandments of the Torah that belong to the category of true opinions. Yet in his subsequent discussion of this commandment (positive commandment no. 4), he mentions only fear of punishment: "We should anticipate the coming of God's punishment at all times." In his *Commentary on the Mishnah*, which antedates both compositions, Maimonides also fails to mention the fear of God that results from the individual's intellectual apprehension. There he relates fear of God to the attainment of the moral virtues, in addition to referring to the fear of punishment. The former type of fear, according to him, precedes the apprehension of the truth and is a necessary condition for it.[13] The fear he describes is the fear of moral failing before the divine presence. This fear is a prerequisite for intellectual as well as moral excellence. It stands between the intellectual awe described in the *Laws of the Principles of the Torah* and the more common type of fear of punishment that is presented in the *Book of the Commandments*. It should be added that Maimonides' approach to love of God in the *Commentary on the Mishnah* is essentially the same as his approach in the *Laws of the Principles of the Torah*. He ties the love of God with the speculative virtues and the apprehension of the truth.[14] In summary, Maimonides' presentation of the notions of love and fear of God underwent a number of significant revisions in his legal works. Worthy of note is the fact that he begins developing his extreme intellectualist approach already in the *Commentary on the Mishnah*, retreats to a more popular approach in the *Book of the Commandments*, and subsequently presents his most extreme intellectualist approach at the beginning of the *Mishneh Torah.*[15]

III

If one should not regard Maimonides' citations from the *Sifre* more than an attempt to supply some justification from authoritative traditional texts for his approach to the love of God, the question remains what were the sources from which he drew his view. It is not my intent to deal here with the non-Jewish sources that strongly influenced Maimonides' thought and in which one can find the love and fear of God tied to the apprehension of God. Ibn Bajja's approach, for example, bears important points of resemblance to that of Maimonides.[16] Maimonides' major contribution in this area is not in the realm of theoretical philosophy, but in the manner in which he interprets the Jewish legal tradition in the light of his philosophy. From this perspective, it is important to see to what extent he drew from attempts of Jewish thinkers before him to view the love and fear of God as divine commandments, and the apprehension of the sciences as the way to fulfill them.

The great tenth-century thinker and legal authority, R. Saadiah Gaon, mentions the love and fear of God in his ground breaking theological treatise, *The Book of Beliefs and Opinions*, a treatise that was known to Maimonides.[17] R. Saadiah concludes his discussion of God's unity in the second part with a description of the importance of this subject:

> Now when a person has achieved the knowledge of this lofty subject by means of rational speculation *(al-naṣra)* and the proof of the miracles and marvels [mentioned in Holy Writ], his soul believes it as true and it is mingled with his spirit and becomes an inmate of its innermost recesses. The result is then that, whenever the soul walks in its temple, it finds it. . . . Moreover, his soul becomes filled with completely sincere love for God, a love which is beyond all doubt, as Scripture expresses it: *And thou shalt love the Lord thy God with all thy heart*, etc. (Deut. 6:5). That servant of God will also grow accustomed to remembering God in the daytime when he does his work and at night when he lies on his bed. . . . Nay it will almost speak—I mean the spirit—moaning [lit., lovesick] at the recollection of God, out of longing and yearning. . . . The more it [the spirit] contemplates His being, the more does it fear and revere Him, as Scripture says: *Therefore am I frightened in His presence; when I consider, I am afraid of Him* (Job 23:15). Also the more it considers His attributes, the greater becomes its praise of Him and the more does it

rejoice in Him. . . . Thus it reaches a point where it loves those that love Him and honors those that honor Him. . . . In this way is it induced to take up His cause and to refute everyone that raises arguments against Him, by the employment of reason *('aql)* and knowledge *(ma'arafa),* not with harshness. . . . It will furthermore laud and praise Him justly and uprightly, not by attributing Him exaggerations and absurdities.[18]

The section dealing with the unity of God comes after the section in which R. Saadiah proves the existence of a single deity. In this manner he shows that the path to the true love of God is by way of knowledge of the existence of God, that there are no other gods, and that God is the incorporeal One. Despite the fact that R. Saadiah mentions the miracles as a means for arriving at the knowledge leading to love of God, it is clear from this passage that speculation plays a more prominent role in this matter. Only by way of speculation, as his subsequent remarks reveal, can one praise God, "justly and uprightly, not by attributing Him exaggerations and absurdities." The similarity between Maimonides' view of the intellectual fear of God and R. Saadiah's approach to fear is also clearly discernible from this passage. The more the individual contemplates God, "the more does he fear and revere Him."

One should not overlook the major differences between these two approaches. Unlike Maimonides' stance in the *Laws of the Principles of the Torah*, but reminiscent of his stance in the *Book of the Commandments*, R. Saadiah emphasizes the public activity to which love of God leads. The individual attempts to educate others in this belief by means of rational argumentation. The passage from the *Sifre* dealing with Abraham, which was cited by Maimonides in the *Book of the Commandments*, influenced R. Saadiah as well. In the *Laws of the Principles of the Torah*, as we have seen, Maimonides refrains from any mention of the public activity associated with love. A more basic difference between the two thinkers lies in the fact that Maimonides, heavily influenced by the Aristotelian philosophic tradition, sees in medieval Aristotelian metaphysics and natural science the requisite knowledge for attaining true love of God. R. Saadiah, who borrows heavily from the theology of the *Kalam*, agrees with the Aristotelian philosophic position in regard to the unity of God, but not the structure of the world.[19] Nor does he mention knowledge of the structure of the world as a necessary condition for attaining love of God.

The most important difference between the two approaches is the legal one. Maimonides enumerates the love and fear of God among the commandments of the Torah. R. Saadiah did not write a legal treatise in which he enumerates the commandments of the Torah. He wrote, however, liturgical poems that include and arrange all the 613 commandments.[20] In one of the poems he opens with fear of God followed by the worship of God in prayer.[21] It is clear that the source for this view is Deut. 6:13: *Your Lord God you shall fear and Him you shall worship*, the same source cited by Maimonides. R. Saadiah, however, does not enumerate the love of God as an independent commandment. He may have regarded it as being included in the commandment to fear God. In a different liturgical poem he writes: "Fear the Master and love Him."[22] Unfortunately, it is not possible to deduce from these poems how he defines the fear of God from a legal standpoint. There is no strong basis for the assumption that his definition would have conformed to his description of fear in his theological treatise. It is interesting to note that R. Saadiah also does not regard knowledge of God's existence as an independent commandment. Neither is the commandment to believe in the unity of God enumerated as a separate commandment. We see from R. Saadiah's liturgical poetry that it is fulfilled by way of the commandment to recite the *Shema* (*Hear O Israel, God is our Lord God is One*—Deut. 6:4).[23] This suggests that R. Saadiah did not consider the fulfillment of any of the commandments as involving the intellect alone, no matter how important the role of the intellect may be in his view of Judaism.[24]

Even closer to Maimonides' approach is that of R. Baḥya Ibn Paquda. R. Baḥya is situated between R. Saadiah and Maimonides not only chronologically but also philosophically. It is almost certain that Maimonides was well acquainted with R. Baḥya's *Duties of the Heart* and drew from it, as the many points of similarity between his compositions and this treatise indicate.[25] R. Baḥya distinguishes between the "duties of the limbs" and the "duties of the heart." He devotes his treatise to the latter duties, and views them as mandated both by intellect and the Torah.

Two of the duties that R. Baḥya mentions are the love and fear of God. The list of the "duties of the heart" is not confined by R. Baḥya to matters that are to be intellectually apprehended, but does include such matters. At the head of the list he enumerates the existence of God and the unity of God. He elaborates on this point as follows: "Knowing for certain that the Creator is the only one who is real, indescribable either by substance or by accident, I recognized the limitations of the mind which cannot conceive of anything indescribable either by substance or by accident. I realized then that it would be impossible for us to conceive of Him by way of His essence and I saw that we must know Him and conceive of His existence by way of His creatures" (Introduction.103).

The last section of the treatise deals with the subject of true love of God. R. Baḥya views the love of God as the, "highest stage and the supreme rank for those who obey God" (10:Introduction.426). All the virtues are treated as stepping-stones to this state. R. Baḥya defines love as the "yearning of the soul, the desire of its very substance to be attached *(tittiṣāl)* to God's supreme light" (10:1.427).[26] In this definition R. Baḥya approaches the Neoplatonic worldview, characteristic also of Sufi mystical thought, that sees in the ontological conjunction of the soul with the higher world its final end.[27] This demands the purification of the soul from all its physical inclinations that distract it from focusing solely on God. In a similar Neoplatonic vein, R. Baḥya proceeds to explain: "The soul is a simple spiritual substance which inclines by its nature to the spiritual beings that are like itself, and rejects by its nature the coarse bodies which are unlike it" (10:1.427).

R. Baḥya explicitly maintains that this love is dependent upon the intellectual apprehension of God's unity. He indicates that this is the reason for the order of the notions in the *Shema*, where love of God (Deut. 6:5) immediately follows knowledge of God's unity (Deut. 6:4).[28] R. Baḥya lists three different types of love of a servant for a master. The most supreme type is described as love for a master, "for his greatness and superiority, out of reverence for his very person and honor, neither from fear nor from hope" (10:2.429).

In the same section R. Baḥya deals also with the fear of God. He regards this fear as, "the goal of asceticism, its supreme end, and the stage closest to that of the love of God" (10:Introduction.427). Fear of God is divided into two types: fear of punishment; and fear that "is based on reverence and awe, on the glorification and exaltation of God's omnipotence . . . this is the gate to the pure love of God and to passionate desire for Him" (10:6.436).[29] In contrast to Maimonides' approach in the *Laws of the Principles of the Torah*, R. Baḥya does not view the love and fear of God as two sides of the same coin. Instead, he arranges them in hierarchical order. Nonetheless, the close affinity between the two approaches is evident. Both thinkers regard true fear as consequent upon the intellectual apprehension of God. Parallels between Maimonides' approach to the relation between love and fear of God, worship and martyrdom and R. Baḥya's approach to the connection between these matters are also noteworthy and should not be overlooked.[30]

The differences in the philosophical conceptions of reality from which these two thinkers drew result in a lack of agreement between them on the particulars of the speculative knowledge that is necessary in order to apprehend God. More significant, however, is the difference in the nature of the compositions themselves. *Duties of the Heart* is not a legal composition in the strict sense of the term. R. Baḥya certainly regards all the matters that he includes in his treatise as duties that obligate a Jew from the standpoint of the Torah and tradition, in addition to the intellect. Yet he makes the point that his treatise is not designed to list and summarize the commandments of the Torah, in contrast to such compositions that already existed in his own day (Introduction). R. Baḥya goes so far as to maintain that while the duties of the Torah are the 613 commandments, the duties of the intellect—which are primarily the "duties of the heart"—are almost infinite in number (3:3). He views his treatise as filling a significant vacuum in the Jewish world by dealing with the latter duties, which he treats as the more important ones.

Maimonides, on the other hand, intended his compositions to serve as summaries of the commandments of the Torah. He may have drawn a number of important ideas from *Duties of the Heart*, but he would not have considered this work a valid *legal* source for the view that the love and fear of God are commandments of the Torah in the technical sense of the term. The two thinkers share much in common in their approach to Judaism. Maimonides follows R. Baḥya in broadening the realm of the law to include both intellectual apprehension and traits of the soul. As opposed to R. Baḥya, he does not accomplish this by creating new legal categories, but by adding to the content of the traditional categories.

The legal work that presents a view closest to that of Maimonides is R. Ḥefeṣ b. Yaṣliaḥ's *Book of Precepts*. This work is a compilation of the 613 commandments, but only fragments of it have survived.[31] Maimonides at times refers to this work, indicating his intimate acquaintance with it.[32] A partial citation of the two opening commandments is brought by R. Judah b. Barzilay of Barcelona in his *Commentary on the Book of Creation*. These commandments are to know that God exists and that God is one.[33] If the opening of the *Book of Precepts* is reminiscent of the manner in which Maimonides opens both of his legal compilations, a fragment that almost certainly represents the continuation of R. Ḥefeṣ's work strengthens the connection between these two legal authorities. R. Ḥefeṣ lists the love of God as the third commandment, fear of God as the fourth, and worship of God as the fifth.[34] Maimonides' indebtedness to R. Ḥefeṣ on the content and order of the commandments with which he opens his legal compositions is apparent.

At the same time, one significant legal difference between the two can be discerned. At the beginning of the fragment is the conclusion of the second commandment, in which the laws of the recitation of the *Shema* are discussed. R. Ḥefeṣ sees in the recitation of the *Shema* a fulfillment of the commandment to believe that God is one. In this matter his approach is similar to that of R. Saadiah.[35] Maimonides, on the other hand, counts these two matters—that is, knowledge of God's unity and the recitation of the *Shema*—as separate commandments.

Maimonides in the *Book of the Commandments* follows R. Ḥefeṣ in listing the worship of God as the commandment that immediately follows the fear of God. As opposed to R. Ḥefeṣ, however, he interprets worship of God as prayer. R. Ḥefeṣ too sees in prayer a commandment of the Torah, but enumerates it as the seventh commandment (after the commandment to remove the impurities and obstacles from our hearts in order to submit ourselves totally to God and His commandments).[36] The worship of God, on the other hand, is defined by R. Ḥefeṣ as the command to martyr oneself when the situation demands self-sacrifice. Maimonides includes this law in the commandment to sanctify the Name of God. In the *Laws of the Principles of the Torah* he lists this commandment immediately after the commandments to love and fear God. In summary, in respect to the title of the commandment that follows the fear of God, Maimonides' *Book of the Commandments* is similar to R. Ḥefeṣ's *Book of Precepts*. In respect to the *content* of the commandment that follows fear of God, Maimonides' *Laws of the Principles of the Torah* is similar to R. Ḥefeṣ's compilation. The major difference between Maimonides and R. Ḥefeṣ on this issue is that Maimonides deals with love and fear of God together, while R. Ḥefeṣ deals with the fear and worship of God together, in accordance with Deut. 6:13.

R. Ḥefeṣ defines the command to love God as follows:

> After attaining knowledge of the unity of the essence of the Creator, we are obligated to love the divine essence with all our being and with all our possessions as it is stated: *You shall love your Lord God.* Our sages said in explaining this [verse]: "Make Him beloved by the people as did Abraham your father." . . . *With all your heart*—with both your inclinations, your good inclination and evil inclination. *With all your soul*—in purifying the rational part of the of the soul's faculties, by which we know our Creator.[37]

In light of the preceding discussion, the similarities between the approaches of R. Ḥefeṣ and Maimonides are easily discernible, as are the differences between them. In contrast to other thinkers with whom Maimonides and R. Ḥefeṣ share much in common, R. Ḥefeṣ provided Maimonides with a well-known *legal* precedent for his view of the love of God.

The far-reaching nature of the legal innovations introduced by Maimonides in his *Laws of the Principles of the Torah* is not called into question here. The view that the apprehension of the theoretical sciences is the ultimate legal obligation—for only by means of this apprehension one fulfills the commandments to know, unify, love, and fear God—was a view that changed the entire way Judaism was to be conceived. Yet Maimonides did not compose his works in a legal or intellectual vacuum. Those who already preceded him in the Jewish world—most notably, R. Saadiah, R. Ḥefeṣ, and R. Baḥya—paved part of the way that Maimonides was to travel.

IV

In the conclusion of the fourth chapter of the *Laws of the Principles of the Torah,* Maimonides divides the *Mishneh Torah* into two parts. The second part begins with the fifth chapter and continues to the very end of Maimonides' legal compendium. The link between the first four chapters and the rest of the composition is not simply a formal one or one of continuity. Maimonides' views in these four chapters leave their imprints throughout the *Mishneh Torah,* though not always in a blatant manner. His use of the term "love" *(ahavah)* and the connection that he draws between it and other notions illustrate how he reveals to his readers by subtle hints a multidimensional world of ideas. While he makes little if any effort to highlight the connection between "love" and "knowledge" in the places that he employs the term "love," his view of this connection in the first four chapters provides the key to a deeper understanding of his approach to a range of legal topics. In many cases, an examination of the *Guide of the Perplexed* casts further light on the hints to his conceptions that he scatters in the *Mishneh Torah,* despite the significant differences between these two compositions.

Maimonides' discussion of the sanctification and profanation of the Name of God in chapter 5 of the *Laws of the Principles of the Torah* reflects the subtle but significant transition from love as consequent upon pure intellection to the expression of love of God in one's physical existence. He presents the talmudic view that one is forbidden to commit idolatry even if it involves the forfeiture of one's life. This view is based on the verse in

Deut. 6:5 that one is to love God with all of one's soul.[38] While one may argue that one should not attach too much significance to Maimonides' citation of the verse since he is following his talmudic source, we shall see that this transition reemerges also in subsequent sections.

The section following *Laws of the Principles of the Torah* is entitled *Laws of Character Traits* (*de'ot*). The connection between these two sections is strengthened by the use of the term *de'ot*. The term is used in the first section to refer to intellects. In the second section Maimonides uses it, instead of the more common term *middot*, to refer to ethical traits.[39] Together these two sections turn intellectual and ethical perfection into legal obligations. In accordance with the philosophic position, Maimonides sees ethical perfection ultimately as serving as a means to intellectual perfection. He maintains: "A person must direct his heart and all of his actions to the knowledge of God alone" (*Laws of Character Traits* 3:2), and goes on to discuss this point in detail. The parallel discussion in *Eight Chapters* 5 mentions also the love of God in this context:

> One should not perform any action, great or small, or utter any speech unless the action or speech leads to a virtue, directly or indirectly. One should first examine and ponder every action and movement to see if it leads to this end or does not lead to it, and only then should one do it. This is the goal that God demands of us in saying: *You shall love your Lord God with all your heart and all your soul* (Deut. 6:5)—that is, with all the parts of your soul. You shall posit the same goal for each of them—to love your Lord God. The prophets also exhorted the people in this matter by saying: *In all of your ways shall you know Him* (Proverbs 3:6).

Maimonides deletes this interpretation of Deut. 6:5 in the *Laws of Character Traits*. Perhaps he does not yet wish to underscore the physical dimension of love of God, even as a means to the intellectual dimension. In his discussion of the commandment to love the convert in *Laws of Character Traits* 6:4, however, he juxtaposes this love with the commandment to love God. In *The Book of the Commandments*, positive commandment no. 207 he makes the same move, citing an unknown midrash as his source. The love of God is treated here as an ethical trait—that is, a trait that belongs to the appetitive faculty of the soul. Thus the physical dimension of the love of God is alluded to, though obliquely. The focus of the discussion, however, is the love of the convert. Love of God is mentioned to stress the importance of loving the convert. It is only at the end of the first book of the *Mishneh Torah*, the *Book of Knowledge*, that Maimonides highlights the physical dimension of love and connects it with the intellectual dimension. This sets the stage for the following book of the *Mishneh Torah*, *The Book of Love (Sefer Ahavah).*

The *Book of Love* contains the following sections: *Laws of the Recitation of the Shema*; *Laws of Prayer and the Priestly Blessing*; *Laws of Mezuzah, Tefillin and Sefer Torah*; *Laws of Ṣiṣit*; *Laws of Blessings*; *Laws of Circumcision.* I am unaware of any source that grouped these topics together under the same label. The immediate questions that arise are: What feature binds these commandments? What is the connection between them and the commandment to love God, which is included in an entirely different book? Adding to the confusion is the fact that when Maimonides discusses the commandment to love God in the *Laws of the Principles of the Torah*, he does not mention any of the commandments he lists in the *Book of Love*, not even in passing. A perusal of the *Book of the Commandments* reveals that this is not simply an oversight on Maimonides' part. There he enumerates most of the commandments found in the *Book of Love* in close proximity to the commandments to love and fear God. The commandment of prayer comes directly on the heels of the latter commandments. In the *Mishneh Torah* he decides to interrupt the continuity and create a substantial interval between these commandments. At the same time he links them by the unifying term, "love."

The key to unraveling these problems is supplied by Maimonides in the last chapter of the *Laws of Repentance*. The tenth and final chapter of this section serves both as a summary of the *Book of Knowledge* and an introduction to the *Book of Love* that immediately follows. This chapter is devoted to the topic of worship of God. Maimonides repeatedly stresses that we are obligated to worship God from a state of love:

> One who worships out of love engages in Torah and its commandments, and walks in the paths of wisdom, for no ulterior motive—not from fear of evil [that is, punishment] nor to inherit the "good" [that is, reward]—but practices what is true because it is true. . . . This is an exceptionally great level that not every sage reaches. This is the level of Abraham our father, whom God called His "beloved" since he worshipped only out of love. This is the level that the Holy One, Blessed be He, through Moses commanded us [to attain], as it says: *You shall love your Lord God.* When a person loves God in an appropriate manner, he performs all the commandments out of love. What is the appropriate love? This is to love God a great, overabundant, exceptionally mighty love, till one's soul is bound up with the love of God and is continuously preoccupied with it. It is as though one is lovesick, and his

mind is completely distracted *('ein da'ato penuyah)* by his love for a certain woman. He is preoccupied with it continuously—whether he is sitting around or going about, or eating and drinking. (*Laws of Repentance* 10:2–3)

Lest one forgets the manner by which true love of God is attained, Maimonides reminds his readers in the final paragraph of the section:

It is well known and evident that the love of God is not secured in a person's heart till one is constantly preoccupied with it in an appropriate manner. Aside from it [love of God], he must forsake [preoccupation with] everything else in the world, as it is commanded: [*You shall love Your Lord God*] *with all your heart and with all your soul.* One loves God only by means of the intellect that apprehends Him. In proportion to one's intellection will be one's love: if little—little; if much—much. Hence a person must devote oneself to an understanding and apprehension of the sciences and areas of knowledge that inform one about the Maker, in accordance with the person's capacity to understand and apprehend. We have already explained this in the *Laws of the Principles of the Torah.*

This paragraph's connection with the commandment to love God, which is fulfilled only by way of intellectual apprehension, is explicit. It's connection with the *Book of Love* that follows is less clear. Maimonides' citation of the verse from the *Shema* in this paragraph provides one important link to the *Book of Love*, which opens with the *Laws of the Recitation of the Shema.* More subtle, but no less significant, is the connection of "constancy"—"one is constantly preoccupied with it." This is an essential feature shared by the commandments that follow in the *Book of Love*. The goal of each of the commandments, and an integral part of their fulfillment, is awareness of God. Moreover, one is required to perform them constantly.

In the last chapter of the *Laws of Repentance* one finds the transition from the commandment to love God, which is fulfilled by means of the activity of the intellect alone, to the worship of God out of love, which demands also physical acts. Maimonides regards the command to love God as the final purpose of all the commandments. The commandments to love and fear God, together with the three other commandments that are discussed in the first four chapters of the *Laws of the Principles of the Torah,* are labeled a "great matter" as we have seen above. All the other commandments are considered in comparison, "a small matter" and described as means to the pursuit of intellectual apprehension or to the cultivation of the world. Thus the worship of God in the context of Maimonides' thought should be viewed primarily as a means to the pursuit of the scientific knowledge by which the love of God is achieved. It also is the practical result of the attainment of the requisite knowledge, and the love that necessarily follows. Maimonides names his second book *Book of Love* in order to indicate that the commandments it contains are the distinctive means intended for the Jewish people to spur them to the true love of God.

This idea appears explicitly in several passages of the *Guide of the Perplexed.* In 3:35 Maimonides describes the commandments appearing in the *Book of Love* (with the notable exception of circumcision, which is transferred to the category of commandments involving sexual intercourse)[40] in the following manner: "The ninth class comprises all the other practices of worship prescribed to everybody, such as prayer and *recitation of Shema.* . . . The utility of this class is manifest, for it is wholly composed of works that fortify opinions concerning the love of the deity and what ought to be believed about Him and ascribed to Him" (p. 531).[41]

The connection between constant worship of God and the command to love God emerges also from the beginning of the *Book of Love: Laws of the Recitation of the Shema* 1:2: "Twice a day, evening and morning, one recites the *Shema.* . . . What does one recite? The three sections which are: *shema* (Deut. 6:4–9); *vehaya 'im shamo'a* (*And if you shall diligently heed my commandments* Deut. 11:13–21); *vayomer* (Numbers 15:37–41). The section *shema* is recited first since it contains the unity of God, the love of Him and the study of Him, for He is the fundamental principle upon which all [existence] is dependent."

In this paragraph Maimonides interprets and expands upon the talmudic notion, "acceptance of the yoke of the kingdom of Heaven" *(kabbalat 'ol malkhhūt shammayim).* This notion is presented in *Mishnah Berakhot* 2:2 in explaining the reason that one recites the section beginning with *Hear O Israel God is our Lord God is One* prior to the others. A simple understanding of this notion suggests that one is obligated to accept God's rule. As is customary for Maimonides in matters such as these, he interprets this notion in accordance with his philosophic position. "Acceptance of the yoke of the kingdom of Heaven" refers to knowledge of the unity of God, an interpretation that he had already advanced in the *Book of the Commandments* (positive commandment no. 2): "They call this commandment 'kingdom' for they say: 'in order that you accept the yoke of the kingdom of Heaven'—that is, the acknowledgment of God's unity and the knowledge of Him." Maimonides outlines this knowledge in the *Laws of the Principles of the Torah.* A further link is established between *Laws of the Recitation of the Shema* and *Laws of the Principles of the Torah* by the phrase "a fundamental principle upon which all is dependent." This phrase appears also in *Laws of the Principles of the Torah* 1:6.[42] He completes his explanation of the reason why the section beginning with the verse *Hear O Israel* is placed first by pointing to some of the other important notions that are mentioned there—for example, love of God. Significantly, these notions are also tied to knowledge of God according to him. In this subtle manner he reinterprets the talmudic tradition to support his philosophic position and give it the status of law. The recitation of the *Shema* serves as a constant reminder to apprehend God and the order of existence in a philosophic manner.

Surprisingly, Maimonides rarely mentions the term "love" in the rest of the book that is so named. The term does not surface at all in *Laws of Prayer*, and not in most of the other sections. As much as Maimonides wishes to establish a link between the commandments included in this book and the love of God, he also wants to preserve the gap between them. In those few places where he introduces the term, his formulation is significant.

One place in which the term "love" appears is *Laws of Mezuzah* 6:13:

> A person must be conscientious in [fulfilling the commandment] of *mezuzah* for it is a constant obligation binding upon everyone. Each time a person enters or exits, he comes in contact with [a reminder of] the unity of God . . . and remembers the love of Him. He awakens from his slumber and preoccupation with temporal vanities. He knows that nothing remains eternal *('ein davar 'omed le-'olam ūl'olmei 'olamim)* except for the knowledge of the *Rock of Eternity*. Immediately he returns to his senses [lit., returns to his intellect] and walks in the ways of the righteous. Our early sages stated (*Menahot* 43b): "Everyone who has *tefillin* (phylacteries) on his head and arm, *ṣiṣit* (fringes) on his garment, and a *mezuzah* on his entrance is fortified against sin for he has many reminders."

Here too Maimonides interprets his sources in accordance with his philosophic-legal conception. While the rabbinic passage he cites deals with avoiding sin in general, he utilizes it to stress the love of God, which he already has shown can be achieved only through knowledge. All the commandments the sages enumerate, and Maimonides includes in the *Book of Love*, are treated by him first and foremost as reminders of the necessity to attain knowledge of God. He goes so far as to allude in this passage to his position in the *Laws of the Principles of the Torah* 4:9 that the immortality of the intellect is dependent upon the attainment of this knowledge:

> The form of this soul *(nephesh)* [the form of the human being of perfect intellect] is not made up of the elements so that it would decompose into its component parts.

Nor is it a faculty of the soul *(neshamah),* dependent upon the soul [for its existence]. Therefore, when the body, which is made up of the elements, decomposes, and the soul *(neshamah)* is corrupted since it exists only with the body. . . . This form will not undergo corruption. . . . It knows and apprehends the intellects *(de'ot)* that are separate from bodies [the Separate Intellects], and it knows the Creator of all. It remains eternal *('omed le-'olam ūl'olmei 'olamim).*

As Maimonides' philosophically well-versed readers would have noted, he refers in this passage to the acquired intellect. This is the intellect that the individual attains as a result of apprehending the incorporeal existents. It too is an incorporeal existent. Only this form of "human" intellect is immortal.[43] The ideal reader of the *Mishneh Torah* is made aware of the fact that in his case the *mezuzah* must serve as a constant reminder not to cease in the effort to perfect of the intellect, which is the only way to achieve immortality.

As often happens, Maimonides immediately covers his tracks after flashing to his readers his deepest thoughts on sensitive issues. The quote from the sages with which he concludes *Laws of Mezuzah* 6:13 serves not only to lend authoritative support to his philosophical approach, but to reassure the average reader who remains within the boundary of more traditional approaches. The quote expresses the view that these commandments function as reminders not to sin—a notion with which all of his readers can feel comfortable. Only his astute readers will be able to tie all the pieces together and grasp his ultimate intent.

The term "love" subsequently appears in the *Laws of Blessings* 10:3: "A person is obligated to bless [God] in good spirit on adverse [events] just as he joyfully blesses on the good, as it is stated: *You shall love your Lord God . . . with all your might.* Even when one is afflicted he should thank and praise [God] joyfully in accordance with the [state of] profuse love we are commanded to attain." Maimonides' source is *Mishnah Berakhot* 9:5 which states: "A person is obligated to bless [God] on the bad just as he blesses on the good, as it is stated: *You shall love your Lord God with all your heart. . . . With all your heart*—with both your inclinations, the good inclination and the bad inclination. *With all your soul*—even if God takes your soul."[44]

While Maimonides' position that one should love God even when afflicted reflects the view of his rabbinic sources, one should also see in it an allusion to his approach to love in *Laws of the Principles of the Torah.* One who intellectually apprehends God is no longer affected by the physical afflictions that he experiences. This view anticipates the conception of providence that Maimonides develops in the *Guide of the Perplexed*. In suffering from afflictions despite his innocence, Job, according to Maimonides, concluded that God does not exercise personal providence. Maimonides attempts to show that this conclusion resulted from Job's initial ignorance of the true state of affairs: "But when he knew God with a certain knowledge, he admitted that true happiness, which is the knowledge of the deity, is guaranteed to all who know Him and that a human being cannot be troubled in it by any of all the misfortunes in question. While he had known God only through the traditional stories and not by the way of speculation, Job had imagined that the things thought to be happiness, such as health, wealth, and children, are the ultimate goal. For this reason he fell into such perplexity and said such things as he did" (3:23.492–93). Maimonides concludes his discourse with the following remarks:

> Just as natural acts differ from those of craftsmanship, so the divine governance of, the divine providence for, and the divine purpose with regard to, those natural matters differ from our human governance of, providence for, and purpose with regard to, the things we govern, we provide for, and we purpose. This is the object of the Book of Job as a whole. . . . If a man knows this, every misfortune will be borne lightly by him. And misfortunes will not add to his doubts regarding the deity . . . but will, on the contrary, add to his love as is said in the conclusion of the prophetic revelation in question (Job 42:6): *Wherefore I abhor myself, and repent of dust and ashes*. As [the Sages], may their memory be blessed, have said (*Shabbat* 88b): "Those who do out of love and are joyful in sufferings."

An understanding of the perfection of the world order, and the true purpose of human life within the order, liberates us from the experience of pain that is tied to our physical condition. This understanding enables us to act from a state of true intellectual apprehension/love of God. Feelings of pain result from our mental involvement with corporeal affairs. A person who lives a life whose sole focus is intellectual apprehension will not be immune from physical misfortunes, but from the resultant suffering they normally cause.[45]

The talmudic quotation brought here by Maimonides appears also in the *Laws of Character Traits* 2:3. This section immediately follows *Laws of the Principles of the Torah* and it deals with moral perfection. There too he describes a reaction to afflictions that derives from intellectual apprehension, and serves also as a preparation to attain intellectual perfection: "Therefore they [the sages] commanded to distance oneself from anger to the point that one feels no anger even in instances that [justifiably] should arouse one's wrath. This is the good path, the path of the righteous. When humiliated they do not humiliate in turn, when ridiculed they do not respond. They act out of love and are joyful in sufferings. Scripture says in regard to them (Judges 5:31): *Those who love Him are like the sun when it appears in its might.*"

Since Maimonides regarded the commandments that he included in the *Book of Love* as the distinctive means for goading the Jew to pursue the true love of God, one would have expected the subject of intention *(kavvanah)* to occupy a prominent place in his discussion. While the purpose of these commandments is to bring about a certain internal state in the individual, and the Talmud deals with the issue of intent in its discussion of the *recitation of the Shema*, Maimonides' remarks on the subject of *kavvanah* are surprisingly meager. He rules, following the view of R. Meir in *Berakhot* 13b:

> One who recites the first verse of the *Shema*—namely, *Hear O Israel*—without intent [lit: without directing one's heart, *ve-lo kivven libo*], does not fulfill one's obligation. If one recites the rest without intent, one fulfills one's obligation. Even if one [reads the *Shema*] in the course of reading the Torah, or in the course of proof reading these sections [of the *Shema* in the scroll of the Torah] at the [mandatory] time of recitation, one fulfills the obligation. This holds true when one [recites] the first verse with intent. (*Laws of the Recitation of the Shema* 2:1)

Maimonides does not add any comment regarding the notion of "intent." Immediately he turns to the problem: under what physical circumstances is one allowed to recite the *Shema*? Overall, the notion of "intent" almost completely disappears amidst all the laws involving technical matters regarding the recitation. One gains the impression that Maimonides is interested in highlighting the points that involve the external activity of the person in fulfilling this commandment. This area is integrally tied with the idea of "constancy" in practice. It is less difficult in being constant in performing a certain physical activity than in being constant in one's state of mind while this activity is being performed. Maimonides only hints to the desired internal state of the individual in this context. This is his manner of presentation. After explicating his position in a relatively clear and open manner at the beginning of the *Laws of the Principles of the Torah*, he relies on the conscientious reader to understand the hints he scatters in the rest of his compendium.

The most significant law regarding the notion of "intent" in the *Laws of the Recitation of the Shema* appears toward the end of the section (4:7): "Everyone who is exempt from the obligation to recite the *Shema* may still recite if he wishes to act more stringently. This holds only if his mind is not distracted *(da'ato penuyah 'alav)*. If the one who is exempt is agitated, he is not permitted to recite until he attains peace of mind *('ad shetityashev da'ato)*." The source for this law is *Mishnah Berakhot* 2:8: "A bridegroom in the first night [after the wedding] may recite the *Shema* if he so wishes. Rabban Shimon b. Gamliel says: Not everyone who wishes to assume a name may assume it [that is, not everyone has the right to act superior]."

Maimonides' position is based upon the first opinion brought in the mishnah.[46] However, he adds a conditional clause dealing with the state of mind of the reciter. Already in the previous mishnah we learn of an incident concerning Rabban Gamliel who recited the *Shema* on the night of his wedding. Rabban Gamliel explained to his students: "I will not heed your view to neglect [my acceptance of] the kingdom of Heaven, even briefly." Maimonides regards the phrase *da'ato penuyah 'alav* as identical to the talmudic phrase *tityashev da'ato 'alav*, which he also employs. The opposite of this state is termed *mevuhal* (agitated), which takes the place of the talmudic term *tarūd* (preoccupied). From a strict legal perspective, Maimonides rules in accordance with the mainstream talmudic tradition. Only in those instances in which one is preoccupied with other commandments and the sages exempted the person from reciting the *Shema*, is one permitted not to recite. When a person is preoccupied with affairs that do not involve the fulfillment of commandments, he is still required to recite.[47] It is evident that if all those who are preoccupied with other matters were exempted from reciting the *Shema*, the all important principle of "constancy" involved in the recitation would be lost. Still, Maimonides does not rule in accordance with the most literal interpretation of the first opinion in the mishnah. In this manner he bridges the first opinion with that of R. Shimon b. Gamliel. According to Maimonides' reasoning, if the sages exempted a person in certain instances from the necessity of being constant in one's practice, then one should demand of the individual who nevertheless desires to observe the commandment that he possess the appropriate internal state. One should not permit an individual in these circumstances to act in a mechanistic manner from force of habit.

It is no coincidence that Maimonides employs here phrases that allude to his discussion in *Laws of the Principles of the Torah*. The reason why the rest of the commandments must precede the commandments involving the apprehension of God is that they insure "the individual's peace of mind"—

miyashvim da'ato shel 'adam (4:13). The "peace of mind" required for the recitation of the *Shema* is reminiscent of the "peace of mind" that is necessary for attaining intellectual apprehension of God. The full implications of the phrase *da'at penuyah* (undistracted mind) emerges from Maimonides' description of the characteristics of the prophet in the continuation of the *Laws of the Principles of the Torah*. In Maimonides' conceptual scheme, the prophet represents the human ideal, the one who has attained intellectual perfection.[48] The subject of prophecy is integrally linked to the subject of knowledge and love of God. Maimonides takes pains that this point should not be lost on the reader. In introducing his discussion of the prophet in 7:1, he uses many of the same notions and terms he employs in the first four chapters of the section. Just as it is a fundamental principle to know that God exists, it is a fundamental principle to know that God bestows prophecy. Just as love of God is achieved by knowledge of *pardes*—metaphysics and natural science—prophecy is achieved by entering into *pardes*, thereby attaining knowledge of all existence. Maimonides goes on to describe the prophet in the following manner:

> He sanctifies himself and distances himself from the ways of the masses, who walk in darkness. He stirs himself and trains his soul not to think at all of the things that avail not, nor of the vanities and machinations of this world. Rather his mind is turned always toward heaven *(da'ato penuyah tamid lema'lah)*, connected to what is under the Throne in order to grasp those holy, pure Forms [that is, the Separate Intellects], and to view the entire wisdom of the Holy One.

The Laws of Prayer contain Maimonides' most important statements regarding the notion of intent. He effectively augments the significance of prayer by ruling in accordance with the prevailing opinion among his predecessors, who regard prayer as a commandment of the Torah.[49] Following the view of the Talmud, he treats intent *(kavvanah)* as a necessary condition for fulfilling this obligation.[50] The proper intent is so integral to the act of prayer that he does not consider prayer without intent to be prayer at all:

> Every prayer that is without intent is not regarded as prayer. If one prayed without intent, one must repeat the prayer with intent. If one's mind is confused and his heart preoccupied, it is forbidden for the individual to prayer until he attains peace of mind *('ad shetityashev da'ato)*. Hence one who has returned from a journey and is tired or troubled is not allowed to pray until he attains peace of mind. The sages said: "One should tarry three days until one rests and becomes calm *(titqarer da'ato)* and then one should pray." (*Laws of Prayer* 4:15)

Despite his emphasis on "constancy" regarding the commandments in the *Book of Love*, and his view of prayer as a commandment of the Torah, Maimonides leaves no room in this area for fulfilling one's obligation merely by the external "physical" act. He appears to adopt a more extreme stance than the position in the Talmud, a position that he does not mention. According to the Talmud, "One must pray all [the blessings of the *Amidah*] with intent. If one cannot pray them all with intent, one should pray one of them with intent" (*Berakhot* 34b).

In the following paragraph, Maimonides goes on to define the requisite "intent": "What is the [proper] intent? A person should clear one's heart *(sheyifaneh 'et libo)* from all thoughts, and see oneself as though standing before the Divine Presence *(shekhinah)*. Hence a person must sit awhile prior to prayer in order to direct one's heart *(le-khavven 'et libo)*, and afterwards pray calmly and with supplications. One should not pray as though bearing a burden that one dumps and leaves."[51]

The first stage in achieving the proper intent is to free oneself from all alien thoughts, till one sees oneself as standing in the presence of God. "Clearing one's heart" *(sheyifaneh 'et libo)* is a preparation for the state in which "one's mind is turned" *(da'ato penuyah)* to what is above, as Maimonides describes the prophet. In his discussion of the preparations for prophecy he also uses the term "intent" *(kavvanah):* "All the prophets do not prophesy any time they so desire. They must direct their minds *(mekhavnim da'atam)*, rest happy, in good spirit and withdrawn" (*Laws of the Principles of the Torah* 7:4).[52] "Direct one's mind" in this context refers to Maimonides' position that the prophet: "views all of the Holy One's wisdom—from the first Form [that is, Separate Intellect] to the navel of the earth—and knows by means of them His greatness" (*Laws of the Principles of the Torah* 7:1). A person who pursues true perfection will understand that this is the deeper significance of Maimonides' view in the *Laws of Prayer.* That one who prays must "see oneself as though standing before the Divine Presence" means that he must direct his mind to the apprehension of the entire order of existence.

In the *Laws of Tefillin* 4:5 Maimonides also alludes to this idea: "How great is the sanctity of *tefillin*. Whenever *tefillin* are on the head and arm of a person, he is humble and fears *(yare')* heaven. He is not drawn to levity and idle chatter. He refrains from thinking bad thoughts, but turns his attention (lit.: turns his heart—*mafneh libo*) to matters of truth and justice." A person cannot concentrate on two matters at the same time. These commandments demand of a person to clear one's heart *(lefanot 'et libo)* from all thoughts in order to turn one's heart *(lifnot libo)* or direct one's mind *(le-khavven 'et da'ato)* to think of God by apprehending the totality of existence and the nature of divine governance. This is the meaning of thinking of "matters of truth and justice."

Maimonides develops this idea in more detail in the *Guide of the Perplexed* 3:51. The prophets are described as follows: "There are those who set their thought to work after having attained perfection in the divine science, turn wholly toward God, may He be cherished and held sublime, renounce what is other than He, and direct all the acts of their intellect toward an examination of the beings with a view to drawing from them proof with regard to Him, so as to know His governance of them in whatever way it is possible" (p. 620). In the continuation of this chapter Maimonides depicts the special worship of those who have attained this state of apprehension of the "true realities."[53] Their worship in effect is the continuous contemplation of God:

> The more they think of Him and of being with Him [lit.: standing before Him], the more their worship increases. . . . This kind of worship ought only to be engaged in after intellectual conception has been achieved. If, however, you have apprehended God and His acts in accordance with what is required by the intellect, you should afterwards engage in totally devoting yourself to Him, endeavor to come closer to Him and strengthen the bond between you and Him—that is the intellect. . . . The Torah has made it clear that this last worship to which we have drawn attention in this chapter can only be engaged in after apprehension has been achieved. . . . Now we have made it clear several times that love is proportionate to apprehension. After love comes the worship to which attention has been drawn by [the sages], may their memory be blessed, who said: *This is the worship of the heart.* In my opinion it consists in setting thought to work on the first intelligible and in devoting oneself exclusively to this as far as this is within one's capacity . . . Thus it is clear that after apprehension, total devotion to Him and the employment of intellectual thought in constantly loving Him should be aimed at. (Pp. 620–21)

Intellect is the link between the individual and God. While one does not contemplate God, the link is broken. Maimonides shows how the commandments, particularly those that are included in the *Book of Love*, should serve as part of the training to establish and strengthen this link:

> Know that all the practices of the worship, such as reading the Torah, prayer, and the performance of the other commandments, have only the end of training you to occupy yourself with His commandments, may He be exalted, rather than with matters pertaining to this world; you should act as if you were occupied with Him,

may He be exalted, and not with that which is other than He. . . . From here on I will begin to give you guidance with regard to the form of this training so that you should achieve this great end. The first thing that you should cause your soul to hold fast onto is that while reciting the *Shema* prayer, you should empty your mind of everything and pray thus. You should not content yourself with being intent while reciting the first verse of the *Shema* and saying the first benediction.[54] When this has been carried out correctly and has been practiced consistently for years, cause your soul, whenever you read or listen to the Torah, to be constantly directed—the whole of you and your thought—toward reflection on what you are listening to or reading. When this too has been practiced consistently for a certain time, cause your soul to be in such a way that your thought is always quite free of distraction and gives heed to all that you are reading of the other discourses of the prophets and even when you read all the benedictions, so that you aim at meditating on what you are uttering and at considering its meaning.[55] (P. 622)

In this passage, Maimonides employs the same terms (at times in Hebrew, but for the most part in their Arabic translation) that can be found in his discussions in the *Laws of the Principles of the Torah*. The true closeness to God, he stresses, is "intellectual worship." In an earlier chapter, 3:32, he goes so far as to allude to the view that the ideal situation is one in which "worship should consist solely in meditation without any works at all" (p. 526). Prayer, *ṣiṣit*, *mezuzah,* and *tefillin* are listed by him as those commandments that are necessary in preparing the individual to achieve the intellectual apprehension of God, which is essentially equivalent to intellectual worship.[56]

Maimonides concludes his discussion in 3:51 with a description of perfection that expands upon his description of love of God in *Laws of Repentance* 10:3 cited above: "We have already explained in preceding chapters that the meaning of knowledge of the Name is: apprehension of Him. It is as if [the psalm] said that this individual is protected because he hath known me and then passionately loved Me. You know the difference between the terms *one who loves* [*oheb*] and *one who passionately loves* [*ḥosheq*]; an excess of love [*mahabbah*] so thought no thought remains that is directed toward a thing other than the Beloved, is passionate love" (p. 627).

In the *Laws of the Principles of the Torah*, Maimonides links love of God with the intellectual apprehension of all of existence, not with knowledge of the commandments of the Torah. He reminds his readers of this point also at the end of *Laws of Repentance*: "Hence a person must devote oneself to an understanding and intellection of the sciences *(ḥokhmot)* and areas of knowledge *(tevunot)* that inform one about the Maker, in accordance with the person's capacity to understand and apprehend" (10:6). Maimonides substitutes the phrase "sciences and areas of knowledge" for Torah. The traditional reader will see this phrase as identical with the commandments of the Torah based on the description of the commandments in Deut. 4:6. The philosophically versed reader, who has followed Maimonides' discourse in *Laws of the Principles of the Torah* carefully, will understand that "sciences" refers to the natural sciences and metaphysics. Regarding this subject too, one can see how Maimonides in the *Guide* elaborates upon the ideas to which he had already alluded in the *Mishneh Torah.*

In the introduction to the *Guide,* Maimonides writes: "It is not the purpose of this Treatise to make its totality understandable to the vulgar or to beginners in speculation, nor to teach those who have not engaged in any study other than the science of the Law—I mean the legalistic study of the Law. For the purpose of this Treatise and all those like it is the science of the Law in its true sense" (p. 5). Maimonides posits a distinction between "science of the Law" and "science of the Law in its true sense." The former deals with the legalistic study of the Torah, while the latter deals with the study of the principles of the Torah. This point emerges from Maimonides' subsequent comments. One who knows how to interpret the Torah and the Books of the Prophets in conformity with true opinions—that is, those attained by a study of the sciences—is the true sage.

Maimonides concludes the *Guide* with a chapter that opens with a discussion of the term "wisdom" or "science" *(ḥokhmah).* This discussion clarifies his usage of these terms in the *Mishneh Torah.* He enumerates four types of wisdom. The most noble is: "the apprehension of true realities, which have for their end the apprehension of Him" (3:54.632). He continues:

> According to this explanation, one who knows the whole of the Law in its true reality is called *wise* in two respects: in respect of the rational virtues comprised in the Law and in respect of the moral virtues included in it. But since the rational matter in the Law is received through tradition and is not demonstrated by the methods of speculation, the knowledge of the Law came to be set up in the books of the prophets and the sayings of the Sages as one separate species and wisdom, in an unrestricted sense, as another species. It is through this wisdom, in an unrestricted sense, that the rational matter that we receive from the Law through tradition, is demonstrated. (P. 633)

In the parable of the king in the palace, Maimonides illustrates the significance of the distinction between these two types of knowledge: "He, however, who has achieved demonstration, to the extent that is possible, of everything that may be demonstrated; and who has ascertained in divine matters, to the extent that it is possible, everything that may be ascertained; and who has come close to certainty in those matters in which one can only come close to it—has come to be with the ruler in the inner part of the habitation" (*Guide* 3:51.619). This individual, as Maimonides indicates in the continuation of his explanation, is the one who achieves perfection in the natural sciences and understands metaphysical science. Those who are still searching for the gate of the palace are: "the jurists who believe in true opinions on the basis of traditional authority and study the law concerning the practice of divine service, but do not engage in speculation concerning the fundamental principles of religion and make no inquiry whatever regarding the rectification of belief" (p. 619).

In light of Maimonides' distinction between *ḥokhmah* (science or wisdom) and Torah, one can see why it was important for him to stress the connection between love of God and knowledge of science. Acceptance on the basis of tradition of the true opinions found in the Torah does not provide the requisite knowledge to experience the true love of God. Practice of the commandments also does not suffice. Only apprehension of the natural and metaphysical sciences leads to love.

This view lies on the basis of Maimonides' approach to the study of Talmud (*gemara*) in the *Laws of the Study of the Torah*. He distinguishes between the Written Law, the Oral Law, and Talmud. The study of *pardes*—that is, metaphysics and the natural sciences—are explicitly included in the study of Talmud. In the early stages of study, the person must divide one's time equally between the Written Law, Oral Law, and Talmud. Maimonides' presentation is highly significant not only for its content but also for the terms he employs. His formulation is designed to strengthen the connection between his approach to Torah study and the position he presents in the *Laws of the Principles of the Torah*. "When one grows in wisdom *(ḥokhmah)* and no longer needs to learn the Written Law, or continuously devote oneself to the Oral Law . . . one should turn *(yifneh)* to [the study] of Talmud alone, in accordance with the broadness of one's understanding [lit.: heart] and one's peace of mind *(yishūv da'ato)*" (*Laws of the Study of the Torah* 1:12).

The importance of *ḥokhmah* (science) in Maimonides' thought emerges also from his legal discussions focusing on leadership.[57] Maimonides' political philosophy is influenced primarily by that of Alfarabi, which in turn is rooted in Plato's notion of the philosopher-king. According to Alfarabi, the individual who is capable of directing society to true felicity is one who has achieved perfection in the speculative sciences, attained the "acquired intellect," and conjoined with the Active Intellect, consequently receiving revelation *(waḥy)*.[58] This model in particular influenced Maimonides' approach to prophecy.[59]

Maimonides' description of the prophet in the beginning of chapter 7 of the *Laws of the Principles of the Torah* should be understood in light of Alfarabi's approach. The prophet, according to Maimonides, is the one who has attained scientific knowledge of all of reality, and conjoins with the Active Intellect *(tit'arev nafsho be-ma'alat ha-mal'akhim ha-niqra'im 'ishim)*.[60] Maimonides also alludes to the view that the prophet attains the acquired intellect—"he understands with his intellect *(da'ato)*, which is not the same as it previously was."[61] While Maimonides goes on to accord the prophet a political role, he is more interested in emphasizing the limits of prophetic authority in this context.[62]

If Alfarabi's approach to the ideal leader is only in part evident from Maimonides' description of the prophet in the *Laws of the Principles of the Torah*, it is far more evident in his description of the messiah in *Laws of Repentance* 9:2. In a highly succinct manner, Maimonides describes the messiah along Alfarabi's model, with the significant qualification of removing from the messiah's province legislative authority. On the surface, he is simply following the description of the messiah found in Isaiah. Yet his discussion in *Laws of the Principles of the Torah* has already prepared his more astute readers to understand the true meaning of the terms he employs: "This king who will arise from the descendants of David will be wiser (or "better versed in the sciences"—*ba'al ḥokhmah*) than Solomon. He will be a great prophet, close to [the level] of Moses our Master. Consequently he will teach the entire nation and instruct them the way of God. All the nations will come to heed him."[63]

In Maimonides' discussion of the requisite characteristics for the members of the high rabbinical court, the *sanhedrin*, one can also detect the influence of Alfarabi's model. In light of the legal-political authority possessed by the members of the *sanhedrin*, Maimonides saw in them some relation to philosopher-kings and treated their qualifications accordingly. This point emerges when one carefully examines Maimonides' interpretation of his primary talmudic source. The Talmud enumerates the qualifications of the members of the *sanhedrin* as follows: "Every member of the *sanhedrin* knows seventy languages, as R. Yohanan indicated: 'One appoints to the *sanhedrin* only those who are wise *(ba'alei ḥokhmah)*, of good appearance, imposing stature, elderly, adepts in magic, and who know seventy languages, in order that they will not require an interpreter to hear [the cases brought to them]'" (*Menaḥot* 65a).

Maimonides introduces a number of changes in his formulation:

> Those appointed to the *sanhedrin*—whether the great one or a small one—must be wise and sagacious people, exceptional in the science of Torah *(muflagin be-ḥokhmat ha-torah),* of profuse intellect *(ba'alei de'ah merubah),* and who know something of the other sciences such as medicine, mathematics, astronomy, astrology, the practices of the soothsayers, magicians and sorcerers, and the vanities of idolatry etc. in order that they know how to judge [cases involving] them. (*Laws of the Sanhedrin* 2:1)

In a subsequent *halakhah* (2:6) Maimonides adds to the list of qualifications: "Just as the [members of the] court are of characterized by consummate justice so too they must not possess any physical blemish.[64] A thorough search should be conducted to insure that all the members are of mature age, of imposing stature, of good appearance, who fathom secrets *(nevonei laḥash)*,[65] and know most of the languages so the *sanhedrin* will not need to hear [cases] by means of an interpreter."

Some of the changes that Maimonides introduces into R. Yohanan's list are blatant. He expands the list of areas of knowledge that the members must know, including both true sciences and false ones.[66] Probably the most significant change in his formulation is one that is less obvious. This is his interpretation of the qualification "wise" that is presented by R. Yohanan. Maimonides employs two phrases instead—"exceptional in the science of Torah" and "of profuse intellect"—before going on to include other areas in which the members of the *sanhedrin* must possess wisdom. According to what we have seen, "science of the Torah" may be interpreted in two ways. It may refer to knowledge of the commandments of the Torah, and to knowledge of its principles by way of tradition. It may also refer to speculative knowledge of the principles of the Torah, which Maimonides equates with knowledge of the theoretical sciences. In this context, he may well have had both meanings in mind. It is clear that the member of the *sanhedrin* must possess knowledge of all the details of the commandments. Yet Maimonides may also be alluding to the view that they must also attain human perfection by way of perfection in the sciences in order to function as the leaders of the Jewish community. The phrase, "of profuse intellect" strengthens this interpretation by creating a linguistic link between Maimonides' description of the qualifications of the members of the *sanhedrin* and his description of the qualifications of the prophet in *Laws of the Principles of the Torah* 7:1:

Prophecy alights only on a sage of exceptional wisdom, valiant in his moral traits. His [evil] inclination never subdues him in anything. By virtue of his intellect he always subdues his inclination. He has an exceptionally broad and penetrating intellect *(ba'al de'ah reḥavah nekhonah 'ad me'od).* A person who possesses all these traits and is perfect of body—when he enters *pardes* and deals with those great and obscure matters, and has a penetrating intellect to understand and apprehend. . . .

We have already seen what Maimonides has to say at the beginning of the *Laws of the Principles of the Torah* (4:8–9) regarding this "intellect" to which immortality is also ascribed: "The exceptional intellect *(ha-da'at ha-yeterah)* found in the soul of the individual is the form of the human being of perfect intellect. . . . This form will not be undergo corruption for it does not require the soul for its activity. It knows and apprehends the intellects *(de'ot)* that are separate from bodies [the Separate Intellects], and it knows the Creator of all. It remains eternal."

Maimonides hints that the members of the *sanhedrin* must endeavor to approach this ideal. It is hard to determine whether Maimonides distinguishes between *de'ah reḥavah* (broad intellect), which characterizes the prophets, and *de'ah merubah* (profuse intellect), which characterizes the members of the *sanhedrin.* At any rate, the similarity between these phrases points to a connection between the two groups. The connection between the prophets and the sages of the Talmud (the members of the *sanhedrin* were seen as belonging to this group) in reference to intellectual perfection and the immortality of the intellect reemerges in Maimonides' discussion in *Guide* 3:51. Even the qualifications he ascribes to members of a three member court, which clearly hold also for members of the *sanhedrin,* are reminiscent of this ideal. These qualifications are: wisdom, fear, humility, disdain of monetary wealth, love of the truth, love of fellow human beings, and a good reputation (*Laws of Sanhedrin* 2:6).[67]

The phrase *de'ah merubah* is reminiscent also of the conclusion of *Laws of Repentance*, where Maimonides links wisdom, intellect and love:

Therefore, one only teaches children, women and the masses in general to worship out of fear and in order to receive a reward till their intellect expands *('ad she-tarbeh da'atam)* and they become exceptionally wise *(ve-yithakhmū ḥokhmah yeterah).* One reveals to them this secret little by little, and one accustoms them to this matter peacefully till they apprehend, know and worship Him out of love. . . . In proportion to one's intellection will be one's love: if little—little; if much—much. Hence a person must devote oneself to an understanding and apprehension of the sciences and areas of knowledge that inform one about the Maker, in accordance with the person's capacity to understand and apprehend. (*Laws of Repentance* 10:5–6)

It is clear from Maimonides' description that very few will reach the final stage of the process and become "exceptionally wise," though he wants to encourage everyone at least to begin moving in this direction.[68] Those who attain this perfection are the sages whom Maimonides regards as the true leaders of the Jewish people, and to whom he refers when he speaks of "physicians of the soul" (*Laws of Character Traits* 2:1), and those to whom we must cleave and learn from their actions *(Laws of Character Traits* 6:2).

The connection between wisdom and love is not confined to the first two books of the *Mishneh Torah*, but is alluded to in other books as well: "Similarly, a man is forbidden to bring about an erection or unchaste thoughts deliberately. If such thoughts do enter his mind, he should direct it away from thoughts of vanity leading to wastage of semen, and back to words of Torah, which is a *hind of love and doe of grace* (Prov. 5:19)" (*Laws of Forbidden Intercourse* 21:19).[69]

Maimonides expands upon this idea in the last *halakhah* of this section (22:21): "But above all this, as the Sages have declared, a man should direct his mind and thoughts to the words of Torah and enlarge his understanding with wisdom *(yarhiv da'ato be-ḥokhmah),* for unchaste thoughts prevail only in a heart devoid of wisdom, and of wisdom it is said, *a hind of love and a doe of grace, let her breasts satisfy thee at all times with her love be thou ravished always*." A person must always devote oneself to the pursuit of wisdom/science in order to attain the true end of humanity, and this pursuit is what guards against being overpowered by one's corporeal desires. The person who, "directs one's heart and all of one's actions to know God" (*Laws of Character Traits* 3:2) makes every effort to detach oneself from all that disturbs this pursuit.[70]

In summary, the commandment to love God, according to Maimonides' approach in the *Mishneh Torah*, is essentially an obligation to pursue true human perfection. This is the perfection of the intellect by means of the apprehension of the sciences. It culminates in the apprehension of God in accordance with human ability. This apprehension, in turn, serves both as a necessary and sufficient condition to experience true love of God. From a strictly Jewish legal standpoint, the commandment applies to Jews alone.[71] From a philosophic standpoint, it binds all humans alike.

The fourth species is the true human perfection; it consists in the acquisition of the rational virtues—I refer to the conception of the intelligibles, which teach true opinions concerning the divine things. This is in true reality the ultimate end; this is what gives the individual true perfection, a perfection belonging to him alone; and it gives him permanent endurance; through it man is man. (*Guide* 3:54.635)

The universality of this pursuit is a central notion in Maimonides' depiction of the messianic period in the *Introduction to Pereq Ḥeleq* and *Laws of Kings and their Wars* 11:4, 12:1. This point finds its expression also in the *Guide*:

> If there were knowledge, whose relation to the human form is like that of the faculty of sight to the eye, they would refrain from doing any harm to themselves and to others. For through cognition of the truth, enmity and hatred are removed and the inflicting of harm by people on one another is abolished. It holds out this promise, saying (Isaiah 11:6–8): *And the wolf shall dwell with the lamp. . . .* Then it gives the reason for this, saying that the cause of the abolition of these enmities, these discords, and these tyrannies, will be the knowledge that men will then have concerning the true reality of the deity. For it says (Isaiah 11:9): *They shall not hurt nor destroy in all My holy mountain; for the earth shall be full of the knowledge of the Lord, as the waters cover the sea.* Know this. (3:11.441)

When Maimonides formulates the commandment to love God (as is also the case with the commandment to know the existence of God) in the *Laws of the Principles of the Torah*, he deletes from its content any matter that is unique to the Jewish People. He did not want his elite readers to make any mistake on this issue. This may also explain why he distances the *Book of Love* from the commandment to love God. One should not conclude that by reciting the *Shema* or by praying one is at the same time fulfilling the commandment to love God. On the other hand, he named the book, *Book of Love* to indicate that the commandments included therein are designed to encourage their adherents to pursue love of God. They serve as a constant reminder to the wise and observant Jew that the true path to the love of God is by means of knowledge of the sciences.

In *Guide* 3:51, Maimonides elaborates upon this idea in his description of the special worship of those pursuing perfection. These individuals utilize the time in which they are engaged in fulfilling the commandments found in the *Book of Love* to direct their mind to a contemplation of God and the world. As they progress in their training, the fulfillment of any of the commandments offers them an opportunity for contemplation. The perfect reach a stage in which they are capable of contemplating God even while they are physically engaged in mundane matters.

One who reads the *Book of Love* carefully can detect the intellectual continuum with the *Guide* on this point. The transition from viewing the purpose of certain commandments as serving to remind the individual of the true goal of existence to viewing them as part of the training in attaining this goal is not a sharp one. In light of Maimonides' definition of "intent" *(kavvanah),* and his use of the phrases "clear one's heart" and "turn one's heart" in the *Mishneh Torah,* the perceptive reader will discern that when one fulfills the commandments in the *Book of Love* one should contemplate the content of the commandment to love God. As for the masses, these commandments will serve as reminders of true notions, particularly the existence and unity of God, though they may be incapable of grasping these notions in the proper manner. This is the primary goal of the Torah in their case.[72] While Maimonides remains loyal to his legal sources in the presentation of the commandments included in the *Book of Love,* at the same time he introduces subtle allusions to the metalegal framework for understanding and properly fulfilling these commandments.

V

The study of Maimonides' use of the term "fear" *(yir'ah)* in the *Mishneh Torah* leads to a far different picture than the one we obtain by the study of the term "love." If the definition of the latter term at the beginning of the *Laws of the Principles of the Torah* casts light on the manner he uses the term in other discussions in the *Mishneh Torah,* and provides a key to glimpsing the more profound significance of his formulations of a variety of laws, the same cannot be said for the definition of "fear." "Fear" in terms of the intellectual awe that results from the same knowledge that leads to love of God gives way in the rest of the *Mishneh Torah* to fear of the divine punishment—the same use that can be found in Maimonides' discussion of the commandment to fear God in the *Book of the Commandments.*[73] Instead of linking the notions of "love" and "fear" in his other discussions and treating them as two sides of the same coin, Maimonides posits a fundamental distinction between them. The divergence in his approaches to "fear" is so glaring that it demands an explanation.

The shift in approach to the notion "fear" occurs as early as the fifth chapter of the *Laws of the Principles of the Torah.* In the context of discussing the commandments to sanctify the Name of God and not to profane the Name of God, Maimonides writes (5:11): "Everyone who avoids transgression, or fulfills a commandment not from any ulterior motive—not trepidation, nor fear *(yir'ah),* nor to seek honor—but for the sake of God . . . sanctifies the Name."

The transition from the notion of "fear of God" as intellectual awe to fear of divine punishment emerges even more clearly from the concluding chapter of *Laws of Repentance* (10:1): "A person should not say: I fulfill the commandments of the Torah and engage in the [study of] its science in order to receive all the blessings that are written in it . . . and I avoid transgressions in order to be spared the curses written in the Torah or not to be cut off from life in the World to Come—it is not appropriate to worship God in this manner. The person who worships in this manner worships from fear. This is not the level of the prophets or of the sages. Only the masses, and women and children worship God in this manner. They are educated to worship out of fear until their intellect develops and they worship out of love."

The gap between wisdom and fear also emerges from Maimonides' discussion in the *Mishneh Torah*: "If he possesses fear [of Heaven] though not wisdom, he is nevertheless installed [as king] in place of his father, and he is taught. Anyone who does not possess fear of Heaven, though he is abounding in wisdom *(ḥokhmato merubah)*—one does not appoint him to any of the appointed positions in Israel" (*Laws of Kings and their Wars* 1:7).

In several places Maimonides cites the rule: "Of everything that pertains only to the heart [that is, involves the private life of the individual] it is said: *You shall fear your Lord*."[74] In these instances where there is no social control over the individual's actions, fear of punishment ensures the desired behavior. Even when Maimonides does not speak of fear in reference to divine punishment, he does not allude to the fear that is consequent upon the intellectual apprehension of God. At best he alludes to the type of fear that helps lead to apprehension.[75] It is clear from Maimonides' approach in the *Mishneh Torah* that he posits different types of fear. This is the same approach that can be discerned in the *Commentary on the Mishnah*. For the most part he treats fear as antithetical to love. At best it serves as a means to attain love.

The novelty in Maimonides' approach in the *Mishneh Torah* is that he opens his compendium with a description of "fear" that is totally within the realm of intellectual apprehension and is integrally tied to the love of God. One may fear God in different ways. Yet one can fulfill the commandment to fear God only when one reaches the highest form of fear that is consequent upon apprehension. Maimonides ceases to allude to this form of fear in the rest of the *Mishneh Torah*, perhaps because the inferior forms of fear play a more important role for the masses' observance of the Law. They also serve as a bridge to the final goal.

VI

Till now, I have treated Maimonides' approach in the *Guide* to the love of God as one in which he takes the ideas he presents in the *Mishneh Torah* and further develops them. The two works should be seen as forming a continuum. The question remains whether his approach to love and fear of God are in fact identical in both works. One would assume that the fundamental difference between the nature of the *Guide* and the *Mishneh Torah* left its mark on Maimonides' discussion of this topic.

In regard to the love of God, it is difficult to detect any modifications in Maimonides' approach when he deals with this topic in the *Guide*. The connection between love and intellectual apprehension is emphasized in the *Guide* as it is in the *Mishnah Torah*. In the course of some of his discussions, Maimonides himself points to the link between his two compositions:

> As for the dictum of Scripture: *And thou shalt love the Lord they God with all thy heart*—in my opinion its interpretation is: with all the forces of your heart; I mean to say, with all the forces of the body, for the principle of all of them derives from the heart. Accordingly the intended meaning is, as we have explained in the commentary on the *Mishnah* and in the *Mishnah Torah*, that you should make His apprehension the end of all your actions. (*Guide* 1:39.89)

> With regard to all the other correct opinions concerning the whole of being—opinions that constitute the numerous kinds of all the theoretical sciences through which the opinions forming the ultimate end are validated—the Law, albeit it does not make a call to direct attention toward them in detail as it does with regard to [the opinions forming ultimate ends], does do this in summary fashion by saying: *To love the Lord*. You know how this is confirmed in the dictum regarding love: *With all thy heart, and with all thy soul, and with all thy might*. We have already explained in *Mishneh Torah* that this love becomes valid only through the apprehension of the whole of being as it is and through the consideration of His wisdom as it is manifested in it. (*Guide* 3:28.512–13)

Maimonides' description cited above of the ecstatic death of one who attains the passionate love of God (*Guide* 3:51) deals with the nature of the immortal state to which this apprehension leads. A parallel passage does not exist in his other writings. Nevertheless, his descriptions at the end of the *Laws of Repentance* of the intense love of one who apprehends God

(10:3, 6), and of the World to Come as the state of immortality of the incorporeal intellect (8:2–3) set the stage for the description in the *Guide*.

While Maimonides' approach in the *Guide* to the love of God parallels his approach in the *Mishneh Torah*, his approach to fear does not. It is surprising that in his theological *magnum opus* Maimonides chose not to highlight the view of the fear of God presented in the beginning of the *Laws of the Principles of the Torah.* For the most part he treats the notion of fear as he does in the other sections of the *Mishneh Torah*. Some passages in the *Guide* may certainly be interpreted as alluding to the notion of fear as intellectual awe, especially Maimonides' discussion of the binding of Isaac.[76] Yet even there he does not present this view of fear explicitly. It is of interest that the passage in the *Guide* that most clearly reflects the notion of fear as intellectual awe concerns the *limitations* in drawing conclusions concerning God rather than the awe one experiences as a result of the conclusions drawn. Fear should keep one from trying to rush forward too fast in one's apprehension, thereby stumbling in the process:

> In the same way we say that man should not hasten too much to accede to this great and sublime matter at the first try, without having made his soul undergo training in the sciences and the different kinds of knowledge, having truly improved his character, and having extinguished the desires and cravings engendered in him by his imagination. When, however, he has achieved and acquired knowledge of true and certain premises and has achieved knowledge of the rules of logic and inference and of the various ways of preserving himself from errors of the mind, he then should engage in the investigation of this subject. When doing this he should not make categoric affirmations in favor of the first opinion that occurs to him and should not, from the outset, strain and impel his thoughts toward the apprehension of the deity; he should rather feel awe and refrain and hold back until he gradually elevates himself. It is in this sense that it is said (Exod. 3:6): *And Moses hid his face, for he was afraid to look upon God.* (*Guide* 1:5.29)[77]

A good example of the fundamental difference between the *Guide* and the *Laws of the Principles of the Torah* on the issue of fear of God is provided by the passage from 3:28 cited above. Maimonides points only to the command to love God to show that the Torah demands one to apprehend all of reality. Immediately beforehand he mentions the notion of fear: "In the same way the Law also makes a call to adopt certain beliefs, belief in which is necessary for the sake of political welfare. Such, for instance, is our belief that He, may He be exalted, is violently angry with those who disobey

Him, and that it is therefore necessary to fear Him and to dread Him and to take care not to disobey" (p. 512). Maimonides alludes here to the fear of punishment. This fear is traced to the belief that God is angry with sinners, a belief that is politically necessary to ensure social welfare. The treatment of fear and love in this context is reminiscent of the last chapter of the *Laws of Repentance*, in contrast to the beginning of the *Laws of the Principles of the Torah*.

Not only can one discern in the *Guide* the notion of fear of God in terms of fear of divine punishment, but also the link between the notion of fear and the acquisition of certain character traits:

> As for the anointing oil, it has two useful functions: it gives a pleasant smell to whatever is anointed with it, and induces the belief that the anointed object is great, sanctified, and distinguished beyond other things of the same species, regardless of whether the thing is a human individual or a garment or a vessel. All this redounds to fear of the Sanctuary, which is a cause of fear of the Lord. For when one came there the soul was affected, so that hard hearts were softened and touched. For the deity with far-away counsels devised this gracious ruse in order that they be softened and become submissive when they came to the Temple, so that they accept God's guiding commands and fear Him. (*Guide* 3:45.580)[78]

Maimonides summarizes his approach to love and fear of God as follows:

> He, may He be exalted, has explained that the end of the actions prescribed by the whole Law is to bring about the passion of which it is correct that it be brought about. . . . I refer to the fear of Him, may He be exalted, and the awe before His command. It says (Deut. 28:58): *If thou will not take care to observe all the words of this Law that are written in this book, that thou mayest fear this glorious and fearful Name, the Lord thy God.* Consider how it is explicitly stated for your benefit that the intention of all the words of this Law is one end, namely, *that thou mayest fear the Name,* and so on. The fact that this end is achieved through actions, you can learn from its dictum in this verse: *If thou wilt not take care to observe*. For it has already been made clear that this refers to actions prescribed by commandments and prohibitions. As for the opinions that the Torah teaches us—namely, the apprehension of His being and His unity, may He be exalted—these opinions teach us love, as we have explained several times. . . . For these two ends, namely love and fear, are achieved through two things: love through the opinions taught by the Law, which include the apprehension of His being as He, may He be exalted, is in truth; while fear is achieved by means of all actions prescribed by the Law, as we have explained. Understand this summary. (*Guide* 3:52.630)

Maimonides views the love of God as tied solely to apprehension. Fear is tied to corporeal activity. The opinions that lead to love are those that are presented in the first four chapters of the *Laws of the Principles of the Torah.* "All the actions prescribed by the Law" refers to all the commandments in the rest of the *Mishneh Torah.* These commandments are intended to bring about "peace of mind" and ensure the "cultivation of this world" (*Laws of the Principles of the Torah* 4:13). In the *Guide* 3:27, Maimonides treats the commandments as either bringing about the "welfare of the body" (the elimination of people wronging each other, and the acquisition of moral qualities) or promoting the "welfare of the soul" (the acquisition of correct opinions). In his presentation of the reasons for many of the particular commandments—for example, the commandments included in the *Book of Love*, the commandments involving sacrifices—he shows how they are designed to fortify these opinions by means of corporeal activities (*Guide* 3:28; 3:32; 3:35). In his summary statement of the notion of fear of God, fear ultimately serves to prepare the appetitive faculty of the soul to cooperate with the rational faculty in the pursuit of intellectual perfection. The appetitive faculty is the one most closely associated with moral traits and the activities resulting from them.[79] While the cooperation between the faculties of the soul is necessary for achieving love of God, this love belongs to the intellect alone. It involves none of the other faculties, not the appetitive or the imagination.

"Fear of God" also designates those moral traits and activities characterizing one who has attained intellectual perfection:

> Just as we apprehend Him by means of that light which He caused to overflow toward us . . . so does He by means of this selfsame light examine us. . . . Know when perfect men understand this, they achieve such humility, such awe and fear of God, such reverence and such shame before Him, may He be exalted—and this in ways that pertain to true reality, not to imagination—that their secret conduct with their wives and in latrines is like their public conduct with other people. (3:52.629)

This passage comes close to suggesting the view of "fear" presented in the *Laws of the Principles of the Torah.* Yet the emphasis here is on the *conduct* resulting from this fear, rather than on the state of one's intellect. This "fear of God" is rooted in the faculties of the soul that are under the guidance of a perfect intellect. Only in the *Laws of the Principles of the Torah* does Maimonides explicitly present the notion of "fear of God" that like "love of God" is not an affect of the corporeal powers of the soul, and that belongs to the intellect alone as a result of its apprehension.

VII

A study of Maimonides' approach to love of God in the *Mishneh Torah* and the *Guide* reveals an overall consistency in the views he presents. The fact that the former composition was intended for a general audience and the latter for an elite group did not lead him to formulate his views differently on this issue. Moreover, there is a surprising similarity in the writing technique he employs in dealing with philosophical topics in these compositions. This point is true also of his *Commentary on the Mishnah*. Maimonides' practice of revealing his views in "flashes" can already be discerned in the *Commentary* and plays an important role in the *Mishneh Torah*.[80]

> If you wish to grasp the totality of what this Treatise contains, so that nothing of it will escape you, then you must connect its chapters one with another; and when reading a given chapter, your intention must be not only to understand the totality of the subject of that chapter, but also to grasp each word that occurs in it in the course of the speech, even if that word does not belong to the intention of the chapter. For the diction of this Treatise has not been chosen at haphazard, but with great exactness and exceeding precision, and with care to avoid failing to explain any obscure point. (*Guide* 1:Introduction.15)

This instruction should be kept in mind also when reading parts of the *Commentary on the Mishnah* and the *Mishneh Torah*. The study of the love of God in the *Mishneh Torah* furnishes a good example. Maimonides links "love" with other notions, employs these terms in the discussion of diverse laws, and in this manner creates a vast conceptual world that is revealed only to one who reads his formulations carefully.

A close reading also reveals problems that otherwise are not immediately evident. Throughout his writings Maimonides treats the fear of God as serving as a means to ensure obedience to the Law, to cultivate desirable character traits and to pursue intellectual perfection. The view of "fear" as a means is true also of Maimonides' sources. In the beginning of the *Mishneh Torah* Maimonides posits a type of fear that is rooted solely in the intellect and belongs to the very goal of human striving. Moreover, only by achieving this type of fear is one said to fulfill the commandment to fear God. This stands in striking contrast to Maimonides' definition of the commandment in the *Book of the Commandments* where fear is defined in terms of fear of the divine punishment.

Maimonides may have decided to modify his approach to fear in formulating this commandment in the *Laws of the Principles of the Torah* due to the problems raised by his definition in the *Book of the Commandments*. A person is required to reach a level in which one no longer fulfills the commandments from the motive of fear of punishment. How then can the Law command something that ideally should be dispensed with? Other definitions, however, were available to Maimonides. In linking fear also with ethical traits, as he does in the *Commentary on the Mishnah*, he could have defined "fear of God" in terms of extreme humility, include this commandment in the *Laws of Character Traits*, and link it with the commandment that opens this section, *You shall walk in His ways,* the commandment of *imitatio Dei*. I am not trying to suggest a more "logical" organization of Maimonides' legal compendium. I only wish to point out that his approach to fear of God in the *Laws of the Principles of the Torah* is so exceptional in relation to the rest of his writings that it arouses astonishment. Instead of linking fear with actions and ethical traits that at best serve as a means to intellectual perfection or result from it, why does he link fear of God with the other commandments that involve intellectual apprehension alone?

Moreover, Maimonides enumerates the love and fear of God as separate commandments, yet he does not distinguish the path by which they are fulfilled. The same knowledge of reality is involved in each case. At first glance, it does not appear that one can fulfill either of the commandments without fulfilling the other. What then does the "fear of God" add to the "love of God"? It is noteworthy that Maimonides not only lists love of God prior to fear—a point that can be explained by regarding love of God as being the more fundamental commandment of the two—but describes it as occurring prior to fear. Traditionally, love of God was viewed as following the fear of God. Just as perplexing is the fact that after defining fear in terms of intellectual awe in the beginning of the *Mishneh Torah,* Maimonides does not appear to leave some trace of this approach in the rest of his compendium as he does in the case of love of God.

In conclusion, the fear that Maimonides describes in the *Laws of the Principles of the Torah* designates a type of humbleness of spirit that belongs to the intellect. It is not an ethical trait or an emotional "feeling." This fear is reminiscent of the philosophic exhortation: "Know thyself." For Maimonides, it is intrinsically bound up with and completes the demand: "Know God." Despite the fact that Maimonides treats love and fear of God as two sides of the same coin, it is important to note the essential distinction between these commands. The former focuses directly on God. The latter command too focuses on God, but involves self-focus. Love always seeks union. The ultimate desire of the lover is to unite with the beloved, to become one. Love of God, if left unchecked, leads to the pursuit of *unio mystica*, which is an impossibility for Maimonides. Fear serves to preserve the gap between the individual and the object of fear.[81] With the fear of God, the person understands one's own nature in the scheme of the world, and by extension one's inability ever to breach God's impenetrable transcendence. The imagery used by Maimonides in describing the fear of God alludes to this point: "And when he thinks of these matters in themselves, he immediately *recoils* (*nirta' le-'ahorav*) from fear and terror. He knows he is a small, lowly, dark creature, with an insignificant and limited intellect, who stands before the Perfect Intellect" (*Laws of the Principles of the Torah* 2:2). Love and fear of God thus represent a form of flow and ebb. Love draws the individual closer, fear pulls the individual back. Love of God alone may result in a form of intellectual hubris. Fear of God, which is defined in terms of intellectual humility, serves to avoid this danger. Maimonides' concern here may have been that his readers not misunderstand the limits in the human striving for the ultimate end, at the same time that he strongly encourages this striving.[82]

In the *Mishneh Torah* Maimonides presents a complex approach to fear of God. He sees fear of God as a means to obedience and the pursuit of perfection. On the highest level it is an integral part of perfection. He treats fear as an emotion. On the highest level it is purely intellectual. The highest level is presented at the beginning of the legal corpus in order to clarify what is the final goal. In other passages he focuses only on the lower levels of fear due to their importance as means. On the other hand, love of God by nature is always regarded as an end. Thus Maimonides constantly alludes to his view that this state is integrally bound up with intellectual perfection.

APPENDIX
Synopsis of the Book

CHAPTER 1

The purpose of most of Maimonides' literary activity must be understood from a political perspective. Maimonides' concern was not in furthering the frontiers of philosophic knowledge, or even in teaching political philosophy per se. Rather, it was in teaching Mosaic Law as the ideal expression of political philosophy. This is as true of his "philosophic" treatise, *The Guide of the Perplexed*, as of his great legal compendium, *Mishneh Torah*. At the same time, Maimonides' goal was to reorient Mosaic legislation to direct its adherents to what was considered to be true happiness in the Aristotelian tradition, while preserving the fabric of the Jewish tradition. Maimonides' life work may be characterized as the practical implementation of political philosophy in reference to the Jewish people. The task was an exceptionally complex one, calling for the delicate balancing of many competing concerns. In this chapter I explore some of the concerns that enter into a number of central topics addressed by Maimonides in the *Guide*, his legal writings, and in some of his public epistles.

1. Maimonides' view of Judaism from the perspective of the political philosophic tradition. His definition of political philosophy in *Treatise on Logic* and the importance of this definition in understanding his literary works.

2. The metaphysical dimensions of political philosophy in medieval Aristotelianism. God is the impersonal First Cause from whom emanates the order of existence. God exercises no direct involvement in human affairs. Society is regarded as necessary for human existence and for the perpetuation of the human species. The natural purpose of the human species is the attainment of intellectual perfection. This is best achieved in societies whose leaders have attained perfection and can direct society to the pursuit of perfection. "Revelation" does not indicate actual speech originating in God, but a special "emanation" from the Active Intellect to the perfect rational faculty and imagination of individuals, strengthening these faculties and allowing them to reach greater heights in their knowledge. Maimonides accepts this picture. The divinity of the Law for him lies in the fact that it is the product of the "revelation" to Moses' perfect intellect, enabling him to lay down a perfect and unique legislation. For social reasons, these philosophic truths must be taught in a veiled manner. The picture of God's "personal" involvement in revealing the Law,

and in reward and punishment, remains the public teaching. Maimonides' view of God's attributes of action and "emanating perfection" is crucial for appreciating his approach to *imitatio Dei* in the human sphere.

3. The role of the prophets and rabbinic sages in adapting Mosaic legislation to their historical period. Maimonides views himself as part of this continuum. *Mishneh Torah* represents his crowning achievement. This work reflects a combination of radical innovation and conservatism. A discussion of some of the competing concerns that characterize this work and how Maimonides mediates between them: the social welfare of Jewish society at large and the intellectual perfection of the elite; the radical inflexibility of Mosaic legislation, and the need for change as social conditions change. Built into the Law, in Maimonides' view, are mechanisms allowing for adaptation, though not allowing for formal change. Maimonides' approach to "oral law."

4. Political institutional authority within Judaism. Maimonides' approach to the authority of the prophet and the considerations underlying his approach. His distinction between private and public prophecy and his attempt to severely limit the latter in his legal writings. The relation between the prophet and the king-messiah in his writings.

5. The ways Abraham and Moses combated idolatry in Maimonides' view. How Maimonides' understanding of these two historical paradigms influenced his own legal-pedagogical approach in promoting his view of monotheism.

6. Idolatry and Maimonides' approach to the reasons for the commandments in the *Guide*. Problems raised by Maimonides' approach. Comparison with his approach in *Mishneh Torah*.

7. Maimonides' discussion of creation in *Guide* in light of the issue of polytheism and idolatry. While Abraham treated as Aristotelian philosopher in *Laws of the Principles of the Torah*, he is treated as anti-Aristotelian philosopher in *Guide*. Maimonides' stance on astrology should also be viewed in light of the threat of polytheism.

8. Commandment to sanctify the Name of God as an example for seeing how different competing concerns enter into Maimonides' discussions. Relation between this commandment and Maimonides' approach to ethics. Comparison between his discussions of this commandment in his various writings, and how various social-pedagogical considerations influenced the formulations of his views.

9. The importance of the critical scholarly approach for the interpretation of Maimonides.

CHAPTER 2

In Aristotelian thought, the practical intellect is a faculty of the rational soul responsible for knowledge of ethics and politics. Maimonides mentions the practical functions of the rational faculty in several writings. In contrast to his sources, however, he never explicitly mentions the practical intellect or practical rational faculty. This omission does not indicate a substantive departure from Aristotelian thought. Maimonides regards ethics and politics as being essentially rooted in the deliberative activity of the rational faculty. These areas, as well as divination, involve the interplay of the rational faculty and the imaginative faculty. Perfect ethical and political systems, together with prophetic divination, involve also the scientific knowledge contained in the theoretical intellect. Maimonides' omission of the term "practical intellect" serves to underline his view that the perfection of the rational faculty lies in the perfection of its theoretical component. By means of the theoretical rational faculty one learns the sciences, wherein lies final human perfection and the immortality of the intellect.

1. The practical intellect in Aristotelian thought. Maimonides' omission in mentioning this faculty despite attributing ethical and political knowledge to the rational faculty.

2. Distinction between "intellect" and "rational faculty" in Maimonides' thought. The intellect possesses only theoretical (scientific) knowledge by means of which one attains the final end and immortality. The rational faculty refers to the human being's power to attain both theoretical and practical knowledge. Ethical knowledge belongs to the rational faculty. Yet this knowledge does not belong to the theoretical intellect. In light of this distinction a number of problematic passages in Maimonides' writings are explored.

3. Discussion of Maimonides' parabolic treatment of the Garden of Eden story in *Guide* 1:2. Adam's sin lies in turning away from constant contemplation of theoretical truths to focusing upon corporeal matters. Maimonides' negative attitude to generally accepted moral knowledge, equated by him with knowledge of "good and evil," does not represent a rejection of the value of this knowledge. His purpose is to stress its inferior value in comparison to knowledge of "true and false"—that is, knowledge of the sciences.

4. Ethical knowledge traced to rational faculty's power of deliberation. Alfarabi's view on this matter is explored.

5. All governance for Maimonides results from the cooperation between the practical rational faculty and the imagination. Maimonides alternately singles out one of these faculties as responsible for governance depending upon the context of the discussion. In discussions of nonperfect governance in contrast to prophetic governance, or governance in contrast to theoretical contemplation, the imaginative component of governance is stressed. Comparison with Alfarabi's views.

6. Discussion of Maimonides' view that Mosaic prophecy alone did not involve an emanation to the imaginative faculty, and the distinction drawn by him between Mosaic Law and non-Mosaic legislations.

7. Discussion of prophetic and nonprophetic divination. Both forms involve

the imagination and the practical rational faculty. The former involves also the theoretical rational faculty.

8. Discussion of those passages in Maimonides' writings that suggest that certain ethical propositions may be known by the theoretical intellect. Basis for distinguishing between different types of ethical knowledge in Maimonides' thought.

CHAPTER 3

Maimonides never uses "good" as a notion describing solely the utility of an action irrespective of the end to which it aims. His definition of a "good and excellent action" as an "action aiming at a noble end and achieves that end" is the primary one underlying his various uses of the term. Actions aiming at imaginary ends are never labeled "good" despite their efficacy. Maimonides implicitly identifies "noble end" with existence. Hence all that exists, and every action that contributes to existence, both to the perpetuation of life and the attainment of one's final end, is considered by him "good."

1. Summary of the interpretations of W. Z. Harvey and Sara Klein-Braslavy of Maimonides' approach to "good." Despite differences between their interpretations, both see at the root of Maimonides' approach his definition of "good" as "an expression applied by us to what conforms to our purpose." According to them, Maimonides' distinction between good and true is between the subjective and objective. Against this view I argue that Maimonides' distinction is the Aristotelian distinction between *praxis* and *theoria*. "Good" is equated by Maimonides with an activity aiming at the actualization of a "noble end." Maimonides' Islamic Aristotelian sources are discussed.

2. Further exploration of Maimonides' treatment of "good" in his interpretation of the Garden of Eden story. Identification of "good" with knowledge of generally accepted moral dictums, which results from Adam's sin, does not contradict the view I have outlined. Adam's "sin" lies in becoming engrossed in corporeal matters instead of remaining focused on the eternal truths of the sciences. Ethics comes into play at this stage since it governs the corporeal life of the individual. This knowledge is to be distinguished from knowledge of unchanging scientific truths. Knowledge of ethics is inferior to theoretical knowledge. Nevertheless, after Adam's "sin," it plays a positive role in governing human existence. Maimonides' complex approach to the well-known moral dictums parallels his approach to those who are said to know good and bad—the nonprophetic rulers and legislators. His treatment of them alternates between positive and negative depending on the context of the discussion.

3. Analysis of the various Arabic terms employed by Maimonides for "good" and "bad" in his various writings. Maimonides does not draw any distinction be-

tween them, despite appearances to the contrary in *Guide* 1:2. Comparison with Alfarabi's usage.

4. Relation between the "good" and God's activity in giving existence to the world. Existence is said to be "good" according to Maimonides since it conforms to God's purpose in creating the world. This "subjective" approach to "good" is designed to negate the notion that there is a final purpose to the world. Maimonides' stance raises the problem whether he regards creation as an arbitrary act of will or consequent upon divine wisdom. In the final analysis Maimonides views existence as having intrinsic value. Thus God's wisdom dictates giving existence to the world. Final purpose of the world is existence itself. This is in conformity with God's wisdom/will.

5. While distinction exists between "good" (realm involving *praxis*) and "true" (realm of *theoria*) in the human realm, there is no such distinction in the divine realm. All existence is the product of divine volition, and necessary for achieving a "noble end"—namely, the chain of existence itself—hence it is "good." All existence is also the object of divine intellection, hence "true." Chapter concludes with a discussion why Maimonides applies the rabbinic notion: "The Torah speaketh in the language of the sons of man" to the verse *And God saw that it was good.*

CHAPTER 4

Maimonides' view of *imitatio Dei* and human perfection is the theme of this chapter. This issue involves a host of others. At the foundation of this issue is the problem of the nature of the human intellect and its relation to the soul and the body on one hand, and its relation to God and the Active Intellect on the other. Maimonides presents a fundamentally coherent approach to human perfection. This is not to say, however, that all the inconsistencies in his writings are more apparent than real, or that he was not at times tentative in his conclusions. There are two aspects of divine and human perfection. The perfection of the intellect characterizes the essence of God and of the perfect individual, despite all the differences between the two intellects. The other aspect involves God's attributes of action. God governs the universe in a perfect manner. Hence one "imitates" God by perfect governance, whether it be of one's self (ethics) or of others (politics). The link between God's essence and activity is the notion of "emanating perfection" in which God's perfection results in giving existence to the entire chain of existence that is beneath God, without a loss of God's own perfection as a result. This type of perfection is true of all the higher level entities—that is, the Separate Intellects and the spheres. In the human plane, emanating perfection involves living the life of constant contemplation while *simultaneously* being physically engaged in governance. Other views of *imitatio Dei* in Maimonides' writings are also explored, as is his view of the relation between this notion and the idea of "holiness" when applied to the human realm.

1. The framework for approaching Maimonides' view of *imitatio Dei* and the problems involved in this issue.

2. Political leadership as *imitating* God whose actions, but not whose essence, can be known. Another model of perfection sees the perfection of the intellect as providing a point of resemblance with God, whose essence is perfect intellect. This perfection leads also to the immortality of the intellect and its eternal felicity.

3. Dissonance between these two views of perfection. One appears to come at the expense of the other. "Emanating perfection" provides key to bridging the two since it posits that both perfections can be practiced at the same time.

4. A discussion of the "acquired intellect," conjunction and immortality in Maimonides' thought. The individual who attains the acquired intellect has two "identities"—one as an intellect separate from matter and the other as a physical existent. Each practices the perfection appropriate to it.

5. How committed was Maimonides to this model in light of all the problems he knew characterized it? Maimonides does not abandon the possibility of attaining the acquired intellect, conjoining with the Active Intellect and achieving immortality, though he appears to be more tentative in his approach to these matters in the *Guide*.

6. Contexts in which Maimonides mentions *imitatio Dei* not involving only the human realm.

7. Holiness and *imitatio Dei*. Relation between holiness and ethical perfection.

8. Contemporary significance of Maimonides' approach to human perfection.

CHAPTER 5

At least five major apparent contradictions emerge from Maimonides' discussions of ethics:

1. Ethics as a means versus ethics as an end in itself, if not the ultimate end.

2. Ethics as a purely social institution that is applicable only in social contexts versus ethics as a domain pertaining to the individual *qua* individual and necessary for perfection even when in a state of isolation.

3. Ethics defined in terms of the doctrine of the mean versus ethics defined in terms of extremism.

4. Ethics as known by reason versus ethics as established solely by social convention or laid down by revelation.

5. All individuals being capable in principle of attaining ethical perfection versus many individuals barred by nature from ever attaining this perfection.

In this chapter I focus on Maimonides' conflicting views whether ethics is necessary only in a social context or whether it is also necessary for the perfection of the individual *qua* individual. From my conclusions on this issue, I draw some implications for understanding Maimonides' ethical thought as a whole. Maimonides does not alternate between fundamentally different approaches to ethics, but between different perspectives on ethics. The apparent inconsistency in his approach results from his desire to stress different points in different discussions, at times even in the same discussion. This leads him to exaggerate a point and treat it as the whole picture, while ignoring the other perspectives. There is no logical inconsistency between the view that the purpose of ethics is communal welfare and the view that ethics is necessary in the quest for individual perfection independent of any social dimension. The inconsistency arises only when Maimonides appears to maintain that the *sole* purpose of ethics is communal welfare. Similarly, Maimonides' conflicting attitudes to the doctrine of the mean, particularly in regard to the practice of asceticism, follow from his different perspectives on the purpose of ethics. Together his views form a coherent picture of ethics, but one that is blurred because of his alternating perspectives. This in turns leads to the problem why Maimonides chose to present his views on ethics in a manner that suggests an inconsistent approach rather than a unified picture. I suggest that these apparent contradictions were introduced on purpose in order to signal the attentive reader that the perspective by which ethics is viewed must constantly be altered to understand the full picture. The nonperceptive reader, on the other hand, remains with the perspective most appropriate for this reader's understanding.

1. Summary of the apparent contradictions in Maimonides' approach to ethics.

2. Ethics as important for the perfection of the individual in Maimonides' writings.

3. Ethics as important for the welfare of society in Maimonides' writings. Some passages suggest that this is the sole purpose of ethics. At the end of the *Guide* Maimonides indicates that ethics is not a perfection that belongs to the individual *qua* individual. Yet he maintains in the conclusion of the chapter that the ultimate perfection of the individual is the practice of loving-kindness, righteousness, and judgment.

4. Two possible solutions to the dilemma: there are two types of moral virtues, one primarily promoting the perfection of the individual and the other the well-being of society; moral virtues contribute simultaneously to both these ends. Problems with both these solutions.

5. Maimonides approaches the role of ethics from two different perspectives. The perspective he adopts depends on the context of the discussion.

6. Two apparently contradictory approaches to asceticism in Maimonides' thought. Maimonides may be interpreted as hinting that extreme asceticism is appropriate for the elite at a certain point in their quest for perfection, and not simply as a therapeutic measure. For society at large he favors the doctrine of the mean. A discussion of the *ḥasid* in Maimonides' thought.

7. Other apparent contradictions in Maimonides' approach to ethics can also be resolved by interpreting Maimonides as constantly switching the perspective from which he approaches the issue. Pedagogical considerations lie at the basis of this style of presentation.

8. How Maimonides' apparently contradictory views on ethics coalesce to form a coherent picture.

CHAPTER 6

Maimonides went to extreme lengths in inculcating the belief in the incorporeality of God. One who does not accept this belief fails to observe a fundamental commandment. Moreover, such an individual is designated a heretic. Belief in God's incorporeality represents the meeting ground between law, philosophy, and public education in Maimonides' thought. His approach, though not entirely without precedent, is quite exceptional in the Jewish legal tradition. The question raised by Maimonides' teachings in this sphere is the reason it was so important for him to inculcate publicly belief in God's incorporeality. The primary answer lies in the type of environment it helps create for the potential elite. This belief holds no epistemic value for the masses who are incapable of grasping it properly. Moreover, Maimonides was well aware that his move reflects a fundamental change of strategy from that of the Torah. While the Torah hints at this belief, it publicly teaches belief in the corporeality of God. The historical changes that led Maimonides to adopt his educational approach and the question whether he was entirely consistent in this approach in the gamut of writings are discussed.

1. The gap between the correct opinions imparted by the Torah, and the knowledge that leads to ultimate perfection.

2. The limited epistemic value for the masses of the correct opinions imparted by the Torah, such as the incorporeality of God, given the fact that from a philosophical standpoint they are incapable of grasping them properly. The need to educate the masses in stages during the course of history.

3. Maimonides saw that the time was ripe to teach publicly that God is incorporeal. and label one who believes in a corporeal deity a heretic. The spread of the monotheistic belief allowed for this change in public teaching. The threat of the belief in many gods no longer posed such a grave danger as it had previously.

4. A discussion of Maimonides' presentation of the belief in the incorporeality of God in the *Laws of the Principles of the Torah.*

5. Not only had historical progress in the spread of the monotheistic idea led Maimonides to adopt his pedagogical-legal stance, but also his view of the intellectual regression of the rabbinic authorities of his period. It was important for him to reach and direct the potential elite by means of his legal writings.

6. An exploration of the question whether Maimonides was consistent in the doctrine of God that he inculcated in his legal writings. Differences between his *Commentary on the Mishnah* and *Mishneh Torah*, on one hand, and *Book of the Commandments* on the other.

7. The conception of God inculcated in the *Guide*. Greater stress on the notion of God as Creator in the *Guide* than in the *Introduction to Pereq Heleq* or *Laws of the Principles of the Torah*. A discussion of the reasons for this stress in Maimonides' theological treatise. Conclude with a discussion of Maimonides' approach to this issue in his *Treatise on Resurrection.*

CHAPTER 7

In *Laws of the Principles of the Torah*, Maimonides treats love and fear of God as divine commandments. The only way to fulfill them is by knowledge of the natural and metaphysical sciences. These commandments—together with the commandments to know that God exists, that God is one, and that there are no other gods—form a unique category. They are fulfilled solely by the activity of the intellect, and involve no physical act at all (or abstention from physical activity), not even speech. This chapter explores Maimonides' approach to the love and fear of God from a number of perspectives.

1. Maimonides' definition of love and fear of God in the *Laws of the Principles of the Torah.*

2. A comparison between the formulation of these commandments in *Laws of the Principles of the Torah*, *Book of the Commandments*, and in the rabbinic sources cited by Maimonides.

3. Discussion of the approaches of R. Saadiah Gaon, R. Baḥya Ibn Paquda, and R. Hefeṣ b. Yaṣliaḥ to love and fear of God. Their views bear marked resemblance to those of Maimonides and appear to have served as the primary sources for his views.

4. Maimonides' definition of love of God in *Laws of the Principles of the Torah* is crucial for appreciating the significance of the organization and formulation of other commandments in the *Mishneh Torah*. Special attention is paid to the *Book of Love*, *Laws of Repentance*, and *Laws of the Sanhedrin*. The use of the term "love" in these contexts should be appreciated in light of his definition. Maimonides' approach to prophecy, wisdom, *kavvanah* (intention), and the qualifications for rabbinic leadership are touched upon in the course of the discussion. Hints scattered by Maimonides in the *Mishneh Torah* to his views on topics related to love of God are further amplified in the *Guide of the Perplexed.*

5. Maimonides' definition of fear of God in *Laws of the Principles of the Torah* in terms of intellectual awe finds no further expression in the rest of the *Mishneh*

Torah. Only inferior forms of "fear," such as fear of divine punishment, are presented. This in itself calls for an explanation.

6. Further discussion of love and fear of God in *Guide of the Perplexed*. While the approach to love parallels that found in *Laws of the Principles of the Torah*, the approach to fear is more reminiscent of Maimonides' other writings.

7. Esoteric writing style characteristic of the *Guide* can be detected in Maimonides' earlier writings. Conclude with a discussion why love and fear of God are treated by Maimonides as two separate commandments, though he draws no distinction between the knowledge by means of which each of these commandments is fulfilled.

NOTES

AJSREVIEW – Association for Jewish Studies Review
HUCA — Hebrew Union College Annual
IOS — Israel Oriental Studies
HTR — Harvard Theological Review
JQR — Jewish Quarterly Review
PAAJR — Proceedings of the American Academy of Jewish Research

Chapter 1. Maimonides' Political Thought: Introductory Essay

1. For a survey of Maimonides' philosophy, see my "Moses Maimonides," in *History of Jewish Philosophy*, ed. Daniel H. Frank and Oliver Leaman (London: Routledge, 1997), 245–80. The history of the two basic approaches to the understanding of Maimonides' philosophy has been traced by Aviezer Ravitzky, "The Secrets of the *Guide of the Perplexed*: Between the Thirteenth and the Twentieth Centuries," in *Studies in Maimonides*, ed. I. Twersky (Cambridge: Harvard University Press, 1990), 159–207.

2. A listing of these treatises has been compiled by Fred Rosner, "Maimonides the Physician: Bibliography," *Bulletin of the History of Medicine* 43 (1969): 221–23.

3. For the most thorough scholarly study of Maimonides' code, see Isadore Twersky, *Introduction to the Code of Maimonides* (New Haven: Yale University Press, 1980).

4. All English citations in this book are from Shlomo Pines's translation of *The Guide of the Perplexed* (Chicago: University of Chicago, 1963). The Arabic edition utilized in this volume is that of Joseph Kafiḥ, *Moreh HaNevukhim* (Jerusalem: Mossad HaRav Kook, 1972). That one should view the *Guide* as a Jewish work rather than a philosophical one has been argued by Leo Strauss in his *Persecution and the Art of Writing* (Glencoe, Ill.: Free Press, 1952), 42–46. See also his introduction to Pines's translation of the *Guide*, "How to Begin to Study the *Guide of the Perplexed*," xiv.

5. See Maimonides' introduction to the *Mishneh Torah*. For a study of Maimonides' stated reasons for writing the code, see Twersky, *Introduction to the Code of Maimonides*, 20–47.

6. See Maimonides' introduction to the *Guide*.

7. More than any other scholar, Leo Strauss has focused on this perspective for understanding Maimonides' thought. See in particular his *Philosophy and Law*, trans. F. Baumann (Philadelphia: Jewish Publication Society, 1987).

8. An English translation of the treatise was published by Israel Efros, "Maimonides' Treatise on Logic," *PAAJR* 8 (1938): 34–65. Efros subsequently published the entire Arabic text in *PAAJR* 34 (1966): 1–42.

9. There is no established date for the treatise, though it long has been regarded as one of Maimonides' first works. Harry Fox has demonstrated that the strongest evidence adduced for an early dating rests on a mistake. See "Maimonides on Aging and the Aged in Light of the Esoterist/Harmonist Debate," in *The Thought of Moses Maimonides*, ed. I. Robinson, L. Kaplan, and J. Bauer (Lewiston, N.Y.: Edwin Mellen Press, 1990), 49–53. One is left to hypothesize at what point in his literary career Maimonides most likely would have written a work of this nature. I find Fox's argument that this work was written close to the writing of the *Guide* unconvincing. For several reasons I continue to view this work as one of Maimonides' earliest.

10. Maimonides lists fourteen principles for determining what is to be counted as a Torah commandment in the *Book of the Commandments*. He divides his *Mishneh Torah* into fourteen books, while calling this treatise also *Yad ha-Ḥazakah* (*yad* meaning "hand," and in gematria having the value of fourteen). In the *Guide* he again divides the commandments into fourteen categories, but not identical ones to those in the *Mishneh Torah*. The number nevertheless remains the same.

11. A similar type of treatise was written by several Islamic philosophers including Alfarabi. Maimonides' classification of the sciences in the wider context of this topic has been explored Harry A. Wolfson, "The Classification of Sciences in Medieval Jewish Philosophy," *HUCA* 2 (1925): 263–315, reprinted in his *Studies in the History of Philosophy and Religion*, ed. I. Twersky and G. Williams, vol. 1 (Cambridge: Harvard University Press, 1973), 493–550. Wolfson returned to the issue of Maimonides' view of political philosophy in "Note on Maimonides' Classification of the Sciences," *JQR* 26 (1936): 369–77, reprinted in *Studies in the History of Philosophy and Religion,* 1:551–60. This issue has attracted much subsequent discussion. See in particular Joel Kraemer, "Maimonides on the Philosophic Sciences in his Treatise on the Art of Logic," in *Perspectives on Maimonides*, ed. Joel Kraemer (Oxford: Oxford University Press, 1991), 77–104. In developing his views Kraemer deals with many of the previous treatments of this subject. Among them are those of Leo Strauss, "Maimonides' Statement on Political Science," *PAAJR* 22 (1953): 115–30; and L. V. Berman, "A Reexamination of Maimonides' Statement on Political Science," *Journal of the American Oriental Society* 89 (1969): 106–11.

12. This translation is based on that of Kraemer, "Maimonides on the Philosophic Sciences," 95–96.

13. See ibid., 98–101.

14. This interpretation is supported by Maimonides' subsequent remarks in the *Guide of the Perplexed* 2:39. Does Maimonides have only Mosaic Law in mind when he speaks of divine commands? Based on Maimonides' subsequent treatment of the other major religions with which he was acquainted—Christianity and Islam—I would argue that he certainly did not wish to label any other legislation, when taken in its entirety, as divine. Neither are they *nomoi* in the strict sense. *Nomoi*, as defined by Maimonides, are presented by their legislators as being of human origin. Maimonides considers the legislation contained in the other religions to be imitations of the divine Law.

15. See Isaac Shailat, ed. and trans., *Letters and Essays of Moses Maimonides* (in Arabic and Hebrew) (Maaleh Adumim, Israel: Maaliyot Press, 1988), 553. For Maimonides' indebtedness to Alfarabi's political philosophy, see in particular Leo Strauss, "Farabi's Plato," in *Louis Ginzberg Jubilee Volume*, ed. A. Marx, S. Lieberman, S. Spiegel, and S. Zeitlin (New York: American Academy of Jewish Research, 1945), 357–93; and Lawrence Berman, "Maimonides: The Disciple of Alfarabi," *IOS* 4 (1974): 154–78.

16. See Warren Zev Harvey, "Political Philosophy and Halakhah in Maimonides" (in Hebrew), *Iyyun* 29 (1980): 198–212. I deal in detail with this issue in chap. 6.

17. See *Politics* 1.2.1252b–1253a.

18. For a discussion of this position, see in particular Herbert Davidson, "Alfarabi and Avicenna on the Active Intellect," *Viator* 3 (1972): 109–78. I discuss this issue in more detail in chap. 4, sections IV–V.

19. See my "Moses Maimonides."

20. More than any other modern scholar, Leo Strauss has made us sensitive to this point. See in particular "How to Begin to Study *The Guide of the Perplexed.*" See also Marvin Fox, *Interpreting Maimonides* (Chicago: University of Chicago Press, 1984). It is precisely because both these scholars were very careful readers who were concerned with the methodological problems involved in interpreting the *Guide* that it is interesting to see how their own ideological propensities influenced the way they understood the text.

21. For a study of Maimonides' philosophic sources, see in particular Pines's introduction to his translation, "The Philosophic Sources of *The Guide of the Perplexed*" lvii–cxxxiv.

22. See chap. 7.

23. The Latin Averroists presented such a dichotomy between philosophic truths and religious truths. Most likely, that they did so for the purpose of avoiding persecution while philosophizing unencumbered by religious dogma. Among Jewish thinkers, Isaac Albalag comes close to presenting a "double truth" theory, and it is clear that it is for this very purpose.

24. See chap. 6 for a further discussion of this point.

25. *Republic* 7.514a–521b.

26. I have dealt in detail with Maimonides' approach to prophecy in my doctoral dissertation, "Theories of Prophecy in Medieval Jewish Philosophy" (Brandeis University, 1981). I am at present working on a book on this subject. Maimonides' views on prophecy are discussed throughout this volume.

27. For a further discussion of this point, see chap. 4, sections IV–V.

28. For the view that Moses was the immediate agent of the Law, see Alvin Reines, "Maimonides' Concept of Mosaic Prophecy," *HUCA* 40 (1969): 350f.; Kalman Bland, "Moses and the Law According to Maimonides," in *Mystics, Philosophers and Politicians*, ed. J. Reinharz and D. Swetschinski (Durham, N.C.: Duke University Press, 1982), 49–66; and Jacob Levinger, *Maimonides as Philosopher and Codifier* (in Hebrew) (Jerusalem: Bialik Institute, 1989), 49–55.

29. See chap. 2, sections V–VI.

30. This point emerges from Maimonides' discussion in *Commentary on the Mishnah: Introduction to Pereq Ḥeleq* (*Sanhedrin* 10). Unfortunately, many readers focus upon the end of the introduction—Maimonides' presentation of the thirteen principles of Judaism—without taking a close look at the rest of the introduction and its implications for understanding his approach. Moreover, few carefully read Maimonides' formulation of the thirteen principles. Rather they rest content with their general meaning. No less than the *Guide*, this introduction contains more than one level of meaning. To grasp the views to which Maimonides alludes requires a close reading of the text in light of his *philosophic* sources. I will return to this point in chap. 6, section VI.

31. For a discussion of negative attributes in the philosophy of Maimonides and his predecessors, see in particular Harry Wolfson, "Maimonides on Negative Attributes," in *Louis Ginzberg Jubilee Volume,* ed. Marx et al., 411–46, reprinted in his *Studies in the History of Philosophy and Religion*, ed. I. Twersky and G. Williams, vol. 2 (Cambridge: Harvard University Press, 1977), 195-230.

32. For a discussion of this point, see Hannah Kasher, "The Myth of 'God's Anger' in the *Guide of the Perplexed*" (in Hebrew), *Eshel Beer Sheva* 4 (1996): 95-111. See also her "Maimonides' Interpretations of the Story of the Divine Revelation in the Cleft of the Rock" (in Hebrew), *Daat* 35 (1995): 29-66.

33. See *Aphorisms of the Statesman*, ed. and trans. D. M. Dunlop (Cambridge: Cambridge University Press, 1961): 54; *The Political Regime*, ed. Fauzi Najjar (Beirut: Imprimerie Catholique, 1964): 80–81. An English translation of this passage has been prepared by Fauzi Najjar and appears in *Medieval Political Philosophy,* ed. Ralph Lerner and Muhsin Mahdi (Ithaca: Cornell University Press, 1972), 37. For a further discussion of this point, see chap. 2, sec. VI.

34. For the reasons for writing the *Mishneh Torah,* see Twersky, *Introduction to the Code of Maimonides,* 20–81.

35. Jacob Levinger has shown that Maimonides basically adopted a conservative stance in the body of his legal rulings, rather than follow his personal views in science and philosophy. See *Maimonides' Techniques of Codification* (in Hebrew)

(Jerusalem: Magnes Press, 1965), 182–89; idem, *Maimonides as Philosopher and Codifier* (in Hebrew) (Jerusalem: Bialik Institute, 1989), 100–111. This point, however, requires further clarification. For an agenda of questions that require further study in regard to Maimonides' legal work, see Gerald Blidstein, "Where Do We Stand in the Study of Maimonidean Halakhah?" in *Studies in Maimonides*, ed. Twersky, 1–30.

36. Twersky's *Introduction to the Code of Maimonides* provides many examples of the importance of this point, as does Levinger's *Maimonides as Philosopher and Codifier*; and *Maimonides' Technique of Codification.* See also Gerald Blidstein, *Political Concepts in Maimonidean Halakha* (in Hebrew) (Ramat Gan, Israel: Bar-Ilan University, 1983); idem, *Prayer in Maimonidean Halakha* (in Hebrew) (Jerusalem: Bialik Institute, 1994). Some scholars have maintained that anything that Maimonides includes in his works indicates also his personal agreement. They tend to see Maimonides exercising far more flexibility in his legal rulings than I have suggested. I am of the opinion that this approach misconstrues the extent of flexibility that any legal authority, even a highly innovative one, has within the system. Often an authority must rule against personal inclinations since the weight of the legal tradition dictates such a ruling. Maimonides' own views emerge primarily from his unconventional rulings or ones that he indicates are not grounded in any source, from the changes he introduces in the formulations found in his rabbinic sources, and from the manner he organizes the legal material. See in particular Blidstein's discussion in the article cited in the previous note.

37. I discuss this point in more detail in chap. 5, section VI.

38. *Introduction to the Commentary on the Mishnah; Introduction to Pereq Ḥeleq* eighth and ninth principles; *Laws of the Principles of the Torah* 9:1; *Laws of Repentance* 3:8; *Guide* 2:39. For the view that the Oral Law was also given at Sinai, see *B.T. Sanhedrin* 99a.

39. There are talmudic passages that suggest the Torah will not undergo any change. See, for example, *B.T. Temurah* 16a. While Nahmanides agrees with Maimonides' position, in his commentary to Deut. 4:2 he indicates that it does not follow from a literal reading of the sages' statements in reference to adding or subtracting to the commandments.

40. For a discussion of the function of prayer in Maimonides' thought, and how different scholars approached this issue, see Ehud Benor, *Worship of the Heart* (Albany: State University of New York Press, 1995), 63–128.

41. See Harvey, "Political Philosophy and Halakhah in Maimonides," 198–212.

42. For a discussion of this issue see Gerald Blidstein, "Traditional and Institutional Authority—On Oral Law in Maimonides" (in Hebrew), *Daat* 16 (1986): 11–27.

43. See above, notes 35 and 36. Some recent papers have tried to show that Maimonides was less conservative than originally thought, and his approach to Oral Law provides the basis for his innovative rulings. Even if this is the case, overall Maimonides' legal corpus is a fairly conservative work in the content of his rulings.

44. See Jacob Levinger, "The Oral Law in Maimonides' Thought" (in Hebrew), *Tarbiz* 37 (1968): 282–93, reprinted in *Maimonides as Philosopher and Codifier,* 56–66. For Maimonides' relation to Karaite thought, see Daniel J. Lasker, "The Influence of Karaism on Maimonides" (in Hebrew), *Sefunot* 5 (1996): 145–61.

45. I deal in detail with this issue in chapters 6 and 7.

46. For an excellent study this subject, with particular reference to the institution of kingship, see Blidstein, *Political Concepts in Maimonidean Halakha.* See also his "Maimonidean Structures of Institutional Authority: Sefer Hamizvot Aseh 172–177," *Dine Yisrael* 17 (1993): 103–26.

47. An undercurrent of an opposing view can also be detected in the Talmud and in the works of subsequent legal authorities. This point, however, is outside the scope of my discussion.

48. See *Epistle to the Jews of Yemen,* in Shailat, *Letters and Essays of Moses Maimonides,* 82–171. This epistle was translated by Abraham Halkin and discussed by David Hartman in their *Crisis and Leadership: Epistles of Maimonides* (Philadelphia: Jewish Publication Society, 1985), 91–207.

49. One is tempted to argue that Maimonides' position emerges from a close reading of the Torah itself. Maimonides cites the verse in which God informs Moses: *And God said to Moses: I will come to you in the thickness of the cloud that the people may hear when I speak with you and have faith in you too forever* (Exod. 19:9). The Torah thereby indicates that it is the speech itself, rather than any other phenomenon, which is the basis for the people's belief. Yet given the Torah's description of this revelation, the embellishments added by the talmudic sages, and the way it was regarded by thinkers prior to Maimonides, such a distinction between belief on the basis of God's speech and belief on the basis of miracles appears to be forced. The Revelation at Sinai is depicted as the crowning miracle, one that combined many miraculous phenomena. Other considerations, rather than a literal reading of the biblical text, clearly underlie Maimonides' approach. It should be noted that Maimonides refrains from entering into the details of this revelation. He treats it as an audible, oracular phenomenon in which God's voice is heard. For a discussion of this issue, see my " 'The Voice of God' in Medieval Jewish Philosophical Exegesis" (in Hebrew), *Daat* 16 (1986): 32–36.

50. For a discussion of Maimonides' approach to authenticating who is a prophet, see my "The Verification of Prophecy in Medieval Jewish Philosophy" (in Hebrew), *Jerusalem Studies in Jewish Thought* 4 (1984–85): 1–18.

51. I will return to this theme in most of the subsequent chapters. See also my "Theories of Prophecy in Medieval Jewish Philosophy."

52. Maimonides' approach to messianism has been the subject of a number of penetrating studies. See in particular Amos Funkenstein, "Maimonides: Political Theory and Realistic Messianism," *Miscellanea Mediaevalia* 9 (1977): 81–103; Aviezer Ravitzky, " 'To the Utmost of Human Capacity': Maimonides on the Days of the Messiah," in *Perspectives on Maimonides,* ed. Kraemer, 221–56.

53. Maimonides tries to "finesse" the issue of the resurrection of the dead that was to take place in this period. This in turn brought against him the charge that he did not believe in resurrection, a charge that he addresses in the *Treatise on Resurrection*. See chap. 6, section VIII.

54. Hartman and Halkin, *Crisis and Leadership,* 124. In the conditions posited by Maimonides for determining whether an individual is the messiah in *Laws of Kings and Their Wars* chapter 11, the notion that the messiah will be a great prophet is not presented explicitly. His description of the messiah in 12:3, however, indicates that this in fact is the case in his view. In the epistle it is important for Maimonides to emphasize that the messiah is a great prophet in order to discredit the false messiah who arose in Yemen.

55. *Guide* 2:13. Cf. 3:29.

56. See Pines, "The Philosophic Sources of *The Guide of the Perplexed*" cxxiii–cxxiv. For a more recent treatment of Sabianism, see Michel Tardieu, "Sabiens Coraniques et 'Sabiens' de Harran," *Journal Asiatique* 274 (1986): 1–44.

57. See *Guide* 3:29–30, 37, 49. See also 1:63.

58. For a further discussion of this point, see chap. 6.

59. See my "The Land of Israel and Prophecy in Medieval Jewish Philosophy" (in Hebrew), in *The Land of Israel in Medieval Jewish Thought*, ed. M. Halamish and A. Ravitzky (Jerusalem: Yad Izhak Ben-Zevi, 1991), pp. 40–51.

60. The term can also be translated "delicate."

61. Cf. *Guide* 3:49. For a study of this commandment in Maimonides' thought, see Josef Stern, "Maimonides on the Covenant of Circumcision and the Unity of God," in *The Midrashic Imagination: Jewish Exegesis, Thought, and History*, ed. M. Fishbane (Albany: State University of New York Press, 1993), pp. 131–54.

62. *Targum Yonatan* to Gen. 4:26; *Mekhilta: ba-Ḥodesh*, 6 (Exod. 20:3).

63. Cf. *Laws of Idolatry* 2:4. It is important to note that Maimonides in the introduction to his *Commentary on the Mishnah* treats the notion that God alone is to be worshipped as one known by the intellect. In his subsequent writings, however, he no longer makes this claim. See Lawrence Kaplan, "Maimonides on the Singularity of the Jewish People," *Daat* 15 (1985): v–xxvi.

64. *Laws of Idolatry* 10:1; *Guide* 1:36, 1:54, 3:29, 3:37.

65. For a discussion of this issue, see my "A Fragment from a Philosophical Commentary on Ruth Ascribed to R. Nissim of Marseilles" (in Hebrew), in *Jerusalem Studies in Jewish Thought* 14 (1998): 160–69.

66. In 3:43 Maimonides refers to the symbolic explanation he gave in the *Mishneh Torah* to the blowing of the ram's horn on Rosh Hashanah. There he indicates that it symbolizes the act of waking up of slumbering souls and calling them to repentance (*Laws of Repentance* 3:4). For the view that in the *Guide* these symbolic explanations play a far more important role in Maimonides' approach to the commandments than I have suggested, see Josef Stern, "The Fall and Rise of Myth in Ritual: Maimonides versus Nahmanides on the *Ḥuqqim*, Astrology, and

the War against Idolatry," *Journal of Jewish Thought and Philosophy* 6 (1997): 213–16.

67. See Twersky, *Introduction to the Code of Maimonides,* 431. It should be kept in mind when studying this topic that the whole purpose of Maimonides' discussion of the commandments in the *Guide* is to show their purpose. This leads him to develop a systematic presentation of his views. In the *Mishneh Torah,* on the other hand, this topic is an incidental one. The purpose of the composition is to present the details of the commandments in a concise, organized manner. Maimonides' comments on the reasons for the commandments are significant but sporadic.

68. This example is cited in Twersky, *Introduction to the Code of Maimonides,* 434.

69. For *de'ot ra'ot* as evil character traits that require repentance, see *Laws of Repentance* 7:3

70. *Laws of Idolatry* 9:4. See also *Laws of Forbidden Foods* 11:7 (ms. Kushta); *Commentary on the Mishnah: Avodah Zarah* 1:3. It is important to note that the references to Christians were censored in many of the printed editions of the *Mishneh Torah.* Despite this view of Christianity, many of Maimonides' statements reflect the fact that he distinguishes between Christians and the idolaters of old. For a study of Maimonides' approach to Christianity, see David Novak, "The Treatment of Islam and Muslims in the Legal Writings of Maimonides," in *Studies in Islamic and Judaic Traditions*, ed. W. Brinner and S. Ricks (Atlanta: Scholars Press, 1986), 233–50. In his *Epistle to the Jews of Yemen*, Maimonides draws a distinction between Jesus' own teachings and the teachings of Christianity. He does not, however, elaborate on this point. It appears from his discussion that he regards belief in the Trinity and in the divine nature of Jesus to be later beliefs that were not part of the initial teaching. Jesus, in Maimonides' view, claimed to be the messiah who would resolve perplexities in the Law. See Hartman and Halkin, *Crisis and Leadership,* 98–99.

71. Joshua Blau, *R. Moses b. Maimon Responsa*, vol. 2 (Jerusalem: Mekize Nirdamim, 1960), 726 (no. 448). See, however, Maimonides' ruling on Moslem wine in Shailat, *Letters and Essays of Moses Maimonides,* 430.

72. *Epistle to the Jews of Yemen* (Hartman and Halkin, *Crisis and Leadership,* 99–100). *Guide* 2:39–40 contains only partially veiled derogatory references to Islam and its founder.

73. See Stern, "The Fall and Rise of Myth in Ritual," 205–16.

74. See Menachem Kellner, *Dogma in Medieval Jewish Thought* (Oxford: Oxford University Press, 1986), 10–65.

75. Significantly, in Maimonides' enumeration of types of heretics, this is the only heresy that is defined in terms of a physical act. All the others are defined in terms of belief alone.

76. In *Guide* 2:5 too Maimonides speaks of the worship of stars as intermediar-

ies. This emphasis is not found in one of Maimonides' most important rabbinic sources, *Mishnah Avodah Zarah* 4:7. The Mishnah speaks of idolatry in terms of worshipping certain objects as deities. The view advanced by Maimonides may be inferred from the discussion in *B.T. Rosh Hashanah* 24b, though it is not presented there explicitly.

77. Cf. 1:54.

78. Maimonides discusses creation in 2:13–31. For a summary of his approach to this issue see my "Moses Maimonides," 256–62.

79. It is important to note that Maimonides, following Alfarabi and Avicenna, does not view God as the *immediate* mover of the diurnal sphere. This task is reserved to the first of the Separate Intellects. See *Guide* 2:4.

80. For a study of this argument, see Herbert Davidson, "Arguments from the Concept of Particularization in Arabic Philosophy," *Philosophy East and West* 18 (1968): 299–314.

81. For a discussion of this point, see chap. 6, section VII.

82. In 1:35 Maimonides insists that the multitude be educated that God is incorporeal, but refrains from dealing with the angels. That the angels are incorporeal is mentioned in 1:49, and subsequently in 2:6–7. In his subsequent *Treatise on Resurrection* Maimonides explicitly maintains that if the masses do not accept this view of the angels they are not considered heretics. See Hartman and Halkin, *Crisis and Leadership,* 215.

83. I have dealt with this issue in "Maimonides' Approach to Astrology" (in Hebrew), *Proceedings of the Eleventh World Congress of Jewish Studies*, vol. 2 (Jerusalem, 1994), 25–32. For other discussions of Maimonides' approach to astrology, see Ralph Lerner, "Maimonides' Letter on Astrology," *History of Religions* 8 (1968): 143–58; Y. Tzvi Langerman, "Maimonides' Repudiation of Astrology," *Maimonidean Studies* 2 (1991): 123–58; Gad Freudenthal, "Maimonides' Stance on Astrology in Context: Cosmology, Physics, Medicine, and Providence," in *Moses Maimonides: Physician, Scientist and Philosopher*, ed. Fred Rosner and Samuel Kotteck (Northvale, N.J.: J. Aronson, 1993), 77–90; and Stern "The Fall and Rise of Myth in Ritual," 185–225.

84. *Commentary on Mishnah: Avodah Zarah* 4:7. Cf. *Guide* 3:29.

85. *Guide* 1:51–54; *Laws of the Principles of the Torah* 1:11.

86. See Kasher, "The Myth of 'God's Anger'," 95–111.

87. See his remarks on this subject in *Treatise on Resurrection* (Hartman and Halkin, *Crisis and Leadership* 215).

88. For a further discussion of this point, see my "Maimonides' Approach to Astrology," 25–32.

89. My translation is based on Joseph Kafiḥ's edition, *Mishnah 'im Perush Rabbenu Moshe b. Maimon: Seder Nezikin* (Jerusalem: Mossad HaRav Kook, 1965), 212.

90. This is how the epistle is generally referred to in English. The Arabic original

is lost. The title in the medieval translation *Iggeret ha-Shemad* is better rendered: *The Epistle on Forced Conversion* (or *Religious Persecution*). For the Hebrew translation, see Shailat, *Letters and Essays of Maimonides,* 30–59. For an English translation, see Hartman and Halkin, *Crisis and Leadership* 15–35.

91. One is said to profane the Name when one does not lay down one's life in situations in which one is commanded to do so. Maimonides, however, treats the wanton disregard of commandments as the prime example of profaning the Name. The former is a crime stemming from weakness of character, the latter from conviction.

92. For a further discussion of this point, see chap. 5, section I.

93. *B.T. Sanhedrin* 74a–b; cf. *B.T. Pesahim* 25b. It should be noted that the medieval rabbinic authorities applied the ruling that one should lay down one's own life rather than take the life of an innocent individual only to cases involving a fellow Jew. Maimonides can be interpreted as considering the prohibition to be more general, yet there are indications that he too followed the prevalent ruling. See in particular his formulation of the related prohibitions of not handing over an innocent hostage for execution and not killing an innocent person for purposes of healing oneself in *Laws of the Principles of the Torah* 5:5–7. This issue is a complex one both from a legal and an ethical perspective. I hope to deal with it in a different context. Suffice to say, this approach should not be interpreted as indicating that it was permissible to murder non-Jews. This was certainly not the case.

94. See, for example, *Laws of the Principles of the Torah* 5:4. Maimonides deals with this point at length in his *Epistle on Martyrdom.*

95. See Hartman and Halkin, *Crisis and Leadership* 17–21.

96. The Arabic edition utilized is that of Joseph Kafiḥ (Jerusalem: Mossad HaRav Kook, 1971), p. 63. The translation is my own. This work has been translated into English by C. B. Chavel based on the medieval Hebrew translation (London: Soncino Press, 1967).

97. The basis for Maimonides' ruling is *B.T. Sanhedrin* 74b.

98. For the relation between love of God and prophecy, see chap. 7, section IV.

99. I deal at length with this point in chap. 7.

100. In *Laws of the Principles of the Torah* 5:7, Maimonides summarizes his stance that one is not to commit idolatry under any circumstances by citing Deut. 6:5—*You shall love God your Lord with all your heart, all your soul and all your might.* This verse appears in the same context in Maimonides' talmudic sources.

101. Conversion to Islam consists of reciting the first *sura* of the Koran by which one acknowledges the one God and the mission of Mohammed. It is the acknowledgment of the mission of Mohammed that is the problematic aspect of the conversion ritual. Note that it is important for Maimonides to emphasize that no one is fooled by this charade, or holds any illusions about the sincerity of the convert. This point is important in light of his position in the *Book of Commandments*. There he indicates that we are not to allow the one who coerces us to think that we deny God

even though we continue to believe in God secretly. In this case, those who coerce the Jews to acknowledge the prophecy of Mohammed know that they are not sincere.

102. This point clearly emerges from Maimonides' own discussion of the situation in the epistle.

103. How solid the legal grounds for his ruling were in Maimonides' own eyes is a point of contention between Haym Soloveichik and David Hartman. See H. Soloveichik, "Maimonides' *Iggeret Ha-Shemad:* Law and Rhetoric," in *Rabbi Joseph H. Lookstein Memorial Volume*, ed. Leo Landman (New York: Ktav, 1980), 281–319; and Hartman in Hartman and Halkin, *Crisis and Leadership,* 46–90. I am in basic agreement with Soloveichik, who argues that Maimonides' position should be viewed more as rhetoric than law. Maimonides was not attempting to expand the borders of the law in this case. The act of conversion may not involve the violation of an explicit commandment, but in Maimonides' own account it inevitably leads to the transgression of commandments. His argument that their acquiescence to the act of conversion is permissible because the forced converts are capable of observing all the commandments is disingenuous in light of the continuation of his remarks describing what happens in reality. For the relation of Maimonides' stance to that of his father, see Eliezer Schlossberg, "The Attitude of R. Maimon, the Father of Maimonides, to Islam and Muslim Persecution" (in Hebrew), *Sefunot* 5 (1991): 95–107.

104. In *Laws of Repentance* 3:9, Maimonides condemns the forced convert who goes on to acquiesce to his conversion and rationalize it.

105. Maimonides' statements concerning the Karaites provide a good example of this phenomenon. Maimonides' changing attitude to the Karaites has been traced in Lasker, "The Influence of Karaism on Maimonides," 145–61. For a study of Maimonides' legal attitude to the Karaites, see Gerald Blidstein, "Maimonides' Approach to the Karaites" (in Hebrew), *Techumin* 8 (1987): 501–10.

106. This is the focus of David Hartman's approach in *Crisis and Leadership.*

107. Blidstein provides an excellent example of this approach in *Political Concepts in Maimonidean Halakha.*

108. For the study of this issue, see in particular *Meaning and Context: Quentin Skinner and His Critics*, ed. James Tully (Cambridge: Polity Press, 1988).

Chapter 2. The Practical Intellect

1. See, for example, *Aphorisms of the Statesman*, ed. and trans. D. M. Dunlop (Cambridge: Cambridge University, 1961), no. 6.

2. An outline of the theoretical sciences, based on Aristotelian sources, is presented by Maimonides in the last chapter of his treatise on logic. See Israel Efros, "Maimonides' Treatise on Logic," *PAAJR* 8 (1938): 62f. Efros edited the Arabic

edition of the treatise, which appears in *PAAJR* 34 (1966): 1–42. See also R. L. Weiss and C. E. Butterworth, *Ethical Writings of Maimonides* (New York: New York University Press, 1975), 158–63. Logic is labeled by Maimonides as a craft *(al-sina'a)*. It is treated by him as an instrument for learning the sciences, rather than as a science *(al-'ilm)* proper. Cf. *The Guide of the Perplexed* 1:34, 3:51.

3. See, for example, *Aphorisms,* no. 6. Cf. Fazlur Rahman, *Avicenna's Psychology* (London: Oxford University Press, 1952), 32. The distinction between theoretical and practical activities of the intellect has its source in Aristotle, *De Anima*, 3.7.431b; and *Nicomachean Ethics*, 6.2.1139a.

4. This is not to say that the theoretical intellect does not serve an important function even in regard to these areas. For a discussion of this point, see below.

5. See Alexander Altmann, "Maimonides on the Intellect and the Scope of Metaphysics," in his *Von der mittelalterlichen zur modernen Aufklärung* (Tübingen: J. C. B. Mohr, 1987), 60–129. Altmann's article not only illuminates Maimonides' views on the intellect and their sources in Aristotelian philosophy, but also provides an excellent response to Shlomo Pines's thought-provoking study, "The Limitations of Human Knowledge according to Al-Farabi, Ibn Bajja, and Maimonides," in *Studies in Medieval Jewish History and Literature*, ed. Isadore Twersky (Cambridge: Harvard University Press, 1979), 82–109. For a more recent detailed response to Pines, see Herbert Davidson, "Maimonides on Metaphysical Knowledge," *Maimonidean Studies* 3 (1992–93): 49–103.

6. See in particular *Aphorisms,* no. 6. A similar description of the rational faculty is presented by Alfarabi also in *The Political Regime*, ed. Fauzi Najjar. (Beirut: Imprimerie Catholique, 1964), 33f. Maimonides repeats much of Alfarabi's description verbatim. For a comparison between Maimonides' *Eight Chapters* and Alfarabi's *Aphorisms*, see Herbert Davidson, "Maimonides' *Shemonah Peraqim* and Alfarabi's *Fuṣūl al-Madani*," *PAAJR* 31 (1963): 116–33; and Jeffrey Macy, "A Study in Medieval Jewish and Arabic Political Philosophy: Maimonides' *Shemonah Peraqim* and Alfarabi's *Fuṣūl al-Madanī*" (Ph.D. diss., Hebrew University, 1982).

7. Alfarabi, *Aphorisms,* nos. 30, 35; idem, *Political Regime,* 34, 71f.; and Richard Walzer, *Al-Farabi on the Perfect State* (Oxford: Clarendon Press, 1985), 208, 218, 244. Alfarabi does not employ the phrase "practical rational faculty" in aphorism no. 6, but he divides the rational faculty into the "theoretical" and "practical." Maimonides adds the term "activities," though he subsequently goes on to refer to the learning of the crafts as a "power" of the rational faculty. For a study of the practical intellect in Alfarabi's thought, see Miriam Galston, *Politics and Excellence: The Political Philosophy of Alfarabi* (Princeton: Princeton University Press, 1990), 76–82.

8. For a detailed discussion of the different forms of intellect in Maimonides' philosophy, see Altmann, "Maimonides on the Intellect." Alfarabi's doctrine of the intellect, which profoundly influenced Maimonides' view, has been analyzed by Fazlur Rahman, *Prophecy in Islam* (London: George Allen and Unwin, 1958), 11–

14; and in far more detail by Herbert Davidson, "Alfarabi and Avicenna on the Active Intellect," *Viator* 3 (1972): 109–51. The importance of evaluating Maimonides' approach to ethics in light of the different types of intellect can be seen from Sara Klein-Braslavy's discussion in *Maimonides' Interpretation of the Adam Stories in Genesis* (in Hebrew) (Jerusalem: Reuven Mass, 1986).

9. Cf. 2:Introduction (propositions 10, 11). The term "intellect" in proposition 10 clearly refers to the hylic intellect. See also *Guide* 2:1.

10. See also the end of 3:51, where perfect knowledge of the intelligibles is described as leading to the passionate love of God.

11. In 3:54 wisdom of the crafts is treated as distinct from the wisdom involved in the rational virtues. Maimonides identifies the rational virtues as knowledge of the intelligibles. See also *Eight Chapters* 1, and *Treatise on Logic* 14.

12. For a discussion of Alfarabi's doctrine of the intellect, see Rahman, *Prophecy in Islam,* 12–14; and Davidson, "Alfarabi and Avicenna on the Active Intellect," 141f. I discuss this issue in more detail in chap. 4, sections IV–V.

13. *Laws of the Principles of the Torah* 4:8–9; *Laws of Repentance* 7:2–3; *Introduction to Pereq Ḥeleq* in *Mishnah 'im Perush R. Moshe B. Maimon: Seder Nezikin* (in Arabic and English), ed. and trans. Joseph Kafiḥ (Jerusalem: Mossad HaRav Kook, 1965), 205; *Guide* 1:30, 1:70, 1:72, 3:8, 3:27, 3:51, 3:54. Cf. *Guide* 1:40, 1:41, 1:74, 3:22. Unfortunately, Maimonides does not enter into detail on this matter. He clearly rules out the possibility of a complete apprehension of the Active Intellect and identity with it. He appears to have accepted the possibility of a partial apprehension of this existent and conjunction with it. See also *Guide* 1:43, 1:49, 1:62; *Laws of the Principles of the Torah* 7:1; *Introduction to Pereq Ḥeleq,* 212. For a discussion of this issue, see chap. 4, sections IV–V.

14. The translation is my own. Cf. *Introduction to Pereq Ḥeleq,* 205.

15. In *Treatise on Logic* 14, the division between these areas is pronounced. Ethics is assigned to the domain of practical philosophy. Cf. *Guide* 1:54, where the two are treated as distinct types of wisdom.

16. For a discussion of these terms and their significance for Maimonides' ethical thought, see chap. 3, section III.

17. See also the connection Maimonides draws between the moral virtues and the rational faculty in his discussion of justice in *Guide* 3:53–54.

18. Cf. *Treatise on Logic* 14; Alfarabi, *Aphorisms,* nos. 30, 34–35, 48, 49, 89.

19. *Guide* 1:2; *Eight Chapters* 6. Cf. *Guide* 2:35, 3:8; *Treatise on Logic* 8.

20. Maimonides' immediate source for this distinction is Alfarabi, *Aphorisms,* no. 13. A similar distinction is brought by R. Baḥya Ibn Paquda in *Duties of the Heart* 7:8. R. Baḥya, however, contrasts one who never sins with one who repents.

21. Maimonides reiterates the view that according to the sages one who subdues his inclination is on a higher level than the one who never sinned in *Laws of Repentance* 7:4.

22. *The Book of Beliefs and Opinions* 3:1–2. For a study of this category of

laws in R. Saadiah's thought, see Alexander Altmann, "Saadya's Conception of the Law," *Bulletin of John Rylands Library* 28 (1944): 320–39.

23. *Mishnah 'im Perush R. Moshe B. Maimon: Seder Nezikin*, 392. For a discussion of this passage, see Hannah Kasher, "Maimonides' Philosophical Division of the Law" (in Hebrew), *HUCA* 56 (1985): 1–7.

24. Reading (according to the better manuscripts) "but *('ela')* from their sages" rather than "and not *(ve-lo')* from their sages." According to the latter reading, one who obeys these laws from rational considerations, rather than belief in revelation, is not even to be considered a philosopher. For a discussion of this issue and its subsequent history in Jewish thought, see Steven S. Schwarzschild, "Do Noachites Have to Believe in Revelation?" *JQR* 52 (1962): 297–365, reprinted in his *The Pursuit of the Ideal*, ed. M. Kellner (Albany: State University of New York Press, 1990), 29–60. Two recent studies have analyzed this paragraph in depth, but more from the perspective of determining the relation between "righteous gentile" and "resident alien" in Maimonides' thought. See Michael Zevi Nehorai, "How a Righteous Gentile Can Merit the World to Come" (in Hebrew), *Tarbiz* 61 (1992): 465–87; and Hannah Kasher, "The Torah as a Means of Achieving the World to Come" (in Hebrew), *Tarbiz* 64 (1995): 301–6. Both studies touch upon the issue of the relation between the gentile sages, those who practice the laws on the basis of the "inclination of the intellect," and those who have a portion in the World to Come. They attempt, in their respective ways, to avoid interpreting Maimonides as maintaining that gentile philosophers necessarily do not attain immortality.

25. See chap. 4, secs. IV–V; chap. 6, sec. V.

26. The seven laws include the prohibition against idolatry and cursing God. They do not explicitly mandate belief in the existence of God. On the surface it appears that they can be fulfilled even by one who does not accept God's existence. In his Torah commentary on Exod. 19:6, Maimonides' son, Abraham, indicates that the gentiles are required to observe the seven laws *and* believe in the unity of God. See *The Torah Commentary of R. Avraham ben HaRambam* (in Hebrew), trans. Ephraim Weisenberg (Jerusalem, 1984), 36. It should be further noted that there existed a tradition prior to Maimonides that gentiles received (or will receive) thirty laws (*B. T. Hulin* 92a; *P. T. Avodah Zarah* 2:1; *Bereishit Rabbah* 98:9). In the list of the thirty noahite laws that is presented by R. Samuel b. Hophni in his commentary on the Torah, he includes belief in the unity of God among the laws that the gentiles are commanded to observe. See Aaron Greenbaum, ed. and trans., *The Biblical Commentary of Rav Samuel ben Hofni* (Jerusalem: Mossad HaRav Kook, 1978), 54–55.

27. Maimonides' interpretation of this story has received two lengthy and distinctly different types of analysis of late. See Marvin Fox, *Interpreting Maimonides: Studies in Methodology, Metaphysics, and Moral Philosophy* (Chicago: University of Chicago Press, 1990), 173–98; and Shlomo Pines, "Truth and Falsehood vs. Good and Evil: A Study in Jewish and General Philosophy in Connection with the *Guide*

of the Perplexed 1.2," in *Studies in Maimonides*, ed. Isadore Twersky (Cambridge: Harvard University Press, 1990), 95–157. In an earlier study, Pines presented in a more summary manner his view of Maimonides' approach. See "Some Traits of Christian Theological Writings in Relation to Moslem Kalam and to Jewish Thought," *Proceedings of the Israel Academy of Sciences and Humanities* 5 (1976): 123–25. For other in-depth treatments of this chapter, see Lawrence Berman, "Maimonides on the Fall of Man," *AJS Review* 5 (1980): 1–16; Warren Harvey, "Maimonides and Spinoza on the Knowledge of Good and Evil" (in Hebrew), *Iyyun* 28 (1979): 167–85; idem, "Maimonides on Genesis 3:22" (in Hebrew), *Daat* 12 (1984): 15–21; and Klein-Braslavy, *Maimonides' Interpretation of the Adam Stories in Genesis,* 40–168. I shall deal in the following chapter with the interpretations advanced by Harvey and Klein-Braslavy on Maimonides' view on knowledge of good and evil.

28. Contrast this with Maimonides' position in *Introduction to Pereq Ḥeleq,* 202, where he lists three classes of readers of rabbinic midrash.

29. The change of identity in Adam is discussed in detail by Klein-Braslavy, *Maimonides' Interpretation of the Adam Stories,* 81–92, 150–68. It should be added that the difference between one's identity as pure intellect and one's identity as a rational corporeal creature also underlies Maimonides' discussion of providence. One attaining intellectual perfection experiences no physical evils (*Guide* 3:51) for his identity is in no way affected by the afflictions occurring to the body. For a discussion of this point among Maimonides' earliest commentators see Zevi Diesendruck, "Samuel and Moses Ibn Tibbon on Maimonides' Theory of Providence," *HUCA* 11 (1936): 341–66.

30. Pines points out the similarity between Maimonides' interpretation of the Fall and that of John Philoponus, who may have indirectly influenced Maimonides on this matter. He stresses that a major difference between the two interpretations lies in Maimonides' substitution of "generally accepted opinions" for the "practical intellect" that appears in Philoponus. I view Maimonides' omission of the practical intellect in this context as due to a question of emphasis rather than substance. The main point of Maimonides' interpretation is to stress the inferiority of the knowledge attained by Adam in relation to the knowledge he possessed initially. This does not mean that Maimonides regarded "generally accepted opinions" in this context as produced by, or directly serving, the imagination.

31. In *Guide* 2:12 Maimonides identifies the imagination with the evil inclination.

32. *Kitāb al-Ishārāt w-al-Tanbīhāt*, ed. J. Forget (Leiden: Brill, 1892), 58f. See Pines, "Some Traits of Christian Theological Writings," 125.

33. In *Healing*, Avicenna explicitly ascribes these opinions to the practical intellect. At the same time, he indicates that the term "intellect" is equivocal when applied to theoretical and practical matters. See Rahman, *Avicenna's Psychology,* 32.

34. Cf. Aristotle, *Topics* 1.1.100a, 10–11.104a–b.

35. Maimonides at times employs the term "intellect" (*'aql)* in regard to practical

matters. Some of these occurrences are in reference to the human intellect's understanding of the Divine Law (*Guide* 3:26; 3:49). This usage is not surprising since Maimonides treats the Law as the product of divine activity and related to nature (2:40). See, however, 3:8, where the term "intellect" is used in reference to practical judgments, and distinguished from "generally accepted opinions" in moral matters. For a further discussion of this passage, see below. I will return to elaborate upon certain aspects of Maimonides' treatment of the story of the Garden of Eden in chap. 3, section II.

36. Maimonides appears to use these terms interchangeably. What, if any, are the differences between these terms, requires a separate study. H. A. Wolfson has studied the term *fikr* at length in his monographs: "The Internal Senses in Latin. Arabic, and Hebrew Philosophic Texts," *HTR* 28 (1935): 69–133, reprinted in H. A. Wolfson, *Studies in the History of Philosophy and Religion*, ed. I. Twersky and G. Williams, vol. 1 (Cambridge: Harvard University Press, 1973), 250–314; and "Maimonides on the Internal Senses," *JQR* 25 (1934): 441–67, reprinted in Wolfson, *Studies,* 344–70. It should be noted that the term *fikr* is often used in the more general sense of focusing one's thought on a particular topic. It is not always clear from the context what meaning Maimonides has in mind. He uses this term in several passages in reference to theoretical matters (*Guide* 2:38, 3:51). Whether Maimonides was of the opinion that similar mental processes are involved in both areas is difficult to determine. It may well be that this is the case. Deliberating about the means to an end would appear to be a form of syllogistic thinking.

37. Cf. Alfarabi, *Aphorisms,* no.7.

38. *Nicomachean Ethics* 6.2.1139a.

39. Alfarabi, *Aphorisms,* nos. 36, 49, 80, 90; idem, *Political Regime,* 73; idem, *The Attainment of Happiness*, trans. Muhsin Mahdi, in *Alfarabi's Philosophy of Plato and Aristotle* (New York: Free Press of Glencoe, 1962), 28f., 32, 45f.

40. Alfarabi, *The Political Regime,* 73. This passage has been translated into English by F. Najjar in *Medieval Political Philosophy*, ed. R. Lerner and M. Mahdi (Ithaca: Cornell University Press, 1972), 34. Cf. *The Perfect State,* 208. See Galston, *Politics and Excellence,* 76–82.

41. Alfarabi, *Political Regime,* 74; *Aphorisms,* nos. 36, 38

42. See note 36.

43. Cf. *Eight Chapters* 1.

44. *Political Regime,* 74.

45. On this point Maimonides appears to be closer to Avicenna's approach than to that of Alfarabi. For a study of Avicenna's approach to the prophetic intellect, see Rahman, *Prophecy in Islam,* 14–20; Davidson, "Alfarabi and Avicenna on the Active Intellect," 163–71; Dmitri Gutas, *Avicenna and the Aristotelian Tradition* (Leiden: E. J. Brill, 1988), 159–76.

46. It appears that Alfarabi does not view the figurative representation of intelligibles by the imagination of the perfect individual as contributing to his own

comprehension of them. Yet it should be noted that in *The Perfect State*, Alfarabi at one point indicates in reference to the visions of particulars and *intelligibles*, "all this is of assistance to the rational faculty (p. 226)." He deals in this context with the prophet himself, making no allusion to the pedagogic value of the visions in educating others. Alfarabi thus may have entertained the notion that the visions contribute to the prophet's intellectual comprehension. See following note.

47. The emanation from the Active Intellect is constant, the differences in its activity depending upon the preparedness of the recipients (*Guide* 2:18). That men of science do not as a rule reach intellectual perfection, often due to bad moral traits, is indicated by Maimonides in 1:34 (see also 2:36). The other reason for the absence of an overflow to the imagination of the philosophers is a defect in the imagination. This would also result for Maimonides in one's inability to reach final perfection. A defect in the imagination indicates a defect in one's natural disposition. Maimonides maintains that defects in one's natural disposition prevent one from attaining ultimate intellectual perfection (2:36). One should keep in mind that for Maimonides, following Alfarabi, knowledge in general is obtained by means of abstraction from sensibilia found in the imagination (1:68). Thus a healthy imagination, faithfully serving the rational faculty, is crucial for all intellection. While Maimonides repeatedly castigates the imagination for the errors to which its activities lead, he also ascribes to it an exceptionally positive role. It is the rationally uncontrolled, or deficient, imagination that is the source of error. In prophecy, the "emanation" to the imagination comes most immediately from the prophet's perfect rational faculty (2:36; 2:38). Based on this "emanation," the imagination creates representations of the intelligible world that aid the intellect's apprehension. This view is presented by Halevi in *Kuzari* 4:5. It is interesting to note that Albert Einstein was once asked: "What internal or mental images, what kind of 'internal words' mathematicians make use of; whether they are motor, auditory, visual or mixed, depending on the subject which they are studying. . . . Do the mental pictures or internal words present themselves in the full consciousness or in the fringe-consciousness?" Einstein replied: "The words or the language . . . do not seem to play any role in my mechanism of thought. The psychical entities which seem to serve as elements in thought are certain signs and more or less *clear images which can be 'voluntarily' reproduced and combined*. . . . Taken from a psychological viewpoint, *this combinatory play seems to be the essential feature in productive thought—before there is any connection with logical construction in words or other kinds of signs which can be communicated to others*" (italics are mine). See Albert Einstein, *Ideas and Opinions* (New York: Dell, 1954), 35.

48. In describing the perfect individual in *The Attainment of Happiness*, Alfarabi equates the imam, philosopher, legislator, and supreme ruler (pp. 46f.). The prophet, who in *The Perfect State* is treated by Alfarabi as one possessing a perfect imagination (p. 224), is conspicuously absent from the list. See Miriam Galston, "Philosopher-King v. Prophet," *IOS* 8 (1978): 205. This fact notwithstanding, a perfect imagination

is ascribed by Alfarabi to the supreme ruler in *The Perfect State* (p. 240). "Revelation" *(waḥy)* for Alfarabi is primarily an overflow to the intellect, and so is not to be equated with "prophecy" *(nabūt)* in his thought. Yet he also describes the revelation attained by the perfect individual as passing from the intellect to the imagination (p. 244). Thus on the ultimate level "revelation" involves a perfect imagination in addition to a perfect intellect. For a detailed analysis of Alfarabi's theory of prophecy, see Richard Walzer, *Greek into Arabic* (Oxford: Oxford University Press, 1962), 206–19. See also Jeffrey Macy, "Prophecy in al-Farabi and Maimonides: The Imaginative and Rational Faculties," in *Maimonides and Philosophy*, ed. S. Pines and Y. Yovel (Dordrecht: Martinus Nijhoff, 1986), 185–201.

49. See *Political Regime,* 84–86; *Attainment of Happiness,* 36–38.

50. *Political Regime,* 80.

51. *Guide* 2:34. Cf. Maimonides' introduction to *Commentary on the Mishnah,* in *Mishnah 'im Perush HaRambam: Seder Zera'im* (in Arabic and Hebrew), ed. and trans. Joseph Kafiḥ (Jerusalem: Mossad HaRav Kook, 1963), 14; *Laws of Principles of the Torah* 9:2. I elaborate upon this point in chap. 1, section IV.

52. Cf. *Laws of Principles of the Torah* 9:1.

53. For a discussion of this issue, see my "A Fragment from a Philosophical Commentary on Ruth Ascribed to R. Nissim of Marseilles" (in Hebrew), *Jerusalem Studies in Jewish Thought* 14 (1998): 160–68.

54. For the view that Moses was the immediate agent of the Law, see chap. 1, section II.

55. For a discussion of this point, see my "Sage and Prophet in the Thought of Maimonides and his Followers" (in Hebrew), *Eshel Bersheva* 3 (1986): 166–69.

56. *Guide* 2:39. Maimonides argues that the Law is completely equibalanced. His illustrations of this point include moral matters. In his view, other laws necessarily fall short of the Divine Law even in this regard.

57. For a discussion of Maimonides' approach to knowledge of good and evil, see chap. 3, sections I–III.

58. *Guide* 2:40; *Treatise on Logic* 14. For a discussion of this point, see chap. 1, section 1.

59. See Maimonides' discussion of the distinction between frivolous and noble actions in *Guide* 3:25.

60. Maimonides on occasion brings examples of generally accepted opinions that are wrong. His examples, however, are in the realm of beliefs, specifically those related to idolatry. See *Guide* 3:29–30, 3:37. I know of no example where he presents a "generally accepted opinion" in moral matters that he rejects.

61. *Guide* 2:38 (Kafiḥ, *Moreh HaNevukhim,* 410).

62. See, however, *Guide* 1:33 (Kafiḥ, *Moreh HaNevukhim,* 74), where Maimonides uses the root *sh-'-r* in regard to the grasping of metaphysical matters.

63. For a detailed study of this term in the context of Avicenna's thought see Gutas, *Avicenna and the Aristotelian Tradition,* 159–76.

64. Though Harry Wolfson does not explicitly discuss divination in his monograph on "Maimonides on the Internal Senses," he gives an indication of his view on this matter in responding to a position advanced by Zevi Diesendruck. Diesendruck attempted to reconcile Maimonides' description of the imagination as an irrational faculty with his description of the imagination of the prophets as being in part rational. The latter type of imagination is treated by Diesendruck as the one associated with parental love. Wolfson shows that parental love is generally ascribed to the estimative faculty, which belongs to all animals. In his view, if Maimonides had in mind a special kind of imagination in his discussion of prophecy, it would be "compositive human imagination" *(mufakkira)*. This type of imagination combines reason and judgment (*Studies,* 360). There is little doubt that Wolfson's view also explains Maimonides' description of divination, which combines imagination and reason.

65. *The Perfect State,* 220. The translation is my own, though I have consulted Walzer's translation. See Herbert Davidson's incisive discussion of this passage in "Alfarabi and Avicenna on the Active Intellect," 146 n. 11.

66. This interpretation is further strengthened by Walzer's reading of a crucial sentence in the text, which he translates, "such things can also be present in the faculty of deliberation without *(bighairi)* having been discovered by deliberation." I have chosen the reading "after" *(ba'ada),* which is found in the Malik library ms. and followed by F. Dieterici in his edition: *Alfarabi's Abhandlung der Musterstaat* (Leiden: Brill, 1964), 51.

67. See Davidson, "Alfarabi and Avicenna on the Active Intellect," 146.

68. *The Perfect State,* 226.

69. See Maimonides' description of prophetic visions in 2:36. In 2:38, however, he clarifies his position by insisting that the overflow to the imagination is always via the rational faculty.

70. For a discussion of this issue, see my "The Verification of Prophecy in Medieval Jewish Philosophy" (in Hebrew), *Jerusalem Studies in Jewish Thought* 4 (1984): 13f.

71. That the prophets possess such knowledge is clearly indicated in *Guide* 3:51.

72. For a discussion of the problem of prophetic error in the thought of the medieval Jewish philosophers, see Charles Touati, "La problème de l'inerrance prophétique dans la théologie juive du moyen âge," *Revue de l'Histoire des Religions* 174 (1968): 169–97.

73. See Alfarabi, *Aphorisms,* no. 89.

74. See Lawrence Kaplan, "Maimonides on the Singularity of the Jewish People," *Daat* 15 (1985): v–xxvi. I have discussed this issue in chap. 1, section VI.

75. The translation is my own based on the Arabic edition of Kafiḥ, *Mishnah 'im Perush HaRambam: Seder Zera'im* 42.

76. *Attainment of Happiness,* 26–28.

77. Note that some of the subsequent legal authorities did try to get around the need to fulfill this command in a literal manner.

78. Immediately preceding his condemnation of drinking parties, Maimonides approvingly cites the example of Pinḥas ben Yair who refrained from partaking his meals in the company of others, including R. Yehudah Hanasi. Maimonides views this as a sign of perfection. Would he regard this too as an act commanded by the "intellect" insofar as it contributes to the individual's perfection? This hardly appears likely. His treatment of the prohibition to attend drinking parties as one that is mandated by the intellect is almost as problematic.

79. See, however, Sara Klein-Braslavy's discussion and defense of the view that Maimonides was in fact positing such a system in *Maimonides' Interpretation of the Adam Stories in Genesis,* 130–68. For a further discussion of this issue, see chap. 3, sections I–III.

80. For a discussion of the ideal morality described by Maimonides at the end of the *Guide,* see chap. 4, section II.

81. For a discussion of this ideal see chap. 4, sections IV–V.

Chapter 3. The Concept "Good"

1. See W. Z. Harvey, "Maimonides and Spinoza on Knowledge of Good and Evil" (in Hebrew), *Iyyun* 28 (1978): 165–85; "Maimonides' Commentary on Genesis 3:22" (in Hebrew), *Daat* 12 (1984): 15–21; "Ethics and Meta-ethics, Aesthetics and Meta-aesthetics in Maimonides," in *Maimonides and Philosophy*, ed. S. Pines and Y. Yovel (Dordrecht: Martinus Nijhoff, 1986), 131–34; Sara Klein-Braslavy, *Maimonides' Interpretation of the Adam Stories in Genesis* (in Hebrew) (Jerusalem: Reuben Mass, 1986), 141–49; idem, *Maimonides' Interpretation of the Story of Creation* (in Hebrew) (Jerusalem: Reuben Mass, 1987), 104–13, 168–74.

2. Klein-Braslavy, *Maimonides' Interpretation of the Adam Stories in Genesis,* 137–49.

3. Harvey, "Maimonides and Spinoza," 172f.

4. *Fī aqsām al-'ulūm al-'aqlīyyah* in *Tis' Rasa'il* (Cairo, 1908), 105. The translation is my own.

5. *Nicomachean Ethics* 6.1.1139a–b. Cf. *De Anima* 3.7.431b.

6. See, for example, *Aphorisms of the Statesman*, ed. and trans. D. M. Dunlop (Cambridge: Cambridge University, 1961), nos. 6, 30–38.

7. *Al-Siyāsah al-Madaniyyah* (The political regime), ed. Fauzi Najjar (Beirut: Imprimerie Catholique, 1964), 72–73, as translated by F. Najjar in *Medieval Political Philosophy*, ed. R. Lerner and M. Mahdi (Ithaca: Cornell University Press, 1972), 34.

8. Translated by W. D. Ross and revised by J. O. Urmson in *The Complete Works of Aristotle*, ed. Jonathan Barnes (Princeton: Princeton University Press, 1985),

1735. In the following chapter Aristotle identifies the happiness of the soul with excellence. "Lovers of what is noble find pleasant the things that are by nature pleasant; and excellent actions are such so that these are pleasant for such men as well as in their own nature" (1.8.1099a; p. 1737). Aristotle concludes his discussion of the first section by noting that some excellences are intellectual in that they belong to the rational part of the soul (this includes both theoretical and practical wisdom). Others are moral in that they belong to the nonrational parts of the soul.

9. In *Eight Chapters* 1, Maimonides defines theoretical knowledge as knowledge of the existents that undergo no change. In chapter 2 he distinguishes between rational virtues and moral virtues. The latter belong to the appetitive faculty. This distinction is clearly based on the distinction between *theoria* and *praxis*. See also *Commentary on Mishnah: Avot* 5:13, in *Mishnah 'im Perush HaRambam: Seder Nezikin* (in Arabic and Hebrew), ed. and trans. Joseph Kafiḥ (Jerusalem: Mossad HaRav Kook, 1965), 42, Maimonides distinguishes between wisdom and practice, and views "the good" *(al-ḵair)* as falling under the latter category.

10. I have dealt with this point in chapter 2, section III. See, however, Harvey, "Maimonides and Spinoza," 179f.

11. I have dealt with Maimonides' interpretation of the story in chapter 2, section III.

12. Maimonides sees these prohibitions as belonging to the "generally accepted" moral dictums in *Eight Chapters* 6. See also *Guide* 2:33. For a discussion of this point, see chapter 2, section VIII.

13. See Maimonides' definitions of theoretical philosophy and practical philosophy in *Treatise on Logic* 14, and his discussion of the rational faculty in *Eight Chapters* 1. Arthur Hyman, too, has argued that Maimonides' distinction between "true" and "good" is between the theoretical and the practical. See "A Note on Maimonides' Classification of the Law," in *American Academy of Jewish Research Jubilee Volume*, ed. S. Baron and I. Barzilay (Jerusalem: American Academy of Jewish Research, 1978), 335f.

14. See Aristotle, *Topics* 1.10.104a.

15. See for example Avicenna's description of the perfect individual in *Kitāb al-Ishārāt w-al-Tanbīhāt*, ed. J. Forget (Leiden: Brill, 1892), 58f.

16. See also *Commentary on Mishnah: Avot* 1:17, 5:13. In his commentary on 2:12, Maimonides regards the study of the sciences as an intellectual virtue. Knowledge belonging to the category of "seeing what is born"—that is, anticipating what will happen—is defined by Maimonides as applying to: "all human concerns that involve the individual's existence." This knowledge, Maimonides indicates, includes the moral virtues.

17. For a detailed discussion of this ideal see chapter 4, sections IV–V. This ideal is similar to the one brought by Judah Halevi in the name of the philosophers and also in his own name. See *Kuzari* 1:1, 1:95.

18. See *Guide* 3:51.

19. Harvey, "Maimonides and Spinoza," 184; Klein-Braslavy, *Maimonides' Interpretation of the Adam Stories,* 147–68.

20. This is the basis for Maimonides' distinction between the "well-known" moral dictums as they appear in the *nomoi* of the nations and the same moral dictums that are found in the Ten Commandments that were given to Moses in revelation. For a discussion of this point see chap. 2, section VI.

21. Cf. 1:72, 3:27.

22. Alfarabi draws a distinction between what is good in accordance with generally accepted opinion, what is good according to a certain religion, and what is really good. See *Attainment of Happiness,* in Muhsin Mahdi, *Alfarabi's Philosophy of Plato and Aristotle* (New York: Free Press of Glencoe, 1962), 32.

23. See *Guide* 1:7, 3:8, 3:49, 3:54; *Commentary on Avot* 5:13.

24. For a detailed discussion of this passage, see Joel Kraemer, "*Shari'a* and *Namus* in the Philosophy of Maimonides" (in Hebrew), *Teudah* 4 (1986): 189. Though there is more than one way for interpreting this passage as Kraemer shows, it is clear that Maimonides sees the ability to govern as crucial for the preservation of the species, and serving as part of the system of divine providence.

25. For a discussion of the acquired intellect in Maimonides' thought, see chap. 4, section VI.

26. For a discussion of this point see chap. 2, section VIII.

27. Kafiḥ, *Mishnah 'im Persuh HaRambam: Seder Nezikin,* 392.

28. See Harvey, "Maimonides' Commentary on Genesis 3:22," 15–21.

29. *Mishnah 'im Persuh HaRambam: Seder Nezikin,* 400.

30. The Arabic edition of this treatise was published by Israel Efros in *PAAJR* 34 (1966). For the terms under consideration, see p. 21 of that issue.

31. *Mishnah 'im Perush HaRambam: Seder Nezikin,* 378.

32. Cf. *Eight Chapters* 2, 4, 5, 7, 8; *Treatise on Logic* 14.

33. Maimonides frequently employs the term *karīm* (noble), at times together with the term *faḍā'il*, or in the same context in which he uses the term *ḥasan*. See *Guide* 3:27–28, 3:38. The term *nafi'* (useful) is also used in reference to the ethical virtues. See *Guide* 3:27, 3:38, 3:54.

34. In 3:8 Maimonides describes the perfect individual for whom even "all the impulses of matter are shameful and ugly *(qabīḥ)* things, deficiencies imposed by necessity" (p. 432).

35. *Guide* 2:40, 3:8, 3:12, 3:33. Maimonides often draws a sharp distinction between the pleasure involving the intellect in attaining knowledge of God and that which belongs to the body. See, for example, 3:51; *Mishnah 'im Persuh HaRambam: Seder Nezikin,* 203–5. See Gabriella Berzin, "The Concept of Happiness in the Teachings of Maimonides and R. Chasdai Crescas" (in Hebrew) (Master's thesis, Ben-Gurion University, 1998), 44–53.

36. *Aphorisms,* nos. 25, 36, 69, 94; *Al-Siyāsah al-Madaniyyah,* ed. Najjar, 72–

73 (= *Medieval Political Philosophy,* ed. Lerner and Mahdi, 34); R. Walzer, *Alfarabi on the Perfect State* (Oxford: Clarendon Press, 1985), 206; *Taḥṣīl al-Sa'ādah* (Hyderabad, 1345 A.H.), 20, 23 (= Mahdi, *Alfarabi's Philosophy of Plato and Aristotle,* 27–30).

37. *Aphorisms,* nos. 25, 36, 37, 69; *Al-Siyāsah al-Madaniyyah* 72, 84; *Taḥṣīl al-Sa'ādah, 15.*

38. *Aphorisms,* nos. 8, 13, 16; Mahdi, *Alfarabi on the Perfect State,* 206.

39. *Aphorisms,* no. 69.

40. Mahdi, *Alfarabi on the Perfect State,* 206; *Al-Siyāsah al-Madaniyyah,* 72; *Taḥṣīl al-Sa'ādah,* 20; *Catalogo de las Ciecias*, ed. A. Gonzalez Palencia (Madrid: Consego Superior de Investigaciones Cientificas, 1953), 90.

41. *Aphorisms,* no. 6; *Al-Siyāsah al-Madaniyyah,* 33.

42. *Aphorisms,* no. 3.

43. In *Al-Siyāsah al-Madaniyyah,* 34, Alfarabi is explicit in rejecting the view that the imagination is the source of knowledge of *al-jamīl* and *al-qabīḥ.*

44. *Taḥṣīl al-Sa'ādah,* 20 as translated by Muhsin Mahdi in Mahdi, *Alfarabi's Philosophy of Plato and Aristotle,* 28.

45. See also Maimonides' arguments in 2:18 against the philosophers' view that the world is without beginning.

46. For a discussion of the issue of the divine attributes of wisdom and will and the problem of the final purpose of the world, see Zevi Diesendruck, "Maimonides' Theory of Teleology and the Divine Attributes" (in Hebrew), *Tarbiz* 1 (1930): 106–36, and 2 (1931): 27–73; Zevi Blumberg, "The Concept of Divine Will in Maimonides' Teachings" (in Hebrew), *Perakim* 4 (1966): 43–55; A. Nuriel, "The Divine Will in Moreh Nevukhim" (in Hebrew), *Tarbiz* 39 (1970): 39–61; A. Ravitsky, "The Hypostasis of Supernal Wisdom in Jewish Philosophy of the Thirteenth Century" (in Hebrew), *Italia* 3 (1982): 7–38; Eliezer Goldman, "On the Purpose of the World in the *Guide of the Perplexed*" (in Hebrew), in *Studies in Honor of Yeshayahu Leibowitz,* ed. A. Kasher and Y. Levinger (Tel Aviv: Papyrus, 1982), 164–91.

47. In Buridan's famous example of this point, the human being is replaced by an ass who finds itself in a similar difficult situation.

48. See S. Van Den Bergh, *Averroes' Tahāfut al-Tahāfut* (London: Luzac, 1954), 18–32.

49. See *Guide* 2:18–19, 3:13.

50. There are two discussions in which Maimonides, following Alghazali, appears to adopt the stance that God chooses between equal possibilities. The first is in the proof of creation based on particularization in *Guide* 2:19. Maimonides maintains that no adequate naturalistic explanation can be offered for the differences between the spheres or planets, whether it be the direction of their motion, their velocity, or their size. The second is in his discussion of the particulars of the commandments in 3:26. Maimonides argues that one should not look for an explanation for such particulars as why a certain animal or a certain number of animals are

sacrificed and not a different animal or quantity. Yet in both discussions Maimonides traces the choice of the particulars to divine wisdom, and not solely to divine will. This suggests that a rational explanation exists for all the particulars, whether in the celestial realm or the realm of the divine law. See Herbert Davidson, "Arguments from the Concept of Particularization in Arabic Philosophy," *Philosophy East and West* 18 (1968): 308–14; Josef Stern, "The Idea of *Ḥoq* in Maimonides' Explanation of the Law," in *Maimonides and Philosophy,* ed. Pines and Yovel, 99–109.

51. See, for example, *Guide* 3:25. It is important to stress that Maimonides often mentions the divine will and divine wisdom in the same context. See 1:69, 2:18, 2:25, 2:27, 2:29, 3:13.

52. See *Book of Beliefs and Opinions* IV:Introduction.

53. For an extensive analysis of this chapter, see Klein-Braslavy, *Maimonides' Interpretation of the Story of Creation* (esp. pp. 104–13, 168–74).

54. For Maimonides' distinction between those things that are intended for their own sake and those that are intended for the existence of something else, see *Guide* 3:13.

55. Maimonides is dealing with the problem of primary intent. Things can be intended for their own sake while at the same time serve to perpetuate the existence of other things. This is true of the Separate Intellects and spheres, for example. Their existence is not brought about for the sake of everything in the sublunar world. Nevertheless, they serve as the cause of all that exists in the sublunar world.

56. It is important to stress that Maimonides is dealing with the remote final end, not the immediate final end that characterizes the species. The immediate final end of human beings, for example, is to perfect their intellect. This final end does not, however, answer the problem of what is the reason for the existence of the human species.

57. This identity is presented in *Guide* 1:69, 2:18, 3:13. See also 1:53, 3:17; *Eight Chapters* 8.

58. For a further discussion of this point, see below.

59. Maimonides dwells on this point in his polemic against Galen appearing at the end of his *Medical Aphorisms*, ed. Suessmann Muntner (Jerusalem: Mossad HaRav Kook, 1982), 324–98. An English translation of the relevant section of the polemic appears on pages xxiv–xxxi. For a discussion of the issue of miracles in Maimonides' thought, see my "Miracles in Medieval Jewish Philosophy," *JQR* 75 (1984): 106–14.

60. See Avraham Nuriel, "The Question of a Created or Primordial World in the Philosophy of Maimonides" (in Hebrew), *Tarbiz* 1964 (33): 372–87. Some of Maimonides' medieval commentators such as Joseph Kaspi and Moses Narboni entertained the same conclusion.

61. Maimonides indicates that Aristotle distinguished between the necessity of the existence of the world and the necessity of the heating action of fire or of the sun (*Guide* 2:20). In his discussion of the attributes of God, Maimonides himself draws

a connection between the essence of God and between the existents that emanate from God: "We apprehend further that the existence of this being, which is its essence, suffices not only for His being existent, but also for many other existents flowing from it, and that this overflow—unlike that of heat from fire and unlike the proceeding of light from the sun—is an overflow that, as we shall make clear, constantly procures for those existents duration and order by means of wisely contrived governance. Accordingly we say of Him, because of these notions, that He is powerful and knowing and willing" (1:58.136). In this context, "will" indicates the nature of the order that flows from God. It does not signify the actualization of one of many equal possibilities, or the bringing into existence of a previously nonexistent thing. This usage of "will" does not stand in opposition to the notion of a primordial world, or to the notion that God's essence necessitates giving existence to the world. In 2:20, on the other hand, Maimonides maintains: "A combination between existing in virtue of necessity and being produced in time in virtue of purpose and will—a combination uniting these two—comes near to a combination of two contraries" (p. 313). According to Maimonides: "The notions of purpose and of particularization only apply to a nonexistent thing for which it is possible to exist just as it was purposed and particularized and for which it is possible not to exist in this fashion" (p. 314). In the following chapter he continues his critique of the philosophers by attacking the notion that God willed and purposed a primordial world. It is clear that Maimonides employs the notion "possible" in entirely different ways. Not in every instance does he see it as standing in contradiction to "necessary," if we interpret "necessary" to mean that which is the effect of an agent whose activity does not change. The combination of necessity and choice reemerges in 2:48. Maimonides explains the notion of God's "command" to human beings: "And who has necessitated this particular free choice in the rational animal" (p. 410). See also the causal chain posited by Maimonides in the beginning of 2:1. Maimonides' approach to the meaning of "possible" varies in accordance with the point of his discussion. For different treatments of the problem of "possibility" in the *Guide,* see J. Guttmann, "Das Problem der Kontingenz in der Philosophie des Maimonides," *MGWJ* 83 (1939): 406–30; H. A. Wolfson, "Hallevi and Maimonides on Design, Chance and Necessity," *PAAJR* 11 (1941): 105–63; E. Fackenheim, "The Possibility of the Universe in Al-Farabi, Ibn Sina and Maimonides," *PAAJR* 16 (1947): 303–33; Harry Blumberg, "Maimonides on the Kalam Doctrine of Tajwiz" (in Hebrew), *Tarbiz* 39 (1970): 268–76; N. L. Rabinovitch, "The Concept of Possibility in Maimonides" (in Hebrew), *Tarbiz* 44 (1975): 159–71; A. Ivry, "Maimonides on Possibility," in *Mystics, Philosophers and Politicians*, ed. J. Reinharz and D. Swetschinski eds. (Durham, N.C.: Duke University Press, 1982), 67–84.

62. See Alexander Altmann, "Essence and Existence in Maimonides," in his *Studies in Religious Philosophy and Mysticism* (Ithaca: Cornell University, 1969), 109–27. For a further discussion of this problem in the thought of Maimonides' commentators, see Aviezer Ravitsky, "Possible and Contingent Existence in the

Exegesis of Maimonides in the Thirteenth Century" (in Hebrew), *Daat* 2–3 (1978): 67–98.

63. See *Nicomachean Ethics* 6.2.1139a–b.

64. See *Guide* 1:57; *Laws of the Principles of the Torah* 1:3–4; *Eight Chapters* 7.

65. See also Maimonides' interpretation of the verse *And the Lord commanded us to do all these statutes to fear the Lord our God for our good always, that He might preserve us alive, as it is at this day* (Deut. 6:24) in *Guide* 3:27 and 3:31. For a discussion of immortality in Maimonides' thought, see chap. 4, sections IV–V.

66. Not in all of his writings does Maimonides maintain this distinction. In *Laws of Repentance* 10:2, Maimonides uses the notion "truth" also in reference to the fulfillment of the commandments: "One does the truth because it is truth."

67. *Yevamot* 71a; *Baba Mezi'a* 31b.

68. For a discussion of Maimonides' use of this saying, see Avraham Nuriel, "The Torah Speaks in the Language of Humans," in *The Guide of the Perplexed* (in Hebrew), in *Religion and Language*, ed. M. Hallamish and A. Kasher (Tel Aviv: University Publishing Projects, 1981), 97–103. Maimonides' use differs from rabbinic usage.

Chapter 4. *Imitatio Dei*

1. For the extensive literature dealing with this topic, see the notes and bibliography in Menachem Kellner, *Maimonides on Human Perfection* (Atlanta: Scholars Press, 1990). See also Ira Robinson, Lawrence Kaplan, and Julien Bauer, eds., *The Thought of Moses Maimonides* (Lewiston, N.Y.: Edwin Mellen Press, 1990), particularly Kaplan's article, " 'I Sleep But My Heart Waketh': Maimonides' Conception of Human Perfection," 130–66; and Joel Kraemer, ed., *Perspectives on Maimonides* (Oxford: Oxford University Press, 1991), particularly the articles of Lawrence Berman, "The Ethical Views of Maimonides within the Context of Islamicate Civilization," 13–32, and Ralph Lerner, "Maimonides' Governance of the Solitary," 33–46. I am indebted to Dr. Hannah Kasher of Bar-Ilan University for sending me a copy of her unpublished manuscript on Maimonides and *imitatio Dei*. This work has provided me with many valuable insights and references. Much of the material in this work was later incorporated in her article, "Maimonides' Interpretations of the Story of the Divine Revelation in the Cleft of the Rock" (in Hebrew), *Daat* 35 (1995): 29–66. For the philosophic background of the concept of *imitatio Dei* in Jewish philosophy, see Alexander Altmann and S. M. Stern, *Isaac Israeli* (Oxford: Oxford University Press, 1958), 197–200; and Lawrence Berman, "The Political Interpretation of the Maxim: The Purpose of Philosophy is the Imitation of God," *Studia Islamica* 15 (1961): 53–61. For a general discussion of this topic in Jewish thought, see David Shapiro, "The Doctrine of the Image of God and

imitatio Dei," *Judaism* 12 (1963): 57–77, reprinted in Menachem Kellner, ed., *Contemporary Jewish Ethics* (New York: Sanhedrin Press, 1978), 127–51.

2. See in particular Alexander Altmann, "Maimonides' 'Four Perfections'," *IOS* 2 (1972): 24. Altmann's subsequent article, "Maimonides on the Intellect and the Scope of Metaphysics," in his *Von der mittelalterlichen zur modernen Aufklärung* (Tübingen: J. C. B. Mohr, 1987), 60–129, is perhaps the most significant study written on the topic of Maimonides' view of human perfection. More recently Herbert Davidson has returned to this subject and written a penetrating study, "Maimonides on Metaphysical Knowledge," *Maimonidean Studies* 3 (1992–93): 49–103. Both Altmann and Davidson attack the position put forward by Shlomo Pines in the study mentioned in the following note.

3. See Shlomo Pines, "The Limitations of Human Knowledge according to Al-Farabi, Ibn Bajja, and Maimonides," in *Studies in Medieval Jewish History and Literature*, ed. Isadore Twersky (Cambridge: Harvard University Press, 1979), 82–109.

4. I have presented this position in a summary manner in my article "Maimonides' View of Prophecy as the Overflowing Perfection of Man," *Daat* 13 (1984): xxi–xxvvi. This basic position has already been advanced by Warren Harvey, "Political Philosophy and Halakhah in Maimonides" (in Hebrew), *Iyyun* 29 (1980): 209–12. For the relation between Maimonides' metaphysical views and political views, see chap. 1, section II. I will enter into more detail concerning the significance of the notion of emanation for understanding Maimonides' approach to human perfection in the continuation of this chapter.

5. Herbert Davidson, in his article "Maimonides' Secret Position on Creation," in *Studies in Medieval Jewish History and Literature,* ed. Twersky, 16–40, maintains that the esoteric/exoteric distinction fails in regard to some of the contradictions in the *Guide* (most notably the problem of creation), which may in fact be inadvertent. While I do not agree with his analysis attempting to show that Maimonides adopts a Platonic view of creation, I think that his view of contradictions in Maimonides' philosophy is essentially correct. One certainly cannot demonstrate that some of the contradictions in the *Guide* are not intentional. Those convinced that Maimonides introduced only purposeful contradictions can always produce arguments to the contrary, as Davidson notes. However, the willingness (if with reluctance) to acquiesce to the possibility that not all contradictions or inconsistencies are of this nature protects us from exaggerated attempts to "reconcile" all contradictions (imagined or otherwise) along esoteric/exoteric lines or to seek out some deeper level of harmony by the use of far-fetched hermeneutics—attempts that at times appear to make a caricature of the text. I am not arguing against the notion that many of the contradictions should be interpreted along esoteric/exoteric lines. I think they should be. I also think that the "harmonists"—those who seek to reconcile apparent contradictions by attempting to show that no real contradictions are in

fact involved—are at times correct. Maimonides occasionally emphasizes seemingly conflicting aspects of what is essentially a coherent picture, as I will attempt to show in the following chapter. Overall, I see no reason why a multifaceted approach should not be adopted to understand this multifaceted work. What ultimately determines one's reading of any given topic must be a careful analysis of the issues and texts involved, together with one's "sense" of the text.

6. See, for example, *Treatise on Logic* and *Commentary to the Mishnah*—particularly his introductions to *Seder Zera'im*, *Avot* (*Eight Chapters*), and *Sanhedrin* 10 (*Pereq Ḥeleq*).

7. For a discussion of this problem, see my article "Miracles in Medieval Jewish Philosophy," *JQR* 75 (1984): 99, 106–14, and the bibliography cited there.

8. For example, Maimonides opens his list by asking: "Why did God give prophetic revelation to this one and not to that?" While the answer he offers is that God willed it, the notion of divine will being incompatible in his view with the notion of an eternal world, he subsequently presents a naturalistic theory of prophecy in conformity with the philosophers' view that the world is eternal. The view that Maimonides believed that the world is eternal *a parte ante* was advanced by some of Maimonides' medieval commentators such as Joseph Kaspi and Moses Narboni, as well as some of his modern ones. See Avraham Nuriel, "The Question of a Primordial or Created World in the Philosophy of Maimonides" (in Hebrew), *Tarbiz* 33 (1964): 372–87; and Warren Harvey, "A Third Approach to Maimonides' Cosmogony-Prophetology Puzzle," *HTR* 74 (1981): 287–301.

9. See Sara Klein-Braslavy, "The Creation of the World and Maimonides' Interpretation of Genesis I–V," in *Maimonides and Philosophy*, ed. S. Pines and Y. Yovel (Dordrecht: Martinus Nijhoff, 1986), 65–78.

10. See F. E. Peters, *Aristotle and the Arabs* (New York: New York University Press, 1968).

11. For a general discussion of the influence of these philosophers on Maimonides, see Shlomo Pines's introduction to his translation of the *Guide*, "The Philosophic Sources of *The Guide of the Perplexed*," lxxviii–cviii.

12. For an analysis of Maimonides' view of the intellect, see Altmann, "Maimonides on the Intellect"; and Davidson, "Maimonides on Metaphysical Knowledge."

13. This in itself is a problematic solution for in the final analysis Maimonides has a great deal to say about God. See Julius Guttmann, "Maimonides' Theology" (in Hebrew), in *Essays in Honour of J. H. Hertz*, ed. I. Epstein, E. Levine, and C. Roth (London: Edward Goldston, 1942): Hebrew Section, 53–69, reprinted in his *Reason and Knowledge* (in Hebrew), ed. S. H. Bergman and N. Rotenstreich (Jerusalem: Magnes Press, 1979), 103–8. The tension between the Neoplatonic and Aristotelian strains in Maimonides' philosophy has recently been analyzed by Alfred Ivry, "Maimonides and Neoplatonism: Challenge and Response," in *Neoplatonism and Jewish Thought*, ed. Lenn E. Goodman (Albany: State University of New York, 1992), 137–56.

14. See Altmann and Stern, *Isaac Israeli,* 198–99.

15. See Joseph Ibn Ṣaddik, *Book of the Microcosm* (in Hebrew), ed. S. Horovitz (Breslau, 1903), p. 65. Maimonides, however, confesses not to have read Joseph's work. See Isaac Shailat, ed. and trans., *Letters and Essays of Moses Maimonides* (in Arabic and Hebrew) (Maaleh Adumim, Israel: Maaliyot Press, 1988), 552.

16. The midrash apparently connects this verse with Moses' request in Exod. 33:13 to be informed of God's "ways." Maimonides too regards this verse as the answer to Moses' request there.

17. The phrase *call by the name of the Lord* appears also in Exod. 34:5, providing the connection between the two verses.

18. The translation is my own, based upon the edition of Louis Finkelstein (New York: Jewish Theological Seminary, 1969), 114. I have consulted the translation of Reuven Hammer (New Haven: Yale University Press, 1986).

19. Reading *'anvehū* as a contraction of I and He *('ani ve-hū').*

20. The *Mishneh Torah,* however, mentions only character traits. For a comparison between these two sources, see Walter Wurzberger, "*Imitatio Dei* in Maimonides' *Sefer Hamitzvot* and the *Mishneh Torah,*" in *Tradition and Transition: Essays Presented to Chief Rabbi Sir Immanuel Jakobovits,* ed. Jonathan Sacks (London: Jews College, 1986), 321–24.

21. In *Book of the Commandments,* positive commandment no. 8, Maimonides explicitly maintains that "God is described by these good activities and noble character traits in a figurative manner." In *Laws of Character Traits* 1:6, he says that "man must conduct himself in accordance with them [the attributes] and imitate Him *(le-hiddamot 'elav)* to the extent of his ability." The term *'elav,* however, does not appear in most of the manuscripts, though it appears in almost all of the printed versions. A similar phrase occurs in *Laws of Slaves* 9:8, where we are commanded to act mercifully with heathen slaves in accordance with the just laws of the Torah: "So too in regard to the attributes of God that we are commanded to imitate *(le-hiddamot ba-hem),* it is written: *And His mercy is upon all His works* (Ps. 145:8)." There is a hint in this passage that Maimonides treats the attributes as attributes of action.

22. For a detailed discussion of this passage see, Gerald Blidstein, "The Concept of Joy in Maimonides" (in Hebrew), *Eshel Beer-Sheva* 2 (1980): 145–64; Isadore Twersky, "On Law and Ethics in the *Mishneh Torah:* A Case Study of *Hilkhot Megillah* II:17," *Tradition* 24 (1989): 138–49; and Lawrence Kaplan, "*Hilkhot Megillah* 2:17 Revisited: A Halakhic Analysis," *Tradition* 26 (1991): 14–21. The notion of *imitatio Dei* also appears in *Laws of Impure Foods* 16:12, where it is regarded as a consequence of holiness. For a discussion of the relation between these two notions, see section VII.

23. The "political" interpretation of *imitatio Dei* in Maimonides has been argued most forcefully by Lawrence Berman in his doctoral dissertation and in a series of articles. See his final study on the subject, "The Ethical Views of Maimonides

within the Context of Islamicate Civilization," 13–32. The implications of this view is that the divine Law itself is the product of Mosaic prophecy, as I have already indicated in chap. 1, section II..

24. In the earlier chapters of the *Guide*, Maimonides' approach to *imitatio Dei* is too general to determine whether the stress is on ethics or politics. In 1:24, the term "to walk," as it appears in the commandment that serves as the basis for *imitatio Dei—And you shall walk in His ways* (Deut. 28:9)—is interpreted by Maimonides simply as, "living a good life" (p. 54)." In 1:38, he interprets the phrase, *walk at the back of the Lord* as "following in obedience to Him and imitating His acts and conducting life in accordance with His conduct" (p. 87).

25. See, for example, 1:34; 2:36; 3:33. Maimonides at times regards the ethical traits as necessary only for the establishment and preservation of society. At other times he treats them as related directly to the attainment of intellectual perfection. For a discussion of this issue see chap. 5, sections II–V.

26. Maimonides consistently treats Moses as having attained the highest level of perfection, but alternates in treating Moses' perfection as paradigmatic or exceptional. His position can be traced to the context of the discussion. When his discussion has a bearing on establishing the uniqueness of the Torah, Maimonides treats Moses' attainment as exceptional and outside the boundaries of nature. This perfection cannot be imitated by the laying down of a new legislation. When Maimonides' discussion turns to final human perfection, on the other hand, he presents Moses as the paradigm case. One can never equal his theoretical and practical virtues, but he represents the model that one strives to approach.

27. For a study of the interpretations of this passage in medieval Jewish philosophy, see Abraham Melamed, "Philosophical Commentaries to *Jeremiah* 9, 22–23 in Medieval and Renaissance Jewish Thought" (in Hebrew), *Jerusalem Studies in Jewish Thought* 4 (1984–85): 31–82.

28. *Laws of the Principles of the Torah* 2:10; *Guide* 1:68. See Aristotle, *Metaphysics* 12.7.1072b; *Nicomachean Ethics* 10.8.1178b. See, however, Ehud Benor, who challenges this point in his "Meaning and Reference in Maimonides' Negative Theology," *HTR* 88 (1995): 339–60. See also Hannah Kasher, "Self-Cognizing Intellect and Negative Attributes in Maimonides' Theology," *HTR* 87 (1994): 461–72.

29. See Warren Zev Harvey, "How to Begin to Study the *Guide of the Perplexed*, I, 1" (in Hebrew), *Daat* 21 (1988): 5–20.

30. The term "intellect" is used equivocally. This led many of the medievals as well as well as moderns to wonder what sense this term has when applied to God. It should be noted that both in his legal writings and in the *Guide* Maimonides introduces a subtle but crucial distinction between two groups of essential attributes. One group, all the attributes that necessarily denote corporeality, Maimonides completely negates in reference to God. A second group—life, power, knowledge, will—is not completely negated of God, but treated as existing in Him in a totally "different sense" than they exist in us. In *Laws of the Principles of the Torah* 1:11, for

example, Maimonides negates from God all the categories pertaining to matter, as well as affections of the soul, without qualification. Life, however, is negated from God "like the life of the living body" and wisdom "like the wisdom of the wise man." See also *Guide* 1:56. For a further discussion of the problem of God's attributes in Maimonides' philosophy see Altmann, "Maimonides on the Intellect," 120–25.

31. See chap. 2, section III.

32. Cf. *Guide* 1:34; 3:28.

33. See also Joseph Kafiḥ, ed. and trans., *Mishnah 'im Perush HaRambam: Seder Zera'im* (in Arabic and Hebrew) (Jerusalem: Mossad HaRav Kook, 1963), 41; *Introduction to Pereq Ḥeleq,* in *Mishnah 'im Perush HaRambam: Seder Nezikin* (in Arabic and Hebrew), ed. and trans. Joseph Kafiḥ (Jerusalem: Mossad HaRav Kook, 1965), 205; *Eight Chapters* 5.

34. See Altmann, "Maimonides on the Intellect," 85–91. For a further discussion of this issue, see below.

35. This notion underlies David Hartman's "integrationist" approach to Jewish law and philosophy in Maimonides' thought in his *Maimonides: Torah and Philosophic Quest* (Philadelphia: Jewish Publication Society, 1976). A similar approach has been advanced more recently by Menachem Kellner, *Maimonides on Human Perfection.* I think that the integrationist approach is essentially correct but misleading. Maimonides integrates philosophy and Jewish law by making the study of philosophy a legal obligation, or to be more precise—*the leading obligation.* He essentially treats the Law as a concrete expression—albeit the ultimate expression—of political philosophy. The final goal of political philosophy is theoretical perfection. This position is already advanced in his *Treatise on Logic* 14, and is maintained consistently throughout all his writings. The Law is framed for a particular society at large in order to bring about, or at least advance, those ends that belong to humanity as a whole. Insofar as it is framed for all of society, it can at best provide "pointers" for the attainment of theoretical perfection by dressing truths in figurative form and mandating belief in them. I have dealt with this issue in chapter 1 and I will deal with it in more detail in chapter 6. Maimonides was very much the disciple of Alfarabi in this area, as correctly argued by Leo Strauss and Lawrence Berman, though he went further than Alfarabi in incorporating philosophic truths in legal contexts. It is noteworthy that neither in *Guide* 1:54 nor in the conclusion of 3:54 does Maimonides identify ultimate perfection with observance of the commandments per se. The perfection he deals with in 1:54 explicitly relates to political leadership. In 3:54 he explicitly treats observance as a means to ethical perfection. Ultimate perfection resides in the practice of the actions resulting from the "divine" attributes. Maimonides does not mention the commandments in this context. He has in mind a type of behavior that results in the performance of the most noble action in any given context, rather than one that is confined to a specific set of actions. For a further discussion of this perfection see below.

36. See, for example, *Guide* 2:36; 3:51. For Maimonides, true felicity is not a function of the feeling accompanying the process of transforming potential knowledge into actual knowledge—that is, the pleasure that comes from the feeling of "progress" in intellection or even from the effort itself. Rather it is a function of the very act of apprehension. The level of felicity is determined by the nobility of the object of apprehension. The more a human progresses in knowledge, the greater the felicity experienced because of the greater nobility of the object of apprehension, not the progress per se. This is true also of the love of God, since it too is treated as a function of knowledge. For the sources and critique of this view, see Warren Zev Harvey, "Crescas versus Maimonides on Knowledge and Pleasure," in *A Straight Path*, ed. R. Link-Salinger (Washington, D.C.: Catholic University of America Press, 1989), 118–23. It should be added that Maimonides is of the view that the perfect individuals will attain a much more elevated apprehension of the incorporeal world with the final separation of their intellects from their bodies, thereby increasing their felicity. He does not, however, believe in progress after this stage, just as there is no progress in the intellection of the celestial or Separate Intellects through all eternity. This does not bring about a gradual loss, or even diminution, of felicity. On the contrary, the unceasing, unchanging, eternal contemplation of the incorporeal world is the intellect's final felicity, whether it be the perfect human intellect or the Separate Intellect. For the clearest expression of this view see Maimonides' *Introduction to Pereq Ḥeleq,* 203–5. See Gabriella Berzin, "The Concept of Happiness in the Teachings of Maimonides and Rabbi Chasdai Crescas" (in Hebrew) (Master's thesis, Ben-Gurion University, 1998).

37. For a discussion of Maimonides' treatment of this story, see chap. 2, section III; chap. 3, section II.

38. *Republic* 7.514a–521b.

39. See Maimonides' approach in *Guide* 2:48 to the meaning of biblical descriptions of the divine "command." The activities of nature, of irrational animals, as well as of human beings, are also described as conforming to the divine "command" though no personal communication from God is involved.

40. This interpretation was already advanced by a number of Maimonides' medieval and modern commentators. See my discussion in "'The Suffering of the Righteous' in Medieval Jewish Philosophy" (in Hebrew), *Daat* 19 (1987): 19–25.

41. For a discussion of the "acquired intellect" in Maimonides and his sources, see Altmann, "Maimonides on the Intellect," 77–84. See also Fazlur Rahman, *Prophecy in Islam* (London: George Allen and Unwin, 1958), 12–20; and Herbert Davidson, "Alfarabi and Avicenna on the Active Intellect," *Viator* 3 (1972): 118–22, 130, 141–44, 151–53, 160.

42. Maurice Bouyges, *Alfarabi: Risalat fi'l 'Aql* (Beirut: Imprimerie Catholique, 1938), 20–31. Arthur Hyman translated this work into English in *Philosophy in the Middle Ages*, ed. Arthur Hyman and James Walsh (New York: Harper and Row, 1967), 215–21.

43. Ed. Fauzi Najjar (Beirut: Imprimerie Catholique, 1964), 79. Najjar translated this passage in *Medieval Political Philosophy*, ed. Ralph Lerner and Muhsin Mahdi (Ithaca: Cornell University, 1972), 36. See also Richard Walzer, *Al-Farabi on the Perfect State* (Oxford: Clarendon Press, 1985), 244–45. A good description of Alfarabi's account is found in Davidson, "Alfarabi and Avicenna" 141–44, 151–53. As Davidson notes, Alfarabi uses both the terms *muttaḥid* (united) and *ittaṣala* (conjoined) to indicate the relation between the acquired intellect and Active Intellect.

44. For Avicenna's view, see Rahman, *Prophecy in Islam* 18–19; and Davidson, "Alfarabi and Avicenna" 168–69. Ibn Bajja's view has been discussed at length by Alexander Altmann, "Ibn Bajja on Man's Ultimate Felicity," in *Harry A. Wolfson Jubilee Volume*, ed. A. Hyman and S. Lieberman (Jerusalem: American Academy of Jewish Research, 1965): English Volume, 47–87, and reprinted in Altmann, *Studies in Religious Philosophy and Mysticism* (Ithaca: Cornell University, 1969), 73–107.

45. Cf. *Laws of Repentance* 8:3, where a similar description is offered by Maimonides.

46. Maimonides does not use the Hebrew term *devekut* (cleavage). In the later translations of his and other Arabic works, as well as in Hebrew philosophical and mystical treatises, this is the standard term used to signify conjunction. This usage already occurs in works prior to Maimonides such as in the Bible commentary of Abraham Ibn Ezra (e.g., Num. 20:8). Maimonides follows the *Sifre, 'Ekev* 49 in interpreting the commandment to "cleave" to God (Deut. 10:20) as meaning to associate with the sages. See *Laws of Character Traits* 6:2. In *Laws of Repentance* 7:6–7, however, his use of this term may be interpreted as a subtle allusion to the conjunction of the intellect.

47. See *Laws of the Principles of the Torah* 2:7.

48. See I Samuel 10:6.

49. Cf. *Political Regime,* 32.

50. See p. 624 of that work. The meanings of "union" *(ittiḥad)* and "conjunction" *(ittiṣāl)* in Maimonides are ambiguous. See Altmann, "Maimonides on the Intellect," 80–84. There is a general agreement that Maimonides did not accept the possibility of a complete union with the Active Intellect. Yet Altmann's limiting of Maimonides' use of "conjunction" to the reception of intelligibles in general is questionable. For a further discussion of this point, see below.

51. See my study "Halevi's Influence on Maimonides: a Preliminary Appraisal," *Maimonidean Studies* 2 (1991): 95–121.

52. The translation is my own, based on David Baneth's Arabic edition (Jerusalem: Magnes Press, 1977), 4–5, and utilizing the Hebrew translations of Ibn Tibbon and Even Shmuel, together with Hartwig Hirschfeld's English translation. See also *Kuzari* 4:19, where Halevi describes the philosophers' view of the dual nature of perfection, consisting both of a theoretical and a practical aspect. In the latter passage the immortality of the acquired intellect is mentioned explicitly.

53. See Berman, "The Political Interpretation of the Maxim," 56. Cf. Halevi's description of the philosophers' view in *Kuzari* 4:19. In Halevi's summary they also confine "assimilation to the Creator" to the practice and legislation of what is good, thereby imitating God's good organization of all things. In the same section Halevi ascribes to the philosophers the view that theoretical perfection is the ultimate end.

54. The highest level assumes the form of legislating for a polity—a level that Maimonides, as opposed to Alfarabi, limits to a single individual. The prophets and sages, however, also practice forms of political leadership. They play the role Alfarabi assigns to the princes of the law. In a crucial sense, Maimonides, both in his capacity as leader of the Egyptian Jewish community and, more important, legal authority and codifier of Jewish law, continues the same political role he ascribes to the prophets and sages of old.

55. That Maimonides sees ultimate ethical perfection in the *Guide* as the obliteration of all psychological traits, thereby imitating God's dispassionate rule over the world, has been convincingly argued by Herbert Davidson, "The Middle Way in Maimonides' Ethics," *PAAJR* 54 (1987): 31–72. Davidson sees a development in Maimonides' thought in this matter. In my opinion, Maimonides comes close to presenting this ideal, albeit in a veiled manner, in his legal writings. He does not explicitly describe there the type of imitation of God that follows the attainment of theoretical perfection, as I have already indicated. The end of the *Guide*, on the other hand, describes the form of *imitatio Dei* characterizing the perfect. This is the practical activity that follows from theoretical perfection since it is determined purely by reason. Yet in his legal writings Maimonides is concerned with the regimen for attaining perfection. He links the training of one's soul to acquire certain character traits—by means of which one "imitates" God—with the process of attaining knowledge of God. The elimination of anger and any feeling of pride is integrally related to this process. Daniel H. Frank has already pointed out the similarity between the *Mishneh Torah* and the *Guide* on this point, and the problem with Davidson's developmental scheme. See "Anger as a Vice: A Maimonidean Critique of Aristotle's Ethics," *History of Philosophy Quarterly* 7 (1990): 269–81. See also "Humility as a Virtue: A Maimonidean Critique of Aristotle's Ethics," in *Moses Maimonides and His Time*, ed. Eric Ormsby (Washington D.C.: Catholic University of America Press, 1989), 89–99. Frank interprets Maimonides as abandoning the "Aristotelian" position and substituting in its place a "rabbinic" position on this issue. I find myself in closer agreement with Raymond Weiss. While stressing the difference between Aristotelian and rabbinic ethics in the case of anger and piety, Weiss notes that Maimonides approaches this issue from the standpoint of the training most "salutary for the contemplative life. The philosophic standpoint supplies the guiding principle for his reconstitution of Jewish morality." See *Maimonides' Ethics: The Encounter of Philosophic and Religious Morality* (Chicago: University of Chicago

Press, 1991), 113. Achieving a state devoid of all passions is both part of the training for intellectual perfection and the consequence of this perfection. I shall have more to say about this point in chap. 5, section VI.

56. *Guide* 1:52–60.

57. This argument is presented by Pines, "The Limitations of Human Knowledge," 82–109. Davidson, in refuting Pines's argument, has presented a detailed analysis of the evidence we have of Alfarabi's position in his lost commentary. See "Maimonides on Metaphysical Knowledge," 55–67.

58. See above, notes 41–43.

59. In *Introduction to Pereq Ḥeleq,* 212–13 (seventh principle), Maimonides indicates that Moses apprehended the level of the angels (= Separate Intellects) and became angelic, with no "veil" remaining that he did not rend. This is a clear reference to the attainment of the acquired intellect and the achievement of conjunction with the Active Intellect. In *Eight Chapters* 7, on the other hand, Maimonides indicates that one "veil" remained that he did not rend—the intellect tied to matter and is not "separate." The differences between the two passages may be traced to their purpose. The former source stresses the uniqueness of Moses' level. This qualifies him for receiving the one divine law. The latter source dwells on the utmost limit of human perfection, as embodied by Moses. This point does not preclude the view that Maimonides did not reach a final conclusion on the issue of the limits of perfection. A similar equivocation occurs in *Laws of the Principles of the Torah.* In 1:10, Maimonides indicates that Moses' intellect remained tied to the body, while in 7:6 he maintains that Moses' intellect was permanently tied to God and he "became sanctified like the angels [= the Separate Intellects]."

60. It is significant that even the philosophers who were aware of Alfarabi's retraction—for example, Ibn Bajja and Ibn Tufayl—continued to accept the possibility of conjunction and immortality.

61. See Altmann, "Maimonides on the Intellect," 85–91. To the sources cited by Altmann should be added *Introduction to Pereq Ḥeleq,* 205; and *Guide* 1:30; 3:8.

62. See Gersonides' discussion in *Wars of the Lord* 1:8–13, translated into English by Seymour Feldman (Philadelphia: JPS, 1984) 1:170–225.

63. See *Metaphysics* 12.7.1072b; *De Anima* 3.5.430a. Maimonides brings this principle in reference to God's intellect in *Guide* 1:68; *Eight Chapters* 8; *Laws of the Principles of the Torah* 2:10.

64. See Davidson, "Alfarabi and Avicenna," 171–75.

65 See the sources cited above, n. 61.

66. See, however, Altmann, "Maimonides on the Intellect," 85–91.

67. Altmann maintains that *Laws of Repentance* 8:3 suggests a different conclusion. The apprehension of the Separate Intellects is treated as one of a wider range of topics—God and the other existents—known to the immortal intellect. The main point, however, is that Maimonides explicitly mentions this topic. Moreover, in

contrast to his mention of the intellect's apprehension of God, the apprehension of the Separate Intellects is not qualified with the phrase "according to its [the intellect's] ability."

68. Maimonides' view of love of God as consequent upon apprehension is a fundamental principle in the *Mishneh Torah* and is found already in the *Commentary on the Mishnah.* I deal at length with this issue in chap. 7.

69. The translation is my own, based on Kafiḥ, *Mishnah 'im Perush HaRambam: Seder Nezikin,* 463–64. Maimonides mentions the apprehension of the Separate Intellects in *Commentary on Avot* 3:20. There he indicates that this apprehension does not result in one's becoming a Separate Intellect. This should be interpreted to mean that some difference remains in their intellection and hence in their ontological status.

70. See Narboni's commentary to *Guide* 1:62, ed. J. Goldenthal (Vienna, 1852), 11a. Several chapters later (1:74), Maimonides also adopts Ibn Bajja's position on the unity of the immortal intellects (cf. 1:70). This may not have been Maimonides' final thought on the matter. See the end of 3:51, where he alludes to different levels of immortal intellects.

71. See also 1:34. Maimonides consistently uses the root *d-r-k* to indicate apprehension, while the roots *'-l-m* and *'-q-l* are used to designate God's Self-knowledge. What, if any, are the differences between these terms is the pivotal problem. It should be noted that in 1:62 he terms the apprehension of the Active Intellect, a "science" *(al-'ilm),* while in 1:68 he appears to use the roots *d-r-k* and *'-q-l* interchangeably.

72. Cf. *Guide* 1:38.

73. See above, section IV.

74. See Avicenna's *De Anima*, ed. F. Rahman (London: Oxford University Press, 1959), 247. For a discussion of this issue, see Davidson, "Alfarabi and Avicenna," 166–69. See also A. M. Goichon, *Lexique de la Langue Philosophique d'Ibn Sina* (Paris: Descléé de Brouwer, 1938).

75. See *Guide* 1:1; 1:18. The former passage is certainly ambiguous on this point. In the latter passage, Maimonides may subtly be referring to prophetic apprehension, rather than normal discursive reasoning. The discussion deals with apprehending God. It should be added that Maimonides holds Alfarabi's view that intelligibles are attained through a process of "abstraction" (1:73). This suggests that the role of the Active Intellect is to enable the human intellect to act, rather than to bestow directly the individual intelligibles as Avicenna maintains. Several scholars, most notably Barry Kogan and Herbert Davidson, have interpreted Maimonides along Avicennian lines. Yet as Davidson notes, the passages cited by Kogan are compatible with Alfarabi's approach. Davidson's own evidence is based on his understanding of a passage in *Guide* 3:8. See B. Kogan, " 'What Can We Know and When Can We Know It?' Maimonides on the Active Intelligence and Human Cognition," in *Moses Maimonides and His Time,* ed. Ormsby, 121–37; Davidson,

"Maimonides on Metaphysical Knowledge," 89. I shall deal with the relevant passage in the continuation of my remarks.

76. Avicenna's *De Anima,* 248. See also F. Rahman, trans., *Avicenna's Psychology* (London: Oxford University Press, 1952), 36. For an analysis of prophetic intuition, see in particular Dmitri Gutas, *Avicenna and the Aristotelian Tradition* (Leiden: E. J. Brill, 1988), 159–76.

77. Davidson notes that Avicenna uses "conjunction" in different ways. Both in *Shifa* and *Najāt,* he posits a permanent form of conjunction occurring upon the culmination of human intellectual development. See "Maimonides on Metaphysical Knowledge," 93.

78. "Form" in the phrase "that through which that form exists" *(allaḏī minna wujidat tilk al-ṣūra)* does not refer to an intelligible that is attained as a result of conjunction. This mistaken interpretation is presented by both Altmann and Davidson. It led them (Altmann implicitly, Davidson explicitly) to view Maimonides as adopting Avicenna's view that conjunction occurs with every act of intellection. In the beginning of the passage cited, Maimonides employs the term *ṣūra* to denote the human form ("individuals who aspire always to prefer . . . what is required by their noble *form*") and *ma'qūl* to denote an intelligible ("mental representation of an *intelligible*"). The subsequent appearance of "form" in the phrase above can only refer to the human being's "noble form"—that is, the intellect—whose source is the Active Intellect. "Conjunction" thus signifies the union of the human intellect with the Active Intellect after the former attains all of the intelligibles. Rather than suggesting Maimonides' adoption of Avicenna's epistemological views on this issue, this passage shows that Maimonides remained loyal to Alfarabi.

79. *Kitāb al-Ishārāt w-al-Tanbīhāt,* ed. J. Forget (Leiden: Brill, 1892), 202–4.

80. Ed. Leon Gauthier ed. (Beirut: Imprimerie Catholique, 1936), 7. Ibn Tufayl employs the term *wuṣūl*. An English translation of this passage by George Atiyeh is found in *Medieval Political Philosophy,* ed. Lerner and Mahdi, 137. It should be noted that in an earlier passage on p. 129, Ibn Sina speaks of a "type of conjunction" *(ittiṣāl mā)* in the attainment of any intelligible from the Active Intellect.

81. See, however, Pines, "Philosophic Sources," cv. Pines treats Ibn Bajja as Maimonides' more probable source.

82. *Guide* 2:24. This chapter deals with astronomical matters. It has been the subject of an in-depth study by Tzvi Langerman, "The True Perplexity: *The Guide of the Perplexed* Part II, Chapter 24," in *Perspectives on Maimonides,* ed. Kraemer, 159–74. The implications of scientific progress for Maimonides' thought has been explored in a number of studies by Menachem Kellner. See his latest study, "Maimonides' Allegiances to Sciences and Judaism," *Torah u-Madda Journal* 7 (1997): 88–104.

83. For the distinction between discursive knowledge and direct apprehension see Davidson, "Maimonides on Metaphysical Knowledge," 92–99. For a comparison between prophets and philosophers see chap. 2, sections V–VI.

84. *Risalat fi'l 'Aql,* 20–31; translated by Hyman in *Philosophy in the Middle Ages,* ed. Hyman and Walsh, 217–20.

85. See Walzer, *Al-Farabi on the Perfect State,* 242–45. The precise relation between the acquired intellect and conjunction in Alfarabi's thought has been subject to conflicting interpretations. See Altmann, "Maimonides on the Intellect," 78 n. 141.

86. The problem whether conjunction occurs only at the moment of death or is possible while one remains tied to the body is one that occupied thinkers prior to Maimonides. See Shlomo Pines, "Shi'ite Terms and Conceptions in Judah Halevi's *Kuzari,*" *Jerusalem Studies in Arabic and Islam* 2 (1980): 211f.; and Ezra Fleischer, *The Proverbs of Sa'id ben Bābshād* (in Hebrew) (Jerusalem: Ben-Zevi Institute, 1990), 144.

87. Compare the end of 3:51, where Maimonides distinguishes between different levels of individuals who attain immortality, and 1:74, where he posits the unity of the immortal human intellects.

88. See *Laws of the Principles of the Torah* 2:6–8.

89. Cf. 1:24, where Maimonides explains the term "going"—as in the verse *to go in His ways* (Deut. 28:9)—in a similar manner.

90. This idea is already found in Alfarabi. See Walzer, *Alfarabi on the Perfect State,* 236–39.

91. I have dealt with this issue in "The Place of Man in the Hierarchy of Existence in the Philosophy of Ibn Gabirol and Maimonides," in *'Alei Shefer: Studies in the Literature of Jewish Thought,* ed. Moshe Hallamish (Ramat-Gan: Bar-Ilan University Press, 1990), English and French section, 100–102.

92. In all probability Maimonides' view of human immortality lies at the foundation of his position. See my "Place of Man," 104–5.

93. For a study of this topic in Jewish thought, see Warren Zev Harvey, "Holiness: a Command to *Imitatio Dei,*" *Tradition* 16 (1976–77): 7–28.

94. Maimonides ascribes this dictum to the *Sifra* on Lev. 11:44 and 19:2 (*Guide* 3:33,47). It does not, however, appear in our editions of the work. In *Book of the Commandments*, root 4, Maimonides traces this dictum to the *Sifre*. It in fact appears in *Sifre, Shelaḥ* 115.

95. This phrase does not appear in the passage in question in our versions of the *Sifre*. However, a similar passage, which includes the imitation of God's holiness (citing Lev. 11:44), appears in the eleventh-century midrashic compilation *Leqaḥ Tov* to Deut. 13:5. See M. M. Kasher, *Torah Shelemah*, vol. 28 (Jerusalem: American Biblical Encyclopedia Society, 1978), 238 n. 281. Maimonides' addition of "holiness" thus may be derived from a rabbinic source. More likely, it reflects a conflation of the passage of the *Sifre* with the verse in Leviticus.

96. The notion of "holiness" occurs in a number of other places in *Laws of the Principles of the Torah:* 4:12 in reference to the celestial spheres; chapter 5 in reference to the commandment "to sanctify the Name"; chapter 6 in reference to the

commandment not to efface the holy names of God; 7:1 in reference to the angels (= Separate Intellects). The command "to sanctify the Name" refers to the realm of human activity. A full discussion of the relation between "holiness" and this activity requires a separate study. Maimonides gives no indication to the meaning of holiness in reference to the celestial spheres or Separate Intellects. Holiness may refer to their ontological status, or it may refer to the perfection of their activity.

97. The translation is my own. I am indebted to Hannah Kasher's unpublished work on *imitatio Dei* for the reference to this passage and discussion of it.

98. See *Laws of Character Traits* 2:1; *Laws of Repentance* 4:5; 7:3; *Laws of Sale* 11:12; *Laws of Ritual Baths* 11:12. With the possible exception of the last passage, *de'ot ra'ot* unequivocally refers to evil character traits. Nor am I aware of any other occurrence of this phrase in the *Mishneh Torah*. In general, Maimonides more frequently uses the term *de'ot* to refer to traits than to intelligibles or intellects, though the latter usage is also common. The phrase *da'atam ha-ra'ah* in *Laws of Idolatry* 1:1 refers to evil thought.

99. Leviticus 11 contains a list of forbidden foods.

100. *Mishnah 'im Perush HaRambam: Seder Zera'im*, 42. See also *Laws of Forbidden Intercourse* 22:21.

101. See also 2:36; 2:40; 3:33; 3:49. For the source in Aristotle, see *Nicomachean Ethics* 3.10.1118b. In 3:12, Maimonides treats concupiscence for eating, drinking, and copulating as the cause of all corporeal and psychical diseases. In his discussion of the virtues and vices in 3:8, he introduces a Platonic motif. The virtues consist of intellectual apprehension, control of desire, and control of anger. This list corresponds to the tripartite Platonic division of the soul.

102. *Berakhot* 10b; *Leviticus Rabbah* 24:6. See 2 Kings 4:9.

103. Exod. 19:10; 19:15. The command to be holy in Lev. 19:2 follows the list of forbidden relations. For the juxtaposition of holiness and forbidden relations, see also *Leviticus Rabbah* 24:6. Cf. S. Buber, ed., *Tanḥuma*: *Qedoshim* 3.

104. Num. 6:5. Cf. Maimonides' remarks in 3:48. For a discussion of Maimonides' contradictory treatment of the nazarite, see chap. 5, section VI.

105. A hint of this view is already found in Maimonides' *Book of the Commandments* root 4. Commenting on the rabbinic interpretation: "*You shall be holy*—you shall be separate (*Sifra* to Lev. 11:44)," Maimonides indicates that one must separate oneself from all bad or disgusting *(qabiḥ)* things against which God warned us. The term *qabiḥ*, as seen from *Guide* 3:33, is used as opposed to "holy" and "pure," particularly in reference to the commandments pertaining to drinking and intercourse. In general Maimonides employs *qabiḥ* in the context of ethical traits and activities. For a discussion of the terms for good and bad in Maimonides' writings, see chapter 3, section III.

106. See Altmann and Stern, *Isaac Israeli,* 185–200.

107. For Maimonides, however, it is not sufficient to negate one's corporeality in order to purify oneself. One must make an active effort to perfect one's intellect

by learning the order of the sciences. For the relation between holiness and the pursuit of truth in Maimonides' thought, see Weiss, *Maimonides' Ethics,* 153–55.

108. See in particular Alasdair MacIntyre, *After Virtue* (Notre Dame, Ind.: University of Notre Dame Press, 1981).

109. The fascination that Spinoza's model continues to exercise on many may in part stem from a similar longing. While Spinoza grounds his model in a far different metaphysical system, it shares with the classical and medieval philosophic approaches the notion that ethics and metaphysics are inseparably intertwined.

Chapter 5. The Problem of Contradictions in Maimonides' Approach to Ethics

1. Aristotle's *Nicomachean Ethics*, a work that exercised a decisive influence in medieval philosophic approaches to ethics, is devoted primarily to this problem. Maimonides offers a concise summary of the Aristotelian approach to ethics in his *Treatise of Logic*, chap. 14. This treatise was translated into English by Israel Efros, "Maimonides' Treatise on Logic," *PAAJR* 8 (1938): 34–65. Efros also edited the Arabic edition of the treatise, which appears in *PAAJR* 34 (1966): 1–42. A number of Maimonides' Aristotelian sources are presented by Joel Kraemer, "Maimonides on the Philosophic Sciences in his Treatise on the Art of Logic," in *Perspectives on Maimonides*, ed. Joel Kraemer (Oxford: Oxford University Press, 1991), 90, 95–96.

2. Aristotle deals with the basis for ethical knowledge in several passages, most notably *Nicomachean Ethics* 5.7.1134b; and *Rhetorica* 1.13.1373b. His views suggest that ethics is known intuitively. His views of the practical intellect in *De Anima* 3.7.431b and *Nicomachean Ethics* 6.2.1139a, on the other hand, suggest that a deliberative process is involved in ascertaining what is good. In yet another passage, *Topics* 1.100a–b, Aristotle deals with dialectical reasoning based upon "generally accepted" opinions. These opinions are distinct from primary intelligibles, "which are believed on the strength not of anything else but of themselves." From the continuation of Aristotle's discussion of dialectical propositions in 1.10–14.104a–105b, it becomes clear that dialectical propositions concern two broad areas—volitional matters (what is to be chosen or avoided) and matters of truth and knowledge. In treating the opinions of the most illustrious philosophers, and not only the opinions of the majority of the masses, as falling into the category of "generally accepted" opinions, Aristotle sees a connection between "generally accepted" opinions and reason. On the basis of this passage, many of the medieval Islamic philosophers, including Alfarabi, treat ethical norms as falling into the category of dialectical opinions. At the same time they trace the distinction between good and bad to the rational faculty. I have dealt with this point in chap. 2, sections I–IV. For a further discussion of this issue, see Israel Efros, "The Approach of Reason to Ethics according to Se'adia and Maimonides" (in Hebrew), *Tarbiz* 28 (1959): 325–29;

Arthur Hyman, "A Note on Maimonides' Classification of the Law," in *American Academy of Jewish Research Jubilee Volume*, ed. Salo Baron and Isaac Barzilay (Jerusalem: American Academy of Jewish Research, 1980), 323–43.

3. See *Nicomachean Ethics* 2.6–9.1106a–1109b. Many medieval philosophic works reflect Aristotle's approach. One that had a direct impact on Maimonides' approach to the subject, particularly as it finds expression in his *Eight Chapters,* is Alfarabi's *Aphorisms of the Statesman*, ed. and trans. D. M. Dunlop (Cambridge: Cambridge University Press, 1961), no. 16. For the relation between Alfarabi's treatise and that of Maimonides, see Herbert Davidson, "Maimonides' *Shemonah Peraqim* and Alfarabi's *Fuṣūl al-Madanī*," *PAAJR* 31 (1963): 116–33; and Jeffrey Macy, A Study in Medieval Jewish and Arabic Political Philosophy: Maimonides' *Shemonah Peraqim* and Alfarabi's *Fuṣūl al-Madanī* (Ph.D. thesis, Hebrew University, 1982).

4. *Nicomachean Ethics* 3.1–3.109b–1113a; 6.2.1139a–b.

5. See *Aphorisms*, nos. 8–15. For the source in Aristotle, see *Nicomachean Ethics* 2.1.1103a–b.

6. Joseph Kafiḥ, ed. and trans., *Mishnah 'im Perush HaRambam: Seder Zera'im* (in Arabic and Hebrew) (Jerusalem: Mossad HaRav Kook, 1963), 41–43; *Eight Chapters* 5, 7; *Guide of the Perplexed* 1:34.

7. *Treatise on Logic* 14; *Eight Chapters* 3–4; *Laws of Character Traits* 1:3–4, 2:1; *Guide* 3:8.

8. Already in Maimonides' *Commentary on the Mishnah* there is some ambiguity in his treatment of these two traits. See *Eight Chapters* 4; *Commentary on Avot* 4:4. This, among other considerations, has led some of Maimonides' modern commentators to question the extent of his acceptance of Aristotle's ethical theory. See Marvin Fox's discussion of this issue, "The Doctrine of the Mean in Aristotle and Maimonides: A Comparative Study," in *Studies in Jewish Religious and Intellectual History*, ed. Siegfried Stein and Raphael Loewe (Tuscaloosa: University of Alabama Press, 1979), 93–120, reprinted in his *Interpreting Maimonides* (Chicago: University of Chicago Press, 1990), 93–123]. Raymond Weiss treats this issue extensively in his *Maimonides' Ethics* (Chicago: University of Chicago Press, 1991). See also Daniel H. Frank, "Humility as a Virtue: A Maimonidean Critique of Aristotle's Ethics," in *Moses Maimonides and His Time*, ed. Eric Ormsby (Washington D.C.: Catholic University of America Press, 1989), 89–99; idem, "Anger as a Vice: A Maimonidean Critique of Aristotle's Ethics," *History of Philosophy Quarterly* 7 (1990): 269–81.

9. This issue has been discussed by a number of scholars. See Jacob Levinger, "Abstinence from Alcohol in Maimonides' *Guide of the Perplexed*" (in Hebrew), *Bar-Ilan* 4–5 (1967): 299–305. Isadore Twersky, *Introduction to the Code of Maimonides* (New Haven: Yale University Press, 1980), 459–68; and Herbert Davidson, "The Middle Way in Maimonides' Ethics," *PAAJR* 54 (1987): 31–72. See section VI of this chapter for a further discussion of the issue.

10. In *Laws of Character Traits* 1:2, Maimonides adopts the position that an individual is born with certain traits. Yet the whole tenor of his discussion is that an individual has the power to change them.

11. Cf. 2:36. This does not imply, however, that training has no effect whatsoever on the modification of bad traits.

12. Several scholars have focused on aspects of this issue. See in particular Miriam Galston, "The Purpose of the Law according to Maimonides," *JQR* 69 (1978–79): 27–51; and Hannah Kasher, "Commandments between Man and God in the Guide of the Perplexed" (in Hebrew), *Daat* 12 (1984): 23–28. For the most extensive treatment of this issue, see Raymond Weiss, *Maimonides' Ethics*. Part of his discussion appears in his earlier study, "The Adaptation of Philosophic Ethics to a Religious Community: Maimonides' *Eight Chapters*," *PAAJR* 54 (1987): 261–87.

13. This point has also been argued by Raymond Weiss in his *Maimonides' Ethics.*

14. *Mishnah 'im Perush HaRambam: Seder Zera'im:* 42–43.

15. Joseph Kafiḥ, ed. and trans., *Mishnah 'im Perush HaRambam: Seder Nezikin* (in Arabic and Hebrew) (Jerusalem: Mossad HaRav Kook, 1965), 208. Cf. Richard Walzer, *Al-Farabi on the Perfect State* (Oxford: Clarendon Press, 1985), 206–7.

16. In Joseph Kafiḥ's edition of Maimonides' commentary the division of the *mishnayot* is slightly different than in the standard editions.

17. Maimonides reiterates in 7:4 the view that "withdrawal" *(hitbodedut)* is among the states necessary for the attainment of prophecy. Both these passages may be referring to physical isolation. There are passages in his writings where the idea of physical isolation as part of the process of attaining perfection is mentioned. See *Guide* 2:36; 3:51. One, however, is not forced to adopt this interpretation of "withdrawal" in the present context. It more likely refers to a form of mental concentration in which the person "withdraws" into the self. For a discussion of this issue, see Moshe Idel, "*Hitbodedut* as Concentration in Jewish Philosophy" (in Hebrew), *Jerusalem Studies in Jewish Thought (Shlomo Pines Jubilee Volume)* 7 (1988): 39–60.

18. The translation from *Sefer ha-Madda'* is my own based on the edition of Jacob Cohen, Moshe Hayim Katzenelebogen, and S. Lieberman (Jerusalem: Mossad HaRav Kook, 1964).

19. For a discussion of the love and fear of God, see chap. 7.

20. For Maimonides' treatment of this story, see chap.2, section III; chap. 3, section II.

21. The notion that human beings are political animals is found in Aristotle's *Politics* 1.2.1252b–1253a. The primary meaning of this notion is that society is required to satisfy the individual's physical needs. Maimonides' usage of this notion in the *Guide* reflects this meaning. In addition, there is a secondary meaning that is mentioned by the medievals, and also hinted at by Aristotle. Humans feels a

need for companionship. Maimonides alludes to this idea in the introduction to his *Commentary on the Mishnah.*

22. See *Mishnah 'im Perush HaRambam: Seder Zera'im,* 43–45.

23. See also *Commentary to Avot* 1:17, 5:13.

24. See *B.T. Ḥagigah* 14b. Maimonides treats *pardes* as a reference to the two types of esoteric knowledge discussed in the second chapter of *Ḥagigah—ma'aseh bereshit (Account of the Beginning)* and *ma'aseh merkavah (Account of the Chariot).* He equates these subjects with physics and metaphysics. See also his *Commentary to Ḥagigah* 2:1.

24. For a detailed discussion of both chapters, as well as 2:39 and 3:28, see Galston, "The Purpose of the Law," 27–51. See also Lawrence Kaplan, " 'I Sleep, but my Heart waketh': Maimonides' Conception of Human Perfection," in *The Thought of Moses Maimonides*, ed. Ira Robinson, Lawrence Kaplan, and Julien Bauer (Lewiston, N.Y.: Edwin Mellen, 1990), 154–59.

25. Galston argues that the chapter deals with two types of legislation—general legislations and Mosaic legislation. The former aims at the welfare of the body and soul. The latter aims at the soul's perfection. In light of the fact that Maimonides explicitly ascribes the aim of "welfare" to Mosaic legislation in this chapter, and the chapter deals exclusively with the divine law (forming part of the section dealing exclusively with the divine law), this argument is difficult to sustain.

26. See Alexander Altmann, "Maimonides' 'Four Perfections'," *IOS* 2 (1972): 15–24.

27. For a comparison with Ibn Bajja on this point, see ibid., 19–21. Aristotle brings the idea that only contemplative activity is self-sufficient in *Nicomachean Ethics* 10.7.1177a. All other virtues are said to necessarily involve other people.

28. See *Mishnah Yoma* 8:9.

29. Hannah Kasher deals with the interpretation of Maimonides' distinction, particularly in reference to the third class of commandments. See "Commandments between Man and God," 26f.

30. See ibid., 26–27.

31. This point is argued by Galston, "The Purpose of the Law," 31–41, 48–51. Her distinction between "noble" *(kirām)* morals aimed at social welfare and moral "virtues" *(faḍā'il)* aimed at individual perfection, however, is difficult to accept. In 3:54, for example, Maimonides uses the term *faḍā'il* for describing moral perfection. In the same context he limits morality to playing only a social role.

32. For a discussion of immortality in Maimonides' thought, see chap. 4, sections IV–V.

33. See Davidson, "The Middle Way," 59–72. For a more detailed discussion of this point, see chap. 4, section IV.

34. In the *Guide* 3:48, Maimonides relates abstinence in eating and drinking to a different trait, *al-qana'a (histapqut).* This trait too is listed in *Eight Chapters* 4.

35. The translation is my own based on Kafiḥ's Arabic edition, *Mishnah 'im Perush HaRambam: Seder Nezikin,* 385.

36. See my article, "Asceticism in the Thought of R. Baḥya Ibn Paquda and Maimonides," *Daat* 21 (1988): vii–xiii.

37. *Yevamot* 63b.

38. For Maimonides' view of holiness, see chap. 4, section VII.

39. Cf. 2:36. Maimonides appears to have in mind someone who is not physically distant from society, but lives an isolated existence within society. This individual continues to rely upon society to provide the basic necessities. For a study of this issue in Maimonides and his sources, see Harry Blumberg, "Alfarabi, Ibn Bajja and Maimonides on the Governance of the Solitary: Sources and Influences" (in Hebrew), *Sinai* 78 (1976): 135–45.

40. For a discussion of this point, see chap. 3, section II.

41. *Mishnah 'im Perush HaRambam: Seder Zera'im,* 42. For the sources of this view in Plato and in subsequent thinkers, see Alexander Altmann and S. M. Stern, *Isaac Israeli* (Oxford: Oxford University Press, 1958), 200f.

42. See *Guide* 1:33. Cf. 1:5, 1:32, 1:34.

43. The distinction between two types of ascetics—those whose asceticism enables them to reach greater spiritual and intellectual heights and those who experience asceticism as a spiritual burden—finds its expression in Judah Halevi, *Kuzari* 3:1.

44. See *'Avodah Zarah* 20b.

45. Maimonides' description of the *ḥasid* as lacking all impulse to do evil has its source in Alfarabi, *Aphorisms,* no. 13.

46. Maimonides cites the story of a certain *ḥasid* who had eliminated all sense of pride to the degree that he felt no insult when defecated upon on a ship. With the realization of his attainment, the *ḥasid* experienced a feeling of great joy. Maimonides indicates that the story is taken from the ethical literature. R. Weiss has identified the source Al-Hujwīrī, *Kashf al-Mahjub*. See *Maimonides' Ethics,* 40 n. 8. The story also appears in the letter ascribed to Maimonides' student and sent to Ḥasdai Halevi. In this source, it is a philosopher, rather than a *ḥasid,* who is the subject of the story. See Isaac Shailat, ed. and trans., *Letters and Essays of Moses Maimonides* (in Arabic and Hebrew) (Maaleh Adumim, Israel: Maaliyot Press, 1988), 681.

47. Shailat, ed., *Letters and Essays of Moses Maimonides* 92.

48. This ideal bears marked similarity to the one presented by R. Baḥya Ibn Paquda. See *Duties of the Heart* 9:7. For a further discussion of this ideal, see chap. 4, sections IV–V.

49. Maimonides' naturalistic approach to the attainment of prophecy allows him to present naturalistic criteria for judging the claimant to prophecy. I have dealt with this issue in "The Verification of Prophecy in Medieval Jewish Philosophy" (in Hebrew), *Jerusalem Studies in Jewish Thought* 4 (1984–85): 1–18.

50. Cf. *Shabbat* 87a.

51. I deal more extensively with this issue in the following chapter.

52. This point has been argued by Jacob Levinger, "Halakhah and Personal Perfection according to Maimonides" (in Hebrew), *Daat* 13 (1984): 61–65, reprinted in his *Maimonides as Philosopher and Codifier* (in Hebrew) (Jerusalem: Bialik Institute, 1989), 149–54.

53. This position has been argued by Sara Klein-Braslavy and Warren Zev Harvey. For a discussion of their interpretations see chap. 3.

54. For a detailed presentation of this point, see chap. 2, sections III, VIII; chap. 3, sections II, III.

55. For a survey of the various approaches to interpreting the *Guide* in both the medieval and modern period, see Aviezer Ravitzky, "The Secrets of the *Guide of the Perplexed:* Between the Thirteenth and the Twentieth Centuries," in *Studies in Maimonides*, ed. Isadore Twersky (Cambridge: Harvard University Press, 1990), 159–207. For problems with the esoteric/exoteric approach, see Marvin Fox, *Interpreting Maimonides,* 47–90.

56. This point is made in passing by Levinger, "Abstinence from Alcohol," 304–5.

57. See *Mishnah 'im Perush HaRambam: Seder Zera'im,* 43–45.

58. Maimonides follows Aristotle in positing two conditions for performing what is good—knowledge and will. Knowledge leads to the proper activity, but in itself does not ensure its practice. See *Eight Chapters* 3.

59. See chap. 4, sections IV–V.

60. This is true even of imperfect forms of rulership, as Maimonides' remarks in *Guide* 2:40 indicate.

61. Yet it should be noted that the two paradigms of human perfection in Maimonides' thought—Abraham and Moses—grew up in imperfect societies. The exceptional individual is able to overcome the deficiencies in the environment, though more obstacles lie in the path.

Chapter 6. Intellectual Perfection, Knowledge of God, and the Role of the Law

1. See *Guide* 1:Introduction, 1:34, 3:27–28, 3:51:27–28, 3:51.
2. See chap. 4, section V.
3. See *Kuzari* 1:95, 2:50, 3:1, 4:3.
4. See chap. 5, section III.
5. For an analysis of this point see Isadore Twersky, *Introduction to the Code of Maimonides* (New Haven: Yale University Press, 1980), 488–507; W. Z. Harvey, "Political Philosophy and Halakhah in Maimonides" (in Hebrew)," *Iyyun* 29 (1980): 198–212; Hannah Kasher, "Talmud Torah as a Means of Apprehending God in Maimonides' Teachings" (in Hebrew), *Jerusalem Studies in Jewish Thought*, 5

(1986): 71–82; idem, "Does 'Ought' Imply 'Can' in Maimonides?" (in Hebrew), *Iyyun* 36 (1987): 13–34.

6. *Laws of the Principles of the Torah*, chaps. 1–4. This topic is the subject of the following chapter.

7. For a detailed discussion of this parable, see Hannah Kasher, "The Parable of the King's Palace in *The Guide of the Perplexed* as a Directive to the Student" (in Hebrew), *AJS Review* 14 (1989): 1–19 (Hebrew Section).

8. Maimonides may be referring to the thirteen principles he presents in his *Commentary on the Mishnah: Sanhedrin 10 (Introduction to Pereq Ḥeleq)*. Most of them, however, have no basis in theoretical philosophy. At the very least the fundamental principles include the existence and unity of God (together with God's incorporeality and eternity), which belong to the science of metaphysics. See, for example, *Guide* 2:29 where the notion of disbelief in the foundations of the Law is used in reference to those who interpret the opening of Genesis (the *Account of the Beginning*) in accordance with the external sense of the text. Knowledge of the principles in this chapter is tied to knowledge of the sciences. The speculation concerning the other principles may well belong to the science of political philosophy in Maimonides' view. For an analysis of the notion of "principles" in Maimonides' thought, together with a discussion of the important scholarly literature on the subject, see Menachem Kellner, *Dogma in Medieval Jewish Thought* (Oxford: Oxford University Press, 1986), 10–65. See also Arthur Hyman, "Maimonides' 'Thirteen Principles,'" in *Jewish Medieval and Renaissance Studies*, ed. Alexander Altmann (Cambridge: Harvard University, 1967), 119–45.

9. For a discussion of "belief" in the thought of Maimonides, see Avraham Nuriel, "Maimonides and the Concept of Faith" (in Hebrew), *Daat* 2–3 (1979): 43–47; idem, "Remarks on Maimonides' Epistemology," in *Maimonides and Philosophy*, ed. S. Pines and Y. Yovel (Dordrect: Martinus Nijhoff, 1986), 36–51; Shalom Rosenberg, "The Concept of 'Emunah' in Post-Maimonidean Jewish Philosophy," in *Studies in Medieval Jewish History and Literature*, ed. I. Twersky, vol. 2 (Cambridge: Harvard University Press, 1984), 273–307.

10. Maimonides presents the categories of attributes that are to be negated of God in *Guide* 1:52.

11. See *Guide* 1:Introduction, 1:33, 2:31, 3:28–30, 3–32.

12. See *Laws of the Principles of the Torah* 1:7–12; *Laws of Repentance* 3:7; *Guide* 1:35–36.

13. Cf. 1:26.

14. See *Guide* 1:35; 1: 60.

15. *Introduction to Pereq Ḥeleq,* principle 3; *Laws of Repentance* 3:7. For the legal consequences of heresy in Jewish law, see Kellner, *Dogma in Medieval Jewish Thought,* 18–21. Following talmudic literature, Maimonides employs a number of terms to designate a heretic—*'epiqoros, min, kofer*. His discussion of heretical beliefs in *Laws of Repentance* 3:6–8 indicates that he sees a distinction between

these terms in accordance with different types of beliefs. *Min* is defined as one who denies the existence of God, divine unity, the incorporeality of God, that God is the First and the Principle of all existents, or one who worships any intermediary. *'Epiqoros* is one who rejects the existence of prophecy, the unique prophecy of Moses, or that God knows human actions. *Kofer ba-Torah* is applied to one who denies that the Torah is from God, rejects the Oral Law, or maintains that God made changes in the Torah. A perusal of Maimonides' other writings, including other passages from the *Mishneh Torah* (ms. Kushta), shows that he was not entirely consistent in his usage. In *Laws of Idolatry* 2:3, Maimonides employs *minūt* as a general term referring to heretical thoughts in general. In *Laws of Ritual Slaughter* 4:14 he applies it to one who rejects the Torah (see also *Commentary on the Mishnah: Hullin* 1:2). In *Laws of a Murderer* 4:10 *min* is used in reference to idolatry (as well as to the wanton transgression of the commandments) as in *Laws of Repentance* 3:6 (and *Laws of Idolatry* 2:5). *'Epiqoros*, however, is defined as one who rejects Torah and divine revelation. Idolaters are listed separately along with *minim* and *'epiqorsin* in *Laws of Robbery* 11:2 though according to *Laws of Repentance* they are defined as *minim*. One who denies the Oral Law is defined as a *min* in *Laws of Mamrim* 3:1. In his *Introduction to Pereq Ḥeleq* Maimonides follows *Sanhedrin* 99b in defining *'epiqoros* as one who behaves contemptuously towards the sages. In *Guide* 3:17 he ascribes to the philosopher Epicurus the view that there is no form of providence and everything happens by chance.

16. Maimonides' legal innovation on this point drew the ire of the Rabad who remarks in his *Hassagot* on *Laws of Repentance* 3:7: "Greater and better than he [Maimonides] held this view [God's corporeality] according to what they saw in the Scriptures."

17. See in particular Averroes' discussion of this issue in George Hourani, *Averroes on the Harmony of Religion and Philosophy* (London: Luzac, 1961). Averroes brings as an example the belief that God is corporeal. He maintains that those who are incapable of giving assent to that which they cannot imagine should continue to believe in the apparent meaning of the text. As in the case of Maimonides, Averroes sees in religion a means for the creation of an ideal society conducive to the study of philosophy, and in the study of philosophy a means for fulfilling a religious obligation to attain true knowledge of God. See W. Z. Harvey, "Averroes and Maimonides on the Obligation of Philosophic Contemplation" (in Hebrew), *Tarbiz* 58 (1989): 75–83.

18. For a further discussion of this point see chap. 1, section V.

19. Maimonides certainly does not think that the monotheistic belief has triumphed completely. In *Laws of Idolatry* 9:4, he categorizes the Christians as idolaters, without elaborating on the basis for his legal ruling. In *Guide* 1:50 he mentions that they affirm the unity of God, though their belief in the Trinity entails a belief in multiplicity. As Harry Wolfson has shown, Maimonides in this passage compares belief in the Trinity with belief in essential attributes, but does not equate the two.

From a logical standpoint, both beliefs violate the Law of Contradiction and entail multiplicity. From a religious standpoint, however, Maimonides does not consider the affirmation of essential attributes as polytheism. He does consider affirmation of the three persons of the Trinity to be such. See Wolfson, "Maimonides on the Unity and Incorporeality of God," *JQR* 56 (1965): 124–34, reprinted in his *Studies in the History of Philosophy and Religion*, ed. I. Twersky and G. Williams, vol. 2 (Cambridge: Harvard University Press, 1977), 445–55. There is a hint in one of his responsa that the deification of Jesus is also a basis for his ruling. See Joshua Blau, *R. Moses b. Maimon Responsa*, vol. 2 (Jerusalem: Mekize Nirdamim, 1960), 726 (no. 448). Nonetheless, Maimonides does not regard Christianity as negatively as he does the idolatrous religion of the Sabians, in large part because the Christians acknowledge the divinity of the Torah. For an analysis of Maimonides' view of both Christianity and Islam, see David Novak, "The Treatment of Islam and Muslims in the Legal Writings of Maimonides," in *Studies in Islamic and Judaic Traditions*, ed. W. Brinner and S. Ricks (Atlanta: Scholars Press, 1986), 233–50.

20. See *Guide* 1:Introduction, 1:26, 1:31, 1:35, 1:46. Maimonides' discussion of parables in the introduction to his treatise is particularly significant. True understanding of a text requires first knowing whether the text is a parable.

21. *R. Moses b. Maimon Responsa,* 726.

22. This point is made most forcefully by Maimonides in his *Epistle to the Jews of Yemen*. There he addresses a situation in which the Jews there faced religious persecution, and had to withstand tremendous pressure exerted upon them to convert. In the *Guide* 2:39–40, Maimonides presents this point in a more veiled manner. For a discussion of this issue, see Novak, "The Treatment of Islam and Muslims in the Legal Writings of Maimonides," 233–50.

23. See R. Saadiah Gaon, *Book of Beliefs and Opinions* 2:8–12; R. Baḥya Ibn Paquda, *Book of Directives of the Heart* 1:8–10; R. Judah Halevi, *Kuzari* 2:1–10.

24. R. Ḥefeṣ b. Yaṣliaḥ treats knowledge of the existence and unity of God as the first two commandments, followed by the commandments to love God and to fear Him. This may well have served as Maimonides' primary source for the opening of his *Book of the Commandments* and *Mishneh Torah*. See Benzion Halper, *A Volume of the Book of Precepts of Ḥefeṣ b. Yaṣliaḥ* (Philadelphia: Jewish Publication Society, 1915), 31f.; Moshe Zucker, "New Fragments from *The Book of Precepts by R. Ḥefeṣ b. Yaṣliaḥ*" (in Hebrew), *PAAJR* 29 (1960–61): 22f., 31f. For a further discussion of this point, see chap. 7, section III.

25. See H. Wolfson, "Maimonides on the Unity and Incorporeality of God," 120f. I disagree with Wolfson when he maintains that Maimonides does not consider the fulfillment of the commandments involving a knowledge of God to be purely mental acts. I will deal with this point in more detail in the following chapter. Wolfson is also incorrect when he infers from Maimonides' formulation in *Laws of Repentance* that heresy is limited to stating certain false beliefs out loud. Society is not in a position to punish a person as a heretic unless the act is a public one, but

Maimonides does not exclude purely mental acts from the category of heresy. See, for example, *Laws of Kings and Their Wars* 11:1, where one who does not *believe (ma'amin)* in the coming of the messiah is described as rejecting *(kofer)* the Torah.

26. A number of philosophical studies are devoted to an exploration of aspects of this work. See especially Leo Strauss, "Notes on Maimonides' Book of Knowledge," in *Studies in Mysticism and Religion Presented to Gershom Scholem*, ed. E. Urbach (Jerusalem: Magnes Press, 1967), 269–83; S. Rawidowicz, "On Maimonides' *Sefer ha-Madda*," in *Essays in Honour of the Very Rev. Dr. J. H. Hertz*, ed. I. Epstein, E. Levine, and C. Roth (London: E. Goldston, 1942), 331–39, reprinted in S. Rawidowicz, *Studies in Jewish Thought*, ed. N. Glatzer (Philadelphia: Jewish Publication Society, 1974), 317–23; I. Twersky, *Introduction to the Code of Maimonides,* 488–507; L. Berman, "Maimonides, the Disciple of Alfarabi," *IOS* 4 (1974): 154–78; J. Kraemer, "Alfarabi's Opinions of the Virtuous City and Maimonides' Foundations of the Law," in *Studia Orientalia Memoriae D. H. Baneth Dedicata,* ed. J. Blau (Jerusalem: Magnes Press, 1979), 107–53; W. Z. Harvey, "Political Philosophy and Halakhah in Maimonides," 198–212; H. Kasher "Does 'Ought' Imply 'Can' in Maimonides?," 13–34.

27. The view that Maimonides' theological positions in his legal works are no less philosophical than the positions he presents in the *Guide* has been argued by Shlomo Pines, "The Philosophical Purport of Maimonides' Halakhic Works and the Purport of the *Guide of the Perplexed*," in *Maimonides and Philosophy,* ed. Pines and Yovel, 1–14.

28. For a more extensive discussion of this point, see the continuation of this chapter and the following one.

29. See also *Guide*: 1:Introduction; *Commentary on the Mishnah: Hagigah* 2:1.

30. This point has been argued by S. Rawidowicz, "On Maimonides' *Sefer ha-Madda,*" 331–39. See also A. Nuriel "Maimonides and the Concept of Faith," 43–47.

31. Cf. *Laws of the Principles of the Torah* 4:13. For an analysis of this point, see Twersky, *Introduction to the Code of Maimonides,* 489f.; Kasher, "Talmud Torah as a Means of Apprehending God," 75f.

32. See Muhsin Mahdi, *Alfarabi's Philosophy of Plato and Aristotle* (New York: Free Press of Glencoe, 1962), 34–41. Cf. Plato, *Republic* 2.376e–412b; 4.421c–427c; 6–7.509d–541b. To what degree Alfarabi felt that the practical implementation of his model was possible is a difficult question. As for the application of this model to Jewish society, no institution equivalent to the caliphate in power existed in Judaism in Maimonides' time (certainly not the exilarchate or gaonate) to make this even a theoretical possibility.

33. For Maimonides indebtedness to Alfarabi in formulating his principles, see Kraemer, "Alfarabi's Opinions of the Virtuous City and Maimonides' Foundations of the Law."

34. *Laws of the Principles of the Torah* 4:13. See Twersky, *Introduction to the Code of Maimonides,* 493f. Twersky points to Maimonides' novel, yet very literal,

interpretation of "great" *(gadol)* and "small" *(qatan)* in terms of nobility. Yet of greater moment is Maimonides' novel and nonliteral interpretation of knowledge of the "discussions *(havvayot)* of Abbaye and Raba" as referring to knowledge of the "forbidden and permitted and their like from the rest of the commandments." That is to say, Maimonides equates the talmudic deliberations of Abbaye and Raba with most of the Oral Law (excluding the commandments involving the apprehension of the natural sciences and metaphysics), as the context of his remarks makes clear. See Harvey, "Political Philosophy and Halakhah in Maimonides," 207.

35. A different variant of this idea is found in *The Laws of Kings and Their Wars* 11:4. The Christians and Moslems are condemned for their promulgation of false beliefs. Nevertheless, Maimonides regards them as helping to prepare the way for the messianic period by publicizing throughout the world the commandments and the notion of the messiah.

36. One has only to look at his remarks in *Guide* 2:6 concerning those who "deem themselves the *Sages of Israel*," or remember where he situates these scholars in relation to God in his parable of the palace in 3:51.

37. See chap. 1, section IV.

38. For a detailed analysis of the conflict among the Maimonidean scholars on this issue see Aviezer Ravitzky, "The Secrets of the *Guide of the Perplexed:* Between the Thirteenth and the Twentieth Centuries," in *Studies in Maimonides*, ed. I. Twersky (Cambridge: Harvard University Press, 1990), 159–207.

39. See in particular Maimonides' exceptionally caustic remarks toward the beginning of his *Treatise on Resurrection,* in *Letters and Essays of Moses Maimonides* (in Arabic and Hebrew), ed. Isaac Shailat (Maaleh Adumim, Israel: Maaliyot Press, 1988), 319–21, 339–43.

40. Cf. 1:Introduction; 1:33–34; 2:11.

41. See Maimonides' dedicatory epistle to his pupil, R. Joseph b. Judah, at the beginning of the *Guide*.

42. In his *Commentary on the Mishnah,* Maimonides writes that he plans to write these two works. According to one of his comments in the introduction to *Pereq Ḥeleq,* it appears that he began writing the former work (p. 213). In the introduction to the *Guide,* he indicates his decision to revise his original plan on the form these works were to assume and to write the present work instead. Whether he incorporated in the *Guide* material that he already had set down in writing his book on prophecy is the subject of a study by Hannah Kasher, "Is There an Early Stratum in the *Guide of the Perplexed*?" *Maimonidean Studies* 3 (1992): 105–29.

43. For a discussion of immortality, see chap. 4, sections IV–V.

44. See the introduction to his *Commentary on the Mishnah,* in *Mishnah 'im Perush HaRambam: Seder Zera'im* (in Arabic and Hebrew), ed. and trans. Joseph Kafiḥ (Jerusalem: Mossad HaRav Kook, 1963): 41 f.

45. This theme is the main focus of chapter 4.

46. For the literature dealing with the principles see above, n. 8.

47. Significantly, Maimonides includes the principle of God's knowledge of particulars and providence as a prelude to the principles concerning reward and punishment, rather than listing it among those that involve God's essence. In the *Guide* too he discusses God's knowledge of particulars in the context of providence rather than divine attributes. This point may have some important ramifications for how one is to interpret Maimonides' view on the subject. Specifically, did Maimonides regard this belief as a true belief about God, as he certainly regarded the principles involving the divine essence, or as a politically necessary one?

48. See above, n. 15.

49. For a discussion of the relation of Maimonides to Avicenna on this issue, see Alexander Altmann, "Essence and Existence in Maimonides," in his *Studies in Religious Philosophy and Mysticism* (Ithaca: Cornell University, 1969), 108–27.

50. This is confirmed by Maimonides' subsequent addendum to this principle. See below for a discussion of this point.

51. The first verse of the Ten Commandments is adduced as the source of the first principle. The verse itself deals with God as Redeemer rather than God as Creator, let alone God as Necessary Existent and First Cause. See W. Z. Harvey, "The First Commandment and the God of History: Halevi and Crescas vs. Ibn Ezra and Maimonides" (in Hebrew), *Tarbiz* 57 (1988): 209–11. The first verse of the *Shema* (Deut. 6:4) is treated as the source for the second principle. This verse hardly suggests, however, the philosophical notion of unity presented by Maimonides. The proof texts for the incorporeality of God are the most numerous, yet the most strained. Maimonides did have a number of Jewish philosophical precedents for his interpretations. See above, n. 35.

52. This point is noted by Joseph Kafiḥ in his edition of *Sefer Mishneh Torah: Sefer ha-Madda'* (Jerusalem: Makhon Mishnat ha-Rambam, 1984), 96 n. 36. Maimonides was not the first to use this phrase in a manner diverging from talmudic usage. He was preceded by R. Hai Gaon (*Otzar ha-Geonim,* ed. B. Lewin, vol. 1 [Haifa, 1928], 131), R. Baḥya Ibn Paquda (*Duties of the Heart* 1:10), R. Judah Halevi (*Kuzari* 5:27), and R. Abraham Ibn Ezra (*Commentary to Genesis* 1:26). Maimonides' usage is most similar to that of R. Baḥya—who like R. Hai Gaon also uses this dictum in reference to corporeal descriptions of God—and may in fact have been influenced by it.

53. See Strauss, "Notes on Maimonides' Book of Knowledge," 269–71. See also W. Z. Harvey, "The Incorporeality of God in Maimonides, Rabad and Spinoza" (in Hebrew), in *Studies in Jewish Thought*, ed. Sara Heller-Wilensky and Moshe Idel (Jerusalem: Magnes Press, 1989), 63–69. No allusion is made to the proofs of the Kalam, based on the notion of a created world, which are utilized by Maimonides in *Guide* 1:73–76. While the proof in the *Guide* for the existence and incorporeality of God is ostensibly based on the conjunction of Aristotelian and Kalamic proofs, Maimonides shows a clear partiality to the Aristotelian ones.

54. Maimonides develops this notion in much fuller detail in the *Guide* 1:57–60.

55. Maimonides already alludes to this notion in the introduction to his *Commentary on Avot* (*Eight Chapters* 8). A similar explanation is given there of the notion of God's *back.* In the *Guide*, on the other hand, God's *back* is interpreted as referring to attributes of action (1:54). See chapter 1, section II.

56. Cf. *Guide* 3:21. See Alfarabi, *Al-Siyāsah al-Madaniyyah* (Hyderabad, 1346 A.H.), 5; Avicenna, *Najāt* (Hyderabad, 1912), 403f.

57. See *Guide* 2:11, 2:22. For an attempt to resolve the apparent contradiction between Maimonides' acceptance of both the doctrine of creation and of emanation, see Arthur Hyman, "Maimonides on Creation and Emanation," in *Studies in Medieval Philosophy*, ed. John F. Wippel (Washington, D. C.: Catholic University of America Press, 1987), 45–61.

58. Maimonides could hardly allow himself to expand upon this point which drew the ire of some of his critics for suggesting that it was unnecessary to study the Talmud. Maimonides dismisses this charge in a letter to R. Pinhas ha-Dayyan. See *Letters and Essays of Moses Maimonides,* ed. Shailat, 539. Nevertheless, he viewed the legal discussions of the Talmud to be subservient to the goal of determining what is the law, as his remarks in the introduction to the *Mishneh Torah* clarify. Thus in a crucial sense, his code serves to replace the primary function of the Talmud. Maimonides certainly had a very negative opinion of those scholars who devoted themselves entirely to legal discussions without rationally exploring the theological foundations of Judaism. See *Guide* 3:51; *Treatise on Resurrection,* in *Letters and Essays of Moses Maimonides,* ed. Shailat, 339–43. In systematically presenting both the laws and the foundations of Judaism, as well as the legal principles in deciding questions of law, Maimonides better accomplishes the purpose he ascribes to the Talmud. Moreover, by including the study of *pardes*—that is, physics and metaphysics—in the command to study Talmud (*Laws of the Study of Torah* 1:12), Maimonides essentially frees the intellectual elite from the necessity of devoting much of their energy to the study of the actual text of the Talmud. Ironically, they fulfill the requirement of Talmud study in Maimonides' view by studying the texts of Aristotle. For a discussion of the explicit reasons Maimonides offers for the writing of the *Mishneh Torah,* see Twersky, *Introduction to the Code of Maimonides,* 61–81.

59. For a study of this issue, see in particular Jacob Levinger, *Maimonides' Techniques of Codification* (in Hebrew) (Jerusalem: Magnes Press, 1965), 182–89; idem, *Maimonides as Philosopher and Codifier* (in Hebrew) (Jerusalem: Bialik Institute, 1989), 100–111. The extent of Maimonides' innovation in his rulings still requires much further study.

60. Maimonides was not the first to write a legal work outlining the 613 commandments. For a summary of this subject, see Salo Baron, *A Social and Religious History of the Jews*, vol. 6 (New York: Columbia University Press, 1958), 90–96. It has been suggested that the critical difference in the formulation of these commandments is that the Book of the Commandments requires belief *('emunah)* in God's

existence and unity, while the *Mishneh Torah* makes the more exacting demand "to know" *(leida')* God's existence and unity. Both Rawidowicz and Nuriel have argued that the commandment to "know" that opens the *Laws of the Principles of the Torah* does not necessarily imply detailed scientific knowledge. Rather it refers to the acceptance of correct opinions, rendering the Arabic *'itiqād*. See above, n. 30. This term is the one used by Maimonides in the *Book of the Commandments* and which was translated by Moses Ibn Tibbon as *'emunah*.

61. I will deal in more detail with this point chap. 7, section II.

62. See above, n. 54.

63. Joseph Kafiḥ, *Mishnah 'im Perush ha-Rambam: Seder Nezikin* (in Arabic and Hebrew) (Jerusalem: Mossad HaRav Kook, 1975), 212. The translation is my own. Cf. *Guide* 1:71.

64. For a further discussion of this point see below.

65. Maimonides speaks of the existents that God created in 2:3 (see also 2:2). The emphasis, however, is on knowledge of the existents themselves and not the fact of their being created.

66. Maimonides labels belief in eternity a "presumptuous assertion with regard to the Deity" (2:23.321), but this phrase is open to a variety of interpretations.

67. See chap. 4, n. 8.

68. For a further discussion of this point, see chap. 1, section VII.

69. On this point I agree with David Hartman's perceptive analysis in his (and Abraham Halkin's), *Crisis and Leadership: Epistles of Maimonides* (Philadelphia: Jewish Publication Society, 1985), 246f. The English translation of the treatise can be found on pages 211–33. The major point on which I disagree with Hartman is on the question whether Maimonides believed in the resurrection of the dead as literally understood. Hartman answers in the affirmative. He maintains that Maimonides sought to limit the significance of this belief in the minds of the Jews, not to deny its validity. On my reading of this treatise in light of the gamut of Maimonides' writings, I would argue that he regarded resurrection as a politically necessary belief but not a literally true one. There are many hints in the *Treatise on Resurrection* that it contains an esoteric level pointing to this conclusion. The only "resurrection" that takes place is the immortality of the perfect intellect. A full discussion of this issue is outside the scope of this book.

70. Hartman and Halkin, *Crisis and Leadership,* 215.

Chapter 7. The Love and Fear of God

1. Much of my analysis in this chapter is based on Prof. Gerald Blidstein's *Prayer in Maimonidean Halakha* (in Hebrew) (Jerusalem: Bialik Institute, 1994), and on ideas that he conveyed to me orally. I am also indebted to Prof. Ezra Fleischer's critical comments on the earlier Hebrew version of this chapter. All translations

from the *Guide of the Perplexed* are taken from Shlomo Pines's translation. All other translations in this chapter are my own unless otherwise indicated.

2. See *Commentary on the Mishnah: Ḥagigah* 2:1; *Guide* 1:Introduction. For a further discussion of this point see chap. 6, section IV.

3. See *Book of the Commandments*, principle no. 9. Maimonides divides the commandments into four categories: opinions, actions, character traits, and speech. Love of God is included in the commandments that consist of true opinions while love of one's fellow is listed among the commandments that involve character traits. The problem whether there exists a category of commandments whose fulfillment is solely by means of intellection is raised by Maimonides in *Eight Chapters* 2. He answers in the affirmative. This sets the stage for opening both the *Book of the Commandments* and the *Mishneh Torah* with commandments that belong to this category. I have discussed this issue in chap. 2, section VI.

4. This is analogous to the problem discussed in the previous chapter on whether Maimonides' depiction of God was the same in all of his works.

5. The Arabic edition utilized is that of Joseph Kafiḥ (Jerusalem: Mossad HaRav Kook, 1971).

6. See Leo Strauss, "Notes on Maimonides' Book of Knowledge," in *Studies in Mysticism and Religion Presented to Gershom Scholem*, ed. E. Urbach (Jerusalem: Magnes Press, 1967), 269–83; W. Z. Harvey, "Political Philosophy and Halakhah in Maimonides" (in Hebrew), *Iyyun* 29 (1980): 198–212.

7. See chap. 6, section VI.

8. In viewing *pardes* as representing certain areas of knowledge rather than a special place, Maimonides strongly influenced subsequent interpretations. Most of Maimonides' predecessors understood this talmudic image in light of the tradition contained in *heikhalot* literature—namely, that the Talmud refers to a heavenly ascent. See, for example Rashi's commentary to *Ḥagigah* 14b; and the responsa of R. Hai Gaon in B. M. Lewin, *Otzar ha-Geonim: Chagigah,* vol. 4 (Jerusalem: Hebrew University Press, 1931), 13–15. For a discussion of this talmudic passage, see David Halperin, *The Merkabah in Rabbinic Literature* (New Haven: American Oriental Society, 1980), 86–97.

9. See in particular Maimonides' comments in the introduction to the third part of the *Guide*.

10. The translation is my own. An English translation of the *Sifre on Deuteronomy* was prepared by Reuven Hammer (New Haven: Yale University Press, 1984).

11. Cf. *Sifre Va-Etḥanan*, 7.

12. See *Laws of Idolatry* 1:3; *Guide* 2:37; 2:39; 3:51. Maimonides does not use the term "love" in reference to the social activity of the prophets, though he draws a connection between their activity and the level of their apprehension. For a further discussion of the prophetic ideal, see chap. 4, sections IV–V. In *Laws of Repentance* 10:2 Maimonides indicates that Abraham was called the "beloved" of God since he worshipped God out of love. See below, section IV.

13. See *Commentary on Avot* 2:6; 2:10; 3:11; 4:14; 5:6. I have utilized the Arabic original and Hebrew translation of this composition, as well as of *Eight Chapters* and *Introduction to Pereq Ḥeleq* (*Sanhedrin*, chap. 10), found in *Mishnah 'im Perush HaRambam: Seder Neẓikin*, ed. and trans. Joseph Kafiḥ (Jerusalem: Mossad HaRav Kook, 1965). Maimonides mentions fear of punishment in the *Introduction to Pereq Ḥeleq,* 132. It appears that this form of fear also underlies his comments on *Avot* 1:3. There he writes: "One who fears will not transgress any prohibition for fear plays an important role [for the observance] of the negative commandments, and even more so, the revelatory commandments [i.e., those commandments that are known solely on the basis of revelation, and not also by way of the rational faculty]." In reference to *Mishnah* 3:20 ("If there is no Torah there is no civilization [lit. 'way of the land'], and if there is no civilization there is no Torah; if there is no wisdom there is no fear, and if there is no fear there is no wisdom"), Maimonides simply states: "In reference to both pairs—each member in the pair is instrumental for the existence of the other and perfects it."

14. *Introduction to Pereq Ḥeleq* 132; *Eight Chapters* 5; *Commentary on Avot* 5:15. In these sources Maimonides deals also with the physical activities that promote these ends. This point is not found in Maimonides' description of the commandment to love God in the *Laws of the Principles of the Torah*, but it emerges clearly from subsequent discussions as I will show below.

15. See chap. 6, section VI.

16. See Alexander Altmann, *Studies in Religious Philosophy and Mysticism* (Ithaca: Cornell University Press, 1969), 90–92. For a study of the Arabic term designating passionate love, *'ishq,* as used by Maimonides and his predecessors, see Steven Harvey, "The Meaning of the Terms Designating Love in Judaeo-Arabic Thought and Some Remarks on the Judaeo-Arabic Interpretation of Maimonides," in *Judaeo-Arabic Studies,* ed. N. Golb (Amsterdam: Harwood Academic Publishers, 1997), 175–96.

17. See my "Judah Halevi's Influence on Maimonides: A Preliminary Appraisal," *Maimonidean Studies* 2 (1991): 98–99, 101–2.

18. *Saadia Gaon: The Book of Beliefs and Opinions*, trans. Samuel Rosenblatt (New Haven: Yale University Press, 1948), 2:13.132–34. For the Arabic terms, I utilized the edition of Joseph Kafiḥ (Jerusalem: Sura Institute, 1970), 112–14.

19. R. Saadiah, for example, regards all existents other than God as being corporeal. This includes the Created Glory, the angels, and the souls of human beings. Their matter is far more pure and refined than that of the body. See *Book of Beliefs and Opinions* 2:5; 2:10; 6:2. This stands in sharp contrast to the Aristotelian view of Separate Intellects, who serve as the movers of the spheres. On the other hand, R. Saadiah does not accept the Kalamic view of atoms. He appears to posit the existence of fixed laws in the world, or "nature," though he continues to think of God's governance of the world as a personal one. See 1:1.

20. See *Siddur R. Saadja Gaon*, ed. I. Davidson, S. Assaf, and B. I. Joel (Jerusalem: Mekitzei Nirdamim, 1963).

21. Ibid., 157.
22. Ibid., 192.
23. Ibid., 157.
24. The fear of God thus would refer to an emotional state when considered from a legal standpoint.
25. Researchers have long assumed that Maimonides was acquainted with *Duties of the Heart* without attempting to prove this point. Maimonides was certainly aware of the existence of this work, since the work is mentioned in one of the letters he received. However, he never cites it explicitly. Blidstein in his *Prayer in Maimonidean Halakha* points to a number of parallels between R. Baḥya and Maimonides in issues touching upon prayer. Support for the view that Maimonides was influenced by R. Baḥya's treatise can be garnered from parallels touching upon other topics as well. My citations are from the translation of Menahem Mansoor, *The Book of Direction to the Duties of the Heart* (London: Routledge and Kegan Paul, 1973).

(1) R. Baḥya's use of the dictum of the Sages—"The Torah speaks as in the language of humankind—which he brings in 1:10 is closely related to Maimonides' use in several passages of his writings (for example, *Laws of the Principles of the Torah* 1:12). R. Baḥya cites this dictum to prove that one should not interpret literally the corporeal descriptions of God in Scripture. The dictum as it appears in the Talmud does not at all touch upon this issue but the problem of the repetition of terms in the Torah. The question the Talmud addresses is whether the repetition of a word is significant, particularly from a legal standpoint. While other thinkers prior to Maimonides also cited this dictum in reference to descriptions of God, there is an exceptionally close affinity between R. Baḥya's discussion and those of Maimonides.

(2) In 2:4 R. Baḥya presents the view that all human *nomoi* are solely directed to matters of this world. In the following chapter he points to God's beneficence to humankind by the fact that "people, despite the great differences in their natures, reach unanimity, agreeing to appoint one of their number to be their leader, undertaking to obey him. . . . For his part, he guards, protects, judges, and directs them in the best interest of all" (p. 172). These positions bear a striking similarity to those presented by Maimonides in *Guide* 2:39–40.

(3) In 2:5 R. Baḥya goes on to maintain "Remark how the things essential for the well-being of the body and its sustenance in this condition until it reaches the term of its life. You will find that their scarcity or abundance depends on the need for them" (p. 173). R. Baḥya points to air, water, and food as that which is most abundant, and to precious stones, gold, silver, and other minerals as that which is scarce. This has its exact parallel in *Guide* 3:12. It should be added that *Duties* 2:5 also brings examples of God's graciousness in nature that appear in Maimonides' description of divine graciousness in 3:32.

(4) The model of asceticism presented by R. Baḥya in 9:3—"they are ascetics

in heart and conscience, but they share with the other inhabitants of the world in its cultivation, construction and reproduction" (p. 409)—is reminiscent of Maimonides' description of perfection in *Guide* 3:51.

26. I have used the Arabic edition of Joseph Kafiḥ (Jerusalem: Akiva-Joseph, 1973), p. 410.

27. One should interpret the term *ittiṣāl* in its technical sense as signifying ontological union. R. Baḥya immediately proceeds to explain "The soul is a simple spiritual substance which inclines by its nature to the spiritual beings that are like itself, and rejects by its nature the coarse bodies which are unlike it" (p. 427). In R. Baḥya's description of the World to Come in 3:3 he uses the same terminology. The most important source for this view is Plotinus, *Enneads* 4.8,1. For a discussion of R. Baḥya's sources, see Mansoor's introduction to his translation, pp. 18–39. Mansoor appears to have overlooked the passage I have cited when he contends: "Baḥya's ascetic ethics approaches Neoplatonism, but there is a difference: Baḥya does not think in terms of freeing the soul for a mystical union with God" (p. 31). Alghazali may have been R. Baḥya's immediate source for the notion of union with the divine light, just as he appears to have been R. Baḥya's source for other central notions in the treatise.

28. 10:Introduction. Cf. 1:Introduction.

29. R. Baḥya points to this type of fear also in the introduction to his treatise and in 8:6. Fear of punishment is mentioned by him in 3:3; 7:5; 7:6.

30. *Duties of the Heart* 1:Introduction. R. Baḥya indicates that the *Shema* contains: duties of the heart, duties of the limbs that involve knowledge and action, duties that involve action alone. In the first category R. Baḥya enumerates the following duties: knowledge of the existence of God, that only God is our Lord, that God is One, to love God and to worship God with a pure heart. This is similar to Maimonides' order in the *Book of the Commandments*. The affinity between R. Baḥya and Maimonides emerges also from R. Baḥya's description of the highest level of worship of God (3:4). There he draws a connection between knowledge, love, the worship of God, and the total submission of one's soul.

31. See Ben Zion Halper, *A Volume of Book of Precepts by Ḥefeṣ b. Yaṣliaḥ* (Philadelphia: Jewish Publication Society, 1911). This treatise is cited by R. Baḥya as an example of a work devoted to a summary of the commandments.

32. See Halper, *Book of Precepts of Ḥefeṣ b. Yaṣliaḥ,* 59–89.

33. Ibid., 31.

34. This fragment was published by Moshe Zucker, together with a Hebrew translation from the Arabic, in "New Fragments from *The Book of Precepts* by R. *Ḥefeṣ b. Yaṣliaḥ,*" *PAAJR* 29 (1960–61): 22f., 31f. The fragment under discussion is almost certainly a continuation of the commandments to know that God exists and that God is one. The only reason there may be some doubt in this matter is that R. Ḥefeṣ numbers the commandments according to category. Every time he begins a

new category, he starts the count anew. The hypothesis that the love and fear of God are a continuation of the category that opens with knowledge and unity of God is further supported by the beginning of the fragment published by Zucker, as we shall see momentarily.

35. In his liturgical enumeration of the commandments, R. Saadiah writes: "Unify Him morning and night." This is a reference to the recitation of the *Shema*. See *Siddur R. Saadja,* 157.

36. Zucker, "New Fragments," 23, 33.

37. Ibid., 23, 31. It should be noted that Zucker skipped a line of the Arabic text in his Hebrew translation.

38. *Sanhedrin* 74a. Maimonides conflates this source with *Berakhot* 61b.

39. This point is noted and explained by Raymond Weiss, *Maimonides' Ethics* (Chicago: University of Chicago Press, 1991), 89–91.

40. See *Guide* 3:49. The reason Maimonides advances for including circumcision in this category is that it diminishes the desire for intercourse. In addition, Maimonides sees circumcision serving as a sign that unites all those who believe in the unity of God. He may well have had in mind the Moslems too in this context. In one of his responsa he acknowledges that they unify God in a correct manner. In the *Mishneh Torah* he rules that from a Jewish legal perspective they are obligated to perform circumcision (*Laws of Kings and their Wars* 10:8). For a study of this issue, see David Novak, "The Treatment of Islam and Muslims in the Legal Writing of Maimonides," in *Studies in Islamic and Judaic Traditions*, ed. W. Brinner and S. Ricks (Atlanta: Scholars Press, 1986): 233–50; Josef Stern, "Maimonides on the Covenant of Circumcision and the Unity of God," in *The Midrashic Imagination: Jewish Exegesis, Thought, and History*, ed. M. Fishbane (Albany: State University of New York Press, 1993), 131–54; Hannah Kasher, "Maimonides' View of Circumcision as a Factor Uniting the Jewish and Muslim Communities," in *Studies in Muslim-Jewish Relations*, ed. R. Nettler (Chur, Switzerland: Harwood Academic Publishers, 1995), 103–8. This point gives added meaning to Maimonides' observation regarding circumcision: "It is also well known what degree of mutual love and mutual help exists between people who all bear the same sign, which forms for them a sort of covenant and alliance. Circumcision is a covenant made by Abraham our Father with a view to the belief in the unity of God. Thus everyone who is circumcised joins Abraham's covenant" (*Guide* 3:49.610). The reason why Maimonides in the *Mishneh Torah* includes circumcision among the commandments belonging to the *Book of Love* may be explained on the basis of *Menaḥot* 43b:

> Our Rabbis taught: Beloved are Israel for the Holy One, Blessed be He, surrounded them with precepts—tefillin on their heads, ṣiṣit on their garments, and mezuzot on their door-posts; concerning these David said: *Seven times a day do I praise Thee because of Thy righteous ordinances* (Psalms 119: 164). And as David entered the bath and saw himself standing naked he exclaimed: "Woe is me that I stand naked without any pre-

cepts about me!" But when he reminded himself of the circumcision in his flesh his mind was set at ease.

See *Menaḥot*, vol. 5 of *The Babylonian Talmud: Seder Kodashim,* trans. Eli Cashdan (London: Soncino Press, 1948). Maimonides refers to the continuation of this talmudic passage in *Laws of Mezuzah* 6:13.

41. Cf. 3:44. In the *Guide* Maimonides lists these commandments even further away from the commandment to love God. For a study of Maimonides' principles of classification in the *Mishneh Torah* and the *Guide,* see Lawrence Berman, "The Structure of the Commandments of the Torah in the Thought of Maimonides," in *Studies in Jewish Religious and Intellectual History*, ed. S. Stein and R. Loewe (Tuscaloosa: University of Alabama Press, 1979), 51–66.

42. In our passage the "fundamental principle" refers to the existence of the deity upon which all other existents are dependent. Maimonides elaborates upon this point in *Laws of the Principles of the Torah* 1:1–3. In the *Laws of the Principles of the Torah* 1:6, on the other hand, the "fundamental principle" refers to *knowledge* of the existence of God, upon which everything (all knowledge and commandments) depends.

43. Maimonides reiterates this view in *Laws of Repentance* 8:3. For a discussion of the acquired intellect and Maimonides' view of immortality, see chap. 4, sections IV–V.

44. Cf. *Sifre, va-Etḥanan* 7.

45. Many Maimonidean scholars—both medieval and modern—advanced this interpretation of Maimonides' approach to providence. For a discussion of this issue, see my "*The Suffering of the Righteous* in Medieval Jewish Philosophy" (in Hebrew), *Daat* 19 (1987): 17–29.

46. Cf. *Commentary on Mishnah: Berakhot* 2:8.

47. See *Berakhot* 16b.

48. For a discussion of the prophetic ideal, see chap. 4, sections III–V.

49. See Blidstein, *Prayer in Maimonidean Halakha,* 23–33.

50. *Berakhot* 30b; *Eruvin* 65b. For a discussion of this issue see Blidstein, *Prayer in Maimonidean Halakha,* 77–122.

51. See *Berakhot* 28b. On this issue too one can discern the affinity between Maimonides' view and the one presented by R. Baḥya in *Duties of the Heart:* "When a man undertakes to perform one of the duties of the heart, the different kinds of which we mentioned at the beginning of this book, then he must free his heart of all thoughts pertaining to this world and its affairs; he must devote his intention and conscience purely to God, driving away from his heart all the cares of this world, using it solely to care for the performing of that act for God's sake" (8:3.364).

52. "Withdrawn" *(mitboded)* may refer to physical isolation. More likely it indicates mental detachment. For a study of this notion, see Moshe Idel, "*Hitbodedut* as Concentration in Jewish Philosophy" (in Hebrew), *Jerusalem Studies in Jewish Thought* 7 (1988): 39–60.

53. See Eliezer Goldman, "The Special Worship of those Apprehending the True Realities" (in Hebrew), *Bar-Ilan* 6 (1968): 287–313. For a philosophic analysis of Maimonides' approach to prayer, see Ehud Benor, *Worship of the Heart* (Albany: State University of New York Press, 1995).

54. As indicated above, Maimonides does not mention in the *Mishneh Torah* that it is sufficient to have intent only while reciting one of the benedictions in order to fulfill the obligation. There he leaves the impression that only if one recites all of the benedictions with the proper intent does one fulfill the obligation. The desired prayer is presented by Maimonides as though it were the minimal obligation. In the *Guide*, Maimonides refers to the minimal requirement of having intent only while reciting one of the benedictions (specifically the first one in his view). His purpose in this context is to depict the *process* by which the individual is gradually able to extend the activities that he performs with "intention."

55. Cf. 3:52.

56. Maimonides indicates that there is no possibility for substituting this type of worship for the one that involves prayer, fasting, and calling upon God in times of misfortune. People would not accept a law that goes against the forms of worship to which they are accustomed. This is analogous, in Maimonides' view, to giving a law to the Israelites leaving Egypt that forbids sacrifice. He distinguishes between the "first intention" of the Law and its "second intention." The second intention refers to those activities that are commanded not because they contribute directly to perfection, but because the people were accustomed to them. Not to include them would pose a grave danger for the popular acceptance of the Law. Sacrifices belong to this category. The first intention refers to the apprehension of God and rejection of idolatry. Maimonides lists as the forms of worship that, "come closer to the first intention and are necessary for its achievement" (p. 529): prayer, *ṣiṣit*, *mezuzah,* and *tefillin*. These are precisely the commandments that are included in the *Book of Love*. As opposed to sacrifices they are obligatory everywhere and upon everyone.

57. For Maimonides' legal approach to the subject of leadership, see Gerald Blidstein, *Political Concepts in Maimonidean Halakha* (in Hebrew) (Ramat Gan, Israel: Bar-Ilan University Press, 1983).

58. *The Political Regime*, ed. Fauzi Najjar (Beirut: Imprimerie Catholique, 1964), 79. Najjar translated this passage in *Medieval Political Philosophy*, ed. Ralph Lerner and Muhsin Mahdi (Ithaca: Cornell University Press, 1972), 36. For a further discussion of Alfarabi's doctrine see chap. 4, sections IV–V.

59. See chap. 1, section I; chap 2, sections V–VII.

60. *Tit'arev*, and not *davek*, is the Hebrew term Maimonides employs for the Arabic term *ittiṣāl* (conjunction). See chap. 4, section IV.

61. *Da'at* in this context is used to translate the Arabic *'aql*. In his translation of the *Guide*, Samuel Ibn Tibbon preferred to translate this term by the Hebrew word *sekhel*. Maimonides employs the Hebrew verb from the same root *(lehaskil)* in *Laws of Repentance* 10:6.

62. For a discussion of this issue, see chap. 1, section III.

63. In his subsequent discussion of the messiah the *Laws of Kings and their Wars* 11:4, Maimonides does not explicitly mention wisdom as one of his characteristics. Yet in the continuation of his description, he ascribes to the messiah the possession of the holy spirit (12:3). The "holy spirit" in Maimonides' legal writings refers to prophecy. See, for example, *Laws of the Principles of the Torah* 7:1. Only in the *Guide* 2:45 does Maimonides introduce a distinction between these two phenomena. The supreme wisdom and prophetic status of the messiah is mentioned by Maimonides in other writings as well. See *Epistle to the Jews of Yemen,* in D. Hartman and A. Halkin, *Crisis and Leadership: Epistles of Maimonides* (Philadelphia: Jewish Publication Society, 1985), p. 123. See also chap. 1, section IV.

64. See *Sanhedrin* 36b.

65. This appears to be another allusion to the fact that they know the esoteric sciences contained in Scripture. *Laḥash* literally means "whisper" and refers to secrets (since they are transmitted by whispering). For the use of this term in reference to the secrets of the Torah, see *Ḥagigah* 14a.

66. In his letter to the Jews of Montpelier regarding astrology, Maimonides testifies that he himself studied many books on astrology and all the works of idolatry that he was able to attain in Arabic. His purpose was to understand the reasons for the commandments. The results of his investigations are to be found in *Guide* 3:29; 3:37.

67. "Love of the truth" may be interpreted as love of God. See *Laws of the Principles of the Torah* 1:4.

68. In 10:2 Maimonides indicates in regard to the stage of worshipping God out of love that "not every sage merits it." In *Guide* 3:51, he distinguishes between the sages who attained final perfection and those who were still on the path.

69. *The Code of Maimonides: The Book of Holiness*, trans. Louis Rabinowitz and Philip Grossman (New Haven: Yale University Press, 1965), 137–8.

70. Cf. *Eight Chapter* 5. In *Laws of Character Traits* Maimonides sees in this way of life "the worship of God." In *Eight Chapters* he links it also with the "love of God." The relation between ethical and intellectual perfection is stressed also in *Guide* 1:34. The "simple" law that Maimonides presents at the end of *Laws of Lulav* attains a much deeper level of meaning in light of what we have seen: "Rejoicing in the fulfillment of a commandment and in love for God who had prescribed the commandment is a supreme act of divine worship. One who refrains from participation in such rejoicing deserves to be punished. . . . One who humbles and makes light of himself on such occasions, achieves greatness and honor, and serves the Lord out of sheer love. . . . True greatness and honor are achieved only by rejoicing before the Lord." See *The Code of Maimonides: The Book of Seasons,* trans. Solomon Gandz and Hyman Klein (New Haven: Yale University Press, 1961), 408.

71. Why Maimonides did not explicitly include this commandment in the seven noahite laws is a complex issue. Among the noahite laws is the prohibition to worship

other Gods. Maimonides accepts the fundamental relation between idolatry and belief in the existence of God, but does not see the two commandments as one. One may believe in the existence of God while committing idolatry. One may not believe in God and not commit idolatry. The prohibition against idolatry, according to Maimonides' approach, does not logically entail belief in the existence of the God. Maimonides finds a way of indirectly including belief in the existence of God among the noahite Laws by positing as one of the conditions for their fulfillment belief in God's revelation. I have briefly dealt with the issue in chap. 2, section II.

72. See chap. 6.

73. See above, section II.

74. See *Laws of the Study of the Torah* 6:2; *Laws of Sale* 14:18.

75. See *Laws of the Study of Torah* 5:8; *Laws of Tefillin* 4:25. Only in the above-cited list of qualifications possessed by the members of a three-member court, may fear be interpreted as alluding to intellectual awe. This, however, would not be the "simple sense" of the text.

76. See 3:24. In 3:52 Maimonides also draws a connection between fear and perfection. The latter passage will be discussed below.

77. The implications of this passage for understanding Maimonides' approach to awe has been discussed by W. Z. Harvey, "Maimonides on Human Perfection, Awe, and Politics," in *The Thought of Moses Maimonides*, ed. I. Robinson, L. Kaplan, and J. Bauer (Lewiston, N.Y.: Edwin Mellen Press, 1990), 6 f.

78. Cf. 3:47. The commandment to fear the sanctuary is found in *Laws of the Chosen Abode,* chap. 7. While Maimonides links the fear of the sanctuary and the fear of God, the laws he enumerates deal with the physical activities that this commandment involves.

79. See *Eight Chapters* 1–2.

80. Jacob Levinger noted that Maimonides began to develop his esoteric writing techniques in his legal compositions. See "Abstinence from Alcohol in Maimonides' *Guide of the Perplexed*" (in Hebrew), *Bar-Ilan* 4–5 (1967): 299–305.

81. I am indebted to Dr. Alan Flashman for this perceptive interpretation.

82. Cf. Maimonides' description of fear of God in *Guide* 1:5, cited above. Maimonides does not introduce the same qualification in his description of the World to Come in the *Introduction to Pereq Ḥeleq*. His discussion suggests the possibility of a type of union with God. There Maimonides wishes to emphasize the significance of the pursuit of the apprehension of God, the great intellectual pleasure that results thereby, and the fact that this state results in the immortality of the intellect. He may have not striven for exactness in this description, given the purpose of his discussion in that work.

SELECT BIBLIOGRAPHY

Editions of Maimonides' Works Cited

Book of the Commandments (Arabic text and Hebrew translation). Edited by Joseph Kafiḥ. Jerusalem: Mossad HaRav Kook, 1971.

Commentary on the Mishnah (Arabic text and Hebrew translation). Edited by Joseph Kafiḥ. Jerusalem: Mossad HaRav Kook, 1963–68.

Ethical Writings of Maimonides. Edited by R. L. Weiss and C. E. Butterworth. New York: New York University Press, 1975.

The Guide of the Perplexed (Arabic text and Hebrew translation). Edited and translated by Joseph Kafiḥ. Jerusalem: Mossad HaRav Kook, 1972. English translation by Shlomo Pines (Chicago: Chicago University Press, 1963).

Letters and Essays of Moses Maimonides (Arabic text and Hebrew translation). Edited and translated by Isaac Shailat. Maaleh Adumim, Israel: Maaliyot Press, 1988. English translations of *Epistle on Martyrdom, Epistle to Yemen,* and *Treatise on Resurrection,* in David Hartman and Abraham Halkin, *Crisis and Leadership: Epistles of Maimonides* (Philadelphia: Jewish Publication Society, 1985).

Medical Aphorisms (Medieval Hebrew translation). Edited by Suessmann Muntner. Jerusalem: Mossad HaRav Kook, 1982.

Mishneh Torah. Warsaw-Vilna edition with commentaries. *The Code of Maimonides: The Book of Seasons*, translated by Solomon Gandz and Hyman Klein (New Haven: Yale University Press, 1961). *The Book of Holiness*, translated by Louis Rabinowitz and Philip Grossman (New Haven: Yale University Press, 1965).

Sefer Ha-Madda' (Book of knowledge). Edited by Jacob Cohen, Moshe Hayim Katzenelenbogen, and Saul Lieberman. Jerusalem: Mossad HaRav Kook, 1964. Joseph Kafiḥ edition with commentary (Jerusalem: Makhon Mishnat ha-Rambam, 1984). N. L Rabinovitch edition with commentary (Maaleh Adumim, Israel: Maaliyot Press, 1990).

Teshuvot ha-Rambam (R. Moses b. Maimon Responsa) (in Arabic and Hebrew). Edited by Joshu Blau. Jerusalem: Mekize Nirdamim, 1960.

Treatise on Logic (Arabic text). Edited by Israel Efros. "Maimonides' Treatise on Logic." *PAAJR* 34 (1966): 1–42. English translation by Efros in *PAAJR* 8 (1938): 34-65.

Other Works Cited

Primary Sources

Al-Farabi. *Aphorisms of the Statesman (Fuṣūl al-Madanī).* Edited and translated by D. M. Dunlop. Cambridge: Cambridge University Press, 1961.

———. *Attainment of Happiness (Taḥṣil al-Sa'āda).* Hyderabad edition (1345 A.H.), translated by Muhsin Mahdi. In *Alfarabi's Philosophy of Plato and Aristotle.* New York: Free Press of Glencoe, 1962.

———. *Enumeration of the Sciences (Ihṣā' al-'Ulūm).* Edited by A. Gonzalez Palencia as *Catalogo de las Ciecias* (Madrid: Consego Superior de Investigaciones Cientificas, 1953). Translated in part by Fauzi M. Najjar in *Medieval Political Philosophy*, ed. R. Lerner and M. Mahdi (Ithaca: Cornell University Press, 1972), 22–30.

———. *Letter on the Intellect (Risālāt fi'l 'Aql).* Edited by Maurice Bouyges. Beirut: Imprimerie Catholique, 1938. Translated by Arthur Hyman in *Philosophy in the Middle Ages*, ed. Arthur Hyman and James Walsh (New York: Harper and Row, 1967), 215–21.

———. *The Political Regime (Al-Siyāsah al-Madaniyyah).* Edited by Fauzi Najjar. Beirut: Imprimerie Catholique, 1964. Translated in part by Fauzi Najjar in *Medieval Political Philosophy*, ed. R. Lerner and M. Mahdi (Ithaca: Cornell University Press, 1972), 31–57

———. *Principles of the Opinions of the People of the Virtuous City (Mabadi' Ārā' Ahl al-Madīna al-Faḍila).* Edited and translated by Richard Walzer as *Al-Farabi on the Perfect State* (Oxford: Clarendon Press, 1985).

Averroes. *Decisive Treatise (Kitāb Faṣl Al-Maqāl).* Translated by George Hourani under the title *Averroes on the Harmony of Religion and Philosophy* (London: Luzac, 1961).

———. *The Incoherence of the Incoherence (Tahāfut al-Tahāfut).* Translated by S. Van Den Bergh. London: Luzac, 1954.

Avicenna. *On the Division of the Rational Sciences (Fī aqsām al-'ulum al-'aqliyyah).* In *Tis' Rasā'il.* Cairo, 1908. Translated in part by Muhsin Mahdi in *Medieval Political Philosophy*, ed. R. Lerner and M. Mahdi (Ithaca: Cornell University Press, 1972), 95–97.

———. *On the Soul (Kitāb al-nafs).* In *Avicenna's "De Anima,"* edited by Fauzi. Rahman. London: Oxford University Press, 1959.

———. *Salvation (Najāt).* Book 2, chap. 6, has been translated by Fauzi Rahman under the title *Avicenna's Psychology* (London: Oxford University Press, 1952).

———. *Theorems and Axioms (Al-Ishārāt w-al-Tanbīhāt).* Edited by J. Forget. Leiden: Brill, 1892.

Avraham ben HaRambam. *Torah Commentary: Genesis and Exodus* (Hebrew translation). Translated by Ephaim Weisenberg. Jerusalem: Keren Hoṣa'at Sifrei Rabbanei Bavel, 1984.

Baḥya Ibn Paquda. *The Book of Direction to the Duties of the Heart* (Arabic text with Hebrew translation). Edited and translated by Joseph Kafiḥ. Jerusalem: Akiva-Joseph, 1973. Translated into English by Menahem Mansoor (London: Routledge and Kegan Paul, 1973).

Gersonides. *Wars of the Lord (Milḥamot ha-Shem)*. Leipzig edition (1866). Translated by Seymour Feldman (Philadelphia: Jewish Publication Society, 1984).

Ḥefeṣ b. Yaṣliaḥ. *Book of Precepts*. Edited by Benzion Halper as *A Volume of the Book of Precepts of Ḥefeṣ b. Yaṣliaḥ* (Philadelphia: Jewish Publication Society, 1915). Moshe Zucker, "New Fragments from *The Book of Precepts by R. Ḥefeṣ b. Yaṣliaḥ*" (in Hebrew), *PAAJR* 29 (1960–61).

Ibn Tufayl. *Hayy ben Yaqdhan*. Edited by Leon Gauthier. Beirut: Imprimerie Catholique, 1936. Translation in part by George Atiyeh in *Medieval Political Philosophy*, ed. R. Lerner and M. Mahdi (Ithaca: Cornell University Press, 1972), 134–62.

Joseph Ibn Zaddik. *Book of the Microcosm (Sefer 'Olam Qatan)*. Edited by S. Horovitz. Breslau, 1903.

Judah Halevi. *Kuzari* (Arabic text). Edited by David Baneth. Jerusalem: Magnes Press, 1977. Medieval Hebrew translation by Judah Ibn Tibbon. Modern Hebrew translation by Yehuda Even Shmuel (Tel Aviv: Dvir, 1972). Translated into English by Hartwig Hirschfeld (New York: Schocken Books, 1964).

Moses Narboni. *Commentary to Guide of the Perplexed* (in Hebrew). Edited by Jacob Goldenthal. Vienna, 1852.

Saadia Gaon. *The Book of Beliefs and Opinions* (Arabic text and Hebrew translation). Edited and translated by Joseph Kafiḥ. Jerusalem: Sura, 1970. Translated into English by Samuel Rosenblatt (New Haven: Yale University, 1948).

———. *Siddur R. Saadja Gaon*. Edited by I. Davidson, S. Assaf, and B. I. Joel. Jerusalem: Mekitzei Nirdamim, 1963.

Samuel ben Hofni. *The Biblical Commentary of Rav Samuel ben Hofni Gaon* (Arabic text and Hebrew translation). Edited and translated by Aaron Greenbaum. Jerusalem: Mossad HaRav Kook, 1978.

Secondary Sources

Altmann, Alexander. "Maimonides' 'Four Perfections'." *IOS* 2 (1972): 15–24.

———. "Saadya's Conception of the Law." *Bulletin of John Rylands Library* 28 (1944): 320–39.

———. *Studies in Religious Philosophy and Mysticism*. Ithaca: Cornell University Press, 1969.

———. *Von der mittelalterlichen zur modernen Aufklärung*. Tübingen: J. C. B. Mohr, 1987.

Altman, Alexander, and S. M. Stern. *Isaac Israeli*. Oxford: Oxford University Press, 1958.

Baron, Salo. *A Social and Religious History of the Jews*. Vol. 6. New York: Columbia University Press, 1958.

Benor, Ehud. "Meaning and Reference in Maimonides' Negative Theology." *HTR* 88 (1995): 339–60.

———. *Worship of the Heart*. Albany: State University of New York Press, 1995.

Berman, Lawrence V. "The Ethical Views of Maimonides within the Context of Islamicate Civilization." In *Perspectives on Maimonides*, edited by Joel Kraemer, 13–32. Oxford: Oxford University Press, 1991.

———. "Maimonides, the Disciple of Alfarabi." *IOS* 4 (1974): 154–78.

———. "Maimonides on the Fall of Man." *AJS Review* 5 (1980): 1–16.

———. "The Political Interpretation of the Maxim: The Purpose of Philosophy is the Imitation of God." *Studia Islamica* 15 (1961): 53–61.

———. "A Reexamination of Maimonides' Statement on Political Science." *Journal of the American Oriental Society* 89 (1969): 106–11.

———. "The Structure of the Commandments of the Torah in the Thought of Maimonides." In *Studies in Jewish Religious and Intellectual History*, edited by S. Stein and R. Loewe, 51–66. Tuscaloosa: University of Alabama Press, 1979.

Berzin, Gabriella. "The Concept of Happiness in the Teachings of Maimonides and Rabbi Chasdai Crescas" (in Hebrew). Master's thesis, Ben-Gurion University, 1998.

Bland, Kalman. "Moses and the Law According to Maimonides." In *Mystics, Philosophers and Politicians*, edited by J. Reinharz and D. Swetschinski, 49–66. Durham, N.C.: Duke University Press, 1982.

Blidstein, Gerald. "The Concept of Joy in Maimonides" (in Hebrew). *Eshel Beer-Sheva* 2 (1980): 145–64.

———. "Maimonidean Structures of Institutional Authority: Sefer Hamizvot Aseh, 172–177." *Dine Yisrael* 17 (1993): 103–26.

———. *Political Concepts in Maimonidean Halakha* (in Hebrew). Ramat Gan, Israel: Bar-Ilan University, 1983.

———. *Prayer in Maimonidean Halakha* (in Hebrew). Jerusalem: Bialik Institute, 1994.

———. "Traditional and Institutional Authority—On Oral Law in Maimonides" (in Hebrew). *Daat* 16 (1986): 11–27.

———. "Where Do We Stand in the Study of Maimonidean Halakhah?" In *Studies in Maimonides*, edited by I. Twersky, 1–30. Cambridge: Harvard University Press, 1990.

Blumberg, Harry Zevi. "Alfarabi, Ibn Bajja and Maimonides on the Governance of the Solitary: Sources and Influences" (in Hebrew). *Sinai* 78 (1976): 135–45.

———. "The Concept of Divine Will in Maimonides' Teachings" (in Hebrew). *Perakim* 4 (1966): 43–55.

———. "Maimonides on the Kalam Doctrine of *Tajwiz*" (in Hebrew). *Tarbiz* 39 (1970): 268–76.

Davidson, Herbert. "Alfarabi and Avicenna on the Active Intellect." *Viator* 3 (1972): 109–51.

———. "Arguments from the Concept of Particularization in Arabic Philosophy." *Philosophy East and West* 18 (1968): 299–314.

———. "Maimonides on Metaphysical Knowledge." *Maimonidean Studies* 3 (1992–93): 49–103.

———. "Maimonides' Secret Position on Creation." In *Studies in Medieval Jewish History and Literature*, edited by Isadore Twersky, 16–40. Cambridge: Harvard University Press, 1979.

———. "Maimonides' *Shemonah Peraqim* and Alfarabi's *Fuṣūl al-Madani*." *PAAJR* 31 (1963): 116–33.

———. "The Middle Way in Maimonides' Ethics." *PAAJR* 54 (1987): 31–72.

Diesendruck, Zevi. "Maimonides' Theory of Teleology and the Divine Attributes" (in Hebrew). *Tarbiz* 1 (1930): 106–36, and 2 (1931): 27–73.

———. "Samuel and Moses Ibn Tibbon on Maimonides' Theory of Providence." *HUCA* 11 (1936): 341–66.

Efros, Israel. "The Approach of Reason to Ethics according to Se'adia and Maimonides" (in Hebrew). *Tarbiz* 28 (1959): 325–29.

Einstein, Albert. *Ideas and Opinions.* New York: Dell, 1954.

Fackenheim, Emile. "The Possibility of the Universe in Al-Farabi, Ibn Sina and Maimonides." *PAAJR* 16 (1947): 303–33.

Fleischer, Ezra. *The Proverbs of Sa'id ben Bābshād* (in Hebrew). Jerusalem: Ben-Zevi Institute, 1990.

Fox, Harry. "Maimonides on Aging and the Aged in Light of the Esoterist/Harmonist Debate." In *The Thought of Moses Maimonides*, edited by I. Robinson, L. Kaplan, and J. Bauer, 49–53. Lewiston, N.Y.: Edwin Mellen Press, 1990.

Fox, Marvin. *Interpreting Maimonides: Studies in Methodology, Metaphysics, and Moral Philosophy.* Chicago: University of Chicago Press, 1990.

Frank, Daniel H. "Anger as a Vice: A Maimonidean Critique of Aristotle's Ethics." *History of Philosophy Quarterly* 7 (1990): 269–81.

———. "Humility as a Virtue: A Maimonidean Critique of Aristotle's Ethics." In *Moses Maimonides and His Time*, edited by Eric Ormsby, 89–99. Washington, D.C.: The Catholic University of America Press, 1989.

Freudenthal, Gad. "Maimonides' Stance on Astrology in Context: Cosmology, Physics, Medicine, and Providence." In *Moses Maimonides: Physician, Scientist and Philosopher*, edited by Fred Rosner and Samuel Kotteck, 77–90. Northvale, N.J.: J. Aronson, 1993.

Funkenstein, Amos. "Maimonides: Political Theory and Realistic Messianism." *Miscellanea Mediaevalia* 9 (1977): 81–103.

Galston, Miriam. "Philosopher-King v. Prophet." *IOS* 8 (1978): 204–18.

———. *Politics and Excellence: The Political Philosophy of Alfarabi.* Princeton: Princeton University Press, 1990.

———. "The Purpose of the Law according to Maimonides." *JQR* 69 (1978–79): 27–51.

Goichon, A. M. *Lexique de la Langue Philosophique d'Ibn Sina.* Paris: Descléé de Brouwer, 1938.

Goldman, Eliezer. "On the Purpose of the World in the *Guide of the Perplexed*" (in Hebrew). In *Studies in Honor of Yeshayahu Leibowitz*, edited by A. Kasher and Y. Levinger, 164–91. Tel Aviv: Papyrus, 1982.

———. "The Special Worship of those Apprehending the True Realities" (in Hebrew). *Bar-Ilan* 6 (1968): 287–313.

Gutas, Dmitri. *Avicenna and the Aristotelian Tradition* (Leiden: E. J. Brill, 1988).

Guttmann, Julius. "Das Problem der Kontingenz in der Philosophie des Maimonides." *MGWJ* 83 (1939): 406–30.

———. *Reason and Knowledge* (in Hebrew). Edited by S. H. Bergman and N. Rotenstreich. Jerusalem: Magnes Press, 1979.

Halperin, David. *The Merkabah in Rabbinic Literature.* New Haven: American Oriental Society, 1980.

Hartman, David. *Maimonides: Torah and Philosophic Quest.* Philadelphia: Jewish Publication Society, 1976.

Hartman, David, and Abraham Halkin. *Crisis and Leadership: Epistles of Maimonides.* Philadelphia: Jewish Publication Society, 1985.

Harvey, Stephen. "The Meaning of Terms Designating Love in Judaeo-Arabic Thought and Some Remarks on the Judaeo-Arabic Interpretation of Maimonides." In *Judaeo-Arabic Studies,* edited by N. Golb, 175–96. Amsterdam: Harwood Academic Publishers, 1997.

Harvey, Warren Zev. "Averroes and Maimonides on the Obligation of Philosophic Contemplation" (in Hebrew). *Tarbiz* 58 (1989): 75–83.

———. "Crescas versus Maimonides on Knowledge and Pleasure." In *A Straight Path*, edited by R. Link-Salinger, 113–23. Washington, D.C.: Catholic University of America Press, 1989.

———. "Ethics and Meta-ethics, Aesthetics and Meta-aesthetics in Maimonides." In *Maimonides and Philosophy*, edited by S. Pines and Y. Yovel, 131–38. Dordrecht: Martinus Nijhoff, 1986).

———. "The First Commandment and the God of History: Halevi and Crescas vs. Ibn Ezra and Maimonides" (in Hebrew). *Tarbiz* 57 (1988): 209–11.

———. "Holiness: A Command to *Imitatio Dei.*" *Tradition* 16 (1976–77): 7–28.

———. "How to Begin to Study the *Guide of the Perplexed*, I, 1" (in Hebrew). *Daat* 21 (1988): 5–20.

———. "The Incorporeality of God in Maimonides, Rabad and Spinoza" (in Hebrew). In *Studies in Jewish Thought*, edited by Sara Heller-Wilensky and Moshe Idel, 63–69. Jerusalem: Magnes Press, 1989.

———. "Maimonides and Spinoza on the Knowledge of Good and Evil" (in Hebrew). *Iyyun* 28 (1979): 167–85.

———. "Maimonides on Genesis 3:22" (in Hebrew). *Daat* 12 (1984): 15–21.

———. "Maimonides on Human Perfection, Awe, and Politics." In *The Thought of Moses Maimonides*, edited by I. Robinson, L. Kaplan, and J. Bauer, 1–15. Lewiston, N.Y.: Edwin Mellen Press, 1990.

———. "Political Philosophy and Halakhah in Maimonides" (in Hebrew). *Iyyun* 29 (1980): 198–212.

———. "A Third Approach to Maimonides' Cosmogony-Prophetology Puzzle." *HTR* 74 (1981): 287–301.

Hyman, Arthur. "Maimonides on Creation and Emanation." In *Studies in Medieval Philosophy*, edited by John F. Wippel, 45–61. Washington D. C.: Catholic University of America, 1987.

———. "Maimonides' 'Thirteen Principles'." In *Jewish Medieval and Renaissance Studies*, edited by Alexander Altmann, 119–45. Cambridge: Harvard University Press, 1967.

———. "A Note on Maimonides' Classification of the Law." In *American Academy of Jewish Research Jubilee Volume*, edited by S. Baron and I. Barzilay, 323–43. Jerusalem: American Academy of Jewish Research, 1980.

Idel, Moshe. "*Hitbodedut* as Concentration in Jewish Philosophy" (in Hebrew). *Jerusalem Studies in Jewish Thought (Shlomo Pines Jubilee Volume)* 7 (1988): 39–60.

Ivry, Alfred. "Maimonides and Neoplatonism: Challenge and Response." In *Neoplatonism and Jewish Thought*, edited by Lenn E. Goodman, 137–56. Albany: State University of New York Press, 1992.

———. "Maimonides on Possibility." In *Mystics, Philosophers and Politicians*, edited by J. Reinharz and D. Swetschinski, 67–84. Durham, N.C.: Duke University Press, 1982.

Kaplan, Lawrence. "*Hilkhot Megillah* 2:17 Revisited: A Halakhic Analysis." *Tradition* 26 (1991): 14–21.

———. " 'I Sleep, But My Heart Waketh': Maimonides' Conception of Human Perfection." In *The Thought of Moses Maimonides*, edited by Ira Robinson, Lawrence Kaplan, and Julien Bauer, 130–66. Lewiston, N.Y.: Edwin Mellen, 1990.

———. "Maimonides on the Singularity of the Jewish People." *Daat* 15 (1985): v–xxvi.

Kasher, Hannah. "Commandments between Man and God in the *Guide of the Perplexed*" (in Hebrew). *Daat* 12 (1984): 23–28.

———. "Does 'Ought' Imply 'Can' in Maimonides?" (in Hebrew). *Iyyun* 36 (1987): 13–34.

———. "Is There an Early Stratum in the *Guide of the Perplexed*?" *Maimonidean Studies* 3 (1992): 105–29.

———. "Maimonides' Interpretations of the Story of the Divine Revelation in the Cleft of the Rock" (in Hebrew). *Daat* 35 (1995): 29–66.

———. "Maimonides' Philosophical Division of the Law" (in Hebrew). *HUCA* 56 (1985): 1–7.

———. "Maimonides' View of Circumcision as a Factor Uniting the Jewish and Muslim Communities." In *Studies in Muslim-Jewish Relations*, edited by R. Nettler, 103–8. Chur, Switzerland: Harwood Academic Publishers, 1995.

———. "The Myth of 'God's Anger' in the *Guide of the Perplexed*" (in Hebrew). *Eshel Beer Sheva* 4 (1996): 95–111.

———. "The Parable of the King's Palace in *The Guide of the Perplexed* as a Directive to the Student" (in Hebrew). *AJS Review* 14 (1989): 1–19 (Hebrew Section).

———. "Self-Cognizing Intellect and Negative Attributes in Maimonides' Theology." *HTR* 87 (1994): 461–72.

———. "Talmud Torah as a Means of Apprehending God in Maimonides' Teachings" (in Hebrew). *Jerusalem Studies in Jewish Thought* 5 (1986): 71–82.

———. "The Torah as a Means of Achieving the World to Come" (in Hebrew). *Tarbiz* 64 (1995): 301–6.

Kellner, Menachem. *Dogma in Medieval Jewish Thought.* Oxford: Oxford University Press, 1986.

———. "Maimonides' Allegiances to Sciences and Judaism." *The Torah u-Madda Journal* 7 (1997): 88–104.

———. *Maimonides on Human Perfection.* Atlanta: Scholars Press, 1990.

Klein-Braslavy, Sara. "The Creation of the World and Maimonides' Interpretation of Genesis I–V." In *Maimonides and Philosophy*, edited by S. Pines and Y. Yovel, 65–78. Dordrecht: Martinus Nijhoff, 1986.

———. *Maimonides' Interpretation of the Adam Stories in Genesis* (in Hebrew). Jerusalem: Reuven Mass, 1986.

———. *Maimonides' Interpretation of the Story of Creation* (in Hebrew). Jerusalem: Reuben Mass, 1987.

Kogan, Barry. " 'What Can We Know and When Can We Know It?' Maimonides on the Active Intelligence and Human Cognition." In *Moses Maimonides and His Time*, edited by Eric L. Ormsby, 121–37. Washington D.C.: Catholic University of America Press, 1989.

Kraemer, Joel. "Alfarabi's Opinions of the Virtuous City and Maimonides' Foundations of the Law." In *Studia Orientalia Memoriae D. H. Baneth Dedicata,* edited by Joshua Blau, 107–53. Jerusalem: Magnes Press, 1979.

———. "Maimonides on the Philosophic Sciences in his Treatise on the Art of Logic." In *Perspectives on Maimonides*, edited by Joel Kraemer, 77–104. Oxford: Oxford University Press, 1991.

———. "*Shari'a* and *Namus* in the Philosophy of Maimonides" (in Hebrew). *Teudah* 4 (1986): 185–202.

Kreisel, Howard Haim. "Asceticism in the Thought of R. Baḥya Ibn Paquda and Maimonides." *Daat* 21 (1988): vii–xiii.

———. "A Fragment from a Philosophical Commentary on Ruth Ascribed to R. Nissim of Marseilles" (in Hebrew). *Jerusalem Studies in Jewish Thought* 14 (1998): 159–80.

———. "Halevi's Influence on Maimonides: A Preliminary Appraisal." *Maimonidean Studies* 2 (1991): 95–121.

———. "The Land of Israel and Prophecy in Medieval Jewish Philosophy" (in Hebrew). In *The Land of Israel in Medieval Jewish Thought*, edited by M. Halamish and A. Ravitzky, 40–51. Jerusalem: Yad Izhak Ben-Zevi, 1991.

———. "Maimonides' Approach to Astrology" (in Hebrew). *Proceedings of the Eleventh World Congress of Jewish Studies*, 2:25–32. Jerusalem, 1994.

———. "Maimonides' View of Prophecy as the Overflowing Perfection of Man." *Daat* 13 (1984): xxi–xxvi.

———. "Miracles in Medieval Jewish Philosophy." *JQR* 75 (1984): 106–14.

———. "Moses Maimonides." In *History of Jewish Philosophy*, edited by Daniel H. Frank and Oliver Leaman, 245–80. London: Routledge, 1997.

———. "The Place of Man in the Hierarchy of Existence in the Philosophy of Ibn Gabirol and Maimonides." In *'Alei Shefer: Studies in the Literature of Jewish Thought*, edited by Moshe Halamish, 100–102. Ramat-Gan, Israel: Bar-Ilan University Press, 1990.

———. "Sage and Prophet in the Thought of Maimonides and his Followers" (in Hebrew). *Eshel Bersheva* 3 (1986): 166–69.

———. " 'The Suffering of the Righteous' in Medieval Jewish Philosophy" (in Hebrew). *Daat* 19 (1987): 19–25.

———. "Theories of Prophecy in Medieval Jewish Philosophy." Ph.D. thesis, Brandeis University, 1981.

———. "The Verification of Prophecy in Medieval Jewish Philosophy" (in Hebrew). *Jerusalem Studies in Jewish Thought* 4 (1984): 1–18.

———. " 'The Voice of God' in Medieval Jewish Philosophical Exegesis" (in Hebrew). *Daat* 16 (1986): 29–38.

Langerman, Tzvi. "Maimonides' Repudiation of Astrology." *Maimonidean Studies* 2 (1991): 123–58.

———. "The True Perplexity: *The Guide of the Perplexed* Part II, Chapter 24." In *Perspectives on Maimonides*, edited by Joel Kraemer, 159–74. Oxford: Oxford University Press, 1991.

Lasker, Daniel J. "The Influence of Karaism on Maimonides" (in Hebrew). *Sefunot* 5 (1996): 145–61.

Lerner, Ralph. "Maimonides' Governance of the Solitary." In *Perspectives on Maimonides*, edited by Joel Kraemer, 33–46. Oxford: Oxford University Press, 1991.

———. "Maimonides' Letter on Astrology." *History of Religions* 8 (1968): 143–58.

Levinger, Jacob. "Abstinence from Alcohol in Maimonides' *Guide of the Perplexed*" (in Hebrew). *Bar-Ilan* 4–5 (1967): 299–305.

———. *Maimonides as Philosopher and Codifier* (in Hebrew). Jerusalem: Bialik Institute, 1989.

———. *Maimonides' Techniques of Codification* (in Hebrew). Jerusalem: Magnes Press, 1965.

MacIntyre, Alasdair. *After Virtue*. Notre Dame, Ind.: University of Notre Dame Press, 1981.

Macy, Jeffrey. "Prophecy in al-Farabi and Maimonides: The Imaginative and Rational Faculties." In *Maimonides and Philosophy*, edited by S. Pines and Y. Yovel, 185–201. Dordrecht: Martinus Nijhoff, 1986.

———. "A Study in Medieval Jewish and Arabic Political Philosophy: Maimonides' *Shemonah Peraqim* and Alfarabi's *Fuṣūl al-Madani*." Ph.D. thesis, Hebrew University, 1982.

Melamed, Abraham. "Philosophical Commentaries to Jeremiah 9, 22–23 in Medieval and Renaissance Jewish Thought" (in Hebrew). *Jerusalem Studies in Jewish Thought* 4 (1984–85): 31–82.

Nehorai, Michael Zevi. "How a Righteous Gentile Can Merit the World to Come" (in Hebrew). *Tarbiz* 61 (1992): 465–87

Novak, David. "The Treatment of Islam and Muslims in the Legal Writings of Maimonides." In *Studies in Islamic and Judaic Traditions*, edited by W. Brinner and S. Ricks, 233–50. Atlanta: Scholars Press, 1986.

Nuriel, Avraham. "The Divine Will in *Moreh Nevukhim*" (in Hebrew). *Tarbiz* 39 (1970): 39–61

———. "Maimonides and the Concept of Faith" (in Hebrew). *Daat* 2–3 (1979): 43–47.

———. "The Question of a Created or Primordial World in the Philosophy of Maimonides" (in Hebrew). *Tarbiz* 1964 (33): 372–87.

———. "Remarks on Maimonides' Epistemology." In *Maimonides and Philosophy*, edited by S. Pines and Y. Yovel, 36–51. Dordrecht: Martinus Nijhoff, 1986.

———. " 'The Torah Speaks in the Language of Humans' in *The Guide of the Perplexed*" (in Hebrew). In *Religion and Language*, edited by M. Hallamish and A. Kasher, 97–103. Tel Aviv: University Publishing Projects, 1981.

Peters, F. E. *Aristotle and the Arabs.* New York: New York University Press, 1968.

Pines, Shlomo. "The Limitations of Human Knowledge according to Al-Farabi, Ibn Bajja, and Maimonides." In *Studies in Medieval Jewish History and Literature*, edited by Isadore Twersky, 82–109. Cambridge: Harvard University Press, 1979).

———. "The Philosophical Purport of Maimonides' Halakhic Works and the Purport of the *Guide of the Perplexed*." In *Maimonides and Philosophy*, edited by S. Pines and Y. Yovel, 1–14. Dordrecht: Martinus Nijhoff, 1986.

———. "The Philosophic Sources of the *Guide of the Perplexed*." In *The Guide of the Perplexed*, translated by Shlomo Pines, lvii–cxxxiv. Chicago: University of Chicago Press, 1963.

———. "Shi'ite Terms and Conceptions in Judah Halevi's *Kuzari*." *Jerusalem Studies in Arabic and Islam* 2 (1980): 211f.

———. "Some Traits of Christian Theological Writings in Relation to Moslem Kalam and to Jewish Thought." *Proceedings of the Israel Academy of Sciences and Humanities* 5 (1976): 123–25.

———. "Truth and Falsehood vs. Good and Evil: A Study in Jewish and General Philosophy in Connection with the *Guide of the Perplexed* 1.2." In *Studies in Maimonides*, edited by Isadore Twersky, 95–157. Cambridge: Harvard University Press, 1990.

Rabinovitch, N. L. "The Concept of Possibility in Maimonides" (in Hebrew). *Tarbiz* 44 (1975): 159–71.

Rahman, Fazlur. *Prophecy in Islam.* London: George Allen and Unwin, 1958.

Ravitsky, Aviezer. "The Hypostasis of Supernal Wisdom in Jewish Philosophy of the Thirteenth Century" (in Hebrew). *Italia* 3 (1982): 7–38

———. "Possible and Contingent Existence in the Exegesis of Maimonides in the Thirteenth Century" (in Hebrew). *Daat* 2–3 (1978): 67–98.

———. "The Secrets of the *Guide of the Perplexed:* Between the Thirteenth and the Twentieth Centuries." In *Studies in Maimonides*, edited by I. Twersky, 159–207. Cambridge: Harvard University Press, 1990.

———. " 'To the Utmost of Human Capacity': Maimonides on the Days of the Messiah." In *Perspectives on Maimonides*, edited by Joel Kraemer, 221–56. Oxford: Oxford University Press, 1991.

Rawidowicz, Simon. *Studies in Jewish Thought.* Edited by N. Glatzer. Philadelphia: Jewish Publication Society, 1974.

Reines, Alvin. "Maimonides' Concept of Mosaic Prophecy." *HUCA* 40 (1969): 325–61.

Rosenberg, Shalom. "The Concept of 'Emunah' in Post-Maimonidean Jewish Philosophy." In vol. 2 of *Studies in Medieval Jewish History and Literature*, edited by I. Twersky, 273–307. Cambridge: Harvard University Press, 1984.

Rosner, Fred. "Maimonides the Physician: A Bibliography." *Bulletin of the History of Medicine* 43 (1969): 221–35.

Schlossberg, Eliezer. "The Attitude of R. Maimon, the Father of Maimonides, to Islam and Muslim Persecution" (in Hebrew). *Sefunot* 5 (1991): 95–107.

Schwarzschild, Steven S. "Do Noachites Have to Believe in Revelation?" *JQR* 52 (1962): 297–365.

Shapiro, David. "The Doctrine of the Image of God and *imitatio Dei*." *Judaism* 12 (1963): 57–77.

Soloveichik, Haym. "Maimonides' *'Igerret Ha-Shemad:* Law and Rhetoric." In *Rabbi Joseph H. Lookstein Memorial Volume*, edited by Leo Landman, 281–319. New York: Ktav, 1980.

Stern, Josef. "The Fall and Rise of Myth in Ritual: Maimonides versus Nahmanides on the *Huqqim*, Astrology, and the War Against Idolatry." *Journal of Jewish Thought and Philosophy* 6 (1997): 185–263.

———. "The Idea of *Ḥoq* in Maimonides' Explanation of the Law." In *Maimonides and Philosophy*, edited by S. Pines and Y. Yovel, 99–109. Dordrecht: Martinus Nijhoff, 1986.

———. "Maimonides on the Covenant of Circumcision and the Unity of God." In *The Midrashic Imagination: Jewish Exegesis, Thought, and History*, edited by M. Fishbane, 131–54. Albany: State University of New York Press, 1993.

Strauss, Leo. "Farabi's Plato." In *Louis Ginzberg Jubilee Volume*, edited by A. Marx, S. Lieberman, S. Spiegel, and S. Zeitlin, 357–93. New York: American Academy of Jewish Research, 1945.

———. "How to Begin to Study the *Guide of the Perplexed*." In *The Guide of the Perplexed*, translated by Shlomo Pines, xi–lvi. Chicago: University of Chicago Press, 1963.

———. "Maimonides' Statement on Political Science." *PAAJR* 22 (1953): 115–30.

———. "Notes on Maimonides' Book of Knowledge." In *Studies in Mysticism and Religion Presented to Gershom Scholem*, edited by E. Urbach, 269–83. Jerusalem: Magnes Press, 1967.

———. *Persecution and the Art of Writing*. Glencoe, Ill.: Free Press, 1952.

———. *Philosophy and Law*. Translated by F. Baumann. Philadelphia: Jewish Publication Society, 1987.

Tardieu, Michel. "Sabiens Coraniques et 'Sabiens' de Harran." *Journal Asiatique* 274 (1986): 1–44.

Touati, Charles. "La problème de l'inerrance prophétique dans la théologie juive du moyen âge." *Revue de l'Histoire des Religions* 174 (1968): 169–97.

Tully, James, ed. *Meaning and Context: Quentin Skinner and his Critics*. Cambridge: Polity Press, 1988.

Twersky, Isadore. *Introduction to the Code of Maimonides*. New Haven: Yale University Press, 1980.

———. "On Law and Ethics in the *Mishneh Torah:* A Case Study of *Hilkhot Megillah* II:17." *Tradition* 24 (1989): 138–49.

Walzer, Richard. *Greek into Arabic*. Oxford: Oxford University Press, 1962.

Weiss, Raymond. *Maimonides' Ethics: The Encounter of Philosophic and Religious Morality.* Chicago: University of Chicago Press, 1991.

Wolfson, Harry A. *Studies in the History of Philosophy and Religion.* Edited by I. Twersky and G. Williams. 2 vols. Cambridge: Harvard University Press, 1973, 1977.

Wurzberger, Walter. "Imitatio Dei in Maimonides' *Sefer Hamitzvot* and the *Mishneh Torah.*" In *Tradition and Transition: Essays Presented to Chief Rabbi Sir Immanuel Jakobovits*, edited by Jonathan Sacks, 321–24. London: Jews College, 1986.

INDEX

Note: Individual sections of Maimonides' *Mishneh Torah* and *Commentary on the Mishnah* are listed *under* the title of the section, e.g., *Laws of Character Traits.*